Library of
Davidson College

BETWEEN TWO ARMIES

DAVIS MEDIEVAL TEXTS AND STUDIES

UNIVERSITY OF CALIFORNIA, DAVIS

General Editor: DANIEL SILVIA
Managing Editor: KEVIN P. RODDY
Editorial Board: SYDNEY R. CHARLES, GERALD HERMAN, DENNIS DUTSCHKE, JAMES J. MURPHY, NEAL W. GILBERT, DAVID A. TRAILL
Production Editor: KATHLEEN CIFRA-PECK

VOLUME TEN

VICTOR MORRIS UDWIN

BETWEEN TWO ARMIES

BETWEEN TWO ARMIES

The Place of the Duel in Epic Culture

BY

VICTOR MORRIS UDWIN

BRILL
LEIDEN · BOSTON · KÖLN
1999

This book is printed on acid-free paper.

Library of Congress Cataloging-in-Publication Data
The Library of Congress Cataloging-in-Publication Data is also available.

Die Deutsche Bibliothek\ - CIP-Einheitsaufnahme
Udwin, Victor Morris:
Between two armies : the place of the duel in epic culture / Victor Morris Udwin. – Leiden ; Boston ; Köln : Brill, 1998
  (Davis medieval texts and studies ; vol. 10)
  ISBN 90–04–11038–0

ISSN 0169-7994
ISBN 90 04 11038 0

© Copyright 1999 by Koninklijke Brill NV, Leiden, The Netherlands

All rights reserved. No part of this publication may be reproduced, translated, stored in a retrieval system, or transmitted in any form or by any means, electronic, mechanical, photocopying, recording or otherwise, without prior written permission from the publisher.

Authorization to photocopy items for internal or personal use is granted by Koninklijke Brill provided that the appropriate fees are paid directly to The Copyright Clearance Center, 222 Rosewood Drive, Suite 910 Danvers MA 01923, USA.
Fees are subject to change.

PRINTED IN THE NETHERLANDS

for Whitney, Trevor, Camden, and Ben

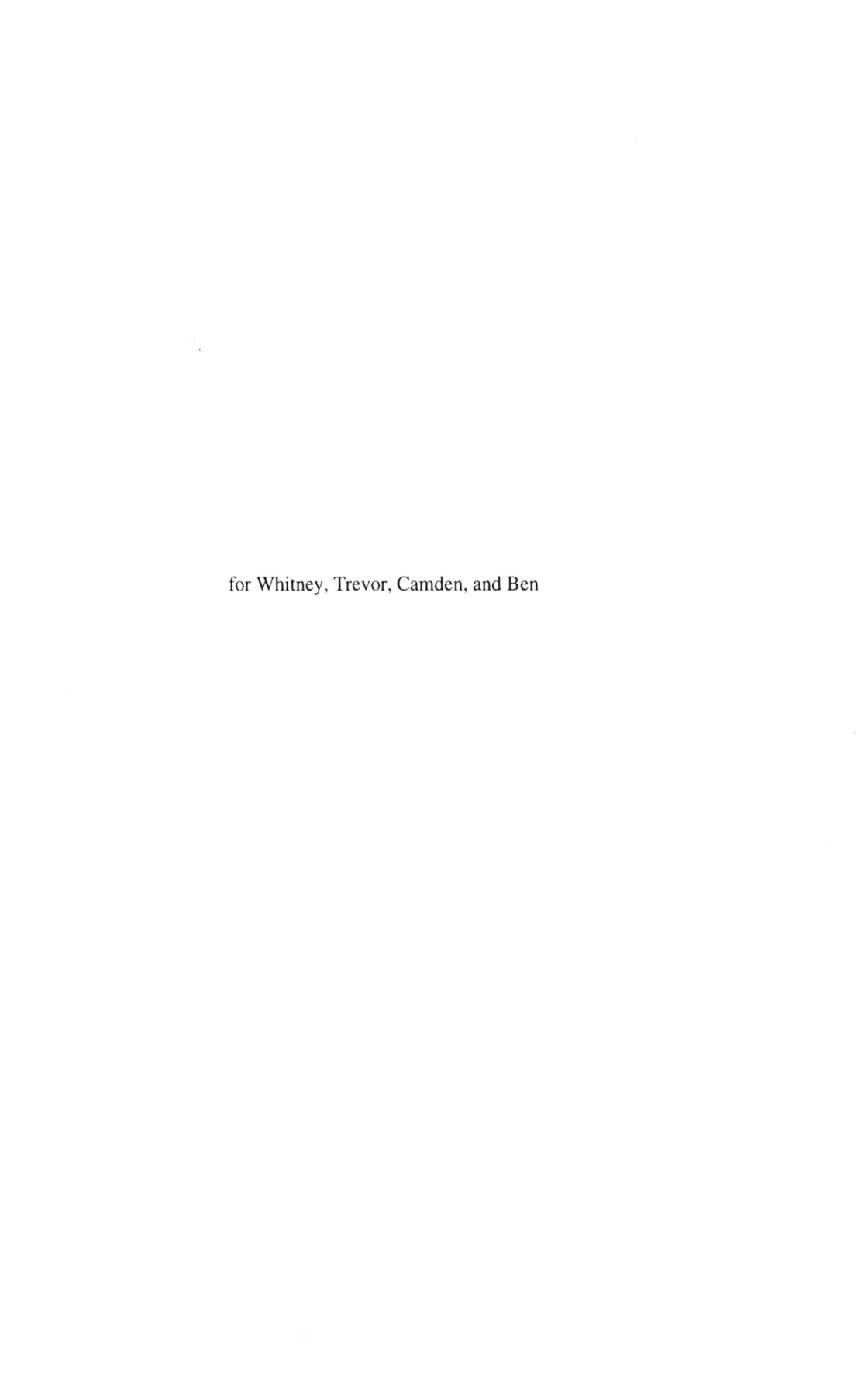

CONTENTS

Acknowledgments ix
Introduction: Working Assumptions 1
1. The Duel in Legend, Lore, and Chronicle 27
2. An Economy of Lives 46
3. The Duel and Its Protocols 79
4. The Champion and His Quest 109
5. The King and His Gifts 136
6. The Queen and Her Lovers 165
7. Hiltibrant and the Problems of Free-Agency 200
8. The Tale-Singer's Function 216
Appendix: The Lay of Hiltibrant—A Translation 225
Works Cited 227
Index 231

ACKNOWLEDGMENTS

In the process of writing this book, I received assistance from a number of friends and colleagues the importance of whose contributions cannot be overstated. Without the benefit of their learning, candid criticism, and thoughtful suggestions, this book would have been less than it is now.

To Sepp Gumbrecht, I wish to express my gratitude for arranging a semester of research as a guest of the Institut für Geistes- und Sozialwissenschaften at the Universität-Gesamthochschule Siegen, where I began to research the discovery of epic culture; to the library at the University of California at Santa Cruz for access to its collections and for providing a beautiful space in which to write; and to Brian and Sharon Beach for the use of their home in Santa Cruz for two successive summers, during which time I wrote the first drafts. To my senior colleagues Paul Rahe (History) and Jacob Howland (Philosophy) I am most deeply indebted for crucial support and encouragement together with suggestions for substantive improvements. Winder McConnell has been this work's good angel. His judicious assessment of an early draft led to numerous revisions; his careful editing of later drafts helped to correct many an error. I wish also to express my heartfelt thanks to him for the confidence he displayed in this work by placing it in a favorable light before the editors of the Davis Series in Medieval Texts and Studies. To Chris Anderson I am indebted for carefully reading and marking the manuscript. Charles Segal, Andrew Miller, Stephen Scully, Ed Haymes, George Odell, Gerhard Richter, Jean Godsall-Myers, Vibs Petersen, Bryn Barnard, and several anonymous readers were all most generous in offering comments, suggestions, and frank criticisms. Tom Benediktson has been unfailingly cheerful and amazingly prompt in responding to my numerous requests for his expert help with the Latin texts. Marc Fitzerman gave of his valuable time to help me with the Hebrew.

Many students have contributed to the ideas expressed in the book as it now stands. Among them, I would like to mention in particular the members of a Senior Seminar in Women's Studies at the University of Tulsa on the subject of "The Queen and Her Lovers." Several classes of honors students at the University of Tulsa have also been most helpful in testing and refining some of the arguments put forward here. Most memorable was the pizza box demonstration of battle dynamics put on by Jim Rion. Wade McKenzie, likely the most brilliant of those I have had the good fortune to have as a student, advised, encouraged, and cajoled with the passion of a co-author. Beyond his many services as a research assistant, I owe him a debt of gratitude for taking on the index, typing the Latin and Greek, and twice proofing the manuscript in its penultimate and ultimate versions.

In readying the book for publication, I had the invaluable assistance of Elena Zorn, who prepared the diagrams. In Carol Kealiher I found the ideal copy editor. I will be endlessly grateful for her devotion to detail, consistency, and accuracy. In addition to her unflagging energy, I cannot say enough about her selfless commitment of time to this project, which she has treated as if it were her own. My esteemed colleague Reggie Hyatte, author of two works published by E. J. Brill, was most thoughtful in providing templates for the book's format. James Kelley proofed the entire manuscript and prepared the camera ready copy. Julian Deahl and the staff of editors and production assistants at Brill showed exceptional patience and tact in their dealings with me as they saw the book through to publication.

The University of Tulsa was most supportive, providing me with several Faculty Development Grants, thus insuring that I had ample time for research and writing. I particularly appreciate the financial support arranged by Al Soltow, Director of Research, and Thomas Horne, Dean of Arts and Sciences; both contributed funds for copy editing and indexing.

Finally, I would like to thank Leah Udwin for contributing in so many ways to this book project. Her interest inspired the work; her steadfast commitment enabled me to complete it. Her critical mind deepened the research; her questions sharpened the writing.

INTRODUCTION

WORKING ASSUMPTIONS

Near the opening of the *Nibelungenlied*, Siegfried, attracted by reports of Kriemhild's beauty, travels with twelve companions deep into hostile territory—all the way to the gates of the court of Burgundy, where he declaims to King Gunther as follows:

"Nu ir sît sô küene,   als mir ist geseit
sone rúoche ich, ist daz iemen   líep óder leit;
ich wil an iu ertwingen   swaz ir muget hân:
lánt únde bürge,   daz sol mir werden undertân."

Den künec hete wunder   und sîne man alsam
umbe disiu mære   diu er hie vernam.[1]

"Now since (as they tell me) you are so brave—and I do not care who minds—I will wrest from you by force all that you possess! Your lands and your castles shall all be subject to me!"
    The King and his vassals were amazed to hear this news that Siegfried meant to deprive him of his lands.[2]

The recipients of the challenge are naturally taken aback to hear Siegfried's astonishing words. Just because of one man's threat, why should they let themselves be intimidated or insulted into giving up control of their kingdom?[3]

But what makes Siegfried's challenge to Gunther particularly audacious is its apparent foolhardiness. Siegfried and his twelve companions would easily

---

[1] *Das Nibelungenlied*, ed. Helmut Brackert (Frankfurt: Fischer, 1977), 110-111,2. Further quotations in the original language will be cited parenthetically in the text by strophe number.

[2] *The Nibelungenlied*, trans. A. T. Hatto (London: Penguin Books, 1988), p. 29. Further quotations in translation will be cited parenthetically in the text.

[3] Edward R. Haymes, in *The "Nibelungenlied": History and Interpretation* (Urbana: Univ. of Illinois Press, 1986), p. 48, describes this as "one of the most surprising scenes in the poem for the modern reader," allowing that "it may well have been equally surprising for the medieval hearer." He recognizes that this scene may be "traditionally patterned" (p. 48), but he emphasizes the fact that, traditional or not, Siegfried's challenge "does not fit into the expectations aroused by the narrative" (p. 48). Haymes consequently sees no need to concern himself with the nature of that traditional pattern and the expectations appropriate to it and thus dismisses as "silly" Siegfried's challenge of his own castle guards in Nibelungenland (p. 102). Further references will be cited parenthetically in the text.

be overwhelmed by the large fighting force ready to obey King Gunther's call, or so it would seem. And yet the Burgundians evidently never consider attacking Siegfried en masse. Siegfried's taunts reflect what we would take to be an unaccountable lack of concern about being so ridiculously outnumbered. Perhaps even stranger still, the Burgundians, though affronted by Siegfried's words, do not calculate their own advantage.[4] Indeed, the fact that they do not, for the moment, make sport of Siegfried and his companions suggests that some understanding restrains the Burgundians from simply putting an end to the brusque challengers—an understanding that protects Siegfried and his men from the Burgundians' obvious tactical advantages. The narrative itself accounts for the Burgundians' inaction by attributing to Siegfried the quality of invulnerability—except for a leaf-shaped spot on his back, his skin is tough as horn. As I hope to show, however, the attribution of magical powers simply thematizes an understanding once accessible through practical experience in the warfare of the times. What, then, is that understanding, and on what set of circumstances does it hinge?[5]

It is my contention that these questions have until now been unasked because to answer them would require access to a premise not articulated by this text and perhaps already lost to the culture for which the text in its

---

[4] Hagen complains: "im heten mîne herren solher leide niht getân" (str. 121,4)—"My lords would never have wronged him so" (p. 30). Ortwin, the only Burgundian willing to fight Siegfried, does not imagine overcoming him with the force of numbers but boasts, in a way similar to Siegfried's, that if the king and his brothers were incapable of serving in their own defense and even if Siegfried were accompanied by a royal army, he, Ortwin, would be able to make Siegfried put aside his arrogant challenge (str. 117).

[5] Winder McConnell, in *The Nibelungenlied* (Boston: Twayne Publishers, 1984), p. 28, has remarked upon this same passage: "Were Siegfried to pursue his claims without relenting, it is difficult to imagine that the Burgundians, despite their knowledge of his virtual invulnerability, would be left with any alternative but to meet force with force. That such a situation does not arise is due solely to the fact that Siegfried, whose thoughts have returned to Kriemhild, allows himself to be mollified by the (sincere) gestures of hospitality and the offer of land made by Gunther." In Werner Schröder's judgment, in *Nibelungenlied-Studien* (Stuttgart: J. B. Metzler, 1968), p. 89, Siegfried's challenge to duel is, in fact, not entirely serious ("Die Herausforderung war von Sivrit im Grunde gar nicht so ernst gemeint gewesen"—p. 89); indeed, a consideration of the purpose of his trip persuades him to discard it. This explanation, however, covers only Siegfried's perspective on "why hostilities do not break out on the spot," as McConnell puts it (p. 28). The Burgundians decide against accepting the challenge despite their overwhelming superior numerical advantage; as McConnell points out, had Gunther "taken a firm stand against Siegfried when confronted by the latter's arrogance in the initial arrival scene in Worms" and met him in single combat, "he might have lost his life then and there, but this, at least, would have spared him depiction as a royal incompetent, a king without answers, a monarch constantly overshadowed by others, including his liegemen" (p. 49). The failure to deal forcefully with Siegfried's challenge must, then, be credited at least in part with the responsibility for Burgundy's destruction.

present version was composed, a time circa A.D. 1200. The missing premise constitutes a key link in what we might for the moment call "Nibelungen culture." To be able to supply the premise is to understand an underlying principle of that culture.

The Nibelungs, of course, for what little we know about them, may well exist only in fiction. Nevertheless, the suppressed premise identified here as our key to Nibelungen culture is anything but fictional, since it had to be borne by the poem's audience. For either there were once people to whom Siegfried's challenge and the Burgundian response made some sense, or some sort of fault has to be found with the text. Modern commentators sometimes place responsibility for this perceived fault with the text's poet.[6] If, however, the text or its author is to be made responsible for the apparent deficit in understanding, then the same fault must be found in a surprisingly large number of completely unrelated epic narratives, for the *Nibelungenlied* is not alone among ancient tales in its reliance on the mysterious unstated principle informing both a challenge in terms of land and people and the response to that challenge. Indeed, passages in other texts bear interesting similarities to the *Nibelungenlied*'s narration of Siegfried's arrival at Worms. These similarities extend not only to the activities depicted but also to the apparent illogic that we associate with Siegfried's audacity.

For our first example, we may turn to I Samuel:

וּפְלִשְׁתִּים עֹמְדִים אֶל־הָהָר מִזֶּה וְיִשְׂרָאֵל עֹמְדִים אֶל־הָהָר מִזֶּה וְהַגַּיְא בֵּינֵיהֶם: וַיֵּצֵא אִישׁ־הַבֵּנַיִם מִמַּחֲנוֹת פְּלִשְׁתִּים גָּלְיָת שְׁמוֹ מִגַּת גָּבְהוֹ שֵׁשׁ אַמּוֹת וָזָרֶת: וְכוֹבַע נְחֹשֶׁת עַל־רֹאשׁוֹ וְשִׁרְיוֹן קַשְׂקַשִּׂים הוּא לָבוּשׁ וּמִשְׁקַל הַשִּׁרְיוֹן חֲמֵשֶׁת־אֲלָפִים שְׁקָלִים נְחֹשֶׁת: וּמִצְחַת נְחֹשֶׁת עַל־רַגְלָיו וְכִידוֹן נְחֹשֶׁת בֵּין כְּתֵפָיו: וְחֵץ חֲנִיתוֹ כִּמְנוֹר אֹרְגִים וְלַהֶבֶת חֲנִיתוֹ שֵׁשׁ־מֵאוֹת שְׁקָלִים בַּרְזֶל וְנֹשֵׂא הַצִּנָּה הֹלֵךְ לְפָנָיו: וַיַּעֲמֹד וַיִּקְרָא אֶל־מַעַרְכֹת יִשְׂרָאֵל וַיֹּאמֶר לָהֶם לָמָּה תֵצְאוּ לַעֲרֹךְ מִלְחָמָה הֲלוֹא אָנֹכִי הַפְּלִשְׁתִּי וְאַתֶּם עֲבָדִים לְשָׁאוּל בְּרוּ־לָכֶם אִישׁ וְיֵרֵד אֵלָי: אִם־יוּכַל לְהִלָּחֵם אִתִּי וְהִכָּנִי וְהָיִינוּ לָכֶם לַעֲבָדִים וְאִם־אֲנִי אוּכַל־לוֹ וְהִכִּיתִיו וִהְיִיתֶם לָנוּ לַעֲבָדִים וַעֲבַדְתֶּם אֹתָנוּ: וַיֹּאמֶר הַפְּלִשְׁתִּי אֲנִי חֵרַפְתִּי אֶת־מַעַרְכוֹת יִשְׂרָאֵל הַיּוֹם הַזֶּה תְּנוּ־לִי אִישׁ וְנִלָּחֲמָה יָחַד: וַיִּשְׁמַע שָׁאוּל וְכָל־יִשְׂרָאֵל אֶת־דִּבְרֵי הַפְּלִשְׁתִּי הָאֵלֶּה וַיֵּחַתּוּ וַיִּרְאוּ מְאֹד:[7]

> And the Philistines stood on a mountain on one side, and Israel stood on a mountain on the other side; and there was a valley between them. And there came out a champion from the camp of the Philistines, named Goliath, of Gath, whose height was six cubits and a span. And he had a helmet of bronze upon his head, and he was armed with a coat of mail; and the weight of the coat was five thousand shekels of bronze. And he had greaves of bronze upon his legs, and a javelin of bronze between his shoulders. And the staff

---

[6] Theodore Andersson, for example, in *A Preface to the "Nibelungenlied"* (Stanford: Stanford Univ. Press, 1987), p. 137, comments that "Siegfried's challenge of the Burgundians at Worms in Adventure 3 has no point and dissolves awkwardly."

[7] I Sam. 17:3-10, *The CD-ROM Bible* (Chicago: Judaica Press, 1995). Further quotations in the original language and translation will be cited parenthetically in the text.

of his spear was like a weaver's beam; and his spear's head weighed six hundred shekels of iron; and a shield bearer went before him. And he stood and shouted to the armies of Israel, and said to them, Why have you come out to set your battle in array? Am I not a Philistine, and you servants to Saul? Choose a man for you, and let him come down to me. If he is able to fight with me, and kill me, then will we be your servants; but if I prevail against him, and kill him, then shall you be our servants, and serve us. And the Philistine said, I defy the armies of Israel this day; give me a man, that we may fight together.

Just as the actions of both Siegfried and the Burgundians imply a tacit avoidance of pitched battle, Goliath's scoffing at the Israelites for drawing up in battle formation expresses his expectation that the Hebrews share his preference for the procedure he is suggesting—a duel. The question "תֵּצְאוּ לַעֲרֹךְ מִלְחָמָה לָמָּה"—"why have you come out to set your battle in array?"—is clearly meant to be rhetorical, for these words are not calculated to persuade Saul's army to accept his offer of single combat. Rather, the Israelites are meant to supply an understanding already in their possession to the effect that a pitched battle can and should be avoided. The Israelites' response, however, is much in keeping with our own. Indeed, the passage's detailed description of Goliath's monstrous size, especially as measured by the weight and size of his armor, seems to account most adequately for their reticence in facing him. To us, it seems perfectly understandable that "אֶת־דִּבְרֵי הַפְּלִשְׁתִּי הָאֵלֶּה וַיֵּחַתּוּ וַיִּרְאוּ מְאֹד׃ וַיִּשְׁמַע שָׁאוּל וְכָל־יִשְׂרָאֵל"—"when Saul and all Israel heard those words of the Philistine, they were dismayed, and greatly afraid" (I Sam. 17:11). So great is their dismay that "וַיִּגַּשׁ הַפְּלִשְׁתִּי הַשְׁכֵּם וְהַעֲרֵב וַיִּתְיַצֵּב אַרְבָּעִים יוֹם׃"—"the Philistine drew near morning and evening, and presented himself for forty days" (I Sam. 17:16)—without anyone coming out to meet him.

It is more the wonder, then, that a slender shepherd boy should step forward to volunteer for the contest. Equally perplexing, however, is Saul's agreement to let him represent Israel against Goliath. Indeed, the Hebrew king would be ill-advised to allow any one of his warriors, even one nearly matching Goliath in size, strength, and self-confidence, to accept the Philistine's challenge. So when the shepherd boy David declares himself willing to face the giant adversary, why does Saul not refuse his offer—not out of any particular concern for David but to protect himself and all Israel from the consequences of David's probable defeat. If David dies, would not Israel be bound to servitude, as specified by the terms laid out by Goliath? Making the same calculation, Gunther and the Burgundians choose not to send a champion against Siegfried.[8] Why, then, would Saul and his army be willing to hazard their communal fate on the luck of any single person—let alone this boy—fighting against such a giant? It can only be that, should

---

[8] Ortwin, Hagen's nephew, does volunteer (str. 116-17) but is rejected by Siegfried as being unworthy, first, because of his rank, and second, because Siegfried does not judge him to be an able enough opponent, declaring that twelve of Ortwin couldn't defeat him ("jane dörften mich dîn zwelve mit strîte nímmér bestân"—118,4).

David be killed, Saul has no intention of abiding by the terms of the treaty. In this respect, Saul, in his ignorance of the logic that compels men to accept the duel as a legitimate and meaningful practice, is perhaps closer to us in our understanding of the situation than he is to Goliath, who is taken aback, even affronted, by the sight of a shepherd boy stepping into the space between the two armies:

וַיַּבֵּט הַפְּלִשְׁתִּי וַיִּרְאֶה אֶת־דָּוִד וַיִּבְזֵהוּ כִּי־הָיָה נַעַר וְאַדְמֹנִי עִם־יְפֵה מַרְאֶה. וַיֹּאמֶר הַפְּלִשְׁתִּי אֶל־דָּוִד הֲכֶלֶב אָנֹכִי כִּי־אַתָּה בָא־אֵלַי בַּמַּקְלוֹת. (I Sam. 17:42-43)

> And when the Philistine looked around, and saw David, he disdained him; for he was but a youth, red haired and good looking. And the Philistine said to David, Am I a dog, that you come to me with sticks?

Goliath and the Philistines are operating under assumptions shared neither by David and the Israelites nor by the modern reader. These, however, appear to be the same as those informing Siegfried's behavior. Goliath and Siegfried, although inhabiting fictional realms entirely alien to one another, appear to behave according to the same wisdom, presumably based upon experiences and circumstances familiar to them but lost to us.

Not only do their understandings direct them to substitute single combat for a pitched battle, but the terms that they propose are uncannily similar. As Siegfried expresses it in his speech to Gunther, the sovereignty of two peoples is to be put at stake:

> "ez enmüge von dînen ellen   dîn lant den fride hân,
> ich wil es alles walten.   und ouch diu erbe mîn,
> erwirbest dus mit sterke,   diu sulen dir undertænec sîn.
>
> Dîn erbe und ouch daz mîne   sulen gelîche ligen.
> sweder unser einer   am andern mac gesigen,
> dem sol ez allez dienen,   die liute und ouch diu lant." (113,2-114,3)
>
> "Unless you can protect your country by your own valour I shall rule the whole of it: but if you can wrest my inheritance from me this shall be subject to you. Now let us stake our patrimonies one against the other, and whichever of us two proves victorious let him be master of both lands and peoples." (29)

At stake in both the duels proposed by Siegfried and Goliath are mastery and servitude—the future relations between two societies.

The recipients of these challenges misunderstand them but in different ways. The Burgundians clearly believe that Siegfried cannot be defeated in a duel. Nor, apparently, can he be beaten in battle, regardless of the Burgundians' overwhelming numerical advantage. But rather than acknowledge his superiority, they seek to bypass combat altogether by inviting Siegfried to enter their court as a guest. From a modern perspective, this strategy seems quite acceptable[9] but, as we shall see, only because of a lack of judgment that proves fatal. The Israelites clearly understand that none of them could survive an encounter with Goliath. They must feel that they have a better chance for victory in a general engagement. They cannot appreciate the opportunity that Goliath seems to be offering, and therefore they will not respect the terms of his challenge.

The "Lay of Hiltibrant," the fragment of a Langobard tale surviving in an Old High German version, presents another variation on the theme of dueling champions, for in this instance the combatants are father and son:

> Ik gihorta ðat seggen,
> ðat sih urhettun ænon muotin,
> Hiltibraht enti Haðubrant untar heriun tuem,
> sunufatarungo iro saro rihtun.
> garutun se iro guðhamun, gurtun sih iro suert ana,
> helidos, ubar hringa, do sie to dero hiltiu ritun.[10]

> I heard it told
> that champions met each other alone,
> Hiltibrant and Hadubrant between two armies,
> son and father, set right their armor,
> belted their battle shirts, girded on their swords,
> the heroes, over chain mail, as they to this battle rode.[11]

Here the narrative leaves us to infer that a truce is already in place, a space between the armies has been cleared, and the troops have laid down their arms. Hiltibrant and Hadubrant meet each other as opposing champions, ignorant at first of each other's identity. The father, however, pauses to inquire into his opponent's clan and parentage. Recognizing himself in his son's description, Hiltibrant somewhat obliquely informs Hadubrant of their

---

[9] Siegfried Beyschlag, for example, describes Gunther as a "responsible" ruler who weighs up "seriously" and "cautiously" the challenges that come his way; strategies that enable him to "master" in "clever coordination" with his brothers the "difficult situation" caused by Siegfried's arrival: "Gunther ist der verantwortliche Herrscher, der die Aufgaben, die ihm entgegentreten, ernst und behutsam abwägt. So meistert er in geschicktem Zusammenspiel mit den Brüdern die schwierige Lage bei Siegfrieds Ankunft"—see Beyschlag, "Das Motiv der Macht bei Siegfrieds Tod," *Germanisch-Romanische Montasschrift* (1952), 95-108; reprinted in *Zur Germanisch-Deutschen Heldensage*, ed. Karl Hauck (Darmstadt: Wissenschaftliche Buchgesellschaft, 1965), p. 207. Further references will be cited parenthetically in the text.

[10] *Das Hildebrandslied*, ed. Hartmut Broszinski (Kassel: Johannes Stauda, 1985), 1-6. Further quotations will be cited parenthetically in the text by line numbers.

[11] See the Appendix for the "Lay of Hiltibrant," my complete translation of the poem fragment.

relationship ("du neo dana halt mit sus sippan man / dinc ni geleitos"—31-32—"you never yet took up combat with a man so closely related") and removes the special bands from his arms to offer as a gift. Hadubrant, however, suspects a trap—a play upon his emotions meant to bring down his guard, a cunning trick to gain the old warrior an advantage against the young man's vigor—and so he refuses to believe his father's words. Hiltibrant then measures his son approvingly and regretfully accepts the necessity of their duel, which, as he recognizes, may make him the killer of his own child.

Of all the duels to which the ancient poems make us witness, the meeting between Hadubrant and Hiltibrant throws this practice into the most doubtful light, for we cannot imagine a bond more compelling than that between parent and child, especially when there is no personal quarrel between them but only between the larger military forces that they represent. Here, victory for either man entails the commission of a most grievous crime—the killing of his nearest kin. Bowing nevertheless to the powerful force of what even he seems to have to acknowledge as an inescapable premise, the father soon accepts the necessity of a duel with his own son.

But what understanding could possibly justify such a decision? Like David and Goliath, Hadubrant and Hiltibrant meet "between two armies," and, like Goliath, they are clad in heavy mail, hefting a spear in one hand, carrying a shield in the other, and wearing a sword slung from the shoulder or waist. Though the terms for the duel are in this case not articulated within the lines of the poetic remnant in our possession, it can be inferred that the long-standing feud between the kings Theodoric and Otachre is now to be settled. The outcome of the duel between Hadubrant and Hiltibrant will therefore have serious consequences for both of their respective armies.

The exchange of terms is also an important feature of the Homeric tale of a duel between Paris and Menelaus in a space especially cleared for them by the Trojan and Achaean armies on the plain before Troy. The action is initiated by Hector:

καί ῥ' ἐς μέσσον ἰὼν Τρώων ἀνέεργε φάλαγγας,
μέσσου δουρὸς ἑλών· τοὶ δ' ἱδρύνθησαν ἅπαντες.
τῷ δ' ἐπετοξάζοντο κάρη κομόωντες Ἀχαιοὶ
ἰοῖσίν τε τιτυσκόμενοι λάεσσί τ' ἔβαλλον·
αὐτὰρ ὁ μακρὸν ἄϋσεν ἄναξ ἀνδρῶν Ἀγαμέμνων·
"ἴσχεσθ'. Ἀργεῖοι, μὴ βάλλετε, κοῦροι Ἀχαιῶν·
στεῦται γάρ τι ἔπος ἐρέειν κορυθαίολος Ἕκτωρ."

Ὣς ἔφαθ'. οἱ δ' ἔσχοντο μάχης ἄνεῴ τ' ἐγένοντο
ἐσσυμένως· Ἕκτωρ δὲ μετ' ἀμφοτέροισιν ἔειπε·
"κέκλυτέ μευ, Τρῶες καὶ ἐϋκνήμιδες Ἀχαιοί,
μῦθον Ἀλεξάνδροιο, τοῦ εἵνεκα νεῖκος ὄρωρεν.
ἄλλους μὲν κέλεται Τρῶας καὶ πάντας Ἀχαιοὺς
τεύχεα κάλ' ἀποθέσθαι ἐπὶ χθονὶ πουλυβοτείρῃ.
αὐτὸν δ' ἐν μέσσῳ καὶ ἀρηΐφιλον Μενέλαον
οἴους ἀμφ' Ἑλένῃ καὶ κτήμασι πᾶσι μάχεσθαι.
ὁππότερος δέ κε νικήσῃ κρείσσων τε γένηται,

κτήμαθ' ἑλὼν εὖ πάντα γυναῖκά τε οἴκαδ' ἀγέσθω·
οἱ δ' ἄλλοι φιλότητα καὶ ὅρκια πιστὰ τάμωμεν."[12]

> He stepped out into no-man's-land, and grasping his spear by the middle thrust back the Trojans' line. They all sat down; but the long-haired Achaeans kept up their archery, making Hector the target for their arrows and stones. King Agamemnon had to intervene. "Argives, enough!" he shouted. "Men, cease shooting. Hector of the flashing helmet is trying to make himself heard."
>
> The troops abandoned their attack and silence was established promptly. Then Hector spoke between the two armies. "Trojans," he said, "and Achaean men-at-arms; hear from me what Paris, who began this trouble, now proposes. He suggests that all the troops should ground their arms while he and the warrior Menelaus fight a duel, between the two armies, for Helen and her wealth. The one who wins and proves himself the better man shall have the lady, goods and all, and take them home with him, while the rest of us make a treaty of peace."[13]

Here, by contrast with I Samuel and the *Nibelungenlied*, the terms articulated by Hector assign to the winner sovereignty, not over the other nation—"land and people"—but only over the woman and her wealth. If, however, one bears in mind not what Siegfried declares in his challenge to Burgundy but what he tells his mother and father at home in Xanten, when he reveals his intention to embark on a wooing expedition to obtain Kriemhild as his wife, the *Nibelungenlied* is also quite like the *Iliad* in that both make possession of a woman the motive for their duels. In Siegfried's strangely doubled purpose (wooing and sovereignty) are combined the quite different motives of Paris (wooing only) and Goliath (sovereignty only).

By contrast with Hiltibrant and Hadubrant, estranged father and son who should by all rights have no personal wish to fight, the confrontation between Menelaus and Paris pits against each other individuals who naturally might feel a great deal of personal animosity for one another; it is for the sake of their rivalry that the Trojan war is said to have been fought. They and their troops, therefore, have every reason to embrace the duel as a means for resolving hostilities. What is incomprehensible here is not the suggestion that they settle their differences in single combat but that the war should have been waged at such terrible cost for so long when a duel between the two men directly concerned could swiftly and appropriately have brought an end to the fighting at the moment when the siege of Troy first began.[14]

---

[12] Homer, *Iliad*, ed. David B. Monro and Thomas W. Allen (London: Oxford Univ. Press, 1969), 3:77-94. Further quotations in the original language will be cited parenthetically in the text.

[13] Homer, *The Iliad*, trans. E. V. Rieu (London: Penguin Books, 1988), p. 66. Further quotations in translation will be cited parenthetically in the text by the book and page numbers of the original-language edition.

[14] Eric Voegelin, in "Order and Disorder," *Critical Essays on Homer*, ed. Kenneth Atchity (Boston: G. K. Hall & Company, 1987), p. 70, ranks this

It is possible from these examples to begin to assemble a list of features common to the practice of dueling: a challenge to a formal duel (I Sam. 17, *Iliad* III, *Nibelungenlied* Av. 3) is issued from the space between opposed armies (*Iliad* III) that then disarm and arrange themselves around the place of the single combat (*Iliad* IV, "Lay of Hiltibrant"). A challenge to a formal duel includes a specification of terms ("we will be your servants . . . [or] you shall be our servants"; "for Helen and her wealth"; or "whichever of us two proves victorious let him be master of both lands and peoples"). The armies arranged in their ranks around the duel's staging place create, as it were, a theater in the round (*Iliad* IV, I Sam. 17). In I Samuel, the opposing mountain slopes form a natural amphitheater. The warriors standing or seated on the slopes thus become spectators—witnesses to the duel, judges of its conduct, and observers of its outcome.

Among the similarities in the protocol that constitutes epic dueling, it may be noted that the only significant observable variation occurs in the spoils: these include either a woman and her wealth or a land and its people. The very sudden shift from wooing expedition to challenge for sovereignty that often takes modern readers quite by surprise suggests that in these narratives the sets of terms overlap. If Paris's relationship with Helen (whether characterized as "rape," "seduction," or "abduction") is likewise understood as a challenge to Achaean sovereignty, then there is no inconsistency in mounting a massive pan-Achaean war effort in response to one prince's absconding with another's wife. The *Nibelungenlied*'s strange equation of wooing and invasion, then, appears rather like the *Iliad*'s equation of abduction with invasion, from which may be surmised that the equation only appears to be out of balance when the behavior patterns constitutive of this culture are no longer understood. Since no state of war exists between Burgundy and Xanten and no armies are in the field, modern readers view Siegfried's challenge as inappropriate to the purpose of his visit to Burgundy. But this is because modern audiences simply have no basis from which to appreciate the fact that not only does Siegfried's audacious challenge to Gunther represent an invitation to a formal duel, but also that, in terms of the set of understandings that constitute his culture, this is an entirely appropriate way for Siegfried to announce himself as Kriemhild's suitor. It would seem, then, that the *Nibelungenlied* and the *Iliad* both presume the same set of behaviors and understandings, one, moreover, that has been lost to us and therefore passes for the most part unnoticed.

---

among the chief questions raised by the conduct of the Trojan war. The questions include: "Why did the Trojans not prevent the war, or at least end it, by restoring Helen to her husband with customary reparations? . . . Why did the warring parties not resort to [single combat] somewhat earlier? . . . And, finally, the question must be answered as to why this attempt to end the war proves abortive even now" (p. 71). Answers to these questions are interrelated as will become clear in the course of the present investigation. Further references to the Voegelin work will be cited parenthetically in the text.

Our examination of this lost culture will focus, then, on the battlefield duel, that signal contest between two warriors, each chosen to represent a king,[15] an army, or a people on terms that generally include the cessation of all hostilities, resolution of the conflict, disposition of the two armies, and, very often, determination of the future sovereignty of those peoples whom the armies serve. In most cases, the losing side forfeits some of its wealth in a one-time payment or an annual tribute. The losing side also forfeits some of its independence. It may have to provide fighting men for the other army. Defeat may well entail ceding sovereignty to the other king or ruler, who assumes a position of superior authority with respect to the defeated king and the people that he rules.

"Nibelungen" culture, as we began by calling it, is clearly not limited to a Nibelungen people, for its practices are shared by "Iliadic" culture, "Philistine" culture, and "Germanic" culture. The same understandings are

---

[15] Walter Donlan is one of many who now eschew the use of misleading terms such as "king," preferring instead to borrow terminology from the anthropologist Morton Fried, thus identifying Homeric society as a "ranked society" occurring "as an evolutionary stage" between "egalitarian" and "stratified" societies—Donlan, "Duelling with Gifts in the *Iliad*: As the Audience Saw It," *Colby Quarterly,* 29 (1993), 155. Further references will be cited parenthetically in the text. Teleological assumptions clearly dominant in such "evolutionary" models are problematized by the very case in which Donlan is interested, for the "ranked society" of the Dark Ages follows immediately *after* an example of the supposedly later "stratified stage" on the same site. The safest path for us would be to refer to things by their right names—ἄναξ ἀνδρῶν ("lord of men") instead of *king*. But working with texts in several languages makes this impracticable, and I prefer, therefore, to use English terms. Here we have the choice between those terms with which we are familiar and which are commonly to be encountered in translations of the narratives and those considered appropriate by anthropologists and archaeologists.

A great many scholars working primarily with ancient narrative have accepted the necessity of borrowing from other disciplines. Donlan, for example, arguing that a "coherent sociology . . . is absolutely necessary," finds before him the question, "should we derive the 'mentalities' from an artificial, totally self-contained poetical universe, as indicated by the 'many layers' theory, or from the empirically verifiable institutions and behaviors of the living society?" (p. 158). Finding the historical tangle within the poems unmanageable except from a stable perspective of empirical verifiability, Donlan turns to the comfort of others' models. The notion that a poetical universe is totally self-contained is itself a product of modern culture, however, and can be argued. Since my methodology is neither anthropological nor archaeological, to adopt their vocabulary indiscriminately would be to prejudice the investigation perhaps even more seriously than the use of traditional terms. To the extent that the experiences, practices, and institutions described in this book represent a cultural system at least aspects of which were heretofore unknown to us, I can see no alternative but to trust that the definition of important terms and the relationships among them will become clearer, more precise, and more accurate as the description of epic culture unfolds.

presumed by the patrons of *Beowulf* and the *Odyssey*. That narratives produced by these societies share such remarkable assumptions suggests that we consider the possibility of cultural similarity or, indeed, of cultural commonality.[16] Nibelungen culture, it seems, is but one manifestation of a more generally occurring phenomenon to which, because much of our access to it is provided by texts commonly categorized as epics, I shall henceforth refer by the more generic designation: epic culture. In combination, the terms "epic" and "culture" will refer specifically to the practice of formal battlefield duels and to the understandings according to which that practice would have been meaningful.

Despite the high profile given single combat by ancient sources, the meeting of champions between armies has rarely been given serious attention by modern historians, even by historians of war. There must, then, be compelling reasons why the duel has not been taken more seriously as a form of military conduct. The first of these, stated quite simply, is that it seems to us to fly in the face of good sense to wager the issue of a battle and the sovereignty of a people on the prowess and fortune of one man. Indeed, as military policy, the agreement to substitute single for general combat runs counter to intuition or, to be more precise, counter to an assumption about warfare so pervasive through the length and breadth of recorded military history that it goes without question, for it seems to be a matter of simple arithmetic that, training and equipment being equal, larger military forces should defeat smaller military forces.[17] The greater the disproportion in

---

[16] Borrowing a concept from archaeology, we can understand the practice of single combat and its related institutions to be "structural homologies"—see Colin Renfrew, "Peer polity interaction and socio-political change," *Peer Polity Interaction and Socio-Political Change*, ed. Colin Renfrew and John F. Cherry (Cambridge: Cambridge Univ. Press, 1986), pp. 3-5. However, Renfrew notes, where the distribution of similar material finds over a defined space prompts the question, "[w]hy should we find these same *structures* (in the architectural sense) repeated through the region of this civilization?" (p. 5)—the discovery of narratival homologies in sources in different languages and presumably created by peoples widely separated in terms of their ethnicity, geography, and time frame prompts rather the following question: why should we find these same structures repeated through different regions and different civilizations? In attempting to answer such a question, archaeology theorizes that these shared features are indicative of "necessary adaptations," that is, as "features which might have evolved quite independently in response to the similar environment in the different communities, each faced with analogous practical problems" (p. 5). Although this is the position adopted at the outset of this study, closer analysis will show that the mechanism of peer polity interaction is strongly in evidence within the epic-cultural domain and may well account for some occurrences of the structural homology with which we are concerned (see Chapter 8 below). Further references to the Renfrew work will be cited parenthetically in the text.

[17] "Actual people never fought in quite the way the *Iliad* suggests," writes G. S. Kirk, in *"The Iliad": A Commentary* (Cambridge: Cambridge Univ. Press, 1985), p. 7. In thus dismissing what the *Iliad* clearly asserts, modern scholarship blinds

numbers, the greater the expectation of victory to the more numerous. Exceptions, such as the victory over Persia by the vastly outnumbered Greeks at Marathon, simply prove the rule, for so unexpected was the outcome of that battle that it catalyzed Greek identity through the Classical period and is even now still celebrated in the twenty-six mile "marathon," which memorializes not so much the Greek success as the impression made by that most improbable outcome on its astonished witnesses, one of whom was inspired to run all the way from the battlefield home to Athens just to say it was so.

The practice of the duel between two armies thus indicates a radical departure from the principle of numerical superiority as a prime factor in determining the outcome of battle. Some epic sources are quite explicit about the fact that an army's success rests with a few of its best warriors and, moreover, that a champion backed by a dozen staunch supporters can rout a much larger enemy force. It has, therefore, seemed reasonable not to take the epic sources too literally on this point. But what if the circumstances associated with the practice of the battlefield duel were to constitute a context so profoundly different from our own as to render it unintelligible to us? This book will work from the assumption that if we can reconstruct some of the conditions of battle lost through the drift of cultural change over millennia, then we might recapture an appreciation for the utility and even necessity of single combat. We might then also read the epics and other ancient sources in a new light.[18]

There is yet another reason why the battlefield duel has not been paid the attention that it deserves, and this has to do with our own expectations and attitudes towards the poetic form in which most ancient narrative comes down to us, for as Pierre Ducrey observes, "nobody is able to separate fact from fiction in the work of Homer," from which assertion he draws the conclusion that warfare, as described in the epic poems, "cannot be considered as historically attested or even as representative of the conflicts supposed to

---

itself to discovering the sense behind a way of fighting quite alien to our own thinking.

[18] The problem presented us by the drift of cultural change is illustrated very nicely with respect to the subject of duels in an article by John Dillery, who recognizes that assumptions shaping Herodotus's understanding are not immediately available to us and thus require recovery—see Dillery, "Reconfiguring the Past: Thyrea, Thermopylae, and Narrative Patterns in Herodotus," *American Journal of Philology*, 117 (1996), 217. The "duel" in Herodotus, as understood by Dillery, is indeed a formal combat but one involving three hundred men on each side. If Herodotus does not clearly distinguish between a two-man and a six hundred-man duel, however, then his assumptions differ not only from our own but also from those of epic culture. In recovering Herodotus's assumptions, Dillery will not, then, have recovered epic assumptions about the duel. This may also explain why he notes that, in Herodotus, such duels fail in their purpose of preventing a large scale conflict and so reducing the loss of life (p. 223).

have taken place in very early times."[19] Ducrey's observation is nearly universally shared by the scholarly community because it stems from assumptions upon which the institution of modern research is itself founded. Indeed, modern scholarship has taken two diametrically opposed yet complementary approaches to narrative, aestheticism and historicism.

Aestheticism treats narrative from the perspective of artistic qualities presumed to apply everywhere and at all times—qualities such as "unity,"[20] "economy,"[21] and "tragedy."[22] From this perspective, any expectation that

---

[19] Pierre Ducrey, *Warfare in Ancient Greece*, trans. Janet Lloyd (New York: Schocken Books, 1986), pp. 15-16.

[20] By "unity" is meant a minimization of internal disjuncture and inconsistency. Schröder, for example, seeks to overcome apparent discrepancies or disjunctures between various aspects of the *Nibelungenlied* by interpreting them as revolving facets of a single personality. The apparent disjuncture between the first and second halves of the *Nibelungenlied* in its present form, then, is a misperception based on the failure to interpret Kriemhild as a consistent character. Schröder proposes that the creation of a new Kriemhild-concept represents the poem's germinal idea and that this new character ultimately constitutes the poem's unity ("die Einheit der Dichtung letztlich konstituiert"—p. 7). When love, suffering, and revenge are properly understood to be compatible aspects of Kriemhild's character, argues Schröder, the poem's unity can be appreciated (p. 112). The problem with such arguments is not that they are untenable or incorrect but that the assumption of "unity" upon which they are based conceives of the poem in terms of an ideal aesthetics of balance, harmony, and closure that is quite static, thus obscuring the dynamics of interaction and change that can occur through the course of a reading. See also footnote 22 on "tragedy" below.

[21] By "economy" is meant a minimization of superfluous realia from the everyday world. Cedric H. Whitman, for example, defines "poetic economy" in terms of maximizing so far as possible language's "presentational" as opposed to its "grammatical" mode, so that an absolute minimum of grammatical "dross" remains—Whitman, "Image, Symbol, and Formula," *Critical Essays on Homer*, p. 87. Further references will be cited parenthetically in the text. See also footnote 22 on "tragedy."

[22] Brian Murdoch points out, in *The Germanic Hero: Politics and Pragmatism in Early Medieval Poetry* (London: Hambledon Press, 1996), p. 19, that when critics expect the hero to end tragically "as if this were part of a definition . . . it is at best questionable." Further references to the Murdoch work will be cited parenthetically in the text. The term "tragedy" is often used to represent the conflict between an individual attempting to live by ideals and the limitations of action in the real world. No Homerist gives clearer expression to the assumptions of traditional literary scholarship than Bernard Knox. In his introduction to the *Iliad*, trans. Robert Fagles (New York: Viking Books, 1990), p. 27, Knox reminds the reader that this poem "celebrates the heroic values war imposes on its votaries." In order to more securely pull this grim narrative of war into the category of art, it is necessary for Knox to aestheticize any possible horror felt by nonvotaries. Knox accordingly recategorizes the epic as a tragedy, beginning by casting Achilles as "a tragic hero, a fully created character whose motives and action form an intelligible unity" (p. 47). "Unity," of course, has a tradition from Aristotle to the European classical age as a characteristic attribute of well-crafted tragedy.

14 INTRODUCTION

the narrative play a direct role in the practical affairs of its audience demeans that narrative, for aesthetic qualities appeal not to the audience's calculation of self-interest but to its higher judgments and finer feelings.

Historicism, on the other hand, is interested in facts as these may be useful in historiography, sociology, anthropology, psychology, and archaeology.[23] And yet it is not solely attitudes towards poetry that have diverted scholarly attention away from the duel between two armies, for the duel is

---

Another Homeric attribute is that he is "economical in the extreme" (p. 47). By applying such neo-Aristotelian criteria to preclassical texts, Knox finds, in short, that "Homer's method is dramatic rather than epic" (p. 47). Knox thus consistently valorizes Achilles for his "godlike, lonely, heroic fury" (p. 46) rather than condemns him, say, for his selfish and destructive vanity. In order to produce the conditions necessary for the hero's "final recognition of human values," Knox must presume a "background" that includes "violence and death," "brutality of war," and "worship of violence" (p. 61). By accepting the worship of violence as a given and assigning it to the "background," however, Knox begs the question of Achilles's culpability for the bloodshed to which the Homeric narrative bears such vivid witness. So humane does Knox make his Achilles that the latter can, in the final assessment, be compared with Socrates, for both are found to be "defying the community, hewing to a solitary line, in loyalty to a private ideal of conduct, of honor. In the last analysis, the bloodstained warrior and the gentle philosopher live and die in the same heroic, and tragic, pattern" (p. 64). Knox has succeeded in making Achilles a tragic hero with the ethics of a martyr. But to do so, he has had to presume upon the narrative for a distinction that it does not license. Achilles was literally a "hero," but as this study will demonstrate, not in the way Knox imagines and, in fact, not in a way that any modern audience can easily appreciate. The fault is not so much Knox's, but it is a fault nevertheless.

[23] Like historicism, Marxist, psychoanalytic, and feminist approaches also consciously and assiduously reject aesthetic categories but only by substituting socio-economic, psychological, or gender theory for text theory, thus betraying their own skepticism towards the text as a reliable and independent source for research into cultural history. Jerold C. Frakes, for example, situates his discussion of Germanic epic both in a theoretical context that "provides a relevant framework for the analysis of the relations among property, power and gender" and in a historical context that provides "an overview of the social and legal possibilities for women's participation in property relations in the early and high Middle Ages in the Germanic territories of central Europe"—Frakes, *Brides and Doom: Gender, Property, and Power in Medieval German Women's Epic* (Philadelphia: Univ. of Pennsylvania Press, 1994), p. 47. Only then, Frakes notes, "the strands are brought together in the detailed examination of these topics in the *Nibelungenlied*" (p. 47). But with so much predetermined, what room remains for discovery? Textual analysis is useful to Frakes only insofar as it illustrates and reflects the conditions anticipated by a contextualizing theory and history. Textual analysis thus practiced can always manage to describe the specific instance in terms laid out by the general theory, but the resulting interpretation is incapable of differing from the theory and thus cannot be used to test it. Further references to the Frakes work will be cited parenthetically in the text.

also mentioned in the relatively sober accounts of Herodotus, Tacitus, Gregory of Tours, Paul the Deacon, and the Danish historian known to us as "Saxo Grammaticus" (see Chapter 1). There is, then, a further distinction at work, one traceable to the foundation of modern scholarship in the latter half of the eighteenth century, a division in attitudes towards the past as either more or less admirable than the present. Homer first, though followed soon after by medieval epic, came to be regarded as the expression of a life nobler and purer than the degraded circumstances of modern commercial, political, and ecclesiastical bureaucracies. At the same time, anthropology at its inception adhered tightly to the view that human history was teleological, beginning from an originary primitiveness and progressing along a rising trajectory towards an ever more complete and sophisticated control of the world, from natural events to human behavior.[24]

These patterns of aestheticism and historicism can be observed even in the small number of scholarly works to have taken up the question of the battlefield duel. In *The Duel and the Oath,* for example, Henry Charles Lea assiduously avoids the use of literary sources, confining his research to written legal code and, where this does not exist, to the presumption of legal practice.[25] Lea's strong prejudice in favor of written law code is directly linked to his assumptions about both literature and history. "When man is emerging from barbarism," he writes, "the struggle between the rising power of reason and the waning supremacy of brute force is full of instruction" (101). Associating the "dark ages" with superstition, violence, and lawlessness, Lea acknowledges the duel's historical practice while disparaging its importance, presumably because it does not advance the cause of reason and law (101). He dismisses battlefield duels, moreover, as "simply expedients to save the unnecessary effusion of blood" (104). Yet a means for reducing bloodshed should seem eminently reasonable.

Attempting to trace the origins of the judicial duel back into the "dark ages," Lea is led into further difficulties. Observing of the judicial duel that "all the tribes which settled in Europe practised the combat with so general a unanimity that its origin must be sought at a period anterior to their separation from the common stock" (108), Lea grants its practice during at least the latter part of the "dark ages," though certainly not as far back as Tacitus, who

---

[24] Johann Gottfried Herder offers paradigmatic expressions of both these attitudes, describing in his private letters in 1773, on the one hand, the proper reading of epic as a conscious escape from scholarly conventions that stifle genuine emotional response, while in his famous prize-winning essay of 1771 on the origin of language, on the other hand, laying the foundations for a teleological anthropology—see "Von deutscher Art und Kunst" in Johann Gottfried Herder, *Herder und der Sturm und Drang,* ed. Wolfgang Pross (1773; Munich: Carl Hanser Verlag, 1984), 1: 477-525 and "Über den Ursprung der Sprache," 2: 251-400.

[25] Henry Charles Lea, *The Duel and the Oath* (1866; Philadelphia: Univ. of Pennsylvania Press, 1974). Further references will be cited parenthetically in the text.

makes "no allusion to such a custom among the Germans of his time" (112). What is documented, in Tacitus and elsewhere, is the tendency to use the battlefield duel as an auspice, one that bespeaks an atmosphere of superstition that Lea's prejudices would never allow him to associate with a reasonable adjudication of law.[26] The concept of the "dark ages" thus is made to obscure what for Lea must be an awkward transition from an irrational age's superstitious use of single combat as auspice to a reasoned application of the same practice for the adjudication of private disputes.

When W. T. H. Jackson objects to the use of literature for historical reconstructions in his book *The Hero and the King*, he works from a similar opposition between poetry and pragmatics but from an aestheticist's perspective, for he complains that among earlier critics "there was more interest in establishing the connection between ancient civilizations and Homer's Trojan War than in analyzing the *Iliad* as a poem, more interest in examining *Beowulf* and the *Nibelungenlied* as evidence for 'Germanic' morality than as works of art."[27]

Jackson's language expresses an ineffable certainty that the *Iliad* "as a poem" exists independently of ancient people and their wars and that *Beowulf* and the *Nibelungenlied* can and should be examined as "works of art," which is to say without any interest in their implications for historiography. "Such an attitude is dangerous," he continues, "not least because it has led to the construction of certain pseudohistorical types of society or behavior which influence even those critics whose major concern is to interpret epics as poetry" (1-2). By placing the label "pseudohistorical" on attempts to use poetic texts in reconstructions of ancient society and behavior, Jackson reminds us that literature describes only pseudorealities and that the project of reconstructing ancient history from literature, therefore, never can succeed, for this would mean allowing that poetry is in some way interwoven into the fabric of reality, thus raising awkward questions about the nature of that relationship. By characterizing the reconstructions as merely pseudohistorical, however, Jackson pulls epic poetry from the clutches of history and restores it to those critics whose major concern is with guarding literature's status as an aesthetic precinct, an Edenic garden outside of history and beyond human law—hence the added distinction between scholars who cannot perform their function because they have been "influenced" by pseudohistory and those who, having kept their vision clear and their principles straight, may proceed without danger of stumbling upon an historical fact.

---

[26] Though the judicial duel is not our concern here, I believe that it will become clear in the course of this book that the judicial duel not only postdates the military duel but very plausibly developed from it. Lea's research will, in that case, be very helpful in establishing that the dates for the practice of the battlefield duel must be earlier than those of the first Germanic, Norse, and English law codes.

[27] W. T. H. Jackson, *The Hero and the King* (New York: Columbia Univ. Press, 1982), p. 1. Further references will be cited parenthetically in the text.

It is not only philologists, comparatists, Homerists, and medievalists who judge it best to separate poetry and legend as far as possible from the analysis of material culture. The same approach is taken by those whose focus is on physical artifacts from the past. Archaeological research has increasingly limited its commentary to pure description. Reports and, indeed, entire books consist of detailed verbal inventories accompanied by figures, illustrations, and photographic plates, maps, and site plans. The peoples with whom the artifacts are to be associated cannot be named, because naming inevitably relies upon legend or history—verbal media that often cannot reliably be linked to material remains. Archaeology has therefore adopted the practice of naming the people responsible for the manufacture or use of materials according to distinguishing characteristics observed in the artifacts ("bell beaker people"), burial style ("urnfielders"), or find site ("La Tène culture"). A principal activity for archaeology consists of scrutinizing numbers of artifacts, graves, and settlements to discover categories of similarity and dissimilarity, allowing, in turn, for a division into sets of objects by their characteristics. Such descriptions are by no means "easier," but previous experience with too-easy correlations between archaeological materials on the one hand and myth and poetry on the other have proven so consistently embarrassing as best now to be avoided. A. M. Snodgrass sums up this attitude when he comments that "[t]he reconstruction of a narrative history . . . is simply an impossibility for the Early Iron Age archaeologist. Even for an analysis of the society of the period . . . one must depend on various archaeological approaches . . . for recent analysis has shown that the Homeric poems, that other potential resource, are as debatable in their application to these questions as are, say, the Geometric vase-paintings."[28]

In Hilda Ellis Davidson we are confronted with the rare example of an archaeologist who, trusting in her ability to recognize useful fact even in narrative poetry, does venture into literary territory for the sake of evidence.[29] Davidson combines a specialized knowledge of weapons recovered from the soils and waters of Britain, Scandinavia, and Northern Europe with a systematic study of English, Norse, and Germanic literature. Facing "the gap between the archaeologist and the student of literature" and mindful of the "diffidence . . . felt in viewing a subject from more than one direction,"

---

[28] A. M. Snodgrass, *An Archaeology of Greece* (Berkeley: Univ. of California Press, 1987), p. 174. Further references will be cited parenthetically in the text.

[29] See Hilda Ellis Davidson, *The Sword in Anglo-Saxon England: Its Archaeology and Literature* (Woodbridge, Eng.: Boydell Press, 1994). A slightly less clear, though perhaps better-known, example is offered by the eminent Biblical historian Yigael Yadin, who writes, in *The Art of Warfare in Biblical Lands in the Light of Archaeological Study* (New York: McGraw-Hill, 1963), p. 267, that the peoples of the Aegean were "accustomed" to using the duel as a method for concluding wars. Though unfortunately Yadin does not cite his evidence for this conclusion, he can have in mind no sources but the *Iliad* and Herodotus or, in other words, poetry and legend. Further references to the Davidson and Yadin books will be cited parenthetically in the text.

18   INTRODUCTION

Davidson remarks that the distant past knew "no such artificial barrier between the practical world of the makers and users of weapons and the imaginative world of poets and story-tellers" (5). Indeed, far from presuming any poetic tendency towards distortion, she considers that an audience "trained from youth to the use of the sword, and bound to prove severe critics of inaccuracy" would demand a technically correct portrayal of battle (3). Nor, she goes on, need the late date at which Anglo-Saxon heroic poetry was written down materially increase the incidence of inaccuracy even of materials stemming from much earlier oral traditions, for "at this time the sword was still an essential and valued weapon, and therefore there was less chance of men misunderstanding earlier traditions concerning it" (3). Directed by her knowledge of the swords and the contexts in which they were found (dated A.D. 100-500), Davidson is able rather precisely to place "before the break-up of the Roman Empire" the period in which the swords found in the bogs of Denmark and Saxony would have been used (2). Considering, then, that Davidson seeks to identify those warriors whose use of the sword effected the Anglo-Saxon settlement of Britain, we can understand why she may have been inclined to the double hypothesis that the Old English heroic tradition was both tolerably accurate and of relatively early date. "The evidence of the literature," Davidson concludes, "suggests that the importance of the duel, fought on foot between adversaries armed with swords, was very great, and continued to be so until late in the Viking Age. It is largely from the various descriptions of single combat which have survived that we can learn something of the technique of swordsmanship" (193).

Despite her exceptional willingness to consider literary sources, however, Davidson's capacity for understanding the use of a duel to decide the issue between two peoples is limited by her decision to take at face value every statement that her sources make regarding the sword and its use. Embracing, for example, Tacitus's interpretation of Germanic dueling custom as "auspices used to forecast the issue of serious wars," Davidson does not find it necessary to wonder about the impact of such a duel upon the resolution of an armed conflict (193-94). To J. G. C. Anderson's musing, "[v]ictory might hearten the tribe that staged the duel, but what would result from a defeat?"[30] Davidson responds simply that "such an objection might be made to any consultation of omens before battle" (194). Here she echoes Lea's view that barbarians are a superstitious folk whose belief in omens cannot be accounted for rationally and must therefore simply be accepted.

As we have already observed, however, poetic sources sometimes describe the duel not as an auspice but as a direct substitute for battle, as an expedient "to save the unnecessary effusion of blood," thus raising again the question of why an army would accept the "expedience" of a defeat predicated upon one man's failure or misfortune. In Davidson's failure to confront this question, we see how modern attitudes towards an earlier age's belief system and its messengers interfere with scholarly research even when, all too rarely,

---

[30] J. G. C. Anderson, ed., *The Germania of Tacitus* (Oxford: Clarendon Press, 1938), p. 82, as cited in Davidson (p. 194).

attention is brought to bear directly on the practice of the duel represented in poetic narrative. Any attempt to employ ancient narratives as primary sources for cultural research thus obliges us to address both the fact that the warriors' experiential domain lies buried beneath layers of cultural detritus left by the millennial drift of environmental, technological, and social transformation and the fact that present-day scholarship has not yet come to terms with the treatment of poetic texts as sources of historical understanding.

Even when one is aware of these pitfalls, however, they cannot be avoided unless the assumptions responsible for them are replaced, as we may learn from a recent attempt at reasoning through these issues by Hans Van Wees.[31] He, too, recognizes that "historians rely heavily on the *Iliad* and *Odyssey* in reconstructing early Greek history," while

> [s]cholars increasingly feel that it is wrong to use the *Iliad* and *Odyssey* as historical sources at all. They hold that the poems are great literature but useless as evidence, except insofar as they corroborate information provided by other, better sources. This is a methodologically safe and sound view, but its implications are revolutionary. In dismissing the *Iliad* and *Odyssey* as sources one discards most of the evidence which supports established views of Dark Age social, economic, political and military organisation. (1)

In short, according to Van Wees, "[d]isregarding the epics means losing a large chunk of Greek history" (2). Rather than accept this loss, he finds it preferable once again to push the rock up the slope, confident that other historians will, when they realize what is at stake, join him in this precarious endeavor. Promising caution, he will rely on "a few methodological guidelines" to "confront the problems" and look for "ways of squeezing out of the poems what information" they hold for historians (2). Pledging himself not to repeat the errors of his predecessors,[32] he observes: "Too often scholars regard as implausible or even impossible what is merely unfamiliar . . . therefore, one should reserve judgment on what is fact and what is fantasy in the epics" (9). "First," he suggests, "one should reconstruct the heroic world as a whole, incorporating not only the seemingly realistic, but also the less plausible and even the blatantly imaginary elements" (9-10). But in the practice of reconstructing another world, Van Wees is unable to escape from his own assumptions, even when the poem clearly emphasizes an altogether different worldview. He concludes, for example, that "in a hypothetical historical counterpart of the heroic world, the prowess of princes could never fully justify the honors they receive, not even if they were excellent warriors doing their utmost in defence of their community" (87). Yet the reasoning

---

[31] Hans Van Wees, *Status Warriors: War, Violence and Society in Homer and History* (Amsterdam: J. C. Gieben, 1992). Further references will be cited parenthetically in the text.

[32] Here Van Wees may have Moses I. Finley's *The World of Odysseus* (New York: Viking Books, 1954) in mind.

from which this conclusion is reached cannot be distinguished from that employed by historicists new and old, for like them he begins with those elements in the poems' descriptive material whose plausibility seems least in doubt. Confronting the fact that in epic fantasy "a prince may be credited with a decisive influence over the course of battle" and that indeed he "turns the tide, saves the city and proves that his honour is well-deserved" (87-88), Van Wees counters: "In *reality*, under conditions of battle as Homer depicts them, with masses of men involved in active combat, no man, whatever his personal prowess or his advantages in equipment and training, could play such a decisive role" (88). Van Wees's ability to make such a distinction is based upon prior establishment of a relatively full, detailed, and plausible description of Iliadic warrior society "as Homer depicts." What Van Wees finds to be plausible in Homer is used as a context against which implausible statements can be tested and excised as "fantasy." The entire procedure is lent credibility by ascribing the interpreter's responsibility for making such excisions to a self-contradiction within the text. What Van Wees finds implausible is set aside on the grounds that it is inconsistent with Homer's descriptions. In addition to using his own judgment of plausibility as an analytical tool, Van Wees is also operating from the aestheticist assumption that the artistic narrative adheres to standards of unity and consistency. He thus simply cannot deliver on his promise to reserve judgment on matters of fact and fantasy, and he is incapable of reconstructing the heroic world, or indeed any world, other than his own.

The Homeric narrative's prominent featuring of impossible princely battle prowess must, nevertheless, still somehow be acknowledged, and Van Wees, echoing new-historicist assumptions, deems it to be of "ideological rather than real importance" (99).[33] Van Wees would thus have us understand the implausible as a function of ideology, which is here viewed as distinct from reality. "The combined efforts of the men of the community would decide the outcome of battle," he reassures, "and no individual display of valour could by itself merit the kind of deference that princes receive from the people" (88). Finally, then, he finds it possible to downgrade the entire issue: "in relations between princes and people, personal qualities, in particular battle-prowess, are not actually as important a source of honour as first appears" (89).

At a similar juncture, Van Wees will find Penelope's selection of a husband by means of a test of strength and skill to be akin to "a folk-tale motif" (100) and therefore never meant to be taken literally. Here, one fictional text is used to discredit another, licensing the conclusion that a "courting competition, therefore, is really a contest of *wealth,* though notionally it is a

---

[33] Stephen Jay Greenblatt's research, for example, in *Shakespearean Negotiations* (Berkeley: Univ. of California Press, 1988), p. 2, proceeds upon the premise that Shakespearean society "generates vivid dreams of access to the linked [human, natural, and cosmic] powers and vests control of this access in a religious and state bureaucracy at whose pinnacle is the symbolic figure of the monarch."

contest of personal excellence" (100). It is well to recognize, then, that apparently incomprehensible claims prompt scholars to insist upon a separation of fact from fiction.[34]

What is needed now is neither another "new criticism" nor another "new archaeology" as yet another way to isolate fact and fiction from each other but instead an approach that places poetic narrative on the same footing with other media. I propose, then, a research stance that regards poetic texts, indeed texts of all sorts, oral as well as written, from a perspective that shares with anthropology and archaeology the goal of reconstructing systems of cultural function.[35] We must distinguish use, which is determined by the user, from function, which is reconstructed only after the fact by a researcher. Just as the excavation of a bowl, a pin, or a figurine immediately raises questions not only about the item's use for holding liquid, fastening clothing, or honoring the gods but also about its function, which may be to display wealth or status, encourage or discourage innovation or contact with foreigners, and so on, so must a poetic text be regarded in light of not only its use, which may be to entertain or to communicate information, but also its function, about which we will have something to say below (see Chapter 8).

An exit from the double cul-de-sac of aestheticism and historicism may begin with a reversal of the founding premise of modern textual studies. Let us assume, then, that poetic texts provide for orientation, organization, and action in a context where survival itself is ultimately at stake. Articulation and defense of this premise would, however, postpone the practice that it is meant to further.[36] In my judgment, the best course to follow at the present juncture would be for me to provide a relatively brief statement of working

---

[34] Like Van Wees, Donlan assumes that "when we peel away the obvious heroizing embellishments and deliberate anachronisms that helped to create the desired 'epic distancing,' the picture of life that emerges matches the observed material and economic conditions of the Dark Age villages. Moreover—and this would seem to clinch the argument—Homeric society conforms both in general and in detail to the anthropological model of the semi-egalitarian ranked society. These congruences give us faith that we see reflected in the epics the image, though admittedly an indirect and distorted one, of a living social order" (p. 157). Contrary to the order of presentation in this sentence, however, it is Donlan's reading of the anthropological model that serves as a criterion for exclusion of some aspects of the narrative as "obvious" fiction. And how do we know that distancing was "desired"? We know only that scholars require some such device in order to distance themselves from troubling aspects of the narrative.

[35] Writing about the folktale, another orally transmitted genre, Michael Hanne comments, in "Peasant Storytelling Meets Literary Theory: The Case of *La Finta Nonna*," *The Italianist*, 12 (1992), 53, that "the tale-type, including all the variants of that tale, is perhaps best viewed as a vast archaeological site, revealing relics left over from (ideological) battles which have taken place at intervals over several hundred years, even millennia."

[36] Indeed, as Snodgrass comments, "the most valid criticism of the new archaeology is surely that, to date, it has preached too much and practiced too little" (p. 9).

assumptions without explanation or defense. And while I am aware that a too-brief articulation will raise more questions than it answers, immediate access to these premises will enable interested readers to engage in independent theorizing in relation to the reconstructions presented in this book.

Reversing the notion of art's disinterest is, of course, no simple matter,[37] for we cannot simply return to a rhetorical approach, as has occasionally been suggested,[38] out of favor since the aesthetic-pragmatic dichotomy was introduced, at least not insofar as such a rhetoric would focus either on authorial motives and intentions or the needs and interests of the authorizing community, for our primary difficulty in dealing with orally-transmitted epic lies in our ignorance of the circumstances in which both poet and community found themselves. If, moreover, poetry, narrative, and other forms of verbal art are to be considered "interested," then this must imply a capacity to effect change. Yet rhetorical theory has for most of its history conceived the capacity for change in terms of conscious decision-making following from judgments based at least in part upon reason. Even where it is quite clear that persuasion is effected subliminally, as in advertising and propaganda, the creation and delivery of such messages follow from conscious planning and reasoned judgments. The same cannot be said for works of literature, however, for the category has been defined, on the one hand, by its apparent resistance to narrow political and business motives and, on the other hand, by a presumption that the creative act is based primarily upon faculties other than reason. Indeed, the very fact that a good many literary texts have survived even the vicissitudes of the most radical historical change seems to demonstrate their ability to transcend the topicality of argument and persuasion, thus lending strength to the supposition that literary texts cannot be analyzed in terms of logical structures such as the enthymeme and *tertium comparitionis*. The extent and vigor of a literary work's suasory powers are nevertheless undeniable, for as soon as a narrative has been given a vehicle for transmission, it no longer requires the assistance of its author or authorizing community but is able to appropriate new audiences for itself. This phenomenon is particularly apparent in the case of written texts, which can be stored and forgotten or even lost for hundreds of years before making a vigorous comeback. It is equally pertinent (though less obvious) to theatrical and oral performance, where every new production or retelling is based upon decisions stemming not from the original producers' or performers' needs and intentions but from new interactions with the work. In order to understand the argumentation of which a poetic work is capable, then, we must seek to define the nature of an audience's interactions with it.

And yet here we seem to be confronted with a paradox, for while a community's needs and interests can only be conceived in terms of historical

---

[37] Immanuel Kant introduced the definition of art as disinterested in his *Kritik der Urteilskraft* (Frankfurt: Suhrkamp, 1974).

[38] See, for example, Terry Eagleton, *Literary Theory* (Minneapolis: Univ. of Minnesota Press, 1983), pp. 205ff.

circumstances, the definition of interactions has to be approached without any regard for such details. It will be objected that to regard texts in light of qualities inherent in the medium is to claim for them a dubious universality but also that to approach texts strictly with regard to their historical circumstantiality is to deny them any capacity to effect change. The problem's paradoxical nature thus requires an apparently paradoxical solution: a theory of change without agents, of agency without intention, of argumentation without reasoning, and of judgments without awareness. What is needed, in short, is a theoretical framework for understanding social organization and historical change in terms of their mediation.

I have elsewhere theorized[39] that interaction between an individual and a poetic or literary text takes the form of an interrupted "reading,"[40] where the interruption follows its own relatively fixed sequence, as follows:

1) smooth conversion of a string of phonemes, lexemes, and other verbal units to construct a context of circumstances and relationships unfolding in time and steadily increasing in detail and complexity (a "world");
2) simultaneous monitoring of this context for the appearance of inconsistencies;
3) discovery of an inconsistency or incongruency within the circumstantial context
4) interruption of the process of adding new elements to the circumstantial context;
5) experimental reconfiguration of one or more of the assumptions employed in producing the circumstantial context
6) simultaneous monitoring of the circumstantial context for an improvement in consistency;
7) continued experimentation until an acceptable measure of consistency and congruency is restored to the circumstantial context;
8) indexing the successful new configuration for retrieval and reuse;
9) resumption of reading with a return to the first activity in the sequence.

According to this model, a narrative's argument works at the level of the assumptions that it subjects to reconfiguration (steps 5-7). While assumptions must be attributed to audiences rather than to texts,[41] the researcher's

---

[39] See Victor Udwin, "Experience Interrupted: The Dynamics of Literary Interpretation" (Ph.D. diss., Univ. of California, 1985); "Reading the Red Ball—A Phenomenology of Narrative Processes," *Papers in Comparative Literature*, 5 (1988), 115-26; and "Autopoiesis and Poetics," *Textuality and Subjectivity*, ed. Eitel Timm (Columbia, S.C.: Camden House, 1991), 1-13.

[40] "Reading" is used here as a metaphor for interactions between an audience and a poetic text or performance. Live performance does, of course, constrain the length and type of interruptions experienced by its audience, but I would suggest that poetic texts in various genres all occasion some such interruptions.

[41] Alain Renoir expresses this relationship in terms of an audience's expectations, its association "consciously or otherwise of certain devices with certain

access to such assumptions occurs in relation to incongruities, inconsistencies, or other problems traceable to features of the narrative itself. By making note of inconsistencies and incongruities observed during the course of a reading, then, the researcher begins to trace the interaction between a narrative and its audience.[42] Because, however, this interaction is approached from the point of an interrupted reading, it can only be observed after the fact via a reconstruction. The "audience" is, therefore, not observable in any objective sense but is itself a construct that must be defined in terms of interaction with the narrative. This approach thus necessarily places emphasis on interactions rather than either the text's form and content or characteristics of an authorizing community. The results generated by such an approach are limited to inferences that can be drawn from precisely those aspects of the culture that are inscribed in the particular medium to which the researcher has access.

A reader's working assumptions are presumed to undergo modification during a reading—a change of which he or she will be unaware. To the extent, however, that the reader has any awareness that something may be at stake during the course of a reading, the range of impact appears to be limited to the "fictional" world existing only in the reader's imagination. If, however, we suppose some of the working assumptions used in building and reacting to an imagined context to be the same as those used in building and reacting to "real-world" contexts, then any change to assumptions in the one would carry over into the other, such that interactions in a literary context could affect interactions in other contexts. The poetic text would thus provide for change based upon judgments made in the course of interaction with it, yet because these judgments remain unarticulated, the text's "argument," along with the reasoning it entails, simply escapes notice.

In contrast to the procedure followed by Van Wees, who uses self-contradiction within the text as a means for setting aside problematic details, we shall assume inconsistency to be the structuring principle of poetic argument. Because language unfolds in time, the appearance of inconsistencies in the circumstantial context can be plotted along the time-line of a narrative's unfolding, and to the extent that interruptions resulting from the encounter

---

situations"—Renoir, *A Key to Old Poems* (University Park: Pennsylvania State Univ. Press, 1988), p. 144. Further references will be cited parenthetically in the text. Renoir also recognizes, though does not reflect on, the fact that expectations aroused by formulaic thematic elements are coupled with and thus color response to "nonthematic aspects of the poem" (p. 144). Yet if these aspects are identifiable with circumstances arising in an audience's activities beyond the storytelling situation, then here we have the basis for a pragmatic connection between an audience's interactions with narrative and those outside this medium.

[42] In contrast with the aestheticists' program of extirpating incongruities and inconsistencies as flaws or accidents of transmission, we should regard these as aspects of narratival argumentation, as signs of the text's structuring of its audience's interactions with it.

with any inconsistencies are addressed before continuing with the narrative, the working assumptions employed by the audience to produce the circumstantial context following an interruption will differ from those in use preceding it. The reconfigured future thus begins to realize itself even before the close of direct interaction with a narrative, giving the audience an opportunity to test its new working assumptions and to repeat the process of modification and adjustment. By the time the end of a given narrative is reached, then, the audience will have had the opportunity not only to develop new assumptions by which to determine a course of action in the face of a given set of circumstances but to prove those assumptions and so to gain confidence in their use, though without ever having become conscious either of the process or the nature of the assumptions involved.[43]

Individuals thus necessarily enter, through their interaction with a narrative, directly into a site of cultural contestation. It is, therefore, proper for the researcher to seize upon the site of an interrupted reading and there to begin the work of discriminating from one another alternative sets of assumptions as these manifest themselves in practices, institutions, distinctions of gender, race, class, and so forth.[44] Analysis of narrative along the lines outlined here has the advantage of catching the target culture at odds with itself and engaged in the process of active reorganization. This method is limited, however, to

---

[43] For two perspectives on the dimension of time in interactions with narrative, see Udwin, "Experience Interrupted" (Chapter 5), and "Der materiale Signifikant," *Materialität der Kommunikation*, ed. H. U. Gumbrecht and Ludwig Pfeiffer (Frankfurt: Suhrkamp, 1988), pp. 858-77.

[44] It should be emphasized that the term "cultural contestation" does not, in this case, refer primarily to the clash between individuals or groups, though such clashes may well occur. Categorical distinctions such as race, class, and gender will be refashioned during a culture's reconfiguration and are thus useful for cultural analysis. The problem, as I see it, is to reconstruct the two systems of organization, the one serving before the event of reconfiguration and the one pertaining afterwards, as these can be inferred from mutually exclusive configurations of each categorical distinction determined at each instance of cultural contestation. Direct application of categories such as gender cannot further the work of such reconstruction because this work requires, in addition to such categories, both a theory of cultural stability and change and a theory appropriate to each medium (such as narrative). Suggesting that "the critic's task . . . is to deal *with* the extant transmitted text," Frakes espouses the following methodological principle: "The *contradictions* of the narrative must be the focus [of the critic's task], for they point up the social contradictions that have been sedimented in the text" (p. 252). The discovery of sedimented social conditions should therefore follow upon analysis of the narrative. Disavowing "conventional scholarship" because it "treats the *Nibelungenlied* as if its cultural context were that of pre-literate, iron-age nomads" (p. 31), however, Frakes's own critical practice defies this principle by eliminating from consideration the sediments of all but one social issue: namely, the exclusion of women from political power as an aspect of the more general phenomenon of declining personal power in favor of institutions circa A.D. 1000-1200, which he makes the focus of his critical practice.

analysis only of those aspects of a culture that are involved in the event of reorganization and inscribed in the particular medium to which the researcher has access. The scope of descriptions that can be developed through such research is thus strictly limited.

CHAPTER ONE

THE DUEL IN LEGEND, LORE, AND CHRONICLE

If modern scholars have understandably missed the importance of the battlefield duel in ancient writings, for the most part dismissing it altogether from consideration as a meaningful practice, early historians, often reporting what had come down to them as legend and lore, do offer occasional descriptions of single combat. A brief survey of these descriptions reveals, moreover, a surprising degree of consistency in the procedures with which such duels were arranged and carried out. Of particular interest to our study, however, is the fact that the accounts provided by chroniclers and historians often include the statement of a reason why the parties at war should agree to allow a duel to substitute for a full-scale military clash involving all available fighting men.

The story of Sinuhe the Egyptian (recorded in the twentieth century B.C.) represents the earliest-known written record of a duel. According to Sinuhe's account (the quotation is in Yadin), when the following incident occurred, he had been living for some time in exile among the Semitic tribes:

> A mighty man of Retenu [i.e., Syria and Palestine] that he might challenge me in my own camp. He was a hero without his peer, and he had repelled all of it [i.e., he had beaten everyone in the land of Retenu]. He said that he would fight me, he intended to despoil me, and he planned to plunder my cattle, on the advice of his tribe. That prince [the host of Sinuhe] discussed it with me and I said: "I do not know him. Certainly I am no confederate of his, so that I move freely in his encampment. Is it the case that I have ever opened his door or overthrown his fences? Rather, it is hostility because he sees me carrying out thy commissions. I am really like a stray bull in the midst of another herd, and a bull of these cattle attacks him. . . ." During the night I strung my bow and shot my arrows [in practice]. I gave free play to my sword and polished my weapons. When day broke, Retenu was come. It had whipped up its tribes and collected the countries of a good half of it. It had thought only of his fight. Then he came to me as I was waiting, for I had placed myself near him. Every heart burnt for me. They said: "Is there another strong man who could fight against him?" Then he took his shield, his battleaxe, and his armful of javelins. Now after I had let his weapons issue forth, I made his arrows pass by me uselessly, one close to another. He charged me, and I shot him, my arrows sticking in his neck. He cried out and fell on his nose. I felled him with his own battleaxe and raised my cry of victory over his back, while every Asiatic roared. I gave praise to Montu, while his adherents were mourning for him. Then I carried off his goods and plundered his cattle. What he had planned to do to me I did to him. I took what was in his tent and stripped his encampment. (72-73)

Sinuhe represents prince and people against a challenger unknown to him personally and against whom he has no personal grudge. His challenger has established a reputation for being "mighty" and "without peer" in combat with other men of Retenu, among whom he seems to have ascended to a position of supremacy. We see also that the people of Egypt appreciate the need to oppose Retenu with a single champion, a man selected for his strength and fighting ability. Nevertheless, this narrative may not indicate an epic-cultural milieu despite displaying features such as a formal challenge and selection of a champion, for as we shall see in Chapter 3, epic culture prohibits the use of archery.

According to the Greek Herodotus (earlier fifth century B.C.), the people of Tegea remember as an important event from their earlier history a duel in defense of land and people. In his *Histories*, Herodotus attributes to the Tegeans the following speech, meant to have been made on the field at Plataea as the Greeks were assuming their battle formation. With these words, the Tegeans lay claim to the honor of a position on the right flank:

τότε εὑρόμεθα τοῦτο διὰ πρῆγμα τοιόνδε· ἐπεὶ μετὰ Ἀχαιῶν καὶ Ἰώνων τῶν τότε ἐόντων ἐν Πελοποννήσῳ ἐκβοηθήσαντες ἐς τὸν Ἰσθμὸν ἱζόμεθα ἀντίοι τοῖσι κατιοῦσι. τότε ὦν λόγος Ὕλλον ἀγορεύσασθαι ὡς χρεὸν εἴη τὸν μὲν στρατὸν τῷ στρατῷ μὴ ἀνακινδυνεύειν συμβάλλοντα. ἐκ δὲ τοῦ Πελοποννησίου στρατοπέδου τὸν ἂν σφέων αὐτῶν κρίνωσι εἶναι ἄριστον. τούτόν οἱ μουνομαχῆσαι ἐπὶ διακειμένοισι. ἔδοξέ τε τοῖσι Πελοποννησίοισι ταῦτα εἶναι ποιητέα καὶ ἔταμον ὅρκιον ἐπὶ λόγῳ τοιῷδε. ἢν μὲν Ὕλλος νικήσῃ τὸν Πελοποννησίων ἡγεμόνα. κατιέναι Ἡρακλείδας ἐπὶ τὰ πατρώια. ἢν δὲ νικηθῇ. τὰ ἔμπαλιν Ἡρακλείδας ἀπαλλάσσεσθαι καὶ ἀπάγειν τὴν στρατιὴν ἑκατόν τε ἐτέων μὴ ζητῆσαι κάτοδον ἐς Πελοπόννησον. προεκρίθη τε δὴ ἐκ πάντων τῶν συμμάχων ἐθελοντὴς Ἔχεμος ὁ Ἠερόπου τοῦ Φηγέος. στρατηγός τε ἐὼν καὶ βασιλεὺς ἡμέτερος. καὶ ἐμουνομάχησέ τε καὶ ἀπέκτεινε Ὕλλον. ἐκ τούτου τοῦ ἔργου εὑρόμεθα ἐν Πελοποννησίοισι [τε] τοῖσι τότε καὶ ἄλλα γέρεα μεγάλα.[1]

"[T]he story goes that when, in company with the Achaeans and Ionians who then occupied the Peloponnese, we marched to the Isthmus to take our stand against the invaders, Hyllus made a proclamation to the effect that there was no need for the two armies to risk their lives in a general engagement; it would suffice, he suggested, if a champion chosen from the Peloponnesian army met him in single combat upon agreed conditions. The Peloponnesians accepted the proposal and engaged upon oath that, if Hyllus were victorious, the Heracleidae should be allowed to resume the ancient rights of their family, and that if he were vanquished, they should withdraw their army and make no further attempt upon the Peloponnese for a hundred years.

"The man chosen to represent the confederate armies was our own commander and king, Echemus, the son of Aeropus, and grandson of Phegeus. He volunteered for the service, engaged Hyllus in single combat, and killed

---

[1] Herodotus, *Herodoti Historiae*, ed. Carolus Hude (Oxford: Oxford Univ. Press, 1975), 9.26.3-5. Further references in the original language will be cited parenthetically in the text.

him; and it was in recognition of this act that we were granted [great gifts]."[2]

Hyllus is an intruder who challenges the Peleponnesians to choose a champion to meet him alone on the battlefield in order to settle the issue of land tenure under dispute. As a reason for the procedure he is suggesting, he claims that there is no need for a battle that will take the lives of many when the issue can be settled by just two men. Echemus, the Tegean king, volunteers for this duty himself, and his victory, which saves all of the Peleponnese from servitude, brings to him and his followers recognition and appreciation in the form of honors and gifts from their neighbors and allies. So great and long-lasting is the prestige accorded the Tegeans as a result of this victory that they can still claim their privileges five hundred years or more later, when the duel belongs to a past so distant that it has become legend.

Diodorus Siculus (floruit 160-130 B.C.) tells a slightly different version of the same story, joining the legend of Hyllus's single combat with another involving Heracles and Eurystheus:

Μετὰ τὴν Ἡρακλέους τοίνυν ἀποθέωσιν οἱ παῖδες αὐτοῦ κατῴκουν ἐν Τραχῖνι παρὰ Κήυκι τῷ βασιλεῖ. μετὰ δὲ ταῦτα Ὕλλου καί τινων ἑτέρων ἀνδρωθέντων. Εὐρυσθεὺς φοβηθεὶς μὴ πάντων ἐνηλίκων γενομένων ἐκπέσῃ τῆς ἐν Μυκήναις βασιλείας. ἔγνω τοὺς Ἡρακλείδας ἐξ ὅλης τῆς Ἑλλάδος φυγαδεῦσαι. διὸ Κήυκι μὲν τῷ βασιλεῖ προηγόρευσε τούς τε Ἡρακλείδας . . . ἢ ταῦτα μὴ ποιοῦντα πόλεμον ἀναδέξασθαι. οἱ δ' Ἡρακλεῖδαι καὶ οἱ μετ' αὐτῶν θεωροῦντες αὐτοὺς οὐκ ἀξιομάχους ὄντας Εὐρυσθεῖ πολεμεῖν. ἔγνωσαν ἑκουσίως φεύγειν ἐκ τῆς Τραχῖνος· ἐπιόντες δὲ τῶν ἄλλων πόλεων τὰς ἀξιολογωτάτας ἐδέοντο δέξασθαι σφᾶς αὐτοὺς συνοίκους. μηδεμιᾶς δὲ τολμώσης ὑποδέξασθαι. μόνοι τῶν ἄλλων Ἀθηναῖοι διὰ τὴν ἔμφυτον παρ' αὐτοῖς ἐπιείκειαν προσεδέξαντο τοὺς Ἡρακλείδας . . . μετὰ δέ τινα χρόνον ἁπάντων τῶν Ἡρακλέους παίδων ἠνδρωμένων. καὶ φρονήματος ἐμφυομένου τοῖς νεανίσκοις διὰ τὴν ἀφ' Ἡρακλέους δόξαν. ὑφορώμενος αὐτῶν τὴν αὔξησιν Εὐρυσθεὺς ἐστράτευσεν ἐπ' αὐτοὺς μετὰ πολλῆς δυνάμεως. οἱ δ' Ἡρακλεῖδαι. βοηθούντων αὐτοῖς τῶν Ἀθηναίων. προστησάμενοι τὸν Ἡρακλέους ἀδελφιδοῦν Ἰόλαον. καὶ τούτῳ τε καὶ Θησεῖ καὶ Ὕλλῳ τὴν στρατηγίαν παραδόντες. ἐνίκησαν παρατάξει τὸν Εὐρυσθέα. κατὰ δὲ τὴν μάχην πλεῖστοι τῶν μετ' Εὐρυσθέως κατεκόπησαν. αὐτὸς δ' ὁ Εὐρυσθεύς. τοῦ ἅρματος κατὰ τὴν φυγὴν συντριβέντος. ὑπὸ Ὕλλου τοῦ Ἡρακλέους ἀνῃρέθη· ὁμοίως δὲ καὶ οἱ υἱοὶ τοῦ Εὐρυσθέως πάντες κατὰ τὴν μάχην ἐτελεύτησαν.

Μετὰ δὲ ταῦτα οἱ μὲν Ἡρακλεῖδαι πάντες περιβοήτῳ μάχῃ νενικηκότες τὸν Εὐρυσθέα. καὶ διὰ τὴν εὐημερίαν συμμάχων

---

[2] Herodotus, *The Histories*, trans. Aubrey de Sélincourt (Suffolk, Eng.: Penguin Books, 1978), pp. 586-87. Further references in translation will be cited parenthetically in the text. The translator has "important privileges" for "γέρεα μεγάλα."

εὐπορήσαντες, ἐστράτευσαν ἐπὶ τὴν Πελοπόννησον Ὕλλου στρατηγοῦντος.³

Now after the deification of Heracles his sons made their home in Trachis at the court of Ceyx the king. But later, when Hyllus and some of the others had attained to manhood, Eurystheus, being afraid lest, after they had all come of age, he might be driven from his kingdom at Mycenae, decided to send the Heracleidae into exile from the whole of Greece. Consequently he served notice upon Ceyx, the king, to banish . . . the Heracleidae [or] submit to war. But the Heracleidae and their friends, perceiving that they were of themselves not sufficient in number to carry on a war against Eurystheus, decided to leave Trachis of their own free will, and going about among the most important of the other cities they asked them to receive them as fellow-townsmen. When no other city had the courage to take them in, the Athenians alone of all, such being their inborn sense of justice, extended a welcome to the sons of Heracles . . . And after some time, when all the sons of Heracles had attained to manhood and a spirit of pride sprang up in the young men because of the glory of descent from Heracles, Eurystheus, viewing with suspicion their growing power, came up against them with a great army. But the Heracleidae, who had the aid of the Athenians, chose as their leader Iolaus, the nephew of Heracles, and after entrusting to him and Theseus and Hyllus the direction of the war, they defeated Eurystheus in a pitched battle. In the course of the battle the larger part of the army of Eurystheus was slain and Eurystheus himself, when his chariot was wrecked in the flight, was killed by Hyllus, the son of Heracles; likewise the sons of Eurystheus perished in the battle to a man.

After these events all the Heracleidae, now that they had conquered Eurystheus in a battle whose fame was noised abroad and were well supplied with allies because of their success, embarked upon a campaign against Peloponnesus with Hyllus as their commander.

Interestingly, no mention is made of a duel in this campaign. Instead, we are given to understand that the armies fought a "μάχην πλεῖστοι"—"pitched battle"—in which chariots played a part (though whether for fighting or only for fleeing cannot be determined[4]). In the end, Eurystheus, his sons, and the "larger part" of his army are all destroyed.

---

[3] Diodorus Siculus, *Diodorus of Sicily with an English Translation by C. H. Oldfather* (Cambridge, Mass.: Harvard University Press, 1953), 4.57.2-4.58.1. Further references in the original language and translation will be cited parenthetically in the text.

4 Robert Drews, *The Coming of the Greeks* (Princeton: Princeton Univ. Press, 1988), discusses at length the probable importance and use of chariots in battle by the Proto-Indo-Europeans, who, he believes, moved into Greece circa 1650-1600 B.C., defeating the military rulers and installing themselves in their place at the top of an already established palatial hierarchy. In *The End of the Bronze Age* (Princeton: Princeton Univ. Press, 1993), Drews puts forward the argument that warfare was radically changed around 1200 B.C. when very lightly armed and fleet-footed harriers ran among the chariot formations. Throwing light javelins, they wounded the vulnerable horses and disabled the chariots, immobilizing the

Hyllus, appearing to have established his fighting prowess in this action, next appears as sole commander of his own forces, at the head of which he issues a challenge to the assembled Peloponnesian defenders to choose one man from among them to meet him in a duel. Here Diodorus Siculus's version of the story confirms and supplements what we have been given by Herodotus:

> Ἀτρεὺς δὲ μετὰ τὴν Εὐρυσθέως τελευτὴν καταλαβόμενος τὴν ἐν Μυκήναις βασιλείαν. καὶ προσλαβόμενος συμμάχους Τεγεάτας καί τινας ἄλλους. ἀπήντησε τοῖς Ἡρακλείδαις. κατὰ δὲ τὸν Ἰσθμὸν τῶν στρατοπέδων ἀθροισθέντων. Ὕλλος μὲν ὁ Ἡρακλέους εἰς μονομαχίαν προεκαλέσατο τῶν πολεμίων τὸν βουλόμενον. ὁμολογίας θέμενος τοιαύτας. εἰ μὲν Ὕλλος νικήσειε τὸν ἀντιταχθέντα. παραλαβεῖν Ἡρακλείδας τὴν Εὐρυσθέως βασιλείαν. εἰ δ' Ὕλλος λειφθείν. μὴ κατιέναι τοὺς Ἡρακλείδας εἰς Πελοπόννησον ἐντὸς ἐτῶν πεντήκοντα. καταβάντος δ' εἰς τὴν πρόκλησιν Ἐχέμου τοῦ βασιλέως τῶν Τεγεατῶν. καὶ τῆς μονομαχίας γενομένης. ὁ μὲν Ὕλλος ἀνῃρέθη. οἱ δ' Ἡρακλεῖδαι κατὰ τὰς ὁμολογίας ἀπέστησαν τῆς καθόδου καὶ τὴν εἰς Τρικόρυθον ἐπάνοδον ἐποιήσαντο.... οἱ δ' ἄλλοι πάντες ἐν Τρικορύθῳ κατοικήσαντες. ὡς ὁ πεντηκονταετὴς χρόνος διῆλθε. κατῆλθον εἰς Πελοπόννησον. (4.58.2-5)

Atreus, after the death of Eurystheus, had taken over the kingship in Mycenae, and having added to his forces the Tegeatans and certain other peoples as allies, he went forth to meet the Heracleidae. When the two armies were assembled at the Isthmus, Hyllus, Heracles' son, challenged to single combat any one of the enemy who would face him, on the agreement that, if Hyllus should conquer his opponent, the Heracleidae should receive the kingdom of Eurystheus, but that, if Hyllus were defeated, the Heracleidae would not return to the Peloponnesus for a period of fifty years. Echemus, the king of the Tegeatans, came out to meet the challenge, and in the single combat which followed Hyllus was slain and the Heracleidae gave up, as they had promised, their effort to return and made their way back to Tricorythus.... [W]hen the fifty-year period had expired, [they] returned to Peloponnesus.

Whereas Herodotus's account ascribes to Hyllus the responsibility both for suggesting the duel[5] and for explaining why the procedure would be a good idea, namely, that "there was no need for the armies to risk their lives in a general engagement," the account of Diodorus Siculus implies that the recipients of the challenge, the Tegeans and Myceneans, already understand the practice of dueling, for it does not need to be explained to them. The more striking discrepancy between the two versions, however, is that Hyllus and

---

charioteers, who were themselves rather too encumbered by their own armor to be able to fight effectively on foot. Drews's interpretation is rather well supported by Diodorus Siculus's scenario concerning the death of Eurystheus.

[5] In Herodotus's narrative, Hyllus "offers counsel" ("ἀγορεύσασθαι") to the Peleponnesians—that is, he publicly informs them of the wisdom of a practice with which they are unfamiliar and whose logic they may not understand.

the Heraclids themselves seem to have adopted the practice of dueling in the time between their "pitched battle" with Eurystheus and their subsequent meeting with his successor, Atreus.

The following incident, cited by the Roman historian Livy, is thought to have occurred in 348 B.C.[6] As he reports, a Roman army having just settled into camp,

> Gallus processit magnitudine atque armis insignis; quatiensque scutum hasta cum silentium fecisset, provocat per interpretem unum ex Romanis qui secum ferro decernat. M. erat Valerius tribunus militum adulescens, qui haud indigniorem eo decore se quam T. Manlium ratus, prius sciscitatus consulis voluntatem in medium armatus processit.[7]

> a Gaul came out to them, remarkable for his great stature and his armour, and, smiting his spear against his shield and thereby obtaining silence, challenged the Romans, through an interpreter, to send a man to fight with him. There was a young tribune of the soldiers, named Marcus Valerius, who, regarding himself as no less worthy of that honour than Titus Manlius had been, first ascertained the consul's wishes, and then armed himself and advanced into the midst.

The Manlius referred to had previously elevated himself by accepting a similar challenge, also related by Livy:

> Bellatum cum Gallis eo anno circa Anienem flumen auctor est Claudius inclitamque in ponte pugnam, qua T. Manlius Gallum, cum quo provocatus manus conseruit, in conspectu duorum exercituum caesum torque spoliavit, tum pugnatam. (6.42.5)

> Claudius relates that the battle with the Gauls took place that year near the river Anio; and that this was the occasion of the famous duel on the bridge in which Titus Manlius slew a Gaul who had challenged him to combat, and despoiled him of his chain, while the two armies looked on.

We may note that, though the Gaul is killed, it was he who issued the challenge to duel, which is fought in a special arena (the bridge) placed between the two armies separated by a river. Finally, in taking the Gaul's chain, Titus indicates his appreciation of the distinction that this confers upon him, though, as we shall see in Chapter 4 below, epic culture has a special use for such honors. While the Gaul is not reported to have offered a reason or even proposed any terms, the armies' interest in the event is evident.

---

[6] For a more complete list of references to duels or possible duels fought by Romans, see S. P. Oakley, "Single Combat in the Roman Republic," *Classical Quarterly*, 35 (1985), 392-410.

[7] *Livy*, trans. B. O. Foster (Cambridge: Harvard Univ. Press, 1960), 7.26.1-2. Further quotations in the original language and translation will be cited parenthetically in the text.

Although the Celts had ransacked Rome in 390 B.C., in confrontations with a well-equipped army, they generally came out the loser, in spite of their warrior traditions. The Roman victories must, in this case, be credited to superior equipment and tactics,[8] though over the long run victory can also be attributed to Rome's organizational efficiency and resources. As a result, Celtic warriors became something of a Roman curiosity.

Hannibal takes advantage of the Celtic predisposition to single combat, putting it on display as a lesson to his own men in preparation for the trials to be faced in the war against the Romans serving under Publius. Details provided by Polybius, ethnically and linguistically a Greek living through the middle of the second century B.C. and the writer of a history of Rome, indicate that, though Hannibal's is not an epic culture, he nevertheless still understands Celtic (or Gaulic) practices:

συναγαγὼν γὰρ τὰ πλήθη παρήγαγε νεανίσκους τῶν αἰχμαλώτων. οὓς εἰλήφει κακοποιοῦντας τὴν πορείαν ἐν ταῖς περὶ τὰς Ἄλπεις δυσχωρίαις. τούτους δὲ κακῶς διετίθετο. παρασκευαζόμενος πρὸς τὸ μέλλον· καὶ γὰρ δεσμοὺς εἶχον βαρεῖς καὶ τῷ λιμῷ συνέσχηντο καὶ ταῖς πληγαῖς αὐτῶν τὰ σώματα διέφθαρτο. καθίσας οὖν τούτους εἰς τὸ μέσον προέθηκε πανοπλίας Γαλατικάς. οἵαις εἰώθασιν οἱ βασιλεῖς αὐτῶν. ὅταν μονομαχεῖν μέλλωσι. κατακοσμεῖσθαι· πρὸς δὲ τούτοις ἵππους παρέστησε καὶ σάγους εἰσήνεγκε πολυτελεῖς. κἄπειτα τῶν νεανίσκων ἤρετο τίνες αὐτῶν βούλονται διαγωνίσασθαι πρὸς ἀλλήλους. ἐφ᾽ ᾧ τὸν μὲν νικήσαντα τὰ προκείμενα λαμβάνειν ἆθλα. τὸν δ᾽ ἡττηθέντα τῶν παρόντων ἀπηλλάχθαι κακῶν. τελευτήσαντα τὸν βίον. πάντων δ᾽ ἀναβοησάντων ἅμα καὶ δηλούντων ὅτι βούλονται μονομαχεῖν. κληρώσασθαι προσέταξε. καὶ δύο τοὺς λαχόντας καθοπλισαμένους ἐκέλευσε μάχεσθαι πρὸς ἀλλήλους. παραυτίκα μὲν οὖν ἀκούσαντες οἱ νεανίσκοι ταῦτα. καὶ τὰς χεῖρας ἐξαίροντες. εὔχοντο τοῖς θεοῖς. σπεύδων ἕκαστος αὐτὸς γενέσθαι τῶν λαχόντων.[9]

Mustering the troops, [Hannibal] brought forward certain young men from among the prisoners he had taken molesting his march in the difficult part of the Alpine pass. He had purposely, with a view to the use he was going to make of them, ill-used them: they wore heavy fetters, they had suffered much from hunger, and their bodies were disfigured by the marks of blows. Placing them in the middle of the meeting he exhibited some Gaulish suits of armour, such as their kings are wont to deck themselves with when about to engage in single combat. In addition to these he placed there some horses and had some rich military cloaks brought in. He then asked the young men which of them were willing to do combat with each other, the prizes exhibited being destined for the victor, while the vanquished would be delivered by death from his present misery. When all shouted out with one voice that

---

[8] See Radomír Pleiner, *The Celtic Sword* (Oxford: Clarendon Press, 1993), especially pp. 33-34 and 157-59.

[9] Polybius, *The Histories*, trans. W. R. Paton, Loeb Classical Library (Cambridge: Harvard Univ. Press, 1979), 3.62.3-8. Further quotations in the original language and translation will be cited parenthetically in the text.

they were willing to fight, he ordered them to draw lots, and the two on whom the lot fell to arm themselves and do combat. The young men, the moment they heard this, lifted up their hands and prayed to the gods, each eager to be himself one of the chosen.

From the Roman perspective, these Celtic warriors appear alien and savage, although in many respects this incident resembles the drawing of lots in the *Iliad* by the Achaean heroes to see which of them will answer Hector's invitation to engage in single combat (7.171-89). In the Roman context, however, Celtic heroic culture no longer functions successfully, as we can infer from the fact that it may be manipulated to serve the rhetorical needs of a Hannibal, a Polybius, or a Caesar.

Perhaps the most extended account of Germanic warrior culture is to be found in Tacitus, whose *Germania* was published in A.D. 98 and was likely based upon the Elder Pliny's *German Wars,* unfortunately lost to us.[10] Though Tacitus may not himself have been an eyewitness to the practices he describes, their details will be of interest because, to the extent that they appear to indicate duelling practices among the Germans, Roman unfamiliarity with such practices increases the report's credibility.

In his chapter on the taking of auspices and reading of omens, Tacitus has several different practices to report. The last one mentioned has to do with predicting the outcome of a war:

> est et alia observatio auspiciorum, qua gravium bellorum eventus explorant. eius gentis, cum qua bellum est, captivum quoquo modo interceptum cum electo popularium suorum, patriis quemque armis, committunt: victoria huius vel illius pro praeiudicio accipitur. (10.5-6)

> They have another method of taking divinations, by means of which they prove the issue of serious wars. A member of the tribe at war with them is somehow or other captured and pitted against a selected champion of their own countrymen, each in his tribal armour. The victory of one or the other is taken as an anticipatory decision.

We have not previously encountered an instance of dueling with a captive, and (as we shall see in Chapter 2) the very fact that the "champion" has been captured bespeaks his unsuitability for a true test of fighting prowess. Therefore, unless such duels were meant simply as a device for encouraging the troops, it may be that Tacitus's uncertainty about the manner in which the opposing champions are selected indicates a misunderstanding on this point.

Another source making mention of the battlefield duel among the Northern Barbarians is Gregory of Tours's *Historiarum Libri Decem* (circa A.D.

---

[10] Tacitus, *Germania*, trans. M. Hutton, in *Agricola, Germania, Dialogus*, Loeb Classical Library (Cambridge: Harvard Univ. Press, 1980). Further quotations in the original language and translation will be cited parenthetically in the text.

609).[11] As they do with Tacitus, so modern historians warn us not to take too literally all that Gregory writes. It is assumed that the Franks themselves, whose history Gregory endeavors to reconstruct, knew little of their own origins and that what Gregory, therefore, has to say on the topic is to be interpreted as the expression of a need to confer status and legitimacy upon the Frankish tenure of land that once had been the northern part of Gaul. Whereas Frankish legend would connect the tribe's origins with the Pannonian plain (the lower Danube), thus associating it with the great Gothic "barbarian success story of the migration period," in fact, the Franks seem to have been a coalition of Rhenish tribal groups that first appear in the Roman records around the middle of the third century as the Iistwaeoni; the common name that they called themselves, the "Franks," means "the brave."[12]

Gregory provides a description of epic dueling practice in the following story of a battle fought in A.D. 406:

> Post haec Wandali a loco suo degressi, cum Gunedrico rege in Galias ruunt. Quibus valde vastatis, Spanias adpetunt. Hos secuti Suebi, id est Alamanni, Gallitiam adpraehendunt. Nec multo pos scandalum inter utrumque oritur populum, quoniam propinqui sibi erant. Cumque ad bellum armati procederent ac iamiamque in conflicto parati essent, ait Alamannorum rex: "Quousque bellum super cunctum populum commovetur? Ne pereant, quaeso, populi utriusque falangae, sed procedant duo de nostris in campum cum armis bellicis, et ipse inter se confligant. Tunc ille, cuius puer vicerit, regione sine certamine obtenebit." Ad haec cunctus consensit populus, ne universa multitudo in ore gladii rueret. His enim diebus Gundericus rex obierat, in cuius loco Trasamundus obtenuerat regnum. Confligentibus vero pueris, pars Wandalorum victa succubuit; interfectoque puero, placitum egrediendi Trasamundus spondit, ut scilicet, praeparatis itineris necessariis, se a finibus Hispaniae removerit. (2.2)

> The next thing which happened was that the Vandals left their homeland and invaded Gaul with Gunderic as their King. When they had ravaged Gaul they attacked Spain. The Suebi, also called the Alamanni, followed the Vandals, and seized Galicia. Not long afterwards a quarrel arose between these two peoples, for their territories were adjacent. They had taken up arms and marched out to war and were on the very point of attacking each other when the King of the Alamanni said: "How much longer is war going to devastate an entire people? In my opinion the armed forces of both peoples should not be slaughtered, but two champions chosen one from each side should meet fully armed on the field of combat and should fight it out between them. That side whose champion is victorious should take over the territory in dispute without further contest." All those present agreed to this, rather than that the entire multitude should rush upon each other's swords. Some

---

[11] *Gregorii Episcopi Turonensis Historiarum Libri Decem*, ed. Rudolf Buchner (Darmstadt: Wissenschaftliche Buchgesellschaft, 1970). Further quotations in the original language will be cited parenthetically in the text.

[12] Patrick J. Geary, *Before France and Germany* (New York: Oxford University Press, 1988), p. 78.

time later King Gunderic died and Trasamund took over the kingship of the Vandals in his place. In the single-combat between the two champions, the man representing the Vandals was beaten and killed. Once he was dead Trasamund gave his word that he would carry out his promise to withdraw and that, as soon as the preparations necessary for the journey back had been made, he would retire from Spain.[13]

In Gregory's narrative we see repeated, even similarly expressed, the notion that general battle will result in the slaughter of both armed forces. The scene is also comparable in other respects to those we have already examined: the specification of terms, selection of a champion, and observation of protocols.[14]

Gregory, writing of another incident, this time perhaps within a year of the event,[15] provides the following account of the Langobard invasion of the Franks, circa A.D. 590:

Ad quem cum adpropinquassent, priusquam flumen, quod diximus, transirent, a litore illo unus Langobardorum stans, lorica protectus et galea, contum manu gestans, vocem dedit contra Francorum exercitum, dicens: "Hodie apparebit, cui Divinitas obtenere victuriam praestit". Unde intellegi datur, hoc signum sibi Langobardi praeparavisse. Tunc pauci transeuntes, contra Langobardum hunc decertantes, prostraverunt eum; et ecce! omnis exercitus Langobardorum in fugam versus praeteriit. (10.3)

[The Franks learned that the Langobards were encamped on the bank of this stream.] They marched towards it, but, before they could cross the watercourse which I have described to you, a Longobard stood up on the opposite bank, wearing a cuirass and with his helmet on his head, and waved a spear at them. He issued a challenge to the Frankish army. "Today we shall find out which side God intends to be victorious!" he shouted. I imagine that this was a signal which the Longobards had agreed upon. A few of the Franks managed to cross. They fought with this Longobard and killed him. Then, lo and behold, all the Longobard army wheeled round in retreat and marched away.

The Langobard warrior gives every evidence of wishing to engage in a duel but the Franks, like the Hebrews confronted by Goliath, seem not necessarily to comprehend the significance of his words. Indeed, it does not seem improbable that Gregory is aware of the parallel with the story in I Samuel, which may even have suggested to him the idea of casting his Franks in the role of uncomprehending but nevertheless victorious Hebrews. If Gregory does have this passage in mind and sees the opportunity provided by the Biblical parallel to illustrate God's preference for the Franks, the idea of

---

[13] Gregory of Tours, *History of the Franks*, trans. Lewis Thorpe (Middlesex: Penguin Books, 1974). Further quotations in translation will be cited parenthetically in the text by the book and page numbers of the original-language edition.

[14] See Chapters 2 and 3 below.

[15] See Thorpe's introduction to *The History of the Franks* (p. 22).

borrowing from Biblical rhetoric must have been suggested to him by appropriate parallels between the two situations. The challenge to engage in single combat is the most notable similarity, but the Langobard flight can also be compared with the Philistines' panic upon the death of their champion, though Gregory has flight followed by an orderly march. It is as though he wished here to give both versions their due—the Biblical model and the actual events as he knew them. An orderly withdrawal of the Lombards accords, of course, with the provisions made by proper observance of the duel's protocols. The Franks' behavior is not as clearly appropriate, for they send "a few" to engage with the Langobard. Does this indicate, as it seems to, a breach of etiquette? Are we to infer that dueling was not understood by these Franks?

Gregory is not our only source for accounts of Langobard proclivity for the duel, for about two centuries after Gregory a Langobard history was composed by Paul the Deacon.[16] The first reported incident of dueling occurs as a small army of Langobards are attempting to pass into Mauringia where the Aspitti block their way "cum magnas hostium copias" (1.11)—"with a great force."[17] The Aspitti are given pause by a rumor spread by the Langobards that they have among them "cynocephalos, id est canini capitis homines"— "dog-headed men"—who "humanum sanguinem bibere" (1.11)—"drink human blood" (20).

> Habebant tamen apud se virum fortissimum, de cuius fidebant viribus, posse se procul dubio optinere quod vellent. Hunc solum pro omnibus pugnaturum obiciunt. Mandant Langobardis, unum quem vellent suorum mitterent, qui cum eo ad singulare certamen exiret, ea videlicet conditione, ut, si suus bellator victoriam caperet, Langobardi itinere quo venerant abirent; sin vero superaretur ab altero, tum se Langobardis transitum per fines proprios non vetituros. Cumque Langobardi, quem e suis potius adversus virum bellicosissimum mitterent, ambigerent, quidam ex servili conditione sponte se optulit, promittit se provocanti hosti congressurum, ea ratione, ut, si de hoste victoriam caperet, a se suaque progenie servitutis naevum auferrent. Quid plura? Gratanter quae postularat sese facturos pollicentur. Adgressus hostem, pugnavit et vicit; Langobardis transeundi facultatem, sibi suisque, ut optaverat, iura libertatis indeptus est. (1.12)

> [The Aspitti] had, however, among them a very powerful man, to whose strength they trusted that they could obtain without doubt what they wanted. They offered him alone to fight for all. They charged the Langobards to send any one of their own they might wish, to go forth with him to single combat upon this condition, to wit; that if their warrior should win the

---

[16] *Pauli Historia Langobardorum*, ed. L. Bethmann and G. Waitz (1878; Hanover: Hahnsche Buchhandlung, 1978). Further quotations in the original language will be cited parenthetically in the text.

[17] *History of the Langobards by Paul the Deacon*, trans. William Dudley Foulke (Philadelphia: Department of History, University of Pennsylvania, 1907), p. 20. Further quotations in translation will be cited parenthetically in the text.

> victory, the Langobards would depart the way they had come, but if he should be overthrown by the other, then they would not forbid the Langobards a passage through their own territories. And when the Langobards were in doubt what one of their own they should send against this most warlike man, a certain person of servile rank offered himself of his own will, and promised that he would engage the challenging enemy upon this condition: that if he took the victory from the enemy, they would take away the stain of slavery from him and from his offspring. Why say more? They joyfully promised to do what he had asked. Having engaged the enemy, he fought and conquered, and won for the Langobards the means of passage, and for himself and his descendants, as he had desired, the rights of liberty. (20-21)

This story also has features in common with the Hebrew account of David's encounter with Goliath, for the Langobard champion, like David, is a volunteer from beyond the military establishment.

If there is any accuracy in the accounts by Gregory of Tours and Paul the Deacon, it could be inferred that the incident related by Paul occurs some time before the one told by Gregory, because the Langobards just east of the Elbe are at an earlier stage in their migration than those in Italy. These details do, in fact, coincide with the Langobard itinerary, which began in the North perhaps on or near Sweden's southern coastline and ended at Ravenna. More interesting, however, than this compatibility among the sources is the implication that when the Langobards first encountered the duel, its practice was alien to them, but they soon adopted it.

Paul describes another battlefield duel bearing the characteristics of epic-cultural understandings. The seventh-century Langobard King Cunincpert is under attack by an Austrian army headed by Alahis.

> Ad quem Cunincpert nuntium misit, mandans ei, ut cum eo singulare certamen iniret, nec opus esset utrorumque exercitum fatigare. Ad quae verba Alahis minime consensit. Cui cum unus e suis, genere Tuscus, ei persuaderet, virium bellicosum fortemque cum appellans, ut contra Cunincpertum audenter exiret, Alahis ad haec verba respondit: "Cunincpert, quamvis ebriosus sit et stupidi cordis, tamen satis est audax et mirae fortitudinis. Nam tempore patris eius quando nos erabamus iuvenculi, habebantur in palatio berbices mirae magnitudinis, quos ille supra dorsum eorum lanam adprehendens, extenso eos brachio a terra levabat; quod quidem ego facere non poteram." Haec ille Tuscus audiens, dixit ad eum: "Si tu cum Cunincperto pugnam inire singulari certamine non audes, me iam in tuo adiutorio socium non habebis." Et haec dicens, proripuit se et statim ad Cunincpertum confugiit et haec ipsa illi nuntiavit. Convenerunt itaque, ut diximus, utraeque acies in campo Coronate. (5.40)

> Cunincpert dispatched a messenger to him, sending him word that he would engage with him in single combat; that there was no need of using up the army of either. To these words Alahis did not at all agree. When one of his followers, a Tuscan by race, calling him a warlike and brave man, advised him to go forth boldly against Cunincpert, Alahis replied to these words:

"Cunincpert, although he is a drunkard and of a stupid heart, is nevertheless quite bold and of wonderful strength. For in his father's time when we were boys there were in the palace wethers of great size which he seized by the wool of the back and lifted from the ground with outstretched arm, which, indeed, I was not able to do." That Tuscan hearing these things said to him: "If you do not dare to go into a fight with Cunincpert in single combat you will not have me any longer as a companion in your support." And saying this he broke away and straightway betook himself to Cunincpert and reported these things to him. Then . . . both lines came together in the field of Coronate. (246-47)

As seen in other examples, the reason for the duel is to save the lives of the men. Personal knowledge of Cunincpert's strength discourages Alahis, however, to which one of the men responds by going over to join the challenger.

Next occurs a rather strange episode reminiscent of Patroclus's donning the armor of Achilles. Here it is a church deacon who begs permission to wear Cunincpert's armor and is subsequently killed in battle. Paul's point, however, is to reveal Alahis's irreverence, for upon discovering that he has killed a churchman he vows that, should he be granted victory, "unum puteum de testiculis impleam clericorum" (5.40)—"I will fill a whole well with the members of churchmen" (248). When the battle lines have formed up and made ready for war:

> Cunincpert ad Alahis iterato in haec verba mandavit: "Ecce, quantus populus ex utraque parte consistit! Quid opus est, ut tanta multitudo pereat? Coniungamus nos ego et ille singulari certamine, et cui voluerit Dominus de nobis donare victoriam, omnem hunc populum salvum et incolomem ipse possideat.' (5.41)

> Cunincpert again sent a message to Alahis in these words: "See how many people there are on both sides! What need is there that so great a multitude perish? Let us join, he and I, in single combat and may that one of us to whom God may have willed to give the victory have and possess all this people safe and entire." (248)

But Alahis again refuses this offer:

> Conseruntur itaque acies perstrepentibus bucinis, et neutra parte locum dante, maxima populorum facta est strages. Tandem crudelis tyrannus Alahis interiit, et Cunincpert, adiuvante se Domino, victoriam cepit. Exercitus quoque Alahis, conperta eius morte, fugae subsidium arripuit. E quibus quem mucro non perculit, Addua fluvius interemit. (5.41)

> Then when the trumpets sounded, the lines of battle joined, and as neither side gave way, a very great slaughter was made of the people. At length the cruel tyrant Alahis perished, and Cunincpert with the help of the Lord obtained victory. The army of Alahis too, when his death was known, took

the protection of flight. And of these whomsoever the point of the sword did not cut down the river Addua (Adda) destroyed. (249)

Whereas Alahis and his men believe that they can be more successful with a mass action on the field, the Lombard king and a Tuscan ally are convinced of the advantages of a duel between the armies' leaders. The dismay felt among the Austrians at the death of their leader, their flight, and their being felled from behind both on land and in the waters of a river all recall what happens to the Trojans when Achilles turns the tide of battle beside Skamandros on the plain of Troy. Indeed, both these narratives reflect patterns of action that include the offer to settle the war through a duel and the failure or refusal of the duel, followed by general slaughter among the ranks of fighting men, thus implicitly making the point that the duel would indeed have been preferable. This particular narrative gives us some indication of an additional important consideration leading to acceptance of the duel as a viable substitute for war: Alahis avoids the duel in order to preserve his own life but dies anyway. This outcome may appear insignificant if it is assumed that Alahis' death was not foreseeable. Yet the Tuscan's decision to change sides suggests otherwise. Indeed, his assessment reflects a sound understanding of battle dynamics, as we shall discover in Chapter 2.

Danish history, at least as recorded circa A.D. 1200 by Saxo Grammaticus, features the duel perhaps even more prominently than that of the Langobards.[18] One of the most striking and detailed accounts includes three instances of single combat.

First Combat

Athisl, king of Sweden, crosses with an army into Denmark, where he provokes Frovin, governor of Schleswig, into a battle resulting in heavy losses on both sides:

> [A]ccidit ipsos agminum duces ita inter se ferro concurrere, ut rem duelli more prosequerentur et praeter publicam belli sortem privati conflictus specie decertarent. Hunc enim congressionis eventum par amborum expetebat affectus, ut virtutem non partium ope, sed propria virium experientia testarentur. Quo evenit, ut, crebrescentibus utrinque plagis, Athislus armis superior, prostrato Frovino, privatae victoriae publicam jungeret, passimque divulsa Danorum agmina profligaret. (162-63)

> The leaders of the armies chanced to run against each other with their swords and conducted the business so much like a duel that the contest went beyond the issue of general fighting and appeared as a personal combat. Both were equally disposed to seek a confrontation in which they could dispense with

---

[18] *Saxonis Grammatici Historia Danica*, ed. Johannes Mattias Velschow and Petrus Erasmus Müller (Copenhagen: Libraria Gyldendaliana, 1839). Further quotations in the original language will be cited parenthetically in the text.

the help of their sides and indulge in a trial of strength to show their worth. As the mutual volley of blows intensified, Athisl proved superior, overthrew Frovin and turned his individual victory into a universal one, so that the Danish ranks were everywhere torn apart and shattered.[19]

In the aftermath of this defeat, Vermund (the Danish king) recognizes Frovin's loyalty by raising his sons Keti and Vigi to the honors of their father's rank. Athisl attacks again but this time is wounded and put to flight by Folki, one of Keti's captains.

Second Combat

Keti and Vigi seek revenge for their father's death by visiting Sweden unaccompanied. They seek out Athisl, who continues to boast about his victory over Frovin. Finding the king in a wood where he takes exercise, they approach him as fugitives from justice. In the course of conversation, he takes credit for killing Frovin in hand-to-hand combat. A few days later, the two boys waylay the king going alone to his exercises and challenge him to combat so that they might have revenge for their father's death. He warns them, however, not to attempt a fight when they have not yet reached their full strength. He offers to compensate them with money. Keti persists in demanding a fight, insisting that the king face him in single combat and promising that his brother will not interfere, for "[d]uos siquidem cum uno decernere ut iniquum, ita etiam probrosum apud veteres credebatur" (168)—"a battle of two against one was ignominious as well as unfair" (105). Athisl counters by inviting both to fight him at once, to which Keti replies that he would rather die—"oblatam certaminis conditionem vitio sibi vertendam existimans" (169)—"for he judged that this type of combat must blemish his reputation" (105). The king acquiesces, though at first restraining himself so as to spare his opponent. Eventually, when Keti gets into difficulty, Vigi cannot refrain from helping his brother, and he kills Athisl. In saving Keti, however, "statutas duelli leges solvisset" (169)—"he had broken the set rules of dueling" (106). Saxo repeats this point: "In proverbium apud exteros ductum, quod prscum dimicandi jus regius labefactasset interitus" 169)—"[A]mong other nations it became a byword that the king's death had shaken the ancient law of combat" (106). From the Danish historian's point of view, dueling proceeds according to set rules established in a forgotten past and rigorously maintained in an unbroken tradition.

---

[19] Saxo Grammaticus, *The History of the Danes*, trans. Peter Fisher (Totawa, N. J.: Rowman and Littlefield, 1979). Further quotations in translation will be cited parenthetically in the text.

CHAPTER ONE

Third Combat

Noting that Vermund is infirm and blind with age, the Saxon king "Daniam duce vacuam ratus" (170)—"believing Denmark lacked a proper leader" (106)—demands through an envoy that the kingdom be handed over to his rule. If the Danish king were to refuse, yet had a son "qui cum suo ex provocatione confligere audeat" (170)—"who would respond to a challenge" (106)—to fight the Saxon king's son, "victorem regno potiri permittat" (170)—"he should allow the victor to command the realm" (106). Vermund, though blind, decides that he will respond to the challenge in person, against which the ambassadors argue on the grounds that such a contest would be absurd and dishonorable. The Danes are paralyzed, "[a]d haec obstupefactis animo Danis subitaque responsi ignorantia perculsis" (170)—"too dismayed to know how to answer" (107)—until Uffi, the king's son, speaks for the first time in his life, offering not only to defend Denmark against the Saxon prince—"sed etiam quemcunque ex gentis suæ fortissimis secum adsciverit" (171)—"but at the same time any one of their nation's most valiant warriors at the prince's side" (107). A time and place are agreed upon. Asked afterwards by the king why he chose to take on two instead of one, he answers that the murder of King Athisl, because it was accomplished by two men, "Danis opprobrio extabat" (171)—"constituted a slur on the Danes"—for which he wished to compensate "unius facinore" (171)—"by a single-handed exploit" (107). In other words, the prince wishes to defend his people, but of even greater importance to him is the restoration of the ancient law of combat broken by his countrymen.

Much is made of finding proper-fitting armor and a stout enough sword, the former a problem because of Uffi's unusually large size, the latter because of his unusual strength. These difficulties, however, only give Uffi credentials as a legitimate champion (for reasons to be discussed in Chapter 2). The king's own sword is dug up from a mound where he had previously buried it. Thus prepared, the young champion proceeds to the battleground, an island in the river Eider, where he succeeds in killing both enemies. "Ita Saxoniae regnum ad Danos translatum post patrem Uffo regendum suscepit" (174)—"So the kingdom of Saxony passed to the Danes and was governed by Uffi after his father's death" (109)—and so ends the tale.

Nearly eight hundred years would have passed between the lifetime of Uffi and that of Saxo. The coincidental preservation of the same story in England suggests, then, the possibility of a premigration source common to both. In addition to Saxo's *History of the Danes*, other sources of this story include one Danish predecessor and three independent English versions, among them, *Widsith*, recorded in the eleventh-century manuscript known as the Exeter Book, considered one of the oldest poems in Germanic literature.[20]

---

[20] R. W. Chambers, trans., *Widsith: A Study in Old English Heroic Legend* (New York: Russell & Russell, 1965), p. 7. Further references will be cited by line number parenthetically in the text.

The poem is couched as a first-person account of the poet's direct personal contact with rulers all over Europe—hence its teller's name Widsith, which means "Farway" or "Widejourney," connoting a minstrel's wanderings. Here, the reference to Uffi (Offa in Old English) is as short as in Saxo it is long.

> ac Offa geslog ærest monna
> cniht wesende cynerica mæst;
> nænig efeneald him eorlscipe maran
> on orette ane sweorde:
> merce gemærde wið Myrgingum
> bi Fifeldore: heoldon forð siþþan
> Engle ond Swæfe, swa hit Offa geslog. (38-44)

> Offa won in combat, the first of men,
> though still a youth, the greatest of kingdoms,
> nor did any men of his time surpass him in deeds of valor
> in a formal duel with a single sword.
> He fixed the boundary against the Myrgingas
> at Fifeldore held from then on
> by Angles and Swaefe, just as Offa had hewn it out.[21]

Where Saxo places the conflict between Danes and Saxons, in *Widsith*, it is between Angles and Myrgingas. In the English sources (Old English and Latin), the name "Offa" refers either to an Angle king of the fifth century or to one of his (purported) descendants in England. The version of this story in *Vitae Duorum Offarum*[22] is actually set among the Western Angles at Warwick, and the tale itself is also somewhat different. Because Offa seems unfit to rule due to his inability to speak, Warmundus is challenged to recognize an heir in his son's place. Offa suddenly gains the power of speech and leads an army against the usurper, killing the latter's two sons "one against two," though in the midst of combat rather than in a formal duel (89).

The Danish version is closer to *Widsith*, which is many centuries older than the *Vitae Duorum Offarum*. Chambers notes that the Danish account has simply made the hero from an Angle into a Dane, as would be appropriate at a time when the Eider served as the frontier between Danes and Germans; it is therefore possible to trace the story in *Widsith* back to a lay brought to England by the Angles but also told continuously, first in Anglian, then in Danish, in the same vicinity where it had originated, which is how it eventually found its way to Saxo, who recorded it in Latin. Chambers concludes that the location of the duel at the Eider and the names Offa/Uffi indicate a common grounding in Schleswig prior to the Angle emigration (90-91).

---

[21] This translation and others from *Widsith* are mine.
[22] See Chambers (p. 89).

44   CHAPTER ONE

Saxo reveals that, following the death of the Danish king in single combat, the neighboring Kurlanders and Swedes, "perinde ac Hotheri morte tributariae sortis onere liberati, Daniam, quam annuis vectigalium obsequiis amplecti solebant, armis aggredi animum induxerunt" (132)—"who used to honour Denmark each year with the payment of taxes, felt as though the death of Høther had liberated them from their oppressive tributary status and had the idea of making an armed attack on the Danes" (79). The Slavs immediately follow suit with their own rebellion. Clearly, the tribute-paying peoples had been subordinate to Denmark through fear and respect for Høther alone. (In Chapter 5, we will examine this phenomenon in connection with Beowulf's death and the subsequent destruction predicted for the Geats.) Without the king in place to maintain dominance, subject lands begin to revolt. In the ensuing conflict, Saxo writes that it emerges that the Slavs have a champion, "vir corporis habitu insignis" (132)—"a man of outstanding physical appearance" (80)—who calls out a challenge to the Danes in the following terms:

> Ut paucorum impendio, inquit, complurium pericula redimantur, publicam stragem privato discrimine praecurrere liceat. Ego vero in hanc confligendi legem non deero, si cui vestrum mutuus decernendi mecum ausus incesserit. In primis autem praetaxata a me conditione utendum postulo, cujus talem sane formulam texui: Si vicero, vectigalium nobis concedatur immunitas; si vincar, pristina vobis tributa solvantur. Aut enim hodie patriam servitutis jugo victor exuam aut victus involvam. In utramque fortunam praedem me vademque recipite. (132-33)

> "As the majority may be bought out of danger at the cost of one or two lives, we could forestall a general catastrophe by hazarding single persons. I won't flinch from these terms of combat if any of you dare attempt to decide the issue with me. But first I demand that we employ a rule for which I have devised the phrasing: 'if I win, grant us immunity from taxes; if I am beaten, the tribute shall be paid to you as of old.' This day I shall either be victorious and relieve my homeland of its slavish yoke, or be conquered and fix it more firmly on. Accept me as a pledge and security for either outcome." (80)

The challenger offers both a reason for the duel and terms depending upon its outcome.

In exchange for the promise of a reward of gold rings from the young king (Høther's son), one of the Danes undertakes to risk his life against the Slav champion. When he is killed with a single blow, however, the Danes apparently hesitate to acknowledge the Slavs' freedom from tribute, for on the following day the Slav champion repeats his challenge, to which the narrative adds the following explanation:

> Fortissimum namque Danorum a se prostratum ratus, nemini illorum secum ulterius provocatione dimicandi spiritum superesse credebat. Unius quoque pugilis occasu totius se exercitus vires labefactasse confisus. (134)

Since he believed he had felled the most valiant Dane, he thought no one was left with the fighting spirit to respond to another summons. He trusted that with the eclipse of one champion the whole army's strength would have wilted. (81)

Saxo's narrative thus attests to the direct connection between dueling practice and an assumption that the strength of an army, thus the outcome of a battle, is measured by its strongest individual (see Chapter 2).

Eventually a second Danish champion, one Ubbi, does step forward. As if citing Agamemnon's treatment of Achilles in the matter of Briseis, he instructs the king to deposit the promised reward of rings with a third party for safekeeping as a guarantee that he will not go back on his word, for as he explains, "Accendit enim pugilum animos irrevocabilis praemii certitudo" (134)—"Champions' souls are only aroused when they can depend on the gift not being withdrawn" (81). Like the *Iliad*, the Danish narrative concerns itself with the champion's problematic preoccupation with material payment for his services (as we will see in Chapter 5). A moment later, however, when the rings are flung into the water, Ubbi insists on fighting without a reward, reversing himself so suddenly and so completely that the narrator is prompted to explain that the initial demand for a guarantee must have been spoken "per ludibrium" (134)—"with his tongue in his cheek" (81). Thus dismissing Ubbi's demand for a gift of rings, Saxo ignores the essential function of a champion's reputation and the symbols of his achievement (to be discussed in Chapter 4).

The accounts that we have just examined suggest that use of the duel may have been relatively widespread, though it is practiced neither by the Greeks from Herodotus' time forward nor by the armies of Rome, except on rare occasions, and then without the giving of terms.[23] And yet, while we repeatedly meet with the same explanation for why the opposing army should accept the challenger's proposition to send a man to meet him in single combat, this reasoning does not stand on its own. For in any battle it is to be expected that many of the men on both sides will perish, and while it may be desirable to save as many lives as possible, warfare is premised on a willingness to risk life and limb for the benefits of victory.

Epic poetry, as we shall see, especially the *Iliad* with its superfluity of detailed battle narration, offers us an opportunity to reconstruct circumstances of battle with which we are otherwise quite unfamiliar, thus enabling us to understand why the outcome of a duel accurately predicts the outcome of a general battle and, once this is well enough understood by the men engaged in this form of warfare, why they will accept the duel as a reasonable alternative to a general engagement.

---

[23] See S. P. Oakley, "Single Combat in the Roman Republic," *Classical Quarterly*, 35 (1985), pp. 392-410

CHAPTER TWO

AN ECONOMY OF LIVES

Two fully-armed warriors step into the open space between their armies to do combat. The outcome of their duel, as previously agreed upon and ratified in solemn public ritual, will resolve the claims at issue between the opposing sides and bring the current war to an end. Such duels, widely known from descriptions in the *Iliad* and the Bible and known also to scholars of Celtic and Germanic lore, seem to have been a staple of ancient song and epic poetry. But to us, such a practice appears to be irrational, for we can see no necessary connection between the outcome of a duel and the outcome of a battle.

Let us assume that the practice of submitting the outcome of a battle to the test of a duel appears irrational due to changes in the conditions under which battles are fought. As we begin to recognize epic culture's assumptions about a single warrior's decisiveness and the culture's equation of wooing and marriage with dueling and sovereignty, the unstated assumptions apparently serving as the basis for practices in battle and even in bed begin to become discernible. By examining these practices more narrowly, we will, in fact, be able to discern a complex continuum of cultural experience and cultural behavior quite alien to our own. We will be led to reconstruct a "logic," a "geometry," and an "economy" that are consistent with each other but so inconsistent with modern experience as to have, until now, entirely escaped our notice. To begin with, we will have to take seriously the seemingly preposterous principle that a single warrior can, in fact, prove to be not only decisive but also virtually invincible, regardless of the number of men by whom he may be opposed. Understanding this proposition requires a reconstruction of action on the battlefield, particularly the connection between the geometry of swordplay and the dismay to which this gives rise among the ranks of warriors as they witness it. The duel is discovered to be not simply a reasonable, economical, and sensible alternative to the bloody clash of arms. Rather, it will emerge that under some conditions the duel is the only available mechanism for averting the annihilation of both armies.

Our immediate task is not to prove that duels actually were fought on ancient battlefields but to show that it was, in fact, the most reasonable measure to prevent a massacre. Instead of presuming that warriors of the past were lacking in the capacity for reason or that logic itself proceeded according to different principles than ours, we should concentrate on differences in the way battle was actually experienced, on the assumption that were we to have the necessary experience, we, too, would be led to the same reasoning as that presumed by the narratives. I wish, therefore, to begin by carefully examining battle descriptions in which no mention is made of the formal duel.

In the *Nibelungenlied*, some time soon after Siegfried enters the Burgundian court as a "guest," the country is attacked by the combined armies of two brothers, the Saxon and Danish kings Liudegast and Liudeger. When envoys first bring news of the impending invasion, Gunther quails. Burgundy has never before in Gunther's lifetime been invaded, and he is now at a loss as to how to meet the threat. Siegfried, however, boasts that with one thousand Burgundians behind him he and his band of twelve could stand off and defeat thirty thousand Saxons and Danes.

Accepted as champion of Gunther and Burgundy, Siegfried rides alone ahead of his forces to reconnoiter the enemy and, encountering King Liudegast, defeats and takes him captive. Thirty thanes coming to Liudegast's rescue fall upon Siegfried at once and are killed—all but one, who is allowed to escape. Upon receiving his report, the Saxon and Danish armies, now said to number forty thousand, mobilize against the far smaller force of Burgundians. The killing begins and soon spills all across the battlefield. But none can match Siegfried for bloodletting:

> man mohte kiesen vliezen   den blúotégen bach
> durch die liehten helme   von Sîvrides hant,
> unz er Liudegêren   vor sînen hergesellen vant.
>
> Drî widerkêre   het er nu genomen
> durch daz her anz ende.   nu was Hagene komen,
> der half im wol ervollen   in sturme sînen muot.
> des tages muose ersterben   vor in manec ritter guot.
>
> Dô der starke Liudegêr   Sîvriden vant,
> und daz er alsô hôhe   truoc an sîner hant
> den guoten Balmungen   und ir sô manegen sluoc,
> des wart der herre zornec   únde grímméc genuoc.
>
> Dô wart michel dringen   und grôzer swerte klanc,
> dâ ir ingesinde   zuo ze ein ander dranc.
> do versúochten sich die recken   beide deste baz.
> die schar begunden wîchen.   sich huop dâ grœzlîcher haz.
>
> Dem vogte von Sahsen   was daz wol geseit,
> sîn bruoder was gevangen: daz was im harte leit.
> wol wesser daz ez tæte   daz Siglinde kint.
> man zêh es Gêrnôten: vil wol erván ér ez sint.
>
> Die slege Liudegêres   die wâren alsô starc
> daz im under satele   strúchté daz marc.
> dô sich daz ross erholte,   der küene Sîvrit
> der gewán ín deme sturme   einen vreislîchen sit.
>
> Des half im wol Hagene   und ouch Gêrnôt,
> Dancwart und Volkêr;   des lag ir vil dâ tôt.
> Sindolt und Hûnolt   und Ortwîn der degen,
> die kunden in dem strîte   zem tôde manegen nider legen.

In sturme ungescheiden   wáren die fürsten hêr.
dô sach man über helme   vliegen manegen gêr
durch die liehten schilde   von der helde hant.
man sach dâ var nâch bluote   vil manegen hêrlîchen rant.

In dem starken sturme   erbeizte manec man
nider von den rossen.   ein ander liefen an
Sîvrit der küene   und ouch Liudegêr.
man sach dâ schefte vliegen   unde manegen scharpfen gêr.

Dô flouc daz schiltgespenge   von Sîvrides hant.
den sic gedâhte erwerben   der helt von Niderlant
an den küenen Sahsen,   der man vil wunder sach.
hei waz dâ liehter ringe   der küene Dancwart zerbrach!

Dô het der herre Liudegêr   ûf eime schilde erkant
gemâlet eine krône   vor Sîvrides hant.
wol wesser daz ez wære   der kréftége man.
der helt zuo sînen friunden   dô lûte rúofén began:

"Geloubet iuch des sturmes,   alle mîne man!
sun den Sigmundes   ich hie gesehen hân,
Sívríden den starken   hân ich hie bekant.
in hât der übele tiuvel   her zen Sáhsén gesant."

Die vanen hiez er lâzen   in dem sturme nider.
vrides er dô gerte,   des werte man in sider,
doch muoser werden gîsel   in Gúnthéres lant.
daz het an im betwungen   des küenen Sîvrides hant. (205,2-217,4)

[A]s his blows fell you could pick out the rivers of blood running down from his enemy's helmets, till at last he came upon Liudeger at the head of his companions.
   Siegfried had cut his way through the enemy there and back for the third time, and now Hagen had come to help him to have his fill of fighting, so that many excellent knights had to die that day from the pair of them. Finding Siegfried before him and seeing him swing his good sword Balmung so high and slay so many of his men, mighty lord Liudeger was seized with fierce anger. There was a grand mêlée and a loud ringing of swords as their retinues closed with each other. Then the two warriors made harsher trial of their prowess, till the Saxons began to give ground. Bitter was the strife between them! The lord of the Saxons had been informed, to his great wrath, that his brother had been taken prisoner, but he was unaware that Siegfried was his captor, since the deed was ascribed to Gernot, though later he learned the truth of it. Liudeger dealt such powerful blows that Siegfried's horse stumbled under him; but when the beast had recovered itself Siegfried raged terribly in the fight. . . . You could see javelins beyond number hurled by warriors' hands flying over helmets and piercing bright shields, with buckler after buckler all stained with blood. Many knights dismounted in

the thick of it—Siegfried and Liudeger assailed each other on foot amid flying spears and keen-edged javelins.

Siegfried of the Netherlands was bent on wresting victory from the brave Saxons, of whom many were now wounded, and the weight of his blows sent the bolts and braces flying from their shields. And oh, the bright mail-corselets that Dancwart burst asunder!

Then, suddenly, lord Liudeger descried a crown painted on Siegfried's shield over the grip, and he knew at once that the mighty man was there.

"Stop fighting, all my men!" the warrior shouted to his friends. "I have just recognized mighty Siegfried, son of Siegmund. The Devil accurst has sent him here to Saxony!" He ordered them to lower their standards, and sued for peace. Peace was later granted him, though, overwhelmed as he had been by fearless Siegfried, he had to be a prisoner in Gunther's land. (39-40)

Liudeger understands something that brings his surrender upon the instant of recognition. Recognizing Siegfried clearly means to him recognizing the inevitability of defeat. Liudeger seems to believe that by surrendering promptly, he can preserve himself and the people still remaining to him, for in his judgment the Saxon and Danish forces otherwise face annihilation at Siegfried's hands. Had Liudeger recognized his adversary sooner, he would the sooner have surrendered, sparing that many more of his people's lives.

Why is Siegfried's mere identity decisive? Liudeger now appears to believe that the outcome of battle will be determined not by the numbers of men fighting but by Siegfried's fighting efficiency and his apparent invincibility. Until the moment of Liudeger's recognition of his opponent, the Saxon seems to have proceeded on the assumption that his own army could outmatch that of the Burgundians. Because they do not expect a warrior of Siegfried's caliber to be among the Burgundians, Liudeger and Liudegast calculate their own advantage against the Burgundians and proceed to make war with the goal of subordinating Burgundy to their own rule. The capture of Liudegast and the course of battle gradually reveal to Liudeger his error. Siegfried, a truly formidable individual warrior, renders irrelevant the number of fighters arrayed on the field and nullifies any advantage previously ascribed to the Saxon and Danish armies. In the presence of such an individual, nothing can preserve the opposing army from total annihilation, except its timely submission. Diplomacy of the type engaged in at Burgundy following upon Siegfried's challenge is not an option for Liudeger, for he is the challenger. From his perspective, the crucial factors determining the battle's outcome, then, are these: timely recognition of an unusually formidable fighter among the enemy forces and assessment of that warrior's abilities when measured against Liudeger's own best fighter—himself.

Liudeger's responsibility as Saxon king appears to include knowledge of enemy strength, and, believing the Saxon forces superior to those of Burgundy, he makes war. Discovering Siegfried among the Burgundians, he instantly reassesses his situation and sues for peace by placing his own life in the hands of his enemy.

The structure of the Nibelungen narrative at this point seems even to underscore the logic implicit in Liudeger's decision. The battle description is foreshortened, jumping right away to the crucial encounter, "unz er Liudegêren vor sînen hergesellen vant" (205,4) when "at last [Siegfried] came upon Liudeger" (39). Having thus marked their encounter as the crux towards which it is moving, the narrative shifts backward in time to elaborate the scene's context. The pluperfect "Drî widerkêre het er nu genomen / durch daz her anz ende" (206,1-2)—"Siegfried *had* cut his way through the enemy there and back for the third time" (39; my emphasis)—subordinates the actions that it now names to the crucial meeting in which they culminate. The hero's wading through the common soldiery and butchering them is presented as a preamble to his meeting with King Liudeger, by whom he is brought to a standstill and put to the test: "do versúochten sich die recken beide deste baz" (208,3)—"the two warriors *made* harsher trial of their prowess" (39; my emphasis). The shift in verb tense now signals an end to the narrative detour and a return to the scene marked by the simple past indicative as central.

The standstill in Siegfried's progress on the battlefield is enacted by another interruption in the forward progress of the narrative. When the two principal warriors stand their ground and muster their most telling blows, the narrative once again moves backwards in time, now providing contextual details from Liudeger's perspective:

> Dem vogte von Sahsen   was daz wol geseit,
> sîn bruoder was gevangen: daz was im harte leit.
> wol wesser daz ez tæte   daz Siglinde kint.
> man zêh es Gêrnôten: vil wol ervánt ér ez sint. (209)

To the leader of the Saxons it *had been accurately reported* that his brother was taken captive, which was very distressing to him. Well he knew that Sieglind's son could have done the deed, but it was ascribed to Gernot. Afterwards [in just a few moments, as we shall see] he found out the truth of the matter.[1]

Here anticipating the future, the narrative assigns responsibility for Liudeger's initial willingness to fight Siegfried to an inadequate intelligence report. Inasmuch as the fighting continues on all sides while Siegfried and Liudeger are "in sturme ungescheiden" (212,1)—"locked in battle" (40)—the inaccurate information reported to Liudeger also must bear the burden of the loss of life in general. While the princes fight each other, with neither able to achieve a victory, their men's shields are "var nâch bluote" (212,4)—"all stained with blood" (40). Many wounded are to be seen (214,3), and clearly even more would have died had not Liudeger, fighting Siegfried at close quarters, suddenly recognized the device painted on his shield. Calling a truce, he sues for peace on Siegfried's terms, which include his own imprisonment in Gunther's land.

---

[1] The translation and emphasis here are mine.

Liudeger's surrender does not make sense unless it is quite unlikely that his forces can defeat the Burgundians. But, as indicated, what convinces Liudeger that this is the case is simply his recognition of Siegfried on the field of battle. In his judgment, Siegfried's presence outweighs all other factors, including the enormous numerical advantage enjoyed by the Saxons. Since Liudeger has not been deceived, so far as we know, about the size of Burgundy's forces, his decision to give up, judging from the passage, is reached without any calculation of numbers. From this, we must infer that at the moment of his decision Liudeger assesses enemy strength not in terms of numbers but solely with regard to his knowledge of Siegfried.

We are not told what precisely constitutes Liudeger's knowledge of Siegfried. It may be, however, that Liudeger has heard the tale of Siegfried's mastery over the Nibelungs. The tale has some currency, we know, because it is the one Hagen tells the Burgundian court when he himself first recognizes Siegfried. Here is the way Hagen's story begins:

> Dâ der helt al eine   âne alle helfe reit,
> er vant vor einem berge,   daz ist mir wol geseit,
> bî Nibelunges horde   vil manegen küenen man;
> . . .
> . . .   ir einer drunder sprach:
> "hie kumt der starke Sîvrit . . ." (88,1-3; 90,2-3)

> Riding unaccompanied past the foot of a mountain (as I was truly told), [Siegfried] chanced upon a host of valiant men whom he had never seen before. . . . "Here comes mighty Siegfried of the Netherlands," said one of them. (27)

Hagen's narrative describes Siegfried for the Burgundians in terms of an incident meant to be definitive of his reputation. This narrative, however, doubles itself in testifying to the fact that Siegfried is already preceded by his reputation when he comes across the Nibelungs, who ask him to help them by making division of their treasure. The *Nibelungenlied*'s narration, then, is the third in this succession, thus intensifying its own presentation of Siegfried and heightening the sense that a truly awe-inspiring warrior may now be at the gate.

Enraged by Siegfried's division, however, the Nibelungs attack him. Hagen's narrative describes the uneven fight as follows:

> Si heten dâ ir friunde   zwélf küene man,
> daz starke risen wâren.   waz kundez si vervân?
> die sluoc sît mit zorne   diu Sîvrides hant,
> und recken siben hundert   twanc er von Nibelunge lant
>
> Mit dem guoten swerte,   daz hiez Balmunc.
> durch die starken vorhte   vil manec recke junc,

> die si zem swerte héten und an den küenen man,
> daz lánt zúo den bürgen si im tâten undertân.
>
> Dar zuo die rîchen künege die sluoc er beide tôt.
> er kom von Albrîche sît in grôze nôt.
> der wânde sîne herren rechen dâ zehant,
> unz er die grôzen sterke sît an Sîvride vant.
>
> Done kúnde im niht gestrîten daz stárké getwerc.
> alsam die lewen wilde si liefen an den berc,
> da er die tarnkappen sît Álbrîche án gewan.
> dô was des hordes herre Sívrit der vréislîche man.
>
> Die dâ torsten vehten, die lâgen alle erslagen. (94-98,1)

"But although they had twelve brave men among their friends there—mighty giants they were—how could it avail them? Siegfried slew them in a fury and he also subdued seven hundred men of Nibelungenland with the good sword Balmung, so that, in dread of this sword and also of brave Siegfried, a host of young warriors yielded the land and its castles to him as their lord. Furthermore he slew the mighty princes Schilbung and Nibelung, and he came in great peril from Alberich who hoped to avenge his masters there and then, till Siegfried's huge strength was brought home to him; for the powerful dwarf was no match for him. They then ran towards the cavern like raging lions, and here he won from Alberich the cloak of invisibility. Thus Siegfried, terrible man, was now lord of all the treasure.

"All who had dared fight lay slain there." (27-28)

Hagen's report conveys Siegfried's ability to slay unaided any and all who dare oppose him, even when they outnumber him more than seven hundred to one. Liudeger apparently finds this report credible enough and, not wishing to measure his own strength against Siegfried's, he yields.

It may seem unlikely to us that any audience would share Liudeger's literal interpretation of tales such as the one Hagen tells. And yet Liudeger's calculation seems to repeat the same strange logic at work in the institution of formal duels that is witnessed in other texts, for when Liudeger meets Siegfried, the clash of armies is reduced to a single decisive meeting between two champions, in whose hands alone appears to rest the fate of all. The Nibelungen narrative, viewed as a whole, seems consistent in its adherence to this one fantastic premise, namely, Siegfried's invincibility.

Making allowances for the fantastic because we find consistency and unity within the text, we might overlook its demands on our gullibility. Indeed, the text makes other fantastic claims that can hardly hope to be taken literally, such as Hagen's report that

> einen lintrachen den sluoc des heldes hant.
> er bádete sich ín dem bluote; sín hût wart húrnín.
> des snîdet in kein wâfen. (100,2-4)

> This hero slew a dragon and bathed in its blood, from which his skin grew horny so that no weapon will bite it. (28)

Here, the narrative appears to make full use of poetic license, flaunting its own fictivity.[2] And yet, the tale of the dragon only underlines other implicit claims for Siegfried's invincibility. We thus discover that the text insistently demands of its audience both explicitly and implicitly the premise of a champion's invincibility—that premise upon which the institution of the duel appears to be founded. Moreover, because other narratives in other languages tell not only of warriors' bare-handed ability to slay dragons (for instance, Beowulf) but also of warriors putting entire armies to rout (like Achilles), we cannot dismiss as pertinent only to one legend the claim of invincibility, nor can it be explained away as the convention of some peculiar poetic genre.

Is there any evidence that could increase this claim's credibility in our eyes? Like the *Nibelungenlied* narrative's claim that its hero "had cut his way through the enemy there and back for the third time," the *Iliad* unapologetically portrays the superior power of its warrior heroes in what appears to be the hyperbolic style of a poetic imagination.[3] The description there of the assault of Diomedes on the Trojan front ranks is, in fact, couched in a simile:

---

[2] It may be argued, of course, that a medieval audience would find dragons and the magic powers of their blood quite plausible. My point is that even those features that, to us, may appear least credible have a basis in fact. If the perception of a warrior's invincibility is to be credible, it must be explainable. Ascription of the warrior's publicly-witnessed invincibility to a bath in dragon's blood does not diminish the plausibility of his invincibility. Rather, it points up that such invincibility has, even for those who might have witnessed it, an aura of the supernatural and the fantastic. Seeing such a warrior fight with one's own eyes would lend credibility to legends linking him to magical dragons or gods.

[3] Whitman comments that the battle books "have been mistakenly neglected"; theirs "is a formal design corresponding to, but not specifically imitating, the natural world. Crystallized and formulaic, its life is not naturalistic but generic, its realism is . . . not that of photographic illusionism" (p. 100). Bernard Fenik, far from neglecting the battles, completed a book-length study entitled *Typical Battle Scenes in the Iliad: Studies in the Narrative Techniques of Homeric Battle Description* (Wiesbaden: Franz Steiner Verlag, 1968). Fenik, however, also takes patterns and typical scenes to be compositional units, a feature of the genre equivalent to phrase formulae. He writes, "The patterns . . . supply the poet with ready-made compositional building blocks. . . . The result of this manner of composition is that in the entire poem *no two combats are exactly alike* even though the battle scenes are almost one hundred percent typical" (p. 45). But why must the similarity in the combats be ascribed to constraints on composition? Should we not consider the possibility that the combat scenes are typical of combat and reflect constraints imposed by circumstances met with on the field of battle? We should then regard in a rather different light Fenik's observation that: "the destructive sweep of a single warrior is a typical battlefield scene" (p. 84). Further references to the Fenik work will be cited parenthetically in the text.

θῦνε γὰρ ἂμ πεδίον ποταμῷ πλήθοντι
ἐοικὼς χειμάρρῳ. ὅς τ' ὦκα ῥέων ἐκέδασσε γεφύρας·
τὸν δ' οὔτ' ἄρ τε γέφυραι ἐεργμέναι ἰσχανόωσιν.
οὔτ' ἄρα ἕρκεα ἴσχει ἀλωάων ἐριθηλέων
ἐλθόντ' ἐξαπίνης. ὅτ' ἐπιβρίσῃ Διὸς ὄμβρος·
πολλὰ δ' ὑπ' αὐτοῦ ἔργα κατήριπε κάλ' αἰζηῶν·
ὣς ὑπὸ Τυδεΐδῃ πυκιναὶ κλονέοντο φάλαγγες
Τρώων. οὐδ' ἄρα μιν μίμνον πολέες περ ἐόντες. (5.87-94)

He stormed across the plain like a winter torrent that comes tearing down and flattens out the dykes. Against its sudden onslaught, backed by the heavy rains, nothing can stand, neither the dykes that were meant to hem it in, nor the stone walls round the vineyards and their sturdy trees. It has its way, and far and wide the farmers see the wreckage of their splendid work. Thus the Trojans in their serried lines collapsed before the son of Tydeus, unable for all their numbers to withstand him.

Diomedes, when alone, is to the Trojans massed together as violent natural forces are to human efforts—the magnitude of the comparands is of an altogether different order.

Unlike the foreshortened depiction of Siegfried's fighting prowess, which offers only the summary of his activity up to the point when he meets Liudeger, the *Iliad*'s presentation of Diomedes at his deadly work offers a relatively detailed view of combat. The narrative begins by naming the father of his first two victims: "Ἦν δέ τις ἐν Τρώεσσι Δάρης. ἀφνειὸς ἀμύμων. ἱρεὺς Ἡφαίστοιο" (5.9-10)—"There was a Trojan called Dares, a wealthy citizen of good repute, who was priest of Hephaestus." Next, the victims are named and supplied with fighting credentials: "δύω δέ οἱ υἱέες ἤστην. Φηγεύς Ἰδαῖός τε. μάχης εὖ εἰδότε πάσης" (5.10-11)—"He had two sons, Phegeus and Idaeus, both trained in every kind of fighting." Only now does the *Iliad* show that action begins:

τώ οἱ ἀποκρινθέντε ἐναντίω ὁρμηθήτην·
τὼ μὲν ἀφ' ἵπποιιν. ὁ δ' ἀπὸ χθονὸς ὄρνυτο πεζός.
οἱ δ' ὅτε δὴ σχεδὸν ἦσαν ἐπ' ἀλλήλοισιν ἰόντες.
Φηγεύς ῥα πρότερος προΐει δολιχόσκιον ἔγχος·
Τυδεΐδεω δ' ὑπὲρ ὦμον ἀριστερὸν ἤλυθ' ἀκωκὴ
ἔγχεος. οὐδ' ἔβαλ' αὐτόν· ὁ δ' ὕστερος ὄρνυτο χαλκῷ
Τυδεΐδης· τοῦ δ' οὐχ ἅλιον βέλος ἔκφυγε χειρός.
ἀλλ' ἔβαλε στῆθος μεταμάζιον. ὦσε δ' ἀφ' ἵππων.
Ἰδαῖος δ' ἀπόρουσε λιπὼν περικαλλέα δίφρον.
οὐδ' ἔτλη περιβῆναι ἀδελφειοῦ κταμένοιο·
οὐδὲ γὰρ οὐδέ κεν αὐτὸς ὑπέκφυγε κῆρα μέλαιναν.
ἀλλ' Ἥφαιστος ἔρυτο. σάωσε δὲ νυκτὶ καλύψας.
ὡς δή οἱ μὴ πάγχυ γέρων ἀκαχήμενος εἴη.
ἵππους δ' ἐξελάσας μεγαθύμου Τυδέος υἱὸς
δῶκεν ἑταίροισιν κατάγειν κοίλας ἐπὶ νῆας. (5.12-26)

These two detached themselves from the rest and advanced against Diomedes in their chariot, while he went to meet them on foot. When they had come within range, Phegeus began the fight by hurling his long-shadowed spear. But the spear-point passed over Diomedes' left shoulder and did not touch him. It was now Diomedes' turn to cast, and his weapon did not leave his hand for nothing. It struck Phegeus in the middle of the breast and tumbled him out of the well-made chariot, which Idaeus then deserted also, with a leap to the rear, not daring to bestride his brother's corpse. And Black Fate would have got him too if Hephaestus had not come to the rescue and wrapped him in night, saving him so that his aged priest might not be utterly broken by grief. The magnificent Diomedes drove the men's horses off and told his followers to take them back to the hollow ships.

Step for step, move for move, the encounter has been documented. By contrast with the sweeping metaphoric description of Diomedes as a torrent of water, the style here is excruciating in its fastidious commitment to detail. And whereas the *Nibelungenlied* passage slows only for the significant encounter between Siegfried and Liudeger, the *Iliad* begins so slowly that it raises to prominence otherwise unknown minor characters, "extras," as it were.

It is difficult to be certain what effect this might be meant to have on the audience of the *Iliad*. The narrative does, however, tell us what effect this scene has on the internal audience—the Trojans and Achaeans who are witnesses to the event:

> Τρῶες δὲ μεγάθυμοι ἐπεὶ ἴδον υἷε Δάρητος
> τὸν μὲν ἀλευάμενον, τὸν δὲ κτάμενον παρ' ὄχεσφι.
> πᾶσιν ὀρίνθη θυμός. . . .
> Τρῶας δ' ἔκλιναν Δαναοί· ἕλε δ' ἄνδρα ἕκαστος
> ἡγεμόνων. (5.27-29, 37-38)

> When the Trojans saw what had happened to Dares' sons, how one was killed beside his chariot and the other put to flight, they were dismayed, for all their bravery. . . .
> As a result, the Danaans thrust back the Trojan line and each of their leaders killed his man.

The sight of "magnificent" Diomedes killing the two sons of Dares turns the tide of the battle. Trojans are "dismayed," Danaans heartened. What follows in the *Iliad* is a series of six short battle narratives, all very much alike, all modeled after the narration of Diomedes's encounter with the hapless brothers Phegeus and Idaeus. Each of the six parallel passages has for its subject the killing of a Trojan by one of the Danaan captains. Though somewhat shorter than the model passage that precedes them, all six contain these elements: identification of the Trojan victim in terms both of paternity and personal qualities, a close-up view of the fatal blow, and death throes. One example serves for all:

υἱὸν δὲ Στροφίοιο Σκαμάνδριον. αἵμονα θήρης.
Ἀτρεΐδης Μενέλαος ἕλ' ἔγχεϊ ὀξυόεντι.
ἐσθλὸν θηρητῆρα· δίδαξε γὰρ Ἄρτεμις αὐτὴ
βάλλειν ἄγρια πάντα, τά τε τρέφει οὔρεσιν ὕλη·
ἀλλ' οὔ οἱ τότε γε χραῖσμ' Ἄρτεμις ἰοχέαιρα.
οὐδὲ ἐκηβολίαι. ᾗσιν τὸ πρίν γ' ἐκέκαστο·
ἀλλά μιν Ἀτρεΐδης δουρικλειτὸς Μενέλαος
πρόσθεν ἕθεν φεύγοντα μετάφρενον οὔτασε δουρὶ
ὤμων μεσσηγύς. διὰ δὲ στήθεσφιν ἔλασσεν.
ἤριπε δὲ πρηνής. ἀράβησε δὲ τεύχε' ἐπ' αὐτῷ. (5.49-58)

Then Menelaus son of Atreus with his sharp-pointed spear killed the hunter Scamandrius son of Strophius. He was a great man for the chase, who had been taught by Artemis herself to bring down any kind of wild game that the mountain forest yields. But Artemis the Mistress of the Bow was of no help to him now, nor were the long shots that had won him fame. For as Scamandrius fled before him, the glorious spearman Menelaus son of Atreus struck him with his lance in the middle of the back between the shoulders and drove it through his chest. He fell face downward and his armour clanged upon him.

Although the six short passages are told sequentially, as they must be when narrative is the medium, all six elaborate the general introductory statement, "The Danaans thrust back the Trojan line and each of their leaders killed his man." The events occur more or less simultaneously. The narrative's descriptive replication is by no means redundant, however, for it conveys the entirety of battle activity at one moment. The six-fold repetition gives the impression that everywhere one looks, the same action is to be seen. In fact, the action is viewed from a position among the fighting men upon the field of battle. The audience finds itself placed in the thick of the action, where battle is inescapable and danger palpable. The "dismay" felt by the Trojans, the heartening of the Danaans—these are emotional responses that, thanks to its deadly proximity to the action, the audience can experience and respond to for itself.

With respect to the audience's placement by the narrative vantage in relative proximity to the violence, the six short passages are not exactly alike. With each successive description, the narrative in the *Iliad* affords its audience a closer and more intimate contact with the violence.

1) "πρώτῳ γὰρ στρεφθέντι μεταφρένῳ ἐν δόρυ πῆξεν / ὤμων μεσσηγύς. διὰ στήθεσφιν ἔλασσε. / δούπησεν δὲ πεσών. ἀράβησε δὲ τεύχε' ἐπ' αὐτῷ" (5.40-42)—"Odius had been the first to fly, and as he turned, Agamemnon caught him in the back with his spear, midway between the shoulders, and drove it through his breast. He fell with a thud and his armour rang about him." Odius's death is witnessed, first, from near enough to permit an unobstructed view of his back as he is struck and, then, from farther away to

afford a sense of the vibrations in the air and earth as his heavily armored body strikes the ground.

2) "τὸν μὲν ἄρ' Ἰδομενεὺς δουρικλυτὸς ἔγχεϊ μακρῷ / νύξ' ἵππων ἐπιβησόμενον κατὰ δεξιὸν ὦμον· / ἤριπε δ' ἐξ ὀχέων. στυγερὸς δ' ἄρα μιν σκότος εἷλε" (5.45-47)—"As Phaestus was getting into his chariot the great spearman pierced his right shoulder with a long javelin. Phaestus crashed down from his car, and hateful night engulfed him." As in the previous passage, the narrative at first assumes a position permitting a clear view of Phaestus and his movements but closes the scene with a perception of night engulfing him, a perception only obtainable from within the circumference of Phaestus's own cognitive field.

3) "ἀλλά μιν Ἀτρεΐδης δουρικλειτὸς Μενέλαος / πρόσθεν ἕθεν φεύγοντα μετάφρενον οὔτασε δουρὶ / ὤμων μεσσηγύς. διὰ δὲ στήθεσφιν ἔλασσεν. ἤριπε δὲ πρηνής. ἀράβησε δὲ τεύχε' ἐπ' αὐτ" (5.55-58)—"For as Scamandrius fled before him, the glorious spearman Menelaus son of Atreus struck him with his lance in the middle of the back between the shoulders and drove it through his chest. He fell face downward and his armour clanged upon him." The narrative position permits short-range observation of the fatal wound and clear perception—even amid the general din—of his armor's clang as it strikes the ground.

4) "τὸν μὲν Μηριόνης. ὅτε δὴ κατέμαρπτε διώκων. / βεβλήκει γλουτὸν κατὰ δεξιόν· ἡ δὲ διαπρὸ / ἀντικρὺ κατὰ κύστιν ὑπ' ὀστέον ἤλυθ' ἀκωκή· / γνὺξ δ' ἔριπ' οἰμώξας. θάνατος δέ μιν ἀμφεκάλυψε" (5.65-68)—"Meriones ran after [Phereclus], and when he caught him up, struck him on the right buttock. The spear-head passed clean through to the bladder under the bone. He dropped on his knees with a scream, and Death enveloped him." Here, the view is surgical, cutting within the body, moving among its organs, shifting back outside the victim to hear his scream, and, then, glimpsing (from whose perspective?) death.

5) "τὸν μὲν Φυλεΐδης δουρικλυτὸς ἐγγύθεν ἐλθὼν / βεβλήκει κεφαλῆς κατὰ ἰνίον ὀξέϊ δουρί· / ἀντικρὺ δ' ἀν' ὀδόντας ὑπὸ γλῶσσαν τάμε χαλκός· / ἤριπε δ' ἐν κονίη. ψυχρὸν δ' ἕλε χαλκὸν ὀδοῦσιν" (5.72-75)—"Meges the mighty spearman caught up [Pedaeus] and struck him with his sharp lance on the nape of the neck. The point came through between his jaws and severed his tongue at the root. He fell down in the dust and bit the cold bronze with his teeth." One can, of course, attribute the coldness of the bronze to oral formulaic patterning, but the descriptive force of "cold" here is consistent with a spatially coherent perspectival displacement within the anatomical ensemble of jaws, tongue, teeth, and lips. The audience is again afforded a vantage point from which the progress of the lance point through the organs is first seen, then felt.

6) "Τὸν μὲν ἄρ' Εὐρύπυλος. Εὐαίμονος ἀγλαὸς υἱός. / πρόσθεν ἕθεν φεύγοντα μεταδρομάδην ἔλας' ὦμον / φασγάνῳ ἀΐξας. ἀπὸ δ' ἔξεσε χεῖρα βαρεῖαν· / αἱματόεσσα δὲ χεὶρ πεδίῳ πέσε· τὸν δὲ κατ' ὄσσε / ἔλλαβε πορφύρεος θάνατος καὶ μοῖρα κραταιή" (5.79-83)—"As [Hypsenor] fled before him, Eurypylus . . . gave chase and slashed at Hypsenor's shoulder with his sword. The man's great arm was shorn off and fell bleeding to the

ground. Fate set her seal on him, and the shadow of Death fell over his eyes." In this instance, it is almost certainly the dying Hypsenor himself to whom alone Death's shadow would have been perceptible.

The perspective from which these perceptions are offered is, in all instances, that of the Trojan victim. The sensations of the Achaean victors are neither reported nor evoked. The audience's access to the battle is carefully orchestrated by a narrative technique designed to cultivate a consistent response. These Trojans are caught in flight. Danaans, in pursuit, are hauling them down from behind. The field is in confusion: "Τυδεΐδην δ' οὐκ ἂν γνοίης ποτέροισι μετείη. / ἠὲ μετὰ Τρώεσσιν ὁμιλέοι ἢ μετ' Ἀχαιοῖς" (5.85-86)—"As for Diomedes himself, you could not have told to which army, Trojan or Achaean, he belonged." Diomedes has been lost sight of now for some time. Considering that his initial success seemed to have touched off the Trojan rout, how much more terrifying must it be for a Trojan to see Diomedes himself coming his way. The terror and brutality conveyed by the six subordinate events thus establish the simile, in whose terms the destruction of the Trojans by Diomedes is the rush of a torrent against earthwork dykes. Diomedes's invincibility is a perception that flows from the dismay first occasioned when the sons of Dares are laid low. By conveying the audience onto the field of battle and placing it among the falling Trojans, the narrative makes the Trojans' dismay palpable, thus carrying the conviction of Diomedes's invincibility.[4]

In addition to evoking this kind of dismay, detailed battle descriptions also make another point. They are perspectival devices to displace the audience's vantage from a position of safety high atop a hill from which the battle is observed in the distance to the battlefield itself among the dismayed Trojans; the audience then stands where they stand, flees when they flee, receives their wounds, tastes the Achaean bronze on their tongues, hears the clang of armor, bites the dust, and sees death's darkness. The narrative establishes battle as a highly personal encounter with an individual and identifiable enemy. Dismay in the face of Diomedes does not come from a rational assessment of his strengths but from a terrified realization of one's own vulnerability.

The distance at which a spear can be thrown forcefully enough to be effective against heavy armor plate is so narrow that it removes the cover of

---

[4] Renoir has observed the same rhetorical effect in the *Beowulf* story, where "the horror of witnessing the aftermath of slaughter" can be compared with "the terror that comes from imagining ourselves on the targeted spot as the agent of destruction approaches" (p. 125). Indeed, as Renoir comments: "The merciless nature of the struggle is impressed upon us because, instead of being asked to see the whole scene from a distance, we are forced to concentrate at close range on a few gruesome details which epitomize the action. . . . As a result . . . the readers or listeners find themselves at the very center of the action rather than merely observing it from a safe distance; and few things are likely to inspire more terror than finding oneself on the very spot where the sinews spring and the bones break" (p. 128).

anonymity. To attack Diomedes means to show oneself to him; to show oneself means to invite his counterattack; and to invite the attack of Diomedes is to welcome death.[5] In order for Diomedes to effect a rout, he will not be required to vanquish many Trojans. According to the passage cited above, the rout is begun with Idaeus's unreflected leap away from the corpse of his brother. Dismay spreads instantly to the rest of the Trojans, who respond like Idaeus, so that Menelaus's spear enters Scamandrius between the shoulders from behind. So, too, the other victims listed are speared in various ways: in the back (1), while mounting the chariot to drive away (2), in the buttock (3), through the nape of the neck (4), and with a sword slash from behind (5). Once Diomedes has caused dismay by his first display of death-dealing might, the Trojans collectively flinch. In the succession of combat deaths, we can see a narrative progression from the initial contact, in which Phegeus and Idaeus are advancing, to the abandonment of his chariot by Idaeus, to the rotation of the Trojans to show their backs, thinking perhaps to reach their waiting chariots. By this time, the entire Trojan force may be imagined in rout, putting all hope of rescue in the speed of their feet.[6]

Achilles's epithet "ποδώκης"—"swift-footed"—has great relevance in this regard, for as an awe-inspiring warrior, he can be expected easily to turn the enemy to flight, but as an especially fleet-footed runner, he is endowed with the ability to catch them from behind expeditiously, hauling them down to their deaths.[7] His name reminds the reader, then, that he is both invincible

---

[5] "Fear of death, of mutilation, of wounds—there we have the chief tactical problem, for the art of war is to achieve victory with the smallest possible losses," writes J. F. Verbruggen in *The Art of Warfare in Western Europe During the Middle Ages* (1954; Woodbridge, England: Boydell Press, 1997) p. 40: "The tactical aim must therefore be to allay fear in one's own army while striving to instil panic into the enemy, if this can be done. This vital aspect of the behavior of men in knightly combat has not been studied by many scholars. Neglect of such an interesting field of investigation throwing a new clear light on the psychology of knights, is doubtless due to the excellent repute noble horsemen have for this. The great individual fighter, as the classic representation of him will have it, knew no fear. . . . This over-simplified picture of undaunted gallantry is not really a true one. Fear in the fighting man in time of war and on the battlefield is easy to see: if it is not quickly mastered men take to their heels, fleeing in whole units, or becoming panic-stricken." Further references will be cited parenthetically in the text.

[6] Fenik characterizes passages like this as "a series of quick, *brutal* slayings (p. 84). He identifies the following elements of underlying similarity:
1. A series of individual slayings.
2. Followed by an unhindered charge.
3. River or fire simile. (p. 85)

He continues, "[t]he description of the Trojan rout is not repeated elsewhere exactly, but it shares a considerable number of details with other such retreat scenes, all of which are generally alike" (p. 85).

[7] Whitman points out that while some epithets can be used interchangeably for many characters and seem to be useful primarily for their metrical qualities,

and inescapable. For those who take the field against him, fate is not even a matter of chance—death is simply ineluctable.

The premise of invincibility derives, as we have seen, from the fact that it is necessary for combatants to face one another at close range. (We shall take up the question of archery further below.) Close-range battle has the effect of fragmenting a mass action into an unlimited number of face-to-face encounters.[8] Precisely as the seven battle narratives examined above all present instances of men working alone or (in the case of Dares's sons) in pairs, we should understand that such battles, no matter how large the forces involved, immediately break down into the configuration of fighting pairs. An example of this breakdown is provided by the *Iliad*'s very first battle description.

> ὡς τότ' ἐπασσύτεραι Δαναῶν κίνυντο φάλαγγες
> νωλεμέως πόλεμόνδε . . . ἀμφὶ δὲ πᾶσι
> τεύχεα ποικίλ' ἔλαμπε. τὰ εἱμένοι ἐστιχόωντο. . . .
>   Οἱ δ' ὅτε δή ῥ' ἐς χῶρον ἕνα ξυνιόντες ἵκοντο.
> σύν ῥ' ἔβαλον ῥινούς. σὺν δ' ἔγχεα καὶ μένε' ἀνδρῶν
> χαλκεοθωρήκων· ἀτὰρ ἀσπίδες ὀμφαλόεσσαι
> ἔπληντ' ἀλλήλῃσι. πολὺς δ' ὀρυμαγδὸς ὀρώρει.
> ἔνθα δ' ἅμ' οἰμωγή τε καὶ εὐχωλὴ πέλεν ἀνδρῶν
> ὀλλύντων τε καὶ ὀλλυμένων. ῥέε δ' αἵματι γαῖα. (4.427-28, 431-32, 446-51)

> And now battalion on battalion of Danaans swept relentlessly into battle.
> . . . The metalled armor that they marched in glittered on every man. . . .
> At last the armies met, with a clash of bucklers, spears and bronze-clad fighting men. The bosses of their shields collided and a great roar went up.

"swift of foot" is not interchanged with other metrical equivalents and is, therefore, specific to Achilles's character (p. 92). Paolo Vivante goes further in "Rose-Fingered Dawn and the Idea of Time," *Critical Essays on Homer*, pp. 51-61, arguing that the selection even of frequently-occurring epithets is appropriate to the context. Michael Lynn-George emphasizes the possibility that "ποδ-άρκης" means "succouring with the feet, running to the rescue"—see Lynn-George, "Aspects of the Epic Vocabulary of Vulnerability," *Colby Quarterly*, 29 (1993), 206 n17. Further references to the Lynn-George work will be cited parenthetically in the text.

[8] Rachel Bespaloff, in "Hector," *Critical Essays on Homer*, pp. 127-31, has observed that there is a connection between battle in the form of a series of duels and each individual participant's constant reassessment of his own chances of survival. "The changing rhythm of the battle," she writes, "pits the defenders' valor against the invaders' fury in a constantly shifting relation which makes every contestant uncertain of the future. This fluctuation of fortune does not stop the Achaians and Trojans from calculating, with a kind of muffled lucidity, their respective chances in the 'indefinite series of duels' whose ensemble is the Trojan war" (p. 130). Further references to the Bespaloff work will be cited parenthetically in the text.

> The screams of the dying were mingled with the vaunts of their destroyers, and the earth ran with blood.

So much for the general and highly metaphorical description that stations the viewer at a safe distance from the front lines, whence all that can be seen is the clash of two glittering but indistinct and impersonal masses. Now the same scene is offered again from a perspective close to the fighting. The narrative follows the same pattern as that observed above:

> Πρῶτος δ' Ἀντίλοχος Τρώων ἕλεν ἄνδρα κορυστὴν
> ἐσθλὸν ἐνὶ προμάχοισι, Θαλυσιάδην Ἐχέπωλον·
> τόν ῥ' ἔβαλε πρῶτος κόρυθος φάλον ἱπποδασείης,
> ἐν δὲ μετώπῳ πῆξε, πέρησε δ' ἄρ' ὀστέον εἴσω
> αἰχμὴ χαλκείη· τὸν δὲ σκότος ὄσσε κάλυψεν.
> ἤριπε δ', ὡς ὅτε πύργος, ἐνὶ κρατερῇ ὑσμίνῃ. (4.457-62)

> Antilochus was the first to kill his man, Echelopus son of Thalysius, who was fighting in full armor in the Trojan front. With the first cast he struck this man on the ridge of his crested helmet. The spear-point, landing in his forehead, pierced the bone; darkness came down on his eyes and he crashed in the mêlée like a falling tower.

If this first spearcast might have selected its victim by chance, the response to it is deliberate:

> τὸν δὲ πεσόντα ποδῶν ἔλαβε κρείων Ἐλεφήνωρ
> Χαλκωδοντιάδης, μεγαθύμων ἀρχὸς Ἀβάντων.
> ἕλκε δ' ὑπὲκ βελέων, λελιημένος ὄφρα τάχιστα
> τεύχεα συλήσειε· μίνυνθα δέ οἱ γένεθ' ὁρμή.
> νεκρὸν γὰρ ἐρύοντα ἰδὼν μεγάθυμος Ἀγήνωρ
> πλευρά, τά οἱ κύψαντι παρ' ἀσπίδος ἐξεφαάνθη,
> οὔτησε ξυστῷ χαλκήρεϊ, λῦσε δὲ γυῖα. (4.463-69)

> He was scarcely down when Prince Elphenor son of Chalcodon and leader of the fiery Abantes seized him by the feet and tried to drag him quickly out of range to spoil him of his armor—an enterprise he did not carry far, for the valiant Agenor saw him dragging the corpse away. With his bronze-headed shaft Agenor caught him on the flank.

Agenor sees, takes aim at, and strikes Prince Elphenor. The narrative readily recognizes individual participants in the battle, easily picking out and identifying each new participant, lingering upon his name and background before dispatching him to dark death. The moment that an individual takes action against one of the heroes, he is recognized, identified, and thus set off from the indiscriminate background of unnamed warriors. As men make themselves visible through their action, they emerge from obscurity and enter immediately into a struggle for their lives.[9]

Still, it is difficult for us to accept the fact that brave men working together in a group would not be capable of standing against and putting an end to even the most formidable individual. Some might lose their lives in such an effort, but the end result would mean victory for the group as a whole. Why would this approach not be tried? Clearly, it must have been, and we must ask, therefore, why it could not succeed.

Again, the *Iliad* as a whole may be taken as a textbook demonstration of this proposition. In order to show the way in which champions operate on the battlefield when the duel is bypassed, the best of the Achaean warriors is subtracted from the equation. The act of removing Achilles's overwhelming power to dismay effectively lifts the limits on the amount of bloodshed to be expected. The bulk of the narrative is then devoted to an explication of the progress of battle without Achilles as a factor.

When Achilles is not on the field, the best men on both sides find themselves nearly evenly matched. The battle sways first one way, then the other. If one of the heroes is wounded or surrounded, he calls for help, and his equals come to his aid. The shifting of a few of the better fighters one way or the other along the battle line thus keeps the fighting balanced. Even when one side is advancing on the other, those in retreat make sure that resistance is evenly matched against the points of greatest pressure. The lesser warriors who die serve as a buffer, taking the shock of a new onslaught and allowing the best fighters to reposition themselves so as to increase resistance where it is most needed. In the process, heroes on both sides, even though they are not killed, are taken out of action by flesh wounds, concussions, and exhaustion. Thus, even as the numbers dwindle, a general balance is maintained between the armies.

The armies prove themselves to be almost perfectly matched. The clearest demonstration of this fact comes in the duel between Hector and Telamonian Aias,[10] at which we shall presently take a closer look. The fact that neither champion can win a decisive victory over the other and that their duel, therefore, must be called off due to darkness and exhaustion simply presages the larger struggle between their two armies. The strength of the armies can in practical fact be measured by their strongest individuals. Quite the opposite of modern group activity, which presumes a team to be stronger

---

[9] The rhetorical force of such perspectival shifts within the battle scenes has been remarked upon by Lynn-George, who sees that in addition to "the sense of isolation in death, the exposure and helplessness of the victim who is struck in the absence of any defender, the construction can also serve to delineate another configuration of battle narrative, one in which the scene widens beyond the helplessness of the victim to include the helplessness of the spectator, the potential protector who, while present, is powerless to do anything" (p. 204).

[10] The more common English form of this name is "Ajax." For consistency with the translation, however, I shall use "Aias."

than its weakest member, the outcome of epic battle depends upon the strongest individual.

In the event of almost perfectly matched forces, the active participation of an Achilles means a slight tipping of the balance. From the perspective of the men in the front ranks, the slightest perceptible imbalance is translated into an immediate rout. Were Achilles to present himself and kill Hector, every Trojan would instantly understand that the battle line must move as quickly as possible back towards the safety of Troy's walls, because none of the remaining Trojans could hope to fare better than Hector against Achilles. Death would take them, and after them those lesser than they, and so on all the way across the plain to the walls of Troy.[11] Mental calculation thus shows the only hope to lie in a lightning-fast retreat. Given the fact that Hector does not trust even himself alone against Achilles, however, the effect of Achilles's addition to the equation on the field must be even more impressive. Hector's hesitation directly to confront Achilles signals to the other Trojans that there is no hope for Troy but the safety of her walls.[12] Without

---

[11] "So much in this world," writes Lynn-George, "hinges upon the necessity and capacity 'to ward off, to defend, protect, succour, aid, come to the rescue.' One of the fundamental constructions in such a world is the wall . . ., the wall erected as εἶλαρ, 'a means of defence or protection,' 'a shelter'" (p. 207). But the wall is always viewed ultimately in terms of its inadequacy and so merely points up the "possibility of destruction" on the one hand, and "the renewed need for defence" on the other (p. 207).

[12] The failure ("οὐκ ἔχραισμε"—14.66) of the ditch and wall to protect the Achaean forces presents Lynn-George with an occasion to characterize Iliadic battle experience in general, as follows:

> The verb *chraismein* does not simply state the effort to secure existence: in the *Iliad* it is always negated, and hence always negates; it forms a construction that is emphatic in its articulation of *ou ti, ou tis*—the "in no way" and "no one" that states what is *of no avail*. On the one hand, the verb *chraismein* belongs to the extensive system of words in Greek that denote help, defence, protection; on the other hand, in its consistent use in a negative construction, it marks the limits of that broad domain, the boundary that defines vulnerability and beyond which human endeavor enters the open, fully exposed space where further effort is potentially futile. In its construction *chraismein* always points to this void, to the absence of help, the collapse of effective protection, the failure of a means of defence; in pronouncing vulnerability the verb sounds a note of profound futility from which the opening of the epic issues and to which the *Iliad* insistently returns. (p. 208)

The "absence," "collapse," "failure" to which the *Iliad* insistently refers stems, in my view, directly from the absence of Achilles from the field, resulting in the futility in wall-building, the failure of the men to contain Hector, and the failure of the wall to hold back the Trojans; these are but extensions of the failure between Achilles and Agamemnon. Thus, where Lynn-George connects the language of epic to the "structures whereby man sought to secure survival" (p. 208), we might include among such structures the duel and other practices attendant upon the institution of championship.

Achilles on the field, the balance beam swings very slowly up and down, now favoring one side, now the other. But when Achilles appears, the effect on the scales is out of all direct proportion to his individual superiority. The conclusion reached from every Trojan's individual mental assessment of the situation amplifies the effect of this change in the balance of power. Dismay acts as an emotional multiplier comparable in modern warfare only to the effects of a "secret weapon." In this way, evenly matched armies can be thrown into a serious imbalance by the addition of a single warrior. In this sense, then, it is fair and accurate to grant, as Van Wees puts it, that Achilles "seems to defeat the Trojans all by himself" (140).

If Siegfried has the reputation for defeating seven hundred Nibelungs singlehanded, this is believable once it is understood that he begins by killing their princes. His challenge to the Burgundians works on the same calculation. We imagine the Burgundians encircling him and cutting him to ribbons. But the Burgundians themselves will look to their best fighter to make the first move. Hagen is probably the man most likely regarded by the Burgundians as their best warrior,[13] but he counsels against accepting Siegfried's challenge, presenting by way of explanation the report he has heard of Siegfried's exploits among the Nibelungs. No matter how many Burgundians there are, none of them will take on Siegfried if they see their best warrior unwilling to do so. Where modern warfare positions the generals behind the lines sending out the lowest ranking men to meet the enemy first, epic warfare depends upon the most prominent military man not only to lead the army into battle but himself to confront and dispose of the enemy's most forceful fighters. Absent such leadership, the army will not stand its ground, not because the common fighter is cowardly but because his function is to protect his champion's flank and then, when the enemy champion has been felled and his cohort routed, to join in running it down and destroying it from behind.

---

[13] Beyschlag calls Hagen the "erster Vasall seines Königs"—the king's first vassal—who makes Burgundy's security his first priority (p. 205). Similarly, Helmut de Boor, in "Hat Siegfried gelebt?" *Beiträge zur Geschichte der deutschen Sprache und Literatur,* 63 (1930), 250-71, reprinted in *Zur Germanisch-Deutschen Heldensage,* pp. 31-51, calls Hagen "die führende burgundische Persönlichkeit in dem Kampf gegen den fremden Emporkömmling"—the leading Burgundian figure in the struggle against the foreign interloper (p. 46), but in his view it is Hagen's hand in Siegfried's murder that establishes the former's special status among the Burgundians. That is, Hagen assumes (or resumes) Burgundy's championship through a deceit, having previously declined to answer Siegfried's challenge. Deceitfulness is, of course, also practiced (with Hagen's approval) by Siegfried and Gunther against Brünhild. But we see from the connection between Hagen's murder of Siegfried and his response to Siegfried's challenge that the opposition is not simply between deceit and honesty, for these are defined specifically in relation to the form of combat and a choice between back-stabbing and an open duel. Further references to the de Boor work will be cited parenthetically in the text.

What makes the *Iliad* a "textbook" case is its careful consideration of two forces comprising warriors evenly matched, equally determined, and similarly equipped. Assuming bronze or iron weapons to be available only to a relative few, only the chiefs or champions would carry long swords in addition to their bronze-tipped spears, while their supporters may not all be equipped even with bronze-tipped spears. Under these conditions, the impact of the few "heroes" will be even more noticeable, the effect of dread far more radical. Assuming also much smaller communities than those to which we are accustomed, variation in the size and weight of individual men would have been greater, so that the biggest may have been bigger by far than the next. Under circumstances such as these, less well armed spear-bearers of lesser stature could act only as back-up to their lead warriors, bringing them fresh weapons and protecting them from encirclement. A battle under such circumstances would more obviously pit the few best warriors on either side against each other, and the outcome of their first encounters would be even more stunningly decisive. The less physically impressive, the less well equipped, and the less experienced the very best man in an army, the more ill at ease will be the rank and file, the more liable to dismay, the more disposed to flight. It is possible to imagine that a visual evaluation of an opponent's size and armor may have been sufficient to settle the issue of a battle. Hence the epic narrative's interest in a visual assessment of its hero's physical attributes and an inventory of his armor.[14]

While the *Iliad* seems to present the case of two armies nearly evenly matched in order to emphasize the difference that can be made when an Achilles is either added to or subtracted from the battlefield equation, actual battle conditions are more likely to have reflected greater disparities in individual physical stature and military equipment. This can again be inferred from battle descriptions—both "natural" and "mythical"—in the *Nibelungenlied*, *Beowulf*, and the "Lay of Hiltibrant," for, while the heroes usually do heft a spear, this weapon most often proves insufficient against another hero, and once it is thrown fighting depends primarily on the sword.[15] Such, for example, is the progress of the duel between Hiltibrant and Hadubrant.

> do lettun se ærist   asckim scritan,
> scarpen scurim,   dat in dem sciltim stont.
> do stoptun to samane   staimbort chlubun,
> heuwun harmlicco   huitte scilti,
> unti im iro lintun   luttilo wurtun,
> giwigan miti wabnum. (63-68)

---

[14] "Within the epic all depends for its existence and survival upon *alkê*, where *alkê* is not simply 'valour' or 'prowess' for its own sake, pure physical might devoid of social meaning, but such a quality specifically in its capacity to help and defend," writes Lynn-George (p. 206). Alkê refers directly to physical might, and thus may indirectly refer to the outward signs of that might, to stature.

[15] Davidson infers from the importance of the sword that it was the weapon of choice for use in the duel (p. 199).

> Then first they both let their ashes stride
> in sharp showers, so that they stood in the shields.
> Then they stepped together. Battle trappings dinned.
> They hewed most harmfully at the bright shields,
> until their linden wood grew small in their fists,
> gouged by the weapons.

Seldom is one of the great champions killed by a spear throw, unless he is ambushed. Siegfried and Beowulf seem, in fact, to rely almost exclusively on their swords, which they swing high over their heads while spears and javelins whiz past them. Being apparently better protected than the rest, the champions find that against each other, the spear is often of little use. When this proves to be the case, their encounter is prolonged, as we have already noted above in the slowing of narrative action during the fight between Siegfried and Liudeger and as occurs in the meeting between Hiltibrant and Hadubrant, who hack and gouge each other's shields. In the duel between Paris and Menelaus, the latter brings his sword down onto the crown of his opponent's helmet, but it shatters. In the duel between Aias and Hector, spears and boulders are first tried; then the champions draw their swords, at which point their friends intervene because of approaching darkness.

For her study of the use of the Anglo-Saxon sword, Davidson cites a passage from *Beowulf* as evidence that sword fighting "was largely a matter of blow and counter-blow, the helmet and shield acting as a defence against the cutting strokes of the sword, brought down upon the head of the adversary" (196). The fight is one between Ongentheow, King of Sweden, and two brothers:

> þær wearð Ongenðiow   ecgum sweorda,
> blondenfex,   on bid wrecen,
> þæt se þeodcyning   ðafian sceolde
> Eafores anne dom.   Hyne yrringa
> Wulf Wonreding   wæpne geræhte,
> þæt him for swenge   swat ædrum sprong
> forð under fexe.   Næs he forht swa ðeh,
> gomela Scilfing,   ac forgeald hraðe
> wyrsan wrixle   wælhlem þone,
> syððan ðeodcyning   þyder oncirde.
> Ne meahte se snella   sunu Wonredes
> ealdum ceorle   ondslyht giofan,
> ac he him on heafde   helm ær gescer,
> þæt he blode fah   bugan sceolde,
> feoll on foldan;   næs he fæge þa git,
> ac he hyne gewyrpte,   þeah ðe him wund hrine.
> Let se hearda   Higelaces þegn
> bradne mece,   þa his broðor læg,

ealdsweord eotonisc, entiscne helm
brecan ofer bordweal; ða gebeah cyning,
folces hyrde, wæs in feorh dropen.[16]

There Ongentheow the gray-haired was brought to bay by sword-blades, and the people's king had to submit to the judgment of Eofor alone. Wulf son of Wonred had struck him angrily with his weapon so that for the blow the blood sprang forth in streams beneath his hair. Yet not for that was he afraid, the old Scylfing, but he quickly repaid the assault with worse exchange, the folk-king, when he turned toward him. The strong son of Wonred could not give the old man a return blow, for Ongentheow had first cut through the helmet of his head so that he had to sink down, smeared with blood—fell on the earth: he was not yet doomed, for he recovered, though the wound hurt him. The hardy thane of Hygelac, when his brother lay low, let his broad sword, old blade made by giants, break the great helmet across the shield-wall; then the king bowed, the keeper of the folk was hit to the quick. [17]

Such a battle, Davidson observes, was not likely to go on for long. From the description, it can be inferred that the sword was a cutting weapon used in a slicing stroke down through the head and dealing a wound in spite of armor (196). Turning to the evidence furnished by multiple wounds on the armored skeletons of warriors who died in battle on the island of Gotland in 1361, Davidson reports that "in several cases the steel coif worn on the head had been cut to pieces and the blows had penetrated the bones of the cranium, while in other cases part of the skull was cut away" (197).

Could not a warrior engaged in swordplay be brought down by a spear or arrow? Indeed, Davidson's analysis of battle practice from the poem on the Battle of Maldon leads her to conclude that "most of the fighting in a battle of the late tenth century was with spears and bows, the sword being used by the leaders for close fighting" (191), and yet "little is said of bows and arrows, here or elsewhere, although they were certainly in use" (191-92), and "battles were often lost and won by close fighting between two adversaries" (193). Pandarus does indeed shoot Menelaus after his victory by default over Paris when the latter suddenly disappears from the field of battle. But in this instance, with the truce formally ratified and in place, neither Menelaus nor any of his companions is guarding against the flight of a missile. Under normal conditions, with the armies opposing each other frontally, javelin throwers and archers behind the front ranks of spearmen, it is to be assumed that any attempt they might make to strike an opposing warrior while he is engaged in a sword duel must be far more likely actually to hit their own champion in the back. Once hand-to-hand fighting is engaged, whether with

---

[16] *Beowulf*, ed. Friedrich Klaeber (Lexington, Massachusetts: D. C. Heath, 1950), 2961-81. Further quotations in the original language will be cited parenthetically in the text by line number.

[17] *Beowulf*, trans. E. Talbot Donaldson (New York: W. W. Norton, 1975). Further quotations in translation will be cited parenthetically in the text.

spear or sword, javelins and arrows must be held or used against ranks not yet so engaged. Archers and javelineers would, in other words, make each other their targets while the champions slashed away with their swords.

The geometry of a slashing sword is quite simple, as shown by the accompanying Diagram 1. The arc of the sword describes a circle. Five circles represent four attackers encircling a lone warrior. Shaded areas show areas of intersection in which the swords of two attackers will interfere with each other. If more than four attackers are used, the interference will occur before the attackers reach the target in the center. Four is therefore the greatest number of swordsmen practical for a synchronized attack, and even here the men fighting side by side must be careful not to move within the circumference of the circle described by their friends' swords, lest they be cut by them or else, interfering with each other's slashing, expose themselves to cuts from the enemy warrior just a few feet away. The geometry of circles thus places a limit on the number of slashing swordsmen able to engage an individual opponent.

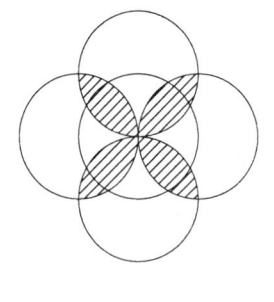

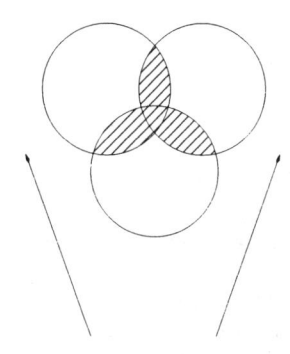

Diagram 1   *Diagram 2*

The geometry thus described presumes, however, that the lone surrounded warrior remain stationary.[18] Should he rush toward any one of his adversaries, however, he would disrupt the synchronicity of their assault, thus engaging them in sequence, albeit a rapid one. Let us further assume that a lone swordsman has at his back companions armed with spears. This immediately reduces to two the number of men capable of mounting a combined attack, even against a stationary swordsman, as shown in Diagram 2. Here we see that the spears flank the lone swordsman on both sides, preventing his encirclement. The combination of swordsman and spearbearers thus further accentuates the tendency to reduce battlefield activity to

---

[18] Fenik's study of the *Iliad* leads him to the observation that there is "no single example of a fight where both men attack each other with their swords or engage in a long sword fight" (p. 6). As we have seen, the men attack first with their spears. When the spear throw is unsuccessful and swords are drawn, one or two blows suffice to end the fight.

AN ECONOMY OF LIVES 69

individual encounters. Diagrams 3-5 presuppose a cadre of twelve to thirteen spearmen taking up a variety of possible formations in support of a single swordsman to the fore. In every case, the swordsman is shown under attack from two opponents.

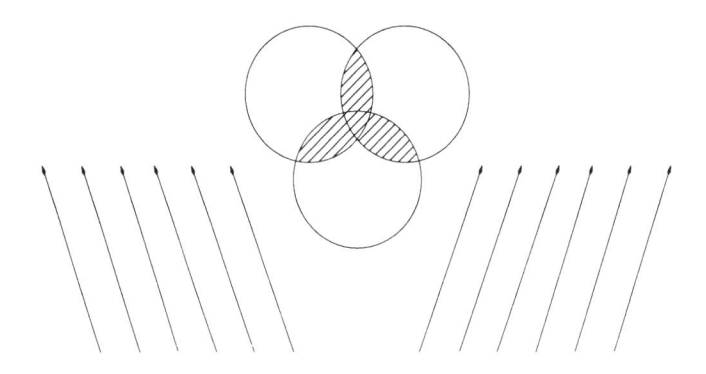

Diagram 3

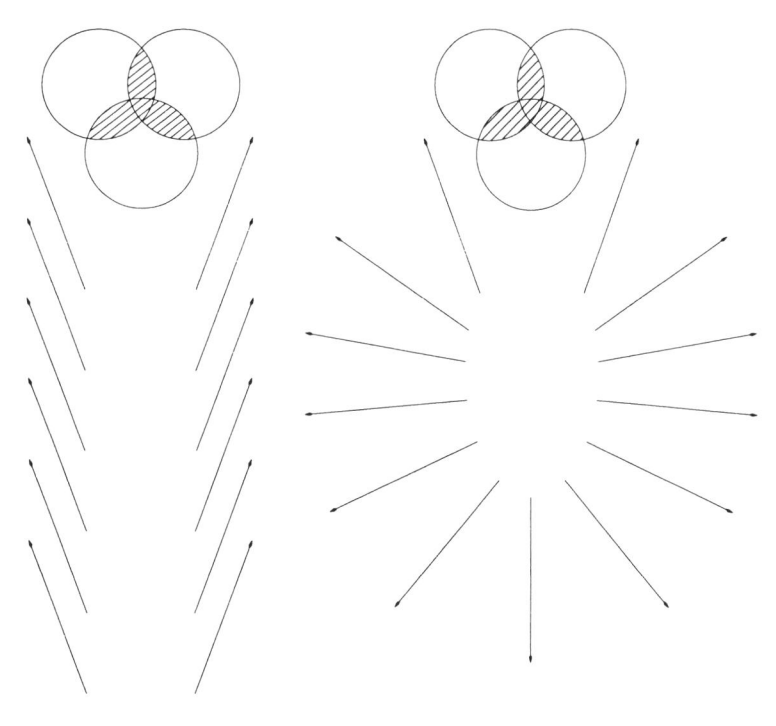

Diagram 4   *Diagram 5*

The constraints of geometry on hand-to-hand combat cannot be overemphasized. We have already seen that when a battle takes the form of numerous instances of single combat, each warrior weighs himself against his adversary in terms of size, strength, skill, and ferocity. Self-confidence therefore plays a crucial role. By undercutting the possibility of concerted action against a single opponent, the geometry of sword arc and thrusting spear intensifies each warrior's sense of isolation and vulnerability. For the modern reader, military violence is imagined to be impersonal and primarily a matter of probability and statistics. As a more general phenomenon, however, the anonymity and impersonal qualities of modern life have become a serious threat to the articulation of a "self." For postenlightenment readers in particular, then, the epic emphasis on the individual has been a feature to be celebrated. The epic warrior's willingness to expose himself to risk may be judged "heroic" because such action appears to express a resistance to the pressures for conformity and subordination to the collective. Epic poetry appears to present an alternative to the horrors of sudden random death. But such a view does not respect the constraints inherent in the conditions presented by epic narrative. For there is, in fact, no safety in numbers on Skamandros's plain, for numbers offer neither anonymity nor protection. In warfare of this kind, the number of greatest significance is one. The only safety is gained by keeping a distance from anyone whose power, size, skill, or courage make him especially formidable. Wherever such heroes go, the men that they face would rather be somewhere else.

For nine years, the Achaean forces are said to have been camped on the beaches before Troy. But how many have been killed? So long as swift-footed Achilles is on the field, the only safety for Trojans lies behind Troy's high walls. In the *Iliad*, the goddess Here, rebuking the Achaeans for their flight from Hector, says, "αἰδώς. Ἀργεῖοι. κὰκ ἐλέγχεα. εἶδος ἀγητοί· / ὄφρα μὲν ἐς πόλεμον πωλέσκετο δῖος Ἀχιλλεύς. / οὐδέ ποτε Τρῶες πρὸ πυλάων Δαρδανιάων / οἴχνεσκον· κείνου γὰρ ἐδείδισαν ὄβριμον ἔγχος" (5.787-90)—"For shame, Argives! . . . In the days when the great Achilles came out and fought, the Trojans never showed themselves in front of the Dardanian gates: they were too fearful of his heavy spear." Only now that Achilles has withdrawn within the walls of his hut on the beach do the Trojans actually make contact with their besiegers, not only for the purposes of this narrative, as is generally thought, *as if* for the first time.[19] For nine years, Achilles has been offered no opposition because victory has always already been conceded

---

[19] Voegelin believes the duel between Paris and Menelaus to result from a chance battlefield encounter in the war's tenth year: "The combat and the truce are not the result of rational action (which could have been taken *at any time*) but of an accident" (p. 72; my emphasis). With Achilles on the field, however, little, if any, combat seems to have occurred, and had there been a duel, Achilles would have been chosen to represent the Achaeans. Only with his absence from the field does combat begin; only in his absence do the Trojans dare consider a duel; and only in his absence does Menelaus emerge as a satisfactory selection as Achaean champion.

to him. As Aeneas declares: "τῷ οὐκ ἔστ' Ἀχιλῆος ἐναντίον ἄνδρα μάχεσθαι" (20.97)—"it is impossible for any man to fight Achilles." Therefore, when he takes the field, the Trojans take shelter in their citadel.

Goliath's daily challenge to Saul's army likewise meets with no response, for no individual dares match himself against the Philistine giant. Liudeger, acquainted with Siegfried's reputation, is ready to acknowledge his superiority without a fight. For Liudeger, no walled citadel stands near at hand into which he can retreat. Originally unaware of Siegfried's presence among the Burgundians, Liudeger had wanted no walls. Quite the contrary—he had come to Burgundy in order to subdue it, to make himself master of its walls. The Achaeans, encamped nine years before Troy, want no protective walls until the withdrawal of Achilles from battle begins to embolden the Trojans. The mere sight of Achilles, however, is still capable of putting the Trojans to rout, as Patroclus knows and demonstrates.

Aias with his "tower" shield is known as the "ἕρκος"—the wall—of the Achaean army.[20] We now see that the image of an individual serving as a protective wall or defensive tower is not nearly as metaphorical as one might think, because one man can quite literally hold off an army. Conversely, a lone Diomedes can break through a line of men, just as water washes out a dyke, not by pushing it down all at once, but by spurting through at one crack, whereupon the rush through the opening tears away ever more of the embankment. But unlike a dyke, which contains a volume by resisting it all along its front at once, the champion holds back the enemy forces by confronting them one individual fighter at a time. If his stature and armaments are gargantuan (like Goliath's), he strikes terror into those arrayed against him, and they will shrink back and refuse to engage him. If, as with Siegfried, he has a reputation for winning even against overwhelming odds, he may demand concessions from his opponents without a fight. And even when he has neither awe-inspiring size nor reputation, a warrior's destructiveness on the field of battle can quickly instill such fear in those who witness it that they will be put to flight. Conversely, should such a warrior fall, it spells defeat for his people. Just so, Hector's death, as Kenneth Atchity puts it, "signals the end of Troy," and as Davidson points out, at the battle of Maldon "the death of the leader proved the turning-point" (193).[21]

When the warriors are equipped with protective armor consisting of a helmet, cuirass, greaves, and heavy shield, every battle, no matter how many individuals may take part, is reduced to a series of duels. The formal duel, then, would appear to be but a specialized case of what must otherwise occur anyway. Once the course of battle is thus understood, the institution of formal duels appears only as a regulated form of what will inevitably come to pass. What remains to be explained, however, is why the staging of a single

---

[20] See the *Iliad* 3.229, 6.5, and 7.211. At 1.284, the term is used for Achilles, while at 4.299 it means a wall of men.

[21] See Kenneth Atchity, "Andromache's Headdress," *Critical Essays on Homer*, p. 162. Davidson links this detail to the observation that "the Teutonic peoples were lovers of single combat" (p. 193).

duel should determine the fate of an entire people. What accounts for the willingness to submit one's fate to the abilities, or even luck, of a champion? Why would the losers ever abide by the terms dictated by the outcome of such a contest?

The acceptance of formal duels is explained by the fact that, since every battle will, in any case, be reduced to a succession of duels in which the two opposing champions will always prevail until eventually they meet one another, it can be seen that the matter will inevitably be determined by an encounter between these two warriors. This conclusion is rather easy to support if we but look for evidence that a meeting between the two champions is bound to occur and that it will always be decisive. The issue for people involved in such a conflict would not be whether to give a champion responsibility for the people's fate but whether the best available warrior has been successfully identified and persuaded to step forward alone to put his life at risk so that the others might be spared.

Siegfried's defeat of the brothers Liudegast and Liudeger provides an almost schematic representation of the advantage in holding the duel sooner rather than later. The clash between Siegfried and Liudegast is the first instance of combat on the field where later rivers of blood will be said to flow. When the warriors chance upon one another between their two armies, both are riding alone. Their meeting, therefore, fulfills the general conditions for a duel, except that the outcome of their meeting, being governed by no agreement between them, has no particular significance beyond the removal of the loser from the field of battle.

The battle itself, which a formal duel would have preempted, is actually ushered in by the report carried back to the Saxons that the Danish king has been taken prisoner. The bloodshed and loss of life that ensue accomplish nothing, except to call Siegfried to Liudeger's attention: "Dô der starke Liudegêr Sîvriden vant, / und daz er alsô hôhe truoc an sîner hant / den guoten Balmungen und ir sô manegen sluoc, / des wart der herre zornec unde grímméc genuoc" (207)—"[S]eeing [Siegfried] swing his good sword Balmung so high and slay so many of his men, mighty lord Liudeger was seized with fierce anger" (39-40). Liudger's recognition of Siegfried thus follows from the prior recognition that Siegfried is responsible for wreaking great havoc among the Saxons and Danes. The battle exists, in this instance, to distinguish Siegfried as best among the Burgundians, but its function can be completed only at the cost of a great many lives on both sides. Once the display of Siegfried's prodigious killing power has been sufficient to call Liudeger's attention to him, the Saxon king moves immediately toward a direct confrontation.

Again, the fight that ensues is, for all practical purposes, a duel, fought this time between and in view of both armies, though again with no formal challenge and no prior agreement. But now, Siegfried is identified, and the Saxon king sues for peace. What the battle has done, if anything, is to make Siegfried recognizable. The cost in Saxon and Danish lives, however, is monstrous. Had Liudegast recognized Siegfried at their chance meeting before the battle and sued then and there for peace, precisely as his brother would later do, neither Saxons and Danes nor Burgundians need have died. Recognizing Siegfried much later, Liudeger is still in time to save the lives of many men: the sooner recognized, the greater the number saved. Had Liudeger not met with Siegfried until much later in the battle, few warriors, if any, would have been alive to witness the outcome. The meeting between the two champions is inevitable, and its outcome appears to be unaffected by what has gone before or what continues to go on around them. But the timing of their meeting is crucial—literally a matter of life and death—to their companions. Timing can make the difference between no loss of life and a massacre.

The sequence of events in which a hero attracts the attention of the enemy leadership by slaying an egregious number of opposing warriors repeats itself more than a few times in the *Iliad*.[22] In the midst of a raging battle, for example, Odysseus witnesses the fall of a comrade, Tlepolemus:

> . . . νόησε δὲ δῖος Ὀδυσσεὺς
> τλήμονα θυμὸν ἔχων. μαίμησε δέ οἱ φίλον ἦτορ. . . .
> ἔνθ' ὅ γε Κοίρανον εἷλεν Ἀλάστορά τε Χρομίον τε
> Ἀλκανδρόν θ' Ἅλιόν τε Νοήμονά τε Πρύτανίν τε.
> καί νύ κ' ἔτι πλέονας Λυκίων κτάνε δῖος Ὀδυσσεύς.
> εἰ μὴ ἄρ' ὀξὺ νόησε μέγας κορυθαίολος Ἕκτωρ·
> βῆ δὲ διὰ προμάχων κεκορυθμένος αἴθοπι χαλκῷ.
> δεῖμα φέρων Δαναοῖσι. (5.669-70, 677-82)

> The excellent Odysseus had observed his fall, but was not to be dismayed. Indeed, it lashed him into fury. . . . Then and there he killed Coeranus, Alastor and Chromius, Alcander and Halius, Noemon and Prytanis. Indeed, the noble Odysseus would have gone on to kill yet more of the Lycians, but for the quick eye of Hector of the glittering helmet, who, when he saw what was afoot, hastened to the forefront in his armor of resplendent bronze, striking terror into the Danaans.

What happens to Odysseus at this juncture we are not told. He appears to withdraw, for Hector now lays low a succession of lesser Argive warriors.

This slaughter, in turn, catches the attention of a very formidable ally of the Achaean cause—the goddess Here. She descends with Athene to the plain of Troy in order to seek out Diomedes and exhort him to return to battle, in

---

[22] Fenik regards this phenomenon as one of the poet's devices. "Every reader of the poem," he writes, " is aware that the battle scenes consist largely of individual encounters related one after the other, and that general or mass scenes of the armies as a whole are relatively rare. At the same time, these single combats do not follow each other in an unending, unbroken chain. One of the many ways the poet breaks or divides the battle scenes up is to organize series of incidents into discrete groups. Such groups are sometimes regular patterns, sometimes they are not. They are usually brought to a close in one of two ways . . . someone on the other side "sees" (ἴδε) or "notices" (ἐνόησε) what is happening (usually an enemy's great success) and moves to stop him. In this way the action takes a fresh turn, and the previous pattern or series of incidents ends" (p. 19).

which she promises to come to his aid against Ares, the god of war, who is siding with the Trojans, in effect, fighting for them as their champion.[23] Diomedes is found away from the front lines, nursing a wound inflicted on him by an arrow. Because of this, he has not been a witness to Hector's rampage. Returning to battle with Athene's aid, Diomedes wounds Ares, who "ὅσσον τ' ἐννεάχιλοι ἐπίαχον ἢ δεκάχιλοι / ἀνέρες ἐν πολέμῳ ἔριδα ξυνάγοντες Ἄρηος. / τοὺς δ' ἄρ' ὑπὸ τρόμος εἷλεν Ἀχαιούς τε Τρῶάς τε / δείσαντας· τόσον ἔβραχ' Ἄρης ἆτος πολέμοιο" (5.860-63)—"let forth a yell as loud as the war cry of nine thousand or ten thousand battling men. The Achaeans and Trojans quaked with terror at that appalling cry from the god who never had his fill of war." The wounded god ascends to Olympus, where he shows his father Zeus his wound. Thus, we see the path by which the battle draws into itself increasingly powerful players on both sides, matching them up in pairs until eventually the two ultimate available powers take the field against one another.[24] The death of lesser fighters calls the attention of their superiors, who, if themselves become wounded, call the attention of even more powerful fighters than themselves. The most powerful of all are inevitably involved. Even the gods cannot remain aloof from a battle in which their own favorites are faring poorly. The gods' intervention here illustrates the principle that pulls towards each other each side's preeminent fighters.

The heroes are not dismayed by the success of an opposing champion, but, stirred to fury by injuries done their own favorites, they move forward through the ranks to offer battle. As the ranks of common fighters fall back in terror, the champions emerge. By this process, the best fighters on both sides sooner or later come to face one another on the field. When they do battle, the outcome is always decisive, for their men are already hanging back behind them, waiting to see who will be victorious. At the moment of decision, the victorious champion's line surges forward, while the fallen champion's followers turn in flight. Only if a new hero steps forth may flight be halted long enough to observe the outcome of this new confrontation. If no new hero comes, the losers will be pursued, hauled down from behind, and killed or enslaved. There is no escape from this logic for the heroes are bound to emerge. The question is one of time, and time can be measured in the flow of blood. If the heroes are recognized before the onset of battle, no other lives need be jeopardized. If recognition is delayed, for whatever cause, the number of lives lost will increase in direct relation to the length of the delay. The delay in no way influences the battle's outcome but

---

[23] I am following the spellings of Athene and Here used by Rieu in his translation of the *Iliad*.

[24] Fenik points to another variation of this process by which one warrior, seeing the enemy's distress, reacts to it by encouraging another to attack him. Not only is the situation typical, but even the language in which the encouragement is offered is standard. Similarly, a warrior who notices an opponent's success and decides to intervene declares his intention to his men in typical words: "I will go to meet this man, whoever he is" (p. 27).

affects only how many of the victors and vanquished will live to see that outcome. In a worst case scenario (such as is seen at the end of the *Nibelungenlied*), when the best warriors finally meet, they are the battle's only survivors.[25] In this case, one "wins" by killing the other, and his victory is genuinely pyrrhic. This is the understanding that provides for the institution of formal duels met with in epic narrative. If these will meet anyway and their meeting will be decisive, then the sooner they meet, the better, for the lives of all their companions and dependents will thus be saved.

The decision for a preeminent warrior is not whether or not to face his counterpart but when. In the best case scenario, the two best men should meet one another at the very outset, but it is not enough that they just meet, for Siegfried and Liudegast do encounter one another alone between the armies. They must meet as champions. A formal truce, presentation and acceptance of terms, and provision for witnesses must also be observed. The Nibelungen narrative offers us the case of a missed opportunity to duel. Indeed, had a truce been declared, and had the warriors revealed their identities to one another, the war could have been ended without a single death, for the Saxons and Danes would have yielded to the Burgundians solely on the strength of Siegfried's reputation.

If the best possible outcome is achieved by the earliest possible duel between champions, the worst possible outcome is achieved by the heroes' latest possible encounter. In this instance, the two heroes are the only remaining living representatives of their respective armies for all other warriors already lie slain. The heroes' encounter then is not a duel in the formal sense, because no truce need be called. The armies in the midst of which they fight are silent in death; the witness they bear is meaningless. The final winner serves nobody. He saves only one life—his own. Nobody remains to tell of his exploits, to give him glory, or to heap him with wealth. Nobody remains as a companion to share a victory feast, to thank the gods with a sacrifice, to drink, to sing, and to make the journey home.

This principle is illustrated by the *Nibelungenlied's* final scenes. The Burgundian forces, headed by King Gunther, his brothers, and their chief vassal, Hagen, arrive as invited guests at Etzel the Hun's court. In attendance on Etzel are many vassals and allies, chief among the former, Rüdiger, and among the latter, Dietrich. A fight breaks out between the guests and their hosts, but for reasons of their own Rüdiger and Dietrich refrain from joining in the bloodshed. As they hesitate, the blood flows in rivers. At one point, the great hall in which the fighting is being conducted becomes so filled with corpses that an armistice has to be declared in order to allow the bodies to be

---

[25] Making the point that scholars have missed the importance of the warrior's fear of death, Verbruggen comments that, according to the classic representation of the great individual warrior, "[u]ndaunted, he continued to fight until his strength was exhausted, even until the last man was driven from the bloody field of battle" (p. 40). Interestingly, the classic representation is an accurate representation of what must occur when the battle proceeds without a duel being fought.

thrown from the windows. Rüdiger eventually finds himself forced to join the fight, and when Rüdiger is killed by Hagen, Dietrich, moved to seek revenge for Rüdiger's death, at last himself offers battle. At the point when Dietrich meets Hagen, of all his own fighting men only old Hildebrand, though wounded, remains alive. Of all the Burgundians, their vassals and allies, only Gunther and Hagen are still living. So when Hagen and Gunther are killed, Dietrich "enjoys" a pyrrhic victory. He can only avenge, not rescue, Rüdiger, his Patroclus.

The *Nibelungenlied* is not the only ancient tale to end in grief. Even though the old king Beowulf is the only man to die in battle with the fire-breathing dragon that has been scorching the Geats' territory, his thane Wiglaf has this to say to his companions:

> "Nu sceal sincþego ond swyrdgifu,
> eall eðelwyn eowrum cynne,
> lufen alicgean; londrihtes mot
> þære mægburge monna æghwylc
> idel hweorfan, syððan æðelingas
> feorran gefricgean fleam eowerne,
> domleasan dæd. Deað bið sella
> eorla gehwylcum þonne edwitlif!" (2884-91)

"Now there shall cease for your race the receiving of treasure and the giving of swords, all enjoyment of pleasant homes, comfort. Each man of your kindred must go deprived of his land-right when nobles from afar learn of your flight, your inglorious deed. Death is better for any earl than a life of blame."

The Geats anticipate the outbreak of war as all their neighbors, hearing of Beowulf's death and remembering past enmities, can now be expected to make their attack.[26]

> swylce giomorgyd sio geomeowle
> æfter Biowulfe bundenheorde
> song sorgcearig, sæde geneahhe,
> þæt hio hyre hearmdagas hearde ondrede,
> wælfylla worn, wigendes egesan,
> hynðo ond hæftnyd. (3150-55a)

"And the Geatish woman, wavy-haired, sang a sorrowful song about Beowulf, said again and again that she sorely feared for herself invasions of armies, many slaughters, terror of troops, humiliation, and captivity."

---

[26] This interpretation of the scene is not as obvious as it might seem. Klaus Von See, for example, in *Germanische Heldensage: Stoffe, Probleme, Methoden* (Frankfurt: Athenäum Verlag, 1971), p. 162, describes Beowulf's death as a self-sacrifice.

Her fate is not unlike that of the Trojan women. Agamemnon foresees the fall of Troy in these terms: "σύν τε μεγάλῳ ἀπέτεισαν. / σὺν σφῇσιν κεφαλῇσι γυναιξί τε καὶ τεκέεσσιν. / εὖ γὰρ ἐγὼ τόδε οἶδα κατὰ φρένα καὶ κατὰ θυμόν· / ἔσσεται ἦμαρ ὅτ' ἄν ποτ' ὀλώλῃ Ἴλιος ἱρή / καὶ Πρίαμος καὶ λαὸς ἐϋμμελίω Πριάμοιο" (4.161-65)—"the transgressors pay a heavy price, they pay with their lives, and with their women and their children too. The day will come—I know it in my heart of hearts—when holy Ilium will be destroyed, with Priam and the people of Priam." Utter destruction of the city, enslavement of the women and children, death of all the men, this is the fate predicted for both the Trojans and the Geats.

And is it not also the fate feared by the Hebrews and probably realized by the Burgundians? The duel proposed by Goliath is meant to determine not whether servitude is necessary but for whom—not whether death is avoidable but for how many. If no Hebrew accepts his challenge, the prosecution of the war will continue until enough of the men are dead to put an end to resistance. Their territories will still fall subject, and their women and children will still be forced into some form of servitude.

We are not informed of Burgundy's future, but what future can be imagined without an army to defend it? Will not old enemies, hearing about the annihilation of the fighting force, rush to the attack? We have only to remember the confrontation initiated by the kings Liudegast and Liudeger. Then, however, the Burgundians had not only an army, but far more significantly they had a champion to defend them.[27] Without a champion, someone to step forward and assume responsibility for the battle's outcome, even a well-equipped army can be lost—which is precisely what occurs to the Burgundians in Hungary at Etzel's court. The murder of Siegfried thus sets up Burgundy's destruction in two ways: directly through Kriemhild's revenge and indirectly by depriving Burgundy of its ablest champion.[28]

---

[27] Siegfried, dying, may allude to this relationship when he asks, "waz helfent mîniu dienest, daz ir mich habet erslagen?" (str. 989,2)—"What good has my service done me now that you have slain me?" (p. 131). But on the other hand, he may also query—what good do my services do *you*, since once I am dead neither my reputation nor my presence can serve *you* further?

[28] I interpret the champion's function to be that of peacemaker. The resolution of conflict comes about not through an absolute prohibition of violence but through the institution of the duel as the most economical expenditure of blood and life. Haymes, commenting on the problem of violence in the *Nibelungenlied*, correctly identifies pacifism through abstinence from battle as a modern notion (p. 106). He therefore is surprised to find the epic apparently preoccupied with the "possibility of preventing bloodshed, or at least mitigating it" (p. 106). Not by chance, perhaps, Haymes compares the unexpectedness of Dietrich's reluctance to fight with the fact that Siegfried has assumed the role of *minneritter*—that is, one who insists on earning his position through service, even though he has a hereditary right to it. Dietrich's attempts at "peacemaking" are, of course, in vain. He is thwarted, in part, by Hagen's unwillingness to jeopardize his honor. We should understand, however, that Hagen is unyielding now because he recognizes the

In all but one of the cases that we have examined so far, then, the story ends in the flow of rivers of blood, decimation of the army, enslavement of women and children, and destruction of all property, both fixed and movable. If we read the survival of the Hebrews as an exception, such survival certainly proves the rule, for David's success is meant to be understood in the light of divine intervention. The death of Goliath at David's hands, David's outliving Saul's plots, and David's ascension to the throne all mark points of radical departure from the set of understandings built around the logic of the duel, but they suggest a departure meant precisely to represent an affront to expectations, since it shows the Israelite survival to be miraculous. All the texts that we have so far discussed assume a link between the proposal that a duel be fought and the preservation of lives. If that link is a strong one, as I believe it must be, then the duel's mismanagement has to be assigned the blame for ensuing destruction.[29]

The institution of the duel is founded on sound principles. Its fundamental premise is an economy of lives. But in order for it to succeed, a great many understandings must come into play, all of them highly significant, because if the duel performs its function properly, at most one life need be lost, but if it fails, the result can mean the annihilation of an army, a city, or an entire population. The effects of such a failure are not less severe than what we now consider to be the ultimate destructive force known to humankind—nuclear weapons. If we recognize that the ancients were witness to destructive power as devastating as (though certainly slower than) a nuclear holocaust, we can appreciate the importance to them of maintaining all of the understandings necessary to hold that destruction in check. The rest of this book is devoted to recuperating these understandings.

---

destructiveness of Siegfried's murder: the tide of violence can no longer be stemmed through pacifism. The peacemaking potential in the function of the champion having been undone by Hagen himself, Hagen has resigned himself to unprecedented bloodshed. Dietrich will eventually accept the necessity of his own participation but persists until the bitter end in peacemaking efforts laudable both from modern and, indeed, some medieval perspectives. They prove a most destructive alternative, however, to the duel and the institution of championship necessary to it. Haymes sees Dietrich as parallel to Hagen (in the first half) and to Gunther's younger brother Gernot, who leads the party of "reconciliation" with Siegfried after his challenge and who opposes "hotheads" like Ortwin, who wish to meet Siegfried in battle on their own terms. To Haymes the former appear to represent a pattern of "reasonable pacification" (p. 110). In fact, Dietrich's reticence, like Hagen's, proves disastrous. He will, like Achilles, be drawn to fight but only by the death of those he would have most wanted to keep alive.

[29] "Not the wrath of Achilles, but the duel between Achilles and Hector . . . is what forms the *Iliad*'s true center and governs its unity and its development," observes Bespaloff (p. 130).

CHAPTER THREE

THE DUEL AND ITS PROTOCOLS

Troy is destroyed not because of the abduction of Helen and the theft of Menelaus's wealth but because of a breach in the etiquette of dueling. In the *Iliad*, Menelaus and the Achaeans accept the terms proposed by Hector in Paris's name: "'Ελένη καὶ κτήμασι πᾶσι" (3.70)—"Helen and her wealth"—to the winner, to the armies—"φιλότητα καὶ ὅρκια πιστὰ" (3.73)—"a treaty of peace." Hector's terms specify, however, not only disposition of the queen and goods but also the conditions under which the duel is to be fought, a formal truce—"ἄλλους μὲν κέλεται Τρῶας καὶ πάντας Ἀχαιοὺς / τεύχεα κάλ' ἀποθέσθαι ἐπὶ χθονὶ πουλυβοτείρῃ. / αὐτὸν δ' ἐν μέσσῳ καὶ ἀρηΐφιλον Μενέλαον" (3.88-90)—"all the troops should ground their arms while [Paris] and the warrior Menelaus fight a duel, between the two armies." To this condition, Menelaus adds two new stipulations: the truce should be solemnized with a sacrifice to the gods, who are thus called upon as witnesses, and Priam himself should come and take an oath that he and his Trojans will abide by all of the terms. Menelaus insists on Priam's participation because "οἱ παῖδες ὑπερφίαλοι καὶ ἄπιστοι. / μή τις ὑπερβασίῃ Διὸς ὅρκια δηλήσηται" (3.106-07)—"he has arrogant and unscrupulous sons, and we do not want to see a solemn treaty wrecked by treachery." Menelaus is clearly concerned about the younger Trojans' reliability as partners in a treaty of peace: "αἰεὶ δ' ὁπλοτέρων ἀνδρῶν φρένες ἠερέθονται· / οἷς δ' ὁ γέρων μετέῃσιν. ἅμα πρόσσω καὶ ὀπίσσω / λεύσσει. ὅπως ὄχ' ἄριστα μετ' ἀμφοτέροισι γένηται" (3.108-10)—"Young men are for the most part unstable, whereas when an old man takes a hand in such affairs, he considers the future as well as the past and does the very best for both parties." The young Trojans are, in his mind, likely to act in view of the past—presumably remembering their injuries at the hands of the Achaeans, which might lead them to break their oaths. The older man will also give some thought to the future—most likely the consequences of breaching the treaty.

Menelaus is right in his assessment of the younger Trojans' disregard for the solemn oaths sworn before the armies and the gods. He is wrong, however, to think that Priam will be more prescient than his sons, for Priam ratifies the treaty, then returns to his citadel without first instructing his men about their proper conduct under the truce. Menelaus expects the Trojan king to exert some measure of restraint or control over his fighting men, but Priam apparently fails to recognize either the likelihood of a breach in discipline or the severity of the consequences to follow from a breach. Priam's omission stems from a failure of nerve: he can't bring himself to watch while his "dear son" risks his life against Menelaus. Thus overcome by the trepidation he feels for his son Paris, the Trojan king exercises neither his judgment nor his authority and leaves open the pathway to the city's total destruction, entailing the death of all his children and grandchildren, including

Hector and Astyanax.[1] Because of his failure properly to charge his men with their duty to observe the truce, Athene has little difficulty in persuading one of the Trojans to violate it. She tells Pandarus, a Trojan ally—"τλαίης κεν Μενελάῳ ἐπιπροέμεν ταχὺν ἰόν. / πᾶσι δέ κε Τρώεσσι χάριν καὶ κῦδος ἄροιο. / ἐκ πάντων δὲ μάλιστα Ἀλεξάνδρῳ βασιλῆϊ. / τοῦ κεν δὴ πάμπρωτα παρ' ἀγλαὰ δῶρα φέροιο. / αἴ κεν ἴδῃ Μενέλαον ἀρήϊον Ἀτρέος υἱὸν / σῷ βέλεϊ δμηθέντα πυρῆς ἐπιβάντ' ἀλεγεινῆς" (4.94-99)—"[i]f you could bring yourself to shoot Menelaus with an arrow, you would cover yourself with glory and put every Trojan in your debt, Prince Paris most of all. He would be the first to come forward with a handsome gift, if he saw the great Menelaus son of Atreus struck down." Pandarus, having no reason to doubt that Paris would approve this covert action, stealthily draws an arrow from his quiver. Screened from view behind the other Trojans, he draws his bow and lets fly at Menelaus.

The bowshot of Pandarus, which only wounds Menelaus, violates the truce and the treaty and leads to Agamemnon's immediate proclamation of destruction for Troy: "σύν τε μεγάλῳ ἀπέτεισαν. / σὺν σφῇσιν κεφαλῇσι γυναιξί τε καὶ τεκέεσσιν" (4.161-62)—"the transgressors pay a heavy price, they pay with their lives, and with their women and their children too." Thinking Menelaus's wound to be fatal, he says: "φίλε κασίγνητε. θάνατόν νύ τοι ὅρκι' ἔταμνον. / οἶον προστήσας πρὸ Ἀχαιῶν Τρωσὶ μάχεσθαι. / ὥς σ' ἔβαλον Τρῶες. κατὰ δ' ὅρκια πιστὰ πάτησαν. / οὐ μέν πως ἅλιον πέλει ὅρκιον αἷμά τε ἀρνῶν / σπονδαί τ' ἄκρητοι καὶ δεξιαί. ἧς ἐπέπιθμεν. / εἴ περ γάρ τε καὶ αὐτίκ' Ὀλύμπιος οὐκ ἐτέλεσσεν. / ἔκ τε καὶ ὀψὲ τελεῖ" (4.155-61)—"My dear brother! . . . It was your death, then, that I swore to when I made the truce and sent you out to fight alone for us against the Trojans, who have shot you now and trampled on their solemn pact. Yet a pact that has been ratified by our right hands and solemnized with wine and in the blood of lambs is not so easily annulled. The Olympian may postpone the penalty, but he exacts it in the end." The transgression that he means is the shot of Pandarus. The penalty for it is Troy's utter destruction, enslavement of women and girls, and brutal murder of old men and boys. As Agamemnon will later say, "τῶν μή τις ὑπεκφύγοι αἰπὺν ὄλεθρον / χεῖράς θ' ἡμετέρας. μηδ' ὅν τινα γαστέρι μήτηρ / κοῦρον ἐόντα φέροι. μηδ' ὅς φύγοι. ἀλλ' ἅμα πάντες / Ἰλίου ἐξαπολοίατ' ἀκήδεστοι καὶ ἄφαντοι" (6.57-60)—"we are not going to leave a single one of them alive, down to the babies in their mothers' wombs—not even they must live. The whole people must be wiped out of existence, and none be left to think of them and shed a tear."

According to legend, Hector's son, Astyanax, whose name means "king of the citadel,"—"οἶος γὰρ ἐρύετο Ἴλιον Ἕκτωρ" (6.403)—"because his father was the one defence of Ilium"—will be flung from the citadel's ramparts in a gesture that signifies both the fall of his father, the so-called "wall of Troy"

---

[1] Andrew Miller pointed out to me in private correspondence that Priam's blameworthy (though humanly comprehensible) faint-heartedness has been forecast by a tiny narrative detail: Priam shudders (3.259) when he first hears from Idaeus that the duel is imminent.

and "tower of Troy," and the destruction of Troy's actual stone walls and towers. As we have seen, because Hector is Troy's champion, the single man who is unto the city its best wall, he must reckon with death, duel or no duel. The life of his son, heir apparent to his strength and, therefore, also his responsibility, can be preserved, however, only if the truce is preserved. Because it is broken, the baby Astyanax will be thrown from the ramparts, dashing out with his life the last hope for Troy's recovery.[2]

The *Iliad*, of course, is not about the destruction of Troy. In consideration of the primary plot, execution of justice must be delayed. Agamemnon even anticipates this delay, correctly recognizing that some items on the cosmic agenda must be subordinated to others. Nevertheless, he is quite clear about the consequences of the Trojan perfidy, and he is able to predict quite correctly that "εὖ γὰρ ἐγὼ τόδε οἶδα κατὰ φρένα καὶ κατὰ θυμόν· / ἔσσεται ἦμαρ ὅτ' ἄν ποτ' ὀλώλῃ Ἴλιος ἱρή . . . / Ζεὺς δέ σφι Κρονίδης ὑψίζυγος, αἰθέρι ναίων. / αὐτὸς ἐπισσείῃσιν ἐρεμνὴν αἰγίδα πᾶσι / τῆσδ' ἀπάτης κοτέων" (4.163-64, 166-68)—"[t]he day will come—I know it in my heart of hearts—when holy Ilium will be destroyed. . . . Zeus, Son of Cronos, from his high seat in Heaven where he lives, will wave his sombre aegis over them all in his anger at this perjury of theirs." Perjury in terms of the duel, then, provides sufficient grounds to destroy Troy.

An understanding of the significance of Trojan perfidy is prepared in the narrative by the note of a sudden shift in mood among the warriors when the terms of the duel are first accepted. Eric Voegelin summarizes the scene as follows: "the soldiers on both sides break their battle lines, joyously put aside their arms, and form a ring of eager spectators around a clearance on

---

[2] The death of Astyanax can be compared to the fate of Siegfried's son Gunther, who is safe at home in the Netherlands at the time of his father's murder in faraway Burgundy, and with that of Hiltibrant's son Hadubrant, who complains that his father's absence left him and his mother "luttila" (l. 20)—"insignificant." Noting that Siegfried's son is in no way poetically necessary or of any significance to action or character development (although references to him reflect directly on Kriemhild's character as a mother), de Boor remarks that the mention of Siegfried's son belongs to relatively older material ("den alten Stoffbestandteilen") that survives in extant forms of the *Nibelungenlied* (p. 48). "Dieser Sohn," he further observes, "ist aller Vorstellung nach unmündig und sein Leben bei der Ermordung des Vaters aufs schwerste bedroht" (p. 48)—"This son is from every indication not yet of age, and his father's death puts his life into gravest jeopardy." While de Boor argues that the immature endangered son of Siegfried reflects a historical situation at the court of Burgundy when a Frankish king Sigibert, brother-in-law to the Burgundian Gundohar, was survived by two sons not yet grown to manhood, I wish to call attention to the fact that the death or extended absence of a champion always endangers his sons, for it is expected—or feared—that they will grow to challenge their father's murderers, whether for justice, power, or both. The stories of Astyanax, Telemachus, and Orestes bear witness to the fact that interest in Siegfried's son is not an idiosyncracy of the *Nibelungenlied* but the remnant of an understanding significant to the epic-cultural system.

which the combat will take place. No matter who the victor, the combat will end the war between Trojans and Achaeans. It looks like an ironclad agreement, and the end of the war within an hour is in sight" (71). After the breakdown in the duel, however, the mood turns grim. "The fate of the Trojans is sealed," Voegelin observes, "for the Achaeans now continue the war with the certainty that the oath-breakers will meet their due fate" (71-72).

The terms of the truce provide for a peaceful parting of Trojans and Achaeans. Had those terms been adhered to, the single combat between Paris and Menelaus would have been the war's final violent act. As it is, "τόφρα δ' ἐπὶ Τρώων στίχες ἤλυθον ἀσπιστάων· / οἱ δ' αὖτις κατὰ τεύχε' ἔδυν. μνήσαντο δὲ χάρμης" (4.221-22)—"the Trojan battle-lines advanced to the attack. So the Achaeans once more put on their armour and turned their thoughts to war." The Trojans have squandered an opportunity to bring the war to a conclusion. One moment before Pandarus shoots his ill-fated arrow, peace and safety lie within reach; a moment later, the Trojans are doomed not only to lose the war but also to be annihilated by it. Prior to the truce, the war had been waged for Helen and Menelaus's stolen wealth. After the truce, the Achaeans wage war in order to avenge themselves for the broken oath, to rid themselves of those who cannot be trusted to keep the peace. Agamemnon exhorts his captains to renewed fighting, saying, "οὐ γὰρ ἐπὶ ψευδέσσι πατὴρ Ζεὺς ἔσσετ' ἀρωγός. / ἀλλ' οἵ περ πρότεροι ὑπὲρ ὅρκια δηλήσαντο. / τῶν ἤτοι αὐτῶν τέρενα χρόα γῦπες ἔδονται. / ἡμεῖς αὖτ' ἀλόχους τε φίλας καὶ νήπια τέκνα / ἄξομεν ἐν νήεσσιν. ἐπὴν πτολίεθρον ἕλωμεν" (4.235-39)—"Perjurers will get no help from Father Zeus. The men who went back on their word and broke the truce are going to have their own smooth flesh devoured by vultures, while we carry off their little children and the wives they love, on board our ships, when we have sacked their stronghold." The chance for a negotiated settlement is past. The Trojans have pushed the only peace-bringing, life-saving mechanism for ending the conflict forever beyond their own reach.

One of the Trojans, Antenor, recognizes this fact. At a counsel among the Trojan leaders, he proposes, "δεῦτ' ἄγετ'. Ἀργείην Ἑλένην καὶ κτήμαθ' ἅμ' αὐτῇ / δώομεν Ἀτρεΐδησιν ἄγειν· νῦν δ' ὅρκια πιστὰ / ψευσάμενοι μαχόμεσθα· τῶ οὔ νύ τι κέρδιον ἡμῖν / ἔλπομαι ἐκτελέεσθαι. ἵνα μὴ ῥέξομεν ὧδε" (7.350-53)—"Let us have done now, and give Argive Helen back to the Atreidae, along with all her property. By fighting on as we are doing, we have made perjurers of ourselves. No good that I can see will ever come of that. We have no choice but to do as I say." He proposes giving Helen back because he is convinced that victory is now impossible, and the reason that he gives is that perjurers cannot win. This logic supports and indeed simply repeats Agamemnon's theology: Zeus will punish Troy.

But there is another explanation for Antenor's proposal. Victory is impossible not because of divine justice but because the only victory ever possible in the absence of a duel is a Pyrrhic one. Even in victory, the male population would be decimated, leaving too few survivors to sustain and defend the city. Far better, in Antenor's mind, to appease the enemy by giving back Helen and her wealth.

Indeed, Antenor makes his unwelcome proposal after witnessing the duel between Aias and Hector—a scene that very well may have brought home to him the realization of how terribly costly the defense of Troy would be. The duel between Aias and Hector is particularly interesting because it is the *Iliad*'s only formal one other than that between Paris and Menelaus. And, in fact, our suppositions about the conditions under which a duel can be held suggest that, once the Trojans have proven themselves unreliable in keeping the terms of a treaty, a contest with them would no longer be meaningful. This is precisely the case in the combat between Aias and Hector. Their duel conforms to all the formal requirements that we have been able to identify— proposal of a truce, a challenge to fight, specification of terms, disarming of the troops, and a single combat in the open space between the armies. The duel is nevertheless rendered meaningless because the terms do not provide any reference to future disposition of the armies. Instead, agreement between the parties is expressly limited to the treatment of the loser's corpse and armor.

The emptiness of the duel between Aias and Hector is accentuated by its similarity to the earlier meeting between Paris and Menelaus. Not only is the language used to present the duels very similar, but the same individuals play the same roles, speaking the same speeches. Yet this is not a case in which one should be satisfied to attribute similarities to the economy of oral formulaic technique. Such an explanation, if it were correct, would argue against making a comparison between the two passages. It would, in essence, deny the differences between the speeches by taking their similarities for granted. If, however, the similarities invite a comparison, and the comparison yields a realization, the one apparently reached by Antenor, then we would do well to scrutinize this second duel.

ῥ' ἐς μέσσον ἰὼν Τρώων ἀνέεργε φάλαγγας.
μέσσου δουρὸς ἑλών· οἱ δ' ἱδρύνθησαν ἅπαντες.
κὰδ δ' Ἀγαμέμνων εἷσεν ἐϋκνήμιδας Ἀχαιούς·
κὰδ δ' ἄρ' Ἀθηναίη τε καὶ ἀργυρότοξος Ἀπόλλων
ἑζέσθην ὄρνισιν ἐοικότες αἰγυπιοῖσι
φηγῷ ἐφ' ὑψηλῇ πατρὸς Διὸς αἰγιόχοιο.
ἀνδράσι τερπόμενοι· τῶν δὲ στίχες ἥατο πυκναί.
ἀσπίσι καὶ κορύθεσσι καὶ ἔγχεσι πεφρικυῖαι.
οἵη δὲ Ζεφύροιο ἐχεύατο πόντον ἔπι φρὶξ
ὀρνυμένοιο νέον· μελάνει δέ τε πόντος ὑπ' αὐτῆς.
τοῖαι ἄρα στίχες ἥατ' Ἀχαιῶν τε Τρώων τε
ἐν πεδίῳ· Ἕκτωρ δὲ μετ' ἀμφοτέροισιν ἔειπε·
"κέκλυτέ μευ, Τρῶες καὶ ἐϋκνήμιδες Ἀχαιοί.
ὄφρ' εἴπω τά με θυμὸς ἐνὶ στήθεσσι κελεύει.
ὅρκια μὲν Κρονίδης ὑψίζυγος οὐκ ἐτέλεσσεν.
ἀλλὰ κακὰ φρονέων τεκμαίρεται ἀμφοτέροισιν.
εἰς ὅ κεν ἢ ὑμεῖς Τροίην εὔπυργον ἕλητε.
ἢ αὐτοὶ παρὰ νηυσὶ δαμήετε ποντοπόροισιν.
ὑμῖν δ' ἐν γὰρ ἔασιν ἀριστῆες Παναχαιῶν·

CHAPTER THREE

> τῶν νῦν ὅν τινα θυμὸς ἐμοὶ μαχέσασθαι ἀνώγει.
> δεῦρ' ἴτω ἐκ πάντων πρόμος ἔμμεναι Ἕκτορι δίῳ.
> ὧδε δὲ μυθέομαι, Ζεὺς δ' ἄμμ' ἐπιμάρτυρος ἔστω·
> εἰ μέν κεν ἐμὲ κεῖνος ἕλῃ ταναήκεϊ χαλκῷ,
> τεύχεα συλήσας φερέτω κοίλας ἐπὶ νῆας,
> σῶμα δὲ οἴκαδ' ἐμὸν δόμεναι πάλιν, ὄφρα πυρός με
> Τρῶες καὶ Τρώων ἄλοχοι λελάχωσι θανόντα.
> εἰ δέ κ' ἐγὼ τὸν ἕλω, δώῃ δέ μοι εὖχος Ἀπόλλων,
> τεύχεα σύλησας οἴσω προτὶ Ἴλιον ἱρήν,
> καὶ κρεμόω προτὶ νηὸν Ἀπόλλωνος ἑκάτοιο,
> τὸν δὲ νέκυν ἐπὶ νῆας ἐϋσσέλμους ἀποδώσω,
> ὄφρα ἑ ταρχύσωσι κάρη κομόωντες Ἀχαιοί,
> σῆμά τέ οἱ χεύωσιν ἐπὶ πλατεῖ Ἑλλησπόντῳ.
> καί ποτέ τις εἴπῃσι καὶ ὀψιγόνων ἀνθρώπων,
> νηῒ πολυκληῒδι πλέων ἐπὶ οἴνοπα πόντον·
> ἀνδρὸς μὲν τόδε σῆμα πάλαι κατατεθνηῶτος,
> ὅν ποτ' ἀριστεύοντα κατέκτανε φαίδιμος Ἕκτωρ.
> ὣς ποτέ τις ἐρέει· τὸ δ' ἐμὸν κλέος οὔ ποτ' ὀλεῖται. (7.55-91)

[Hector] stepped out into no-man's land, and grasping his spear by the middle thrust back the Trojan lines. They all sat down, and Agamemnon made the Achaean soldiers do the same. Athene and Apollo of the Silver Bow also sat down, in the form of vultures, on the tall oak sacred to aegis-bearing Zeus. They enjoyed the sight of all these Trojan and Achaean warriors sitting there on the plain, rank upon rank, bristling with shields, helmets and spears, like the darkened surface of the sea when the West Wind begins to blow and ripples spread across it.

Hector stood between the two armies and said: "Trojans and Achaean men-at-arms, hear a proposal that I wish to make. Zeus, from his high seat in heaven, has not allowed our truce to last. It is clear that he means us all to go on suffering till the day when you bring down the towers of Troy, or succumb to us yourselves by your much-travelled ships. Now you have in your army the finest men of all Achaea. Is one of these prepared to fight me? If so, let him step forward from among his friends as your champion against Prince Hector. And here are the conditions I lay down, with Zeus for witness. If your man kills me with his long-pointed spear, he can strip me of my arms and take them to your hollow ships; but he must let them bring my body home, so that the Trojans and their wives may burn it in the proper manner. If Apollo lets me win and I kill your man, I shall strip his armour off and bring it into sacred Ilium, where I shall hang it on the wall of the Archer-King's shrine; but I shall send back his corpse to your well-found ships, so that the long-haired Achaeans may give him burial rites and make a mound above him by the broad Hellespont. Then one day some future traveller, sailing by in his good ship across the wine-dark sea, will say: 'This is the monument of some warrior of an earlier day who was killed in single combat by illustrious Hector.' Thus my fame will be kept alive for ever."

Although many formal qualities of this challenge echo those of the challenge uttered earlier by Hector on behalf of Paris, we are confronted by numerous novelties. First, Athene and Apollo here appear as vultures—carrion birds who feed on corpses. And in the character of vultures, they take delight in the sight of rank upon rank of armored men, anticipating that soon all of these will be theirs to devour. Second, Hector explicitly acknowledges the broken truce of the first duel, though placing the fault for its breach with Zeus. Implicit in this acknowledgment seems to be Hector's anticipation of an Achaean refusal to enter into a new treaty, and he indicates that his present proposal is not meant to change the will of Zeus or, in other words, the course that the war must take in coming to its protracted and bloody conclusion. Granting that there is no hope for a change in this dismal destiny, Hector makes it plain that fighting now has nothing to accomplish except to secure personal glory, the reputation that survives an individual once he is dead. Hector appeals to the Achaeans on the understanding that the determination of victory is no longer a matter of personal concern. The gods alone will determine victory, but more important, only they and future travelers will be left to judge the action. Death is at hand for the combatants. The question for them is neither who will win the victory nor who will survive to see it but rather only what will remain to be said about the way they fought and died. The truce does not usher in new hope, as did the first one, when Menelaus said, "ἡμέων δ' ὁπποτέρῳ θάνατος καὶ μοῖρα τέτυκται. / τεθναίη· ἄλλοι δὲ διακρινθεῖτε τάχιστα" (3.101-02)—"One of us must die— Fate has already marked him out for death—and then the rest of you will soon be reconciled." By sharp contrast, the new truce solemnly marks a new fatalism made appropriate by the breaking of the first truce.

The combat between Aias and Hector only underscores the hopeless deadlock in whose grip scores of men in both armies must perish. This is because neither is able to establish a clear advantage over the other. Even though the terms agreed upon are empty, the duel could nevertheless hasten victory for one side or the other if it were to end decisively. Just as the killing of Dares's sons by Diomedes dismays the Trojans, the killing of Hector, "Troy's bulwark," or Aias, who carries "a shield like a tower," would dismay his comrades. Because with Achilles sidelined they are recognized as the best among their fellows, the removal of either from the battle would reduce one army's ability to prosecute the battle. Without Hector to protect them against Aias or Aias against Hector, every individual would become keenly aware of an increase in his own vulnerability. With either Aias or Hector dead, his survivors, had they the temerity to stand and fight, would inevitably also fall to the opposing champion, the first few, the best and bravest, perhaps only after putting up a valiant effort, but those coming after succumbing more and more quickly in proportion to the increasing difference in strength, size, skill, and experience between themselves and their rampaging enemy. In fact, the calculation of this disproportion alone would eventually suffice to put the army to flight.

We have seen that it is inevitable that the champions eventually face one another: the sooner they meet, the more lives will be saved. And if they meet under the terms of a formal duel, all further bloodshed can be avoided. The formal duel works because it translates a psychologically decisive event into an articulated legal decision. A formal duel has precisely the function of guaranteeing decisiveness. But because the duel between Hector and Aias has no legal force, it is a matter of the champions' whim whether or not to bring their fight to a decisive conclusion. Since they prove to be equally matched, neither sees the prospect of gaining much glory even from an eventual victory. In fact, as their struggle lengthens, it becomes clear that both will slowly weaken, succumb to their relatively minor but increasingly numerous wounds, and then die.

Whether Aias and Hector fight until both are finished or break off their fight with neither killed, the hope to gain even a limited advantage over the enemy through the removal of such a formidable warrior proves to have been vain. Indeed, the inconclusiveness of their meeting must usher in the direst consequences for both armies.

At the outset of their empty duel, Aias boasts to Hector:

"νῦν μὲν δὴ σάφα εἴσεαι οἰόθεν οἶος
οἷοι καὶ Δαναοῖσιν ἀριστῆες μετέασι.
καὶ μετ' Ἀχιλλῆα ῥηξήνορα θυμολέοντα.
ἀλλ' ὁ μὲν ἐν νήεσσι κορωνίσι ποντοπόροισι
κεῖτ' ἀπομηνίσας Ἀγαμέμνονι, ποιμένι λαῶν·
ἡμεῖς δ' εἰμὲν τοῖοι οἵ ἂν σέθεν ἀντιάσαιμεν
καὶ πολέες." (7.226-32)

> You are now going to discover, in single combat, what sort of champions the Danaans have at their disposal, even when they cannot count on Achilles, the lion-hearted breaker of men. At the moment he is lying idle by his beaked seagoing ships, nursing a quarrel with Agamemnon, our Commander-in-Chief. But for all that, we have men who can stand up to you—yes, plenty of them.

In retrospect, when neither Aias nor Hector is able to kill the other, Aias's boast reveals that the "sort of champions" fielded by the Danaans will not easily break the Trojans. Because neither Aias nor Hector proves himself superior, neither dismays the enemy, and no rout is produced. Neither, therefore, will be able to save his own men from protracted battle and heavy losses. Because the champions have proven themselves to be evenly matched, the large-scale battle that ensues will be fought at a stalemate, costing ever more lives as both sides struggle for an ever less meaningful victory. This war will reach its conclusion only through the depletion of one side's forces.

Not only is the duel between Aias and Hector robbed of any legal force by the limits placed on its terms, but also these limitations deprive their duel of even its psychological value. From the perspective of saving lives and bringing the war to a conclusion, their duel ends in the worst possible way. The champions having fought to a draw with neither one killed, the armies retire to prepare for the next day's battle. What this means is that Aias and Hector will have to fight again, sooner or later. When that occurs, it is to be expected that their meeting in single combat will once again be long, exhausting, and perhaps again inconclusive. While they fight, the others will also be fighting. Matched up against their equals, all will be worn away by fatigue and wounds until eventually they begin to drop. Casualties will occur more or less equally on both sides until both armies are so reduced that nothing remains of them except their corpses, for which there will be no survivors left to build a barrow and carry out burial rites. Theirs will be the worst fate imaginable to a Greek warrior—to become carrion for dogs and birds. Indeed, perhaps what makes this the worst fate of all is its signification of the war's utter futility; glory is only possible when survivors remain to remember and praise the heroic deeds of their dead.

The worst outcome is, in fact, the most probable. The duel ends in a draw because, had the terms been not empty but full of significance, nobody would have dreamed of calling a halt before one of the champions lay dead. Even a contest between two equally matched champions, if continued long enough, would lead eventually to the death of one of them. No matter how slow this process, its finality would accomplish the duel's central function—to convince the loser's companions of the victor's invincibility. They would thus be persuaded to yield their land, their wealth, and even some of their political autonomy in order to preserve their own and their people's lives.

Because the duel between Aias and Hector is empty and because neither one seems able to dominate or destroy the other, there seems to them to be no point in continuing their fight to the death. Since their duel is not attended with contractual significations, it cannot prevent further bloodshed. And since the duel does not produce a display of dominance, it does not embolden either army. Quite the contrary—it reveals how slow, difficult, and hard-fought the war will be. Its spectators are left with the bleakest assessment of what lies in store for them.

Antenor, having just witnessed the duel, thus proposes to the Trojans that they return Helen and her wealth to Menelaus forthwith. Aias meanwhile counsels the Achaean leadership to build a defensive wall along the line of ships and huts on the beach. The Achaeans would, of course, never have needed a wall if, instead of Aias, they had had Achilles to send against Hector. Realizing this, they also soon begin to take steps to propitiate their champion. The Trojans, however, have only one avenue to avoid annihilation—giving up Helen. Pandarus's flagrant abuse of the peace treaty has closed off to his companions the only other avenue to peace, once and for all, sealing their fate. Every deadly encounter, even the inevitable meeting between Hector and Achilles, is now robbed of any possible broader significance. Because all the Trojans must die, every individual Trojan death is rendered meaningless.

With their fate so clearly before them, the fighters turn grim. Because of the dawning recognition that all will die, the distinction between friend and enemy erodes, and heroes from both sides begin to identify with each other as the victims of a hopelessly mired political and military policy. This is revealed most clearly in Glaucus's and Diomedes's recognition of each other as friends. Discovering in their past a common bond, the bond between host and guest whose transgression is said to be the cause of this war, Diomedes and Glaucus exchange gifts instead of blows. But this very substitution reveals again how great the cost of forgetting the institution of the duel, for in swearing friendship for one another, Diomedes and Glaucus are concerned neither for the prosecution of the war nor for the preservation of their companions' lives. As Diomedes says, "ἔγχεα δ' ἀλλήλων ἀλεώμεθα καὶ δι' ὁμίλου· / πολλοὶ μὲν γὰρ ἐμοὶ Τρῶες κλειτοί τ' ἐπίκουροι. / κτείνειν ὅν κε θεός γε πόρῃ καὶ ποσσὶ κιχείω. / πολλοὶ δ' αὖ σοὶ Ἀχαιοὶ ἐναιρέμεν ὅν κε δύνηαι" (6.226-29)—"let us avoid each other's spears, even in the mêlée, since there are plenty of Trojans and their famous allies for me to kill, if I have the luck and speed to catch them, and plenty of Achaeans for you to slaughter, if you can." Diomedes is now assuming that the bloodshed will not abate, that there is no measure to be taken to prevent it. In other words, he accepts the inevitability of his people's destruction, while ignoring the inevitability of champions meeting in battle, for if Diomedes and Glaucus both can and do catch and kill hosts of each other's allies, they must almost certainly, when all others have been killed, once again come face to face. Their only hope for this not to happen is if Glaucus should first meet Aias or Diomedes should first meet Hector, because then death would intervene. For Aias and Hector, breaking off their duel likewise postpones death, but in their case it is probable that they themselves, if they prove indeed to be each the best among his peers, must meet again at last to settle the issue. (They do meet at 14.402-32.) The postponement of a future meeting reveals the recognition and fatalistic acceptance of violence's unboundedness and the meaninglessness of their own deaths.

Postponement of a decisive combat between Hector and Aias occurs, however, within the context of a far more significant postponement, that of the combat between Hector and Achilles. Indeed, the delay in this latter duel is the governing trope for the entire narrative. How is it that nine years of war pass by without a meeting between these two? Hector, for all his courage and integrity, clearly judges Achilles to be his better, as is made clear by his behavior when finally the two do meet. When Hector does then stand before the city's ramparts to face Achilles, he does so with the reflection that it would be better "ἄντην ἢ Ἀχιλῆα κατακτείναντα νέεσθαι. / ἠέ κεν αὐτῷ ὀλέσθαι εὐκλειῶς πρὸ πόληος" (22.109-10)—"to stand up to Achilles, and either kill him and come home alive or myself die gloriously in front of Troy." But this thought only occurs to him because he has just realized that Achilles's slaughter of Trojans (Book 21) is due to his own poor judgment, for he did not order a withdrawal into the city as he should have (22.103). Rather, "ἧφι βίηφι πιθήσας ὤλεσε λαόν" (22.107)—he had "trusted in his own right arm and lost an army." Hector exposes his men to Achilles on the premise that he will put himself between them and Achilles. This he has not done, thus opening himself to the reproach that now forms the basis for his decision to take a stand. In this scene, then, we see the fundamental principles of the epic duel laid out, for when the best warrior declines to meet his opposite in single combat, his friends pay for it with their lives. Delay gains nothing. Even if it is the case that the opposing champion seems the better warrior, as Priam judges, telling Hector that Achilles "πολὺ φέρτερός ἐστι"

(22.40)—"is far stronger"—Hector realizes that his death is necessary and therefore "ἐϋκλειῶς"—"glorious." Yet, as Hector reflects, Achilles cannot be placated. He does not want peace but lives. Hector has thus missed the opportunity for a peace-bringing death, and thus also for full praise.

Hector slowly comes to terms with this fact as he imagines offering Achilles the return of Helen and the property taken with her, adding to these half the wealth in Ilium (22.111-21). As he realizes that this course of action would be fruitless, the audience may recall the terms of the duel between Paris and Menelaus, which provided for the return of Helen and the stolen property (3.70-72). Had that duel been carried out properly, Hector would not now find himself facing his death. And had Hector fought Achilles nine years before in a formal duel, he would have died, but at least his death would have meant the salvation of his family, though Helen and her wealth would have to have been returned. Hector's present shame, then, prompts him to die a needless death, all because his calculation of the necessity for single combat comes too late.

The delay in Hector's thinking stems from his fear or rather his accurate assessment of Achilles's superiority. It is the fear that now prompts him to take flight three times around Troy's walls. Only when tricked into thinking that his brother Deiphobus will stand beside him does he stop his flight and regain his composure. But reliance on a companion is forbidden by the protocols of the formal duel. Now it proves to have been an illusion as Deiphobus simply vanishes.

When Hector determines, then, to face Achilles as he should have done some time ago, he attempts to articulate the terms of an agreement, just as should have occurred, had the two met before the death of Patroclus and before Pandarus's ill-conceived bowshot. Now, however, the terms for which Hector asks bear only upon the treatment of his corpse. The duel no longer has any bearing upon the living, only upon the dead. And even this Achilles refuses. The moment for a formal duel is forever past, and thus the meeting between the great champions only underscores the many failures of judgment and missed opportunities. Priam's admonition to Hector not to face Achilles may prompt the audience to consider, for example, that if he was unwilling to pit his son Hector against Achilles, then he had no basis for refusing to yield Helen to the Achaeans when first they arrived in pursuit of her.

We have seen that the single understanding most significant to the functioning of epic culture is the conviction that any military conflict will inevitably be determined by single combat between the best fighters from both sides. Best of all, therefore, would be to arrange for such a meeting to take place before the onset of the general mêlée. Such arrangements, however, are both delicate and complex. In order for the duel to succeed in its function, numerous conditions must be met. Failure to observe any one of the conditions results in a return to battle and the annihilation or near-annihilation of both armies. There are, as we shall see, a great many points at which the agreements can break down. Because of this institution's complexity and fragility, it must be very carefully managed.

As a signal of acceptance of the duel and its provisions, the armies usually lay down their arms and take up positions from which to view the contest. Because the duel is not simply a battlefield encounter but a formal event of exceptional significance, the spectators have the role of referees, watching intently to ensure that all the conditions are met. One of the most important conditions is, naturally, that the fight be fair. In the arena, the champions are exposed on all sides, without companions to cover their flanks. During the duel, it is therefore imperative that nobody interfere in any way with either of the champions. The men ringing the arena must see to it that this condition is met.

Since the duel is meant to put an end to all hostilities, it is essential that all issues lying between the warring parties be addressed before the duel is fought. A formal agreement announced to the assembled armies helps guarantee fulfillment of the agreement's terms. Those who make and announce such an agreement must themselves be distinguished individuals, duly recognized by all parties as having the authority proper to their function. As we have seen, Priam himself must come down from Troy's citadel to ratify the treaty.

The truce allowing for negotiations, preparations, and the duel itself must be scrupulously observed. A ritual sacrifice may be called for in order to ratify the truce. Menelaus instructs: "οἴσετε ἄρν'. ἕτερον λευκόν. ἑτέρην δὲ μέλαιναν. / Γῇ τε καὶ Ἡελίῳ· Διὶ δ' ἡμεῖς οἴσομεν ἄλλον" (3.103-04)—"Bring a couple of sheep, a white ram and a black ewe, for Earth and the Sun; and we will bring one for Zeus." The force of this ritual is to solemnize the proceedings, to signify how much hangs in the balance, to warn of the extreme gravity of a breach. A truce of this kind can only be made once in the course of a war. If it is tried and fails because of an infraction against any one of its conditions, then the parties at fault will thenceforth be held incapable of keeping their oaths. When agreements cannot be made, there is no alternative to violence without end. Truce-breakers face annihilation. Discipline, therefore, is crucial to the successful management of a duel.

Aside from the explicit agreements entered into, the management of a duel also requires adherence to conventions based on understandings so central that they need not be articulated. Chief among these is the selection of weapons. Armor, as it is described in the texts we have been considering, is surprisingly uniform. Champions are usually attired in chest mail, greaves, and a helmet. They carry a massive shield, broadsword, and long bronze-tipped javelins. But occasionally, other weapons are used. Diomedes, Aias, and Achilles all lift and throw boulders. Siegfried does the same in the contest for Brünhild's hand in marriage. And Beowulf relies on the strength of his bare hands to come to grips with Grendel. One principle governing the choice of weapons is that they should be of the same type. A second principle is to prefer weapons that afford more intimate contact and require greater physical strength. Bare-handed combat between giants appears to be the most impressive form of combat.[3] Slender delicate-featured archers are least suitable as champions.

Of course, virtually every army has its complement of archers, but it should be clear by now that archery can play no role in a duel. Because the bowman works from afar, he can maintain anonymity or, if recognized, he can make good his escape. The bow does not, therefore, allow its user to display invincibility, the one quality absolutely essential in a champion. If both sides have skillful archers, a war of arrows will result only in attrition of the fighting forces. The use of bows thus results in losses without producing a resolution. The entire principle of the bow is antithetical to the project of the duel. While champions are usually skilled in the use of a bow, as they demonstrate in contests or while hunting, in battle they shun it, and in a duel it is taboo.

When Odysseus packs for the war, he leaves his bow in the armory. Philoctetes, the bowman without whom, according to augury, Troy cannot be taken, is abandoned on a deserted island by his Achaean companions because they are disgusted by the fetid stench of an open sore. The revulsion felt for Philoctetes, however, is easily explainable in terms of his archery, which is itself to be loathed and reviled, at least so long as there is another means for achieving victory. After Achilles's death when he is wounded by a poisoned arrow, Philoctetes is recalled and fetched to Troy, for without Achilles the Achaeans cannot dominate the battlefield and victory in pitched battle will cost them the greater part of their army. Troy must be brought down by cunning, deceit, and trickery.

These are the qualities in which Odysseus, "he of many contrivances," distinguishes himself, and so it is that he, not a towering hero like Achilles or Aias, is given responsibility for bringing down Troy. It is also no coincidence that Odysseus is the one who persuades the archer Philoctetes to bring his bow to Troy. Indeed, the bowman and the trickster are naturally allied; they are two aspects of the same character. Both are occasionally reviled, frequently suspect, and generally held in lower esteem than their sword-wielding companions. Nevertheless, the occasion does arise when the use of a bow or trickery is required and appropriate, although even then their use does not in and of itself confer glory. Rather, a good reputation is sometimes achieved despite the resort to archery or cunning.

Such is the story of Odysseus's homecoming. If the display of heroic virtue that intimidates the enemy is best effected with a show of physical might, why does Odysseus not arrive openly, declaring his name to all and challenging his wife's suitors to meet him squarely in combat? Presumably, it is for the same reason that the Trojans, once they reveal their untrustworthiness, must be defeated by a cunning stratagem. It is no coincidence that Achilles's death results from a poisoned arrow, shot by Paris. The poison

---

[3] Davidson recognizes that "a hero is evidently permitted to use wrestling tactics, as Beowulf did, or any available weapon such as a club, like Halfdan and Gram in Saxo's stories," but the inference is "that for a duel with an adversary whom he respects, the sword must be the chosen weapon" (pp. 198-99).

adds cunning to archery[4] and defeats even the greatest champion, though without benefit to its user. In returning to Ithaca, Odysseus is not invulnerable to treachery. Knowing his adversaries at home as well as he has learned to know the Trojans abroad, Odysseus rightly elects to employ inglorious cunning, preferring it to a bravado that would have been as fatal to him as it already had been to Agamemnon, who returned from Troy resplendent in his war cart, only to be snared and butchered in his bathtub by his wife and her lover.

Penelope's suitors are not to be trusted, first and foremost, because they never went to Troy. Because they do not share the values or abilities that compel a man to leave home to join the war, it seems probable that they would not know, understand, or respect battlefield etiquette. Furthermore, the manner of their wooing reveals that not a single one of them possesses the courage to confront and drive off his competitors. Instead, they plot together as a mob to set an ambush for Telemachus, who has not yet even reached manhood. Rather than defending Penelope, the suitors devote themselves to consuming her wealth; her flocks, her grain, and her wine. They have, therefore, no legitimate claim to her. The contest proposed by Penelope reveals that they are so far beneath a legitimate suitor's might that they cannot even string Odysseus's great bow.

Odysseus has no intention of impressing, intimidating, or negotiating terms with the suitors. Just like the Trojans whose perfidy immediately condemns them to death, the suitors must all die because there can be no security for Odysseus in living among them. Odysseus understands that they cannot be trusted, not for an instant, not a single one of them. And so he, who had devised a stratagem to get the Achaeans inside Troy's walls, sets about getting inside the walls of his own hall. Once there and armed with his bow, he blocks the suitors' exit and then picks them off one by one until none remains. Odysseus's crooked bow, like that of Philoctetes and like the stratagem of the wooden horse, makes itself useful only after the more economical means available, the duel, proves fruitless or inappropriate.[5]

---

[4] Michael N. Nagler, in "Penelope's Male Hand: Gender and Violence in the *Odyssey*," *Colby Quarterly*, 29 (1993), 245-46, points out Odysseus's special distinction in being granted the use of poison for his arrows. The bow is prohibited in battle, the use of poison strictly regulated even for peacetime use. Use of poisoned arrows is thus reserved, according to Nagler, for those "under protection of Zeus himself" (246) or, in other words, those who have proven themselves trustworthy: first, to have the ability to analyze both the circumstances in which a bow may be used and, further, in which poisoned arrows may be fired, and then to have the self-discipline never to misuse these weapons. Further references to the Nagler work will be cited parenthetically in the text.

[5] Nagler argues that the appropriate sphere for the bow's use is not a distinction "between war and hunting but between enemies and one's own community" (p. 245). In the symbolic code of the *Odyssey*, the bow "stands for violence used to control one's own community. *Toxon* ('bow') corresponds roughly to the functions of the Justice Department and law enforcement" (pp. 250-51). The difference between the Departments of Defense and State, between war and punishment, is

Pandarus, the bowman responsible for breaking the truce, himself comes to realize the error in his thinking. Regretting his use of the bow, he puts it aside—too late, of course. His own fate, like that of all the Trojans, has already been sealed. Sensing this, he reflects at length upon his earlier decision to shoot Menelaus from behind the cover of his companions rather than advancing in a chariot, spear in hand, to the forefront. He tells Aeneas:

"ἦ μέν μοι μάλα πολλὰ γέρων αἰχμητὰ Λυκάων
ἐρχομένῳ ἐπέτελλε δόμοις ἔνι ποιητοῖσιν·
ἵπποισίν με κέλευε καὶ ἅρμασιν ἐμβεβαῶτα
ἀρχεύειν Τρώεσσι κατὰ κρατερὰς ὑσμίνας·
ἀλλ' ἐγὼ οὐ πιθόμην—ἦ τ' ἂν πολὺ κέρδιον ἦεν—
ἵππων φειδόμενος, μή μοι δευοίατο φορβῆς
ἀνδρῶν εἰλομένων, εἰωθότες ἔδμεναι ἄδην.
ὣς λίπον, αὐτὰρ πεζὸς ἐς Ἴλιον εἰλήλουθα
τόξοισιν πίσυνος· τὰ δέ μ' οὐκ ἄρ' ἔμελλον ὀνήσειν.
ἤδη γὰρ δοιοῖσιν ἀριστήεσσιν ἐφῆκα,
Τυδεΐδῃ τε καὶ Ἀτρεΐδῃ, ἐκ δ' ἀμφοτέροιιν
ἀτρεκὲς αἷμ' ἔσσευα βαλών, ἤγειρα δὲ μᾶλλον.
τῶ ῥα κακῇ αἴσῃ ἀπὸ πασσάλου ἀγκύλα τόξα
ἤματι τῷ ἑλόμην ὅτε Ἴλιον εἰς ἐρατεινὴν
ἡγεόμην Τρώεσσι, φέρων χάριν Ἕκτορι δίῳ.
εἰ δέ κε νοστήσω καὶ ἐσόψομαι ὀφθαλμοῖσι
πατρίδ' ἐμὴν ἄλοχόν τε καὶ ὑψερεφὲς μέγα δῶμα,
αὐτίκ' ἔπειτ' ἀπ' ἐμεῖο κάρη τάμοι ἀλλότριος φώς,
εἰ μὴ ἐγὼ τάδε τόξα φαεινῷ ἐν πυρὶ θείην
χερσὶ διακλάσσας· ἀνεμώλια γάρ μοι ὀπηδεῖ." (5.193-216)

"There in the palace before I left for the front, my father Lycaon, the old spearman, told me time and again that I ought to lead the men from a chariot and pair when we engaged the enemy. But I would not listen to him—better for me if I had. I thought of my horses, who had always had enough to eat, and was afraid that fodder might run short in the congested city. So I left and came to Ilium on foot, relying on archery. Not that archery was going to do me any good. For I have already shot at a couple of their best men, Diomedes and Menelaus, and in each case I scored a hit and drew blood—

---

not, then, one of numbers, for the hero is far outnumbered in both instances. On the battlefield, however, he can (and must) defeat an army by relying entirely on the power of his sword, while at home he must be wary enough to use even a bow to gain advantage over unscrupulous miscreants. As Lynn-George points out, Telemachus is unable "to envisage the possibility that they might engage their opponents unaided," especially considering the great number of the suitors, to which Odysseus counters that, in the absence of other help one must seek the help of the gods, for "they will support—and secure—rightful vengeance" (p. 215). The use of poisoned arrows can, then, be attributed to the gods but only for their judgment, through human hosts, that Odysseus is worthy to own and make use of these instruments.

there is no doubt about it. But I only roused them to greater efforts. Yes, I did an unlucky thing when I took my crooked bow from its peg, that day I set out with my company for your lovely town to please Prince Hector. But if ever I get home again and set eyes on my own country and my wife and the high roof of my great house, I shall be ready to let anybody cut off my head then and there, if I don't smash this bow with my own hands and throw it in the blazing fire. The thing is of no earthly use to me."

It is ironic that Pandarus brings his bow to Troy but promises to smash it if he gets home—precisely the reverse of what Odysseus does. Aeneas now agrees with Pandarus that "πάρος δ' οὐκ ἔσσεται ἄλλως. / πρίν γ' ἐπὶ νὼ τῷδ' ἀνδρὶ σὺν ἵπποισιν καὶ ὄχεσφιν / ἀντιβίην ἐλθόντε σὺν ἔντεσι πειρηθῆναι" (5.218-20)—"nothing can be done to stop [Diomedes] till you and I get into a chariot and attack him with other weapons." So Pandarus goes to meet his death—one death among many caused by the wound he himself inflicted with an arrow, a mere flesh wound to Menelaus but a mortal blow to the truce, fatal both to Pandarus and Troy.

Paris always feels most comfortable with his bow. Like Pandarus, he has it with him when the course of battle puts him in range of Diomedes. Unlike Pandarus facing Diomedes, however, Paris sees no reason not to pull off a shot with it. His attempt to kill the mighty spearman reveals much about the bow's limitations against bronze-clad warriors and about attitudes towards the bow:

Ἀλέξανδρος. Ἑλένης πόσις ἠϋκόμοιο.
Τυδεΐδῃ ἔπι τόξα τιταίνετο. ποιμένι λαῶν.
στήλῃ κεκλιμένος ἀνδροκμήτῳ ἐπὶ τύμβῳ
Ἴλου Δαρδανίδαο. παλαιοῦ δημογέροντος.
ἤτοι ὁ μὲν θώρηκα Ἀγαστρόφου ἰφθίμοιο
αἴνυτ' ἀπὸ στήθεσφι παναίολον ἀσπίδα τ' ὤμων
καὶ κόρυθα βριαρήν· ὁ δὲ τόξου πῆχυν ἄνελκε
καὶ βάλεν. οὐδ' ἄρα μιν ἅλιον βέλος ἔκφυγε χειρός.
ταρσὸν δεξιτεροῖο ποδός· διὰ δ' ἀμπερὲς ἰὸς
ἐν γαίῃ κατέπηκτο· ὁ δὲ μάλα ἡδὺ γελάσσας
ἐκ λόχου ἀμπήδησε καὶ εὐχόμενος ἔπος ηὔδα·
"βέβληαι. οὐδ' ἅλιον βέλος ἔκφυγεν· ὡς ὄφελόν τοι
νείατον ἐς κενεῶνα βαλὼν ἐκ θυμὸν ἑλέσθαι.
οὕτω κεν καὶ Τρῶες ἀνέπνευσαν κακότητος.
οἵ τέ σε πεφρίκασι λέονθ' ὡς μηκάδες αἶγες."

Τὸν δ' οὐ ταρβήσας προσέφη κρατερὸς Διομήδης·
"τοξότα. λωβητήρ. κέρᾳ ἀγλαέ. παρθενοπῖπα.
εἰ μὲν δὴ ἀντίβιον σὺν τεύχεσι πειρηθείης.
οὐκ ἄν τοι χραίσμῃσι βιὸς καὶ ταρφέες ἰοί·
νῦν δέ μ' ἐπιγράψας ταρσὸν ποδὸς εὔχεαι αὔτως.
οὐκ ἀλέγω. ὡς εἴ με γυνὴ βάλοι ἢ πάϊς ἄφρων·
κωφὸν γὰρ βέλος ἀνδρὸς ἀνάλκιδος οὐτιδανοῖο.
ἦ τ' ἄλλως ὑπ' ἐμεῖο. καὶ εἴ κ' ὀλίγον περ ἐπαύρῃ.

ὀξὺ βέλος πέλεται, καὶ ἀκήριον αἶψα τίθησι.
τοῦ δὲ γυναικὸς μέν τ' ἀμφίδρυφοί εἰσι παρειαί,
παῖδες δ' ὀρφανικοί· ὁ δέ θ' αἵματι γαῖαν ἐρεύθων
πύθεται. οἰωνοὶ δὲ περὶ πλέες ἠὲ γυναῖκες." (11.369-95)

Paris, the husband of Helen of the lovely hair, drew a bow on Tydeides the great captain, leaning for cover against the column on the mound which men of a bygone age had made for their chieftain, Ilus, son of Dardanus. As Diomedes was engaged in pulling the burnished cuirass from the stalwart Agastrophus' breast, the shield from his shoulder, and the heavy helmet from his head, Paris drew the centre of his bow, and shot. The arrow did not leave his hand for nothing. Hitting Tydeides on the flat of his right foot, it went right through and stuck in the earth. Paris, with a happy laugh, leapt out from his ambush and gloated over Diomedes. "You are hit," he cried; "I did not shoot for nothing. I only wish I had hit you in the belly and shot you dead. Then the Trojans, who quake before you like bleating goats before a lion, would have some respite from this blight."

Unperturbed, the mighty Diomedes answered him: "Bowman and braggart, with your pretty lovelocks and your glad eye for the girls; if you faced me man to man with real weapons, you would find your bow and quiverful a poor defence. As it is, you flatter yourself. All you have done is to scratch the sole of my foot. And for that I care no more than if a woman or a naughty boy had hit me. A shot from a coward and milksop does no harm. But *my* weapons have a better edge. One touch from them, and a man is dead, his wife has lacerated cheeks, and his children have no father; the earth turns red with his blood, and there he rots, with fewer girls than vultures at his side."

Diomedes is caught by Paris's arrow while he is bent over to strip the bronze from a slain warrior. In order to wound him, Paris has to find a spot not covered by bronze. It is the bronze itself that limits archery's effectiveness, and because archers shoot from cover, they seem to be avoiding the dangers of a direct confrontation "man to man." Archery thus comes to be viewed as cowardly and effeminate or even childish. The heroic definitions not only of warfare but of manhood, courage, and the heroic physique follow from the refinement of protective armor, which reduces archery's effectiveness. Protective armor forces the warriors to meet face to face in more intimate tests of their strength and courage, relegating archery to a peripheral role. Used improperly, it can bring doom upon its adherents. The arrow thus comes to be regarded with mistrust, and its use is henceforth poisoned. Its effects spread like a contagion that cannot be checked.

Indeed, the metaphorical association between archery and contagion must have been a commonplace, for Homer employs it even in reverse in the *Iliad* (1), when he describes the plague visited upon the Achaeans by an angry Apollo in terms of the archer-god's sharp arrows:

τοῦ δ' ἔκλυε Φοῖβος Ἀπόλλων.
βῆ δὲ κατ' Οὐλύμποιο καρήνων χωόμενος κῆρ,
τόξ' ὤμοισιν ἔχων ἀμφηρεφέα τε φαρέτρην·

ἔκλαγξαν δ' ἄρ' ὀϊστοὶ ἐπ' ὤμων χωομένοιο.
αὐτοῦ κινηθέντος· ὁ δ' ἤϊε νυκτὶ ἐοικώς.
ἕζετ' ἔπειτ' ἀπάνευθε νεῶν, μετὰ δ' ἰὸν ἕηκε·
δεινὴ δὲ κλαγγὴ γένετ' ἀργυρέοιο βιοῖο·
οὐρῆας μὲν πρῶτον ἐπῴχετο καὶ κύνας ἀργούς,
αὐτὰρ ἔπειτ' αὐτοῖσι βέλος ἐχεπευκὲς ἐφιεὶς
βάλλ'· αἰεὶ δὲ πυραὶ νεκύων καίοντο θαμειαί. (1.43-52)

> Phoebus Apollo . . . came down in fury from the heights of Olympus with his bow and covered quiver on his back. As he set out, the arrows clanged on the shoulder of the angry god. . . . He sat down opposite the ships and shot an arrow, with a dreadful twang from his silver bow. He attacked the mules first and the nimble dogs; then he aimed the sharp arrows at the men, and struck again and again. Day and night innumerable fires consumed the dead.

Disease, coming unseen like an arrow, strikes senselessly, indiscriminately, and threatens universal destruction. The metaphor in this case is not the product of a poetic imagination but of a painful recognition that does not exhaust itself in the composition of epic song; it creates and supports arcane military prohibitions, like the one regulating the use of arrows on the battlefield.

Epic culture must be ever vigilant against the bow, and the champion must shun its use. The men must be disciplined to employ it only when conditions preclude a duel or ritual battle. Self-discipline thus becomes associated with rejection of the bow. In a metaphorical expression of self-control, for example, Hrothgar instructs Beowulf not to allow the success won by his physical prowess to induce him to relax his guard against pride, "se þe of flanbogan fyrenum sceoteð" (1744)—"whose bow shoots treacherously." The arrow is treacherous because "him bebeorgan ne con" (1746b)—the warrior "cannot protect himself." Archery is dangerous because it is insidious, and it catches the unwary. Against it, the careful warrior is safe. Its use thus becomes a touchstone for vigilance, courage, and self-discipline. Against it, the greatest warriors will seem magically protected. Achilles is said to have been dipped in the Styx, the river crossed by dead souls on their way to the underworld, so that he is thus made invincible to wounds everywhere except on the heel by which he was lowered into the water. Siegfried is similarly protected by having bathed in a dragon's blood, which leaves him vulnerable only at a single spot in the middle of his back. Both heroes can be brought down only from behind. They are vulnerable only to a cunning and cowardly assassination, a deed that would prove itself worthless to the doer.

If archery undermines the institution of the duel by denying the principle of invincibility, a champion's election to use no weapon at all and to meet the enemy with his bare hands stands as the strongest possible reinforcement of understandings that make the duel viable as a means for stanching the flow of blood on the field of battle.

Beowulf is such a champion. Hearing of the Gar-Danes' suffering at the hands of a monster, he crosses the sea with fourteen companions to offer

King Hrothgar his services: "ond nu wið Grendel sceal, wið þam aglæcan, ana gehegan ðing wið þyrse" (424b-26b)—"I alone," he boasts, "shall settle affairs with Grendel, the monster, the demon." In the next breath, however, Beowulf imposes his own terms on Hrothgar for ridding the hall, Heorot, of its monster.

        Ic þe nu ða,
brego Beorht-Dena, biddan wille,
eodor Scyldinga, anre bene,
þæt ðu me ne forwyrne, wigendra hleo,
freowine folca, nu ic þus feorran com,
þæt ic mote ana ond minra eorla gedryht,
þes hearda heap, Heorot fælsian.
Hæbbe ic eac geahsod þæt se æglæca
for his wonhydum wæpna ne recceð;
Ic þæt þonne forhicge swa me Higelac sie,
min mondrihten, modes bliðe,
þæt ic sweord bere oþðe sidne scyld,
geolorand to guþe, ac ic mid grape sceal
fon wið feonde ond ymb feorh sacan,
lað wið laþum. (426b-40a)

Therefore, lord of the Bright-Danes, protector of the Scyldings, I will make a request of you, refuge of warriors, fair friend of nations, that you refuse me not, now that I have come so far, that alone with my company of earls, this band of hardy men, I may cleanse Heorot. I have also heard say that the monster in his recklessness cares not for weapons. Therefore, so that my liege lord Hygelac may be glad of me in his heart, I scorn to bear sword or broad shield, yellow wood, to the battle, but with my grasp I shall grapple with the enemy and fight for life, foe against foe.

Beowulf insists upon fighting the monster alone and on its own terms, fairly, using only his bare hands. Clearly, with Grendel, because he is a monster and because he acts only for himself and is champion of no army, there will be no treaty, no contract, no terms to specify future relations between warring parties. If Grendel wins, Beowulf anticipates, "byreð blodig wæl, byrgean þenceð, eteð angenga unmurnlice" (448-49)—"he will bear away my bloody flesh meaning to savor it, he will eat ruthlessly"—and that will be the sole consequence of Grendel's victory, because Beowulf's challenging the monster puts Hrothgar's people under no obligation.

If Beowulf wins, on the other hand, Heorot will again fill with people, and normal life will be resumed by the Gar-Danes. It will be as if Beowulf has won a formal duel providing for peace between the warring peoples. Of course, these results could be achieved by killing Grendel by any means, fair or foul. The duel in this instance has no apparent life-saving economy to justify it, for Grendel is a monster, not a champion. Nevertheless, Beowulf insists upon fighting Grendel under the conditions of a formal duel. As it turns out, these are the only conditions under which Grendel can be defeated, because Grendel has magic properties that enforce all the conditions appropriate to a formal duel. While appearing to live beyond the pale of law and custom and thus perhaps inviting unlawful or uncustomary methods of suppression, Grendel actually provides the ideal test for a would-be champion, for only by adhering rigorously to the principles that regulate the formal duel does Beowulf evade the monster's magic.[6]

Before Beowulf deals Grendel his death wound, the audience is told for the first time that swords are useless against him.

                      þær genehost brægd
eorl Beowulfes   ealde lafe,
wolde freadrihtnes   feorh ealgian,
mæres þeodnes,   ðær hie meahton swa.
Hie þæt ne wiston,   þa hie gewin drugon,
heardhicgende   hildemecgas,
ond on healfa gehwone heawan þohton,
sawle secan.   þone synscaðan
ænig ofer eorþan   irenna cyst,
guðbilla nan,   gretan nolde,
ac he sigewæpnum   forsworen hæfde,
ecga gehwylcre. (794b-805a)

There more than enough of Beowulf's earls drew swords, old heirlooms, wished to protect the life of their dear lord, famous prince, however they might. They did not know when they entered the fight, hardy-spirited warriors, and when they thought to hew him on every side, to seek his soul, that not any of the best of irons on earth, no war-sword, would touch the evil-doer: for with a charm he had made victory-weapons useless, every sword-edge.

---

[6] As Renoir has so clearly remarked, the passages describing Beowulf and Grendel emphasize the quality of physical strength in each: "mightiest in strength among mankind" on the one hand, "a savage demon" on the other, so that "the two are perfectly matched, and it is only fitting that, just as the monster always fights 'alone against all' (154a: 'ana wið eallum'), so his human opponent should vow to face the giant alone (425b-426a: 'ana gehegan / ðing wið þyrse')" (p. 116). Murdoch sees a similarity between Siegfried and Grendel, particularly insofar as both are outside forces threatening an established court (pp. 152-53). I would go further, because they threaten not by leading an army in an offensive military action but as individuals who cannot be turned aside even by an army, from whose perspective such challengers therefore appear to be quite monstrous. When met by Beowulf, however, Grendel is not regarded as a monster but as an opponent deserving respect expressed through the acceptance of dueling protocol. Murdoch may miss this fine point when he judges the monsters in *Beowulf* to be "the equivalent of the Vikings at Maldon" (p. 64), for in this text the monsters act alone, while in "Maldon" the Vikings fight rather as a unit, though it could be argued that individual mettle plays a decisive role here too.

The monster's magic accomplishes what among human beings is effected only through the formalities of a duel—it renders the champion's companions powerless to interfere, converting them from warriors to spectators. So even though no treaty specifies that the men should sit down, the magic disarms them, and the integrity of this duel is guaranteed. An infraction against the duel's formalities is impossible. While no treaty is made with the inhuman Grendel, the monster's personal qualities bring about the very conditions that a treaty would have stipulated.

The monster's magic contrives not only the conditions of a formal duel, but it also dictates the qualities of the champion who will succeed in defeating him. Hrothgar and his people have, in fact, learned the hard way what it means not to possess these qualities:

> Ful oft gebeotedon   beore druncne
> ofer ealowæge   oretmecgas
> þæt hie in beorsele   bidan woldon
> Grendles guþe   mid gryrum ecga.
> Ðonne wæs þeos medoheal   on morgentid,
> drihtsele dreorfah,   þonne dæg lixte,
> eal bencþelu   blode bestymed,
> heall heorudreore. (480-87a)

> Full often over the ale-cups warriors made bold with beer have boasted that they would await with grim swords Grendel's attack in the beer-hall. Then in the morning this mead-hall was a hall shining with blood, when the day lightened, all the bench-floor blood-wet, a gore-hall.

Men armed with swords will never harm Grendel, for someone has to take the monster directly into his grip. And this means that the monster must be taken on by a single challenger fully confident in his own strength; no ambush can touch Grendel. While not formally prohibited, weapons are rendered useless, since within the confines of the hall, there is insufficient scope for the play of arrows and spears. Swords are harmless against this monster's skin. Finally, an opponent must resort to bare hands. The qualifications for the challenger, then, are that he work alone and rely on his own physical strength as his ultimate weapon.

The bare-handed fight here is noteworthy for its ferocity. Grendel enters the hall at night as Beowulf's fourteen companions sleep. Snatching up the first one by the door, he "bat banlocan, blod edrum dranc, / synsnædum swealh; sona hæfde / unlyfigendes eal gefeormod, fet ond folma" (742-45a)—"bit into his bone-locks, drank the blood from his veins, swallowed huge morsels; quickly he had eaten all of the lifeless one, feet and hands." Then he reaches for Beowulf, but Beowulf is ready and seizes Grendel's hand.

> Sona þæt onfunde   fyrena hyrde,
> þæt he ne mette   middangeardes,
> eorþan sceata,   on elran men

```
          mundgripe maran; . . .
     . . .           ne wæs his drohtoð þær
     swylce he on ealderdagum        ær gemette. (750-57)
```

Straightway the fosterer of crimes knew that he had not encountered on middle-earth, anywhere in this world, a harder hand-grip from another man. . . . What he met there was not such as he had ever before met in the days of his life.

A wrestling match ensues—Grendel trying to break free, Beowulf refusing to let him go.

```
     [E]oten wæs utweard;       eorl furþur stop.
     Mynte se mæra,       þær he meahte swa,
     widre gewindan       ond on weg þanon
     fleon on fenhopu;       wiste his fingra geweald
     on grames grapum.       þæt wæs geocor sið
     þæt se hearmscaþa       to Heorute ateah!
     Dryhtsele dynede;       Denum eallum wearð,
     ceasterbuendum,       cenra gehwylcum,
     eorlum ealuscerwen.       Yrre wæron begen,
     reþe renweardas.       Reced hlynsode.
     þa wæs wundor micel,       þæt se winsele
     wiðhæfde heaþodeorum,       þæt he on hrusan ne feol,
     fæger foldbold. (761-73a)
```

The giant was pulling away, the earl stepped forward. The notorious one thought to move farther away, wherever he could, and flee his way from there to his fen-retreat; he knew his fingers' power to be in a hateful grip. That was a painful journey that the loathsome despoiler had made to Heorot. The retainers' hall rang with the noise—terrible drink for all the Danes, the house-dwellers, every brave man, the earls. Both were enraged, fury-filled, the two who meant to control the hall. The building resounded. Then was it much wonder that the wine-hall withstood them joined in fierce fight, that it did not fall to the ground, the fair earth-dwelling.

So violent is their struggle that the hall seems ready to burst or collapse, and it is saved only by the fact that its walls are reinforced with iron. The benches and tables, however, pop loose from the floor. Then, from the building, comes a terrible noise:

```
                  Norð-Denum stod
     atelic egesa,       anra gehwylcum
     þara þe of wealle       wop gehyrdon,
     gryreleoð galan       Godes ondsacan,
     sigeleasne sang,       sar wanigean
     helle hæfton.       Heold hine fæste
```

se þe manna wæs   mægene strengest
on þæm dæge   þysses lifes. (783b-90)

> Horrible fear came upon the North-Danes, upon every one of those who heard the weeping from the wall, God's enemy sing his terrible song, song without triumph—the hell-slave bewail his pain. There held him fast he who of men was strongest of might in the days of this life.

The violence of this struggle not only shows Beowulf's strength to exceed that of the monster, but it makes the claim that Beowulf is the strongest man alive. This is a central qualification to be champion.

The huge monster, whose frame fills a gateway, who is able to swallow down a full-grown man in a few gulps, becomes puny in Beowulf's grip. "Licsar gebad / atol æglæca; him on eaxle wearð / syndolh sweotol, seonowe onsprungon, / burston banlocan" (815b-18)—"The awful monster had lived to feel pain in his body, a huge wound in his shoulder was exposed, his sinews sprang apart, his bone-locks broke." Beowulf literally crushes the huge creature. After this, who would doubt his invincibility?

The fight with Grendel is not unusual in its emphasis on raw physical strength. Every battle must see its share of close fighting, its mêlée when friend and enemy are too densely packed to permit the shooting of an arrow or the wielding of a long-shafted spear. It is then that the men draw their swords, but the armor of helmet, cuirass, greaves, and above all, massive shield protect the warrior's skin, warding off every blow as if a magic spell were upon him. The great warriors fling away their swords to pick up huge boulders heavy enough to crush even armor. In the *Iliad*, Diomedes, for example, when challenged by Pandarus, the erstwhile archer, and Aeneas, who approach together in a single chariot, first casts his spear, which kills Pandarus. After this, Diomedes picks up a rock:

> μέγα ἔργον. ὅ οὐ δύο γ' ἄνδρε φέροιεν.
> οἷοι νῦν βροτοί εἰς'· ὁ δέ μιν ῥέα πάλλε καὶ οἶος.
> τῷ βάλεν Αἰνείαο κατ' ἰσχίον. ἔνθα τε μηρὸς
> ἰσχίῳ ἐνστρέφεται. κοτύλην δέ τέ μιν καλέουσι·
> θλάσσε δέ οἱ κοτύλην. πρὸς δ' ἄμφω ῥῆξε τένοντε·
> ὦσε δ' ἀπὸ ῥινὸν τρηχὺς λίθος. (5.303-08)

> Even to lift it was a feat beyond the strength of any two men bred to-day, but Diomedes handled it alone without an effort. With this he struck Aeneas on the hip, where the thigh turns in the hip-joint—the cup-bone as they call it. He crushed the cup-bone, and he broke both sinews too—the skin was lacerated by the jagged boulder.

When Aias fights Hector, we observe in detail how, when spears prove ineffective, they may be abandoned in favor of boulders:

Ἦ ῥα, καὶ ἀμπεπαλὼν προΐει δολιχόσκιον ἔγχος,
καὶ βάλεν Αἴαντος δεινὸν σάκος ἑπταβόειον
ἀκρότατον κατὰ χαλκόν, ὅς ὄγδοος ἦεν ἐπ' αὐτῷ.
ἓξ δὲ διὰ πτύχας ἦλθε δαΐζων χαλκὸς ἀτειρής,
ἐν τῇ δ' ἑβδομάτῃ ῥινῷ σχέτο· δεύτερος αὖτε
Αἴας διογενὴς προΐει δολιχόσκιον ἔγχος,
καὶ βάλε Πριαμίδαο κατ' ἀσπίδα πάντοσ' ἐΐσην.
διὰ μὲν ἀσπίδος ἦλθε φαεινῆς ὄβριμον ἔγχος,
καὶ διὰ θώρηκος πολυδαιδάλου ἠρήρειστο·
ἀντικρὺ δὲ παραὶ λαπάρην διάμησε χιτῶνα
ἔγχος· ὁ δ' ἐκλίνθη καὶ ἀλεύατο κῆρα μέλαιναν.
τὼ δ' ἐκπασσαμένω δολίχ' ἔγχεα χερσὶν ἅμ' ἄμφω
σύν ῥ' ἔπεσον λείουσιν ἐοικότες ὠμοφάγοισιν,
ἢ συσὶ κάρποισιν, τῶν τε σθένος οὐκ ἀλαπαδνόν.
Πριαμίδης μὲν ἔπειτα μέσον σάκος οὔτασε δουρί,
οὐδ' ἔρρηξεν χαλκός, ἀνεγνάμφθη δέ οἱ αἰχμή.
Αἴας δ' ἀσπίδα νύξεν ἐπάλμενος· ἡ δὲ διαπρὸ
ἤλυθεν ἐγχείη, στυφέλιξε δέ μιν μεμαῶτα,
τμήδην δ' αὐχέν' ἐπῆλθε, μέλαν δ' ἀνεκήκιεν αἷμα.
ἀλλ' οὐδ' ὣς ἀπέληγε μάχης κορυθαίολος Ἕκτωρ,
ἀλλ' ἀναχασσάμενος λίθον εἵλετο χειρὶ παχείῃ
κείμενον ἐν πεδίῳ, μέλανα, τρηχύν τε μέγαν τε·
τῷ βάλεν Αἴαντος δεινὸν σάκος ἑπταβόειον
μέσσον ἐπομφάλιον· περιήχησεν δ' ἄρα χαλκός.
δεύτερος αὖτ' Αἴας πολὺ μείζονα λᾶαν ἀείρας
ἧκ' ἐπιδινήσας, ἐπέρεισε δὲ ἶν' ἀπέλεθρον,
εἴσω δ' ἀσπίδ' ἔαξε βαλὼν μυλοειδέϊ πέτρῳ,
βλάψε δέ οἱ φίλα γούναθ'· ὁ δ' ὕπτιος ἐξετανύσθη
ἀσπίδι ἐγχριμφθείς. (7.244-72)

With this, [Hector] poised his long-shadowed javelin and cast. He struck the formidable, sevenfold shield of Aias on its metal sheath, the eighth and outermost layer. The untiring bronze tore through six layers, but was held up by the seventh hide. Then royal Aias in his turn launched his long-shadowed spear. The heavy weapon struck the round shield of Priam's son. It pierced the gleaming shield, forced its way through the ornate cuirass, and pressing straight on, tore the tunic on Hector's flank. But he had swerved, and so avoided death. And now the pair, when each had pulled his long spear out, fell on each other like flesh-eating lions, or like wild boars, whose strength is not to be despised. Hector struck Aias with a spear on the centre of his shield. But the bronze did not break through: the stout shield turned its point. Then Aias leaping in caught Hector on the shield. Hector was brought up short and the spear passed clean through his shield with force enough left to reach his neck and bring the dark blood gushing out. Yet even so, Hector of the flashing helmet did not give up the fight. He drew back a little and with his great hand picked up a large and jagged piece of black rock that was lying on the ground, hurled it at Aias' formidable sevenfold shield and struck it in the middle on the boss, making the bronze ring out. But Aias then picked up an even bigger rock, which he swung and hurled at Hector with such tremendous force that the great boulder crumpled his shield and swept him off his feet. Hector, jammed in the shield, lay stretched on his back.

We see that the final outcome of this duel is a matter of who can lift the heaviest boulder. A great premium is placed on raw physical might.

The same principle is demonstrated when Beowulf has to grapple with Grendel's mother. On this occasion, he will even fight his adversary in her own element—the waters at the bottom of the lake. Fully armed, he plunges into the waters, where it was "hwil dæges, / ær he þone grundwong ongytan mehte" (1495b-96)—"a part of a day before he might see the bottom's floor." Seeing his approach, Grendel's mother "[g]rap þa togeanes, guðrinc gefeng / atolan clommum" (1501-02a)—"groped toward him, took the warrior in her awful grip." She, like her son, uses no sword, and Beowulf soon finds his own sword useless against her.

>   mægenræs forgeaf
> hildebille,   hond sweng ne ofteah,
> þæt hire on hafelan   hringmæl agol
> grædig guðleoð.   Ða se gist onfand,
> þæt se beadoleoma   bitan nolde,
> aldre sceþðan,   ac seo ecg geswac
> ðeodne æt þearfe;   ðolode ær fela
> hondgemota,   helm oft gescær,
> fæges fyrdhrægl;   ða wæs forma sið
> deorum madme,   þæt his dom alæg. (1519b-28)

He gave a great thrust to his sword—his hand did not withhold the stroke—so that the etched blade sang at her head a fierce war-song. Then the stranger found that the battle-lightning would not bite, harm her life, but the edge failed the prince in his need: many a hand-battle had it endured before, often sheared helmet, war-coat of man fated to die: this was the first time for the rare treasure that its glory had failed.

There are adversaries against whom one's weapons have no power. In such a situation, what is to be done?

> Eft wæs anræd,   nalas elnes læt,
> mærða gemyndig   mæg Hylaces:
> wearp ða wundenmæl   wrættum gebunden
> yrre oretta,   þæt hit on eorðan læg,
> stið ond stylecg;   strenge getruwode,
> mundgripe mægenes.   Swa sceal man don,
> þonne he æt guðe   gegan þenceð
> longsumne lof;   na ymb his lif cearað. (1529-36)

But still he was resolute, not slow of his courage, mindful of fame, the kinsman of Hygelac. Then, angry warrior, he threw away the sword, wavy-patterned, bound with ornaments, so that it lay on the ground, hard and steel-edged: he trusted in his strength, his mighty hand-grip. So ought a man to do when he thinks to get long-lasting praise in battle.

The weapon of last resort is one's grip; the ultimate test is of one's strength. In this instance, though Beowulf resolutely throws away his sword in favor of his fingers, it is his armor that saves him, and a found weapon that ultimately delivers victory. The sword he finds, however, is one that he alone and no other human has the strength to use: "buton hit wæs mare ðonne ænig mon oðer / to beadulace ætberan meahte" (1560-61)—"it was larger than any other man might bear to war-sport."

Archers like Pandarus eventually throw down their bows and pick up spears. But when heroes meet, their spears also prove ineffective. They unsheath their swords. And when their swords splinter, they turn to heaving boulders, or they wrestle. Wrestling is a demonstration of championship because evenly matched champions may eventually have to resort to this. As we have seen, the more evenly matched the champions, the longer, more grueling, and physically demanding will be their struggle. In such struggles, the men appear likely to outlast their weapons. This is not to say that arrows, javelins, and swords are not dangerous but that, in the final analysis, the hierarchy of weapons will assert itself.

A fine demonstration of this principle is provided by the Hebrews and their antichampion, David. It never crosses Goliath's mind that his challenge to the Hebrews will be answered by a boy carrying only a staff and a sling.

וַיַּבֵּט הַפְּלִשְׁתִּי וַיִּרְאֶה אֶת־דָּוִד וַיִּבְזֵהוּ כִּי־הָיָה נַעַר וְאַדְמֹנִי עִם־יְפֵה מַרְאֶה.וַיֹּאמֶר הַפְּלִשְׁתִּי אֶל־דָּוִד הֲכֶלֶב אָנֹכִי כִּי־אַתָּה בָא־אֵלַי בַּמַּקְלוֹת. (I Sam. 17:42-43)

And when the Philistine looked around, and saw David, he disdained him; for he was but a youth, red haired and good looking. And the Philistine said to David, Am I a dog, that you come to me with sticks?

Goliath never recognizes David as the Hebrew champion, nor do the rest of the Philistines, for when Goliath falls they do not abide by the terms set forth in his challenge: "לָכֶם לַעֲבָדִים וְאִם־אֲנִי אוּכַל־לוֹ וְהִכִּיתִיו וִהְיִיתֶם לָנוּ לַעֲבָדִים_עֲבַדְתֶּם אֹתָנוּ׃ אִם־יוּכַל לְהִלָּחֵם אִתִּי וְהִכַּנִי וְהָיִינוּ" (I Sam. 17:9)—"If he is able to fight with me, and kill me, then we will be your servants; but if I shall prevail against him, and kill him, then shall you be our servants, and serve us." Instead of submitting to David and the Hebrews as their servants, the Philistines, dismayed indeed, turn to flight, and warfare resumes. The men of Israel and Judah pursue them, wounding many. Saul and his people are rid of Goliath but not the war.

David is not, however, disciplined or even upbraided for his breach of etiquette. Does this mean that the Hebrews have no understanding of battle economy and the crucial role to be played by the duel? If they are ignorant of duelling practice and its conventions, then they must also be unaware of the consequences of their ignorance. Their monotheism distinguishes them from their neighbors, including the Philistines, as well as from their rough contemporaries in Asia Minor, Crete, and the Balkans. David is most conscious of this particular difference, and in place of a personal boast to the Philistine champion whom he is about to fight for his life, David articulates his novel understanding of the relationship between warfare and theology:

אַתָּה בָּא אֵלַי בְּחֶרֶב וּבַחֲנִית וּבְכִידוֹן וְאָנֹכִי בָא־אֵלֶיךָ בְּשֵׁם יְהוָה צְבָאוֹת אֱלֹהֵי מַעַרְכוֹת
יִשְׂרָאֵל אֲשֶׁר חֵרַפְתָּ. הַיּוֹם הַזֶּה יְסַגֶּרְךָ יְהוָה בְּיָדִי וְהִכִּיתִךָ וַהֲסִרֹתִי אֶת־רֹאשְׁךָ מֵעָלֶיךָ וְנָתַתִּי
פֶּגֶר מַחֲנֵה פְלִשְׁתִּים הַיּוֹם הַזֶּה לְעוֹף הַשָּׁמַיִם וּלְחַיַּת הָאָרֶץ וְיֵדְעוּ כָּל־הָאָרֶץ כִּי יֵשׁ אֱלֹהִים
לְיִשְׂרָאֵל. וְיֵדְעוּ כָּל־הַקָּהָל הַזֶּה כִּי־לֹא בְּחֶרֶב וּבַחֲנִית יְהוֹשִׁיעַ יְהוָה כִּי לַיהוָה הַמִּלְחָמָה וְנָתַן
אֶתְכֶם בְּיָדֵנוּ׃ (I Sam. 17:45-47)

You come to me with a sword, and with a spear, and with a javelin; but I come to you in the name of the Lord of hosts, the God of the armies of Israel, whom you have defied. This day will the Lord deliver you into my hand; and I will strike you, and take your head off you; and I will give the carcass of the camp of the Philistines this day to the birds of the air, and to the wild beasts of the earth; that all the earth may know that there is a God in Israel. And all this assembly shall know that the Lord saves not with sword and spear; for the battle is the Lord's and he will give you into our hands.

Although the death of Goliath is literally to be effected with a weapon worthy only of his disdain, the Philistine's fall is to be attributed to the venerable hand grip of a hero whose physical strength is prodigious, for the great hand of the Hebrew champion hangs not from David's slender arm but from the long arm of David's god. David anticipates that the significance of his victory will derive precisely from its improbability. His very unsuitability as champion makes him well suited to display an inconspicuous precept of epic culture—namely, the expectation that a champion will step forward to help his lesser companions when he sees them in danger. In the *Iliad*, just as Aeneas steps forward to protect the fallen Pandarus and the goddess Aphrodite rushes quickly to the aid of her son Aeneas, where he lies crushed beneath the boulder Diomedes hurled, David has faith that, regardless of his own unsuitability to be champion, his god will shield him from harm by defeating Goliath. Just so, the god Apollo answers a Trojan prayer by smiting Patroclus:

στῆ δ' ὄπιθεν. πλῆξεν δὲ μετάφρενον εὐρέε τ' ὤμω
χειρὶ καταπρηνεῖ. στρεφεδίνηθεν δέ οἱ ὄσσε.
τοῦ δ' ἀπὸ μὲν κρατὸς κυνέην βάλε Φοῖβος Ἀπόλλων . . .
πᾶν δέ οἱ ἐν χείρεσσιν ἄγη δολιχόσκιον ἔγχος.
βριθὺ μέγα στιβαρὸν κεκορυθμένον· αὐτὰρ ἀπ' ὤμων
ἀσπὶς σὺν τελαμῶνι χαμαὶ πέσε τερμιόεσσα.
λῦσε δέ οἱ θώρηκα ἄναξ Διὸς υἱὸς Ἀπόλλων.
τὸν δ' ἄτη φρένας εἷλε. λύθεν δ' ὑπὸ φαίδιμα γυῖα.

στῆ δὲ ταφών· ὄπιθεν δὲ μετάφρενον ὀξέϊ δουρὶ
ὤμων μεσσηγὺς σχεδόθεν βάλε Δάρδανος ἀνήρ.
Πανθοΐδης Εὔφορβος. (16.791-93, 801-09)

> Phoebus Apollo stood behind [Patroclus] now, and striking his broad shoulders and back with the flat of his hand, he made the eyes start from Patroclus' head and knocked off his visored helmet. . . . Not only that, but the long-shadowed spear, huge, thick and heavy with its head of bronze, was shattered in Patroclus' hands; the tasselled shield with its baldric fell from his shoulder to the ground; and King Apollo Son of Zeus undid the corslet on his breast. Patroclus was stunned; his shapely legs refused to carry him; and as he stood there in a daze, a Dardanian called Euphorbus came close behind and struck him with a sharp spear midway between the shoulders.

Hellenic polytheism's portrayal of bickering gods offers a ready explanation for their frequent failure to protect their human suppliants. By contrast, David looks beyond the human conflict, since, from the outset, he anticipates divine intervention that he believes will not be withheld. With monotheism, God's own omnipotence and omniscience are called into question whenever one of his people is endangered. David simply recognizes this fact and uses the only means he knows to summon his champion—he exposes himself to danger, while at the same time declaring his faith. Were he to be slaughtered by Goliath, his premise may appear to be proven false.

The story of David and Goliath is indeed a cross-cultural clash, but the difference lies not in the understanding of battlefield economics but in each people's approach to the problem of displaying its champion's might. The head severed from Goliath's body may be read as a sign of the unseen Hebrew champion's formidable protective powers. The glorification of God through the defeat of Goliath is actually intended by David to fulfill precisely the function of a formal duel—namely, to prevent further bloodshed. The shepherd boy's victory is meant to be reported far and wide, producing the inference in "כָּל־הָאָרֶץ"—"all the earth"—that "יֵשׁ אֱלֹהִים לְיִשְׂרָאֵל"—"there is a God in Israel"; in other words, Israel has a champion capable of defeating even the largest and mightiest opponent. If David's gambit does not work, it is because the Philistines do not ascribe David's victory to the presence of an unseen champion. It is, in fact, a disadvantage for David that his champion cannot be seen with the naked eye. Even Saul does not recognize that God is acting through David. What the Philistines see is a rule-breaker and the flaunting of etiquette. They see, additionally, a race of people that cannot ever be trusted and a neighbor with whom peaceful relations of any kind must prove impossible.

Beowulf regards Grendel, nobody's champion, as a formal challenger because he understands that his own success as a champion depends most of all on a public demonstration of his prowess. This is actually the same logic as that expressed inversely by David, who takes on a known champion even when his own diminutive stature so obviously proclaims his unsuitability. David attempts, thus, to make manifest the presence of an unseen champion, whose stature, though invisible, can be measured against that of Goliath. What is at stake in both cases is not only immediate survival and settlement of the present conflict but the avoidance of future conflict, which can be achieved by a champion of such stature that he causes all would-be attackers to shrink back. Size and might are visible signs of the champion's ability to defend his people. This is why champions who are establishing a reputation must prefer wrestling and boulder-throwing to archery, spear-throwing, and even swordplay. It also explains why champions are so concerned about their trophies and their fame.

Just as heroes in the *Iliad* are forever preoccupied with stripping slain foes of their arms, which they display as trophies, Beowulf, fighting a foe whose only weapons are his two flesh-and-bone arms, literally tears one of these from Grendel's torso and mounts it in Heorot's rafters as a trophy of his victory:

> Hæfde Eastdenum
> Geatmecga leod   gilp gelæsted,
> . . .
> . . .   þæt wæs tacen sweotol,
> syþðan hildedeor   hond alegde,
> earm ond eaxle   —þær wæs eal geador
> Grendles grape—   under geapne hrof. (828b-36)

The man of the Geats had fulfilled his boast to the East-Danes.... That was clearly proved when the battle-brave man set the hand up under the curved roof—the arm and the shoulder: there all together was Grendel's grasp.

Hrothgar's people inspect the trophy, the monster's footprints, and the bloody waters of the lake to which Grendel had slunk to die, and then they pronounce their judgment of Beowulf:

> Ðær wæs Beowulfes
> mærðo mæned;   monig oft gecwæð,
> þætte suð ne norð   be sæm tweonum
> ofer eormengrund   oþer nænig
> under swegles begong   selra nære
> rondhæbbendra,   rices wyrðra. (856b-61)

There was Beowulf's fame spoken of; many a man said—and not only once—that, south nor north, between the seas, over the wide earth, no other man under the sky's expanse was better of those who bear shields.

The champion's success is not measured simply by his opponent's death. He must effect the judgment that he can defeat all comers.

We see, then, how the duel's protocols function within the logic of battlefield dynamics and an economy of lives. The truce between the armies is not a simple formality to enable the assembled warriors to await and witness the duel's outcome. It signals, rather, the observance of numerous spoken and unspoken protocols and implies acknowledgment by all parties of the solemnity of these proceedings. To ensure that the seriousness of the occasion is properly understood, the truce may be further elaborated. Not only do men cease their fighting, but they may disarm, be seated, or be called upon to witness or participate in animal sacrifice or other similarly signifying practices. The truce provides, moreover, an opportunity for all to hear the terms that are meant to bind them. Their observance of the truce and participation in its various protocols after hearing the announcement of the duel's terms implies their willingness to acquiesce in whatever stipulations are attached to the duel's outcome. Furthermore, the protocols according to which the warriors gather around a clearing to witness the duel help to assure its fairness. The terms of fairness include absolute prohibitions against assistance or interference as well as against the use of cunning or trickery. There is also an expectation that the champions will use similar weapons, with preference for hand-to-hand combat. The bow is disallowed, both because it constitutes a form of cunning and also because the bowman has no power to dismay and thus cannot put an army to rout.

The formal battlefield duel has two crucial functions—depriving one army of its most potent battlefield threat and unequivocally demonstrating to every individual warrior that he is no match for the opposing champion and must therefore surely die if he continues fighting. Both of these functions must be accomplished if the duel is to have its desired effect of bringing to an end the otherwise ceaseless flow of blood and endless loss of life. Those who mistakenly believe, like Pandarus, that it would be sufficient to kill the opposing champion without observing the protocol of the duel, eventually pay not only with their own lives but with the knowledge that the life of their entire community must now end. Conversely, for those armies capable of observing all the protocols involved in a formal duel, it is possible to establish a bond of trust between the two societies, such that the parties to a conflict may part in peace—even as friends and allies.

CHAPTER FOUR

THE CHAMPION AND HIS QUEST

We have already observed how, in the course of battle, heroes distinguish themselves as those who are able and willing to hold their ground against the enemy's most daunting fighters. It is they who come to the aid of beleaguered companions. Emerging from the obscurity of the ranks, they draw to themselves the attention of their enemy counterparts, who then approach to face off in a decisive meeting. The special situation of a duel, however, no longer requires that the champion catch the attention of his worthiest opponent. Indeed, in the event that a formal duel is to substitute for a battle of attrition, champions must be selected prior to the engagement in which they would otherwise have emerged in due course. The mechanism of the duel must by-pass the battlefield selection process if it is to bring the two heroes together directly. The selection process is thus displaced from its original setting to a new venue especially suited to the purpose. And because the fate of each polity will rest entirely with the success of its champion, the matter of his selection becomes an issue of utmost importance. The institution of the duel thus imposes new constraints and exacts new disciplines.

Contests, games, and hunting parties provide three obvious means for testing, measuring, and comparing the merits of candidates for championship. Our sources, in fact, abound in descriptions of and references to tournaments, funeral games, hunting expeditions, and sporting contests. Yet nowhere are we given to understand that the explicit purpose of such contests was the selection of a champion. At this point, we must therefore conjecture about the function of such practices. The Greek practice of holding funeral games following the ritual burning of a fallen warrior's body, for example, makes perfect sense in view of the immediate need to select a new champion. The games give the survivors an opportunity to reassess their relative strengths and to select a successor to their fallen hero. Funeral games might also, of course, fulfill other important functions aside from the identification of new champions. As becomes evident in Achilles's management of the games in honor of his companion Patroclus, the ritual context allows for a demonstration of kingly qualities appropriate to maintaining peacetime relations among hierarchically aligned allies. To this aspect of the contest, however, we will return later.

There is another means by which champions can be identified and credentials gathered about which our sources are quite explicit—namely, the warrior's quest for battle. Traveling abroad, the warrior seeks an opportunity to attach himself to one of two contesting parties, specifically the beleaguered underdog, to whom he offers himself as champion. In return, he requires only that he be allowed to fight unassisted, so as most clearly to put his own merits on display. If he wins, the victor then need only secure for himself some sign or token of his victory—usually the arms of the champion he defeats—to take home as supporting evidence for his claims to championship of his own people as their sole protector.[1]

Beowulf, in his mission to rescue Hrothgar, presents the ideal case of a warrior in quest of a championship. For he requires of Hrothgar that he be allowed to fight the monster alone. In fighting Grendel, he eschews the use of weapons so as to meet his adversary on an equal footing. In lieu of "arms," he takes Grendel's arm itself as the trophy of his victory, and this he places on display in the rafters at Heorot for all to witness. For himself, he wishes nothing more than to be able to report his success to Hygelac, his own ruler.

Hrothgar's plight is ideal for Beowulf's purposes, for this king of the Gar-Danes must welcome the offer of any volunteer who comes along to fight Grendel. In the case of a formal duel, this would not be prudent because the king would not place his people under constraint to accept the enemy's terms unless he were convinced that the volunteer champion was more likely to win a victory than the king himself or any of his vassals.[2] Hrothgar is, in any case, already living in banishment from his own hall, which is made uninhabitable at night by Grendel's nocturnal predations. And because the monster lives outside the law and beyond all customary relationships, Beowulf's battle with him has no possible legal ramifications for Gar-Danish sovereignty. Grendel's inhuman qualities make him an ideal opponent for the young and relatively untried Beowulf. By thus exploiting its capacity to design a fantastic adversary for Beowulf, the narrative more sharply defines the process by which a younger warrior gains credentials for service as a formal champion.

---

[1] The phenomenon of individuals traveling in quest of battle and presenting themselves at foreign courts to sue for dominion over land and people is attributed by E. A. S. Butterworth, in *Some Traces of the Pre-Olympian World in Greek Literature and Myth* (Berlin: Walter de Gruyter & Company, 1966), p. 104, to a matrilineal system of royal succession according to which a son cannot succeed his father to the throne and must therefore seek his kingdom abroad. Butterworth makes two assumptions that should, however, be more critically appraised. He opines, first, that princes must seek kingdoms to rule—that they have no other viable or attractive options and, second, that a lone warrior would be capable of overcoming a well-supported incumbent. It is my view that only under conditions of epic-cultural battle does this latter assumption prove true, in which case other reasons for the quest also come into play, as I am presently arguing, for even when a male member of the ruling family stands to inherit the throne, he must still establish his reputation. As Siegfried explains, "Ich bin ouch ein recke und solde krône tragen. / ich wil daz gerne füegen daz si von mir sagen / daz ich habe von rehte liute unde lant" (109,1-3)—"I am also a warrior and am destined to wear a crown. / I am intent upon seeing to it that it is said of me / that I hold my people and territory by right" (my translation).

[2] A case in point is Gunther's silence upon Ortwin's offer to fight Siegfried for control of Burgundy (117-19). While Siegfried explicitly rejects Ortwin as an unworthy opponent, Gunther is waiting for Ortwin's uncle, Hagen, to step forward ("daz der sô lange dagete, daz was dem künege leit"—119.3).

Beowulf's success in establishing his name as a champion is indicated by the changed regard in which Hrothgar holds him following his victory over Grendel. When, on the next night, the hall is ravaged by a new menace, Grendel's avenging mother, Beowulf will no longer have to stipulate that he fight her alone, for, as we have seen, of him it can now be said that "suð ne norð be sæm tweonum / ofer eormengrund oþer nænig / under swegles begong selra nære / rondhæbbendra" (858-61a)—"south nor north, between the seas, over the wide earth, no other man under the sky's expanse was better of those who bear shields." Hrothgar acknowledges Beowulf with the words: "Nu is se ræd gelang / eft æt þe anum" (1376b-77a)—"Now once again is the cure in you alone." No longer is Beowulf simply a volunteer, nor is he simply a hero. He has become Hrothgar's champion, the only man alive considered capable of defending Heorot.

At home among the Geats following his return, Beowulf is held in high esteem. As a token of his respect, King Hygelac bestows gifts upon him—most significant among them, an ancient sword, described as "Hreðles lafe" (2191b)—"heirloom of Hrethel"—of which it is said, "næs mid Geatum ða sincmaðþum selra on sweordes had" (2192b-93)—"[t]here was not then among the Geats a better treasure in sword's kind." This the king laid in Beowulf's lap. This best of swords, a treasure inherited by the king from his father, is reserved to be given, if it is given at all, to signify a bond between the king and his best warrior, the protector of the people, their champion. The close relationship in status between king and champion is later confirmed by Beowulf's ascension to Hygelac's throne upon the king's death: "syððan Beowulfe brade rice / on hand gehwearf; he geheold tela / fiftig wintra" (2207-09a)—"then the broad kingdom came into Beowulf's hand. He held it well fifty winters."

Siegfried takes a more direct path towards establishing himself as protector of his people. Where no war exists, he makes one.[3] His wooing expedition to Burgundy actually has a dual motive—the winning of Kriemhild as a bride and the establishment of his own reputation as a champion. In fact, while the wooing of Kriemhild is first announced by Siegfried as the purpose of his trip, the evidence suggests that the wooing itself is subordinate to Siegfried's need to display his virtuosity as a warrior. From this perspective, he would bring Kriemhild home as a token of his mastery over the Burgundians.

---

[3] In this respect, the champion as defender hardly differs from the champion as destroyer—the same individual can easily be both, and indeed, there would be no need for the "good" defender if it were not for the "evil" predator. Under these circumstances, good and evil are purely circumstantial and perspectival attributes, though some of the tale-tellers and modern critics through whose hands the poems pass do attempt to fix these attributes in the protagonists' identities. Renoir, for example, comments: "Positive and negative must perforce adhere to the same structure, but they are nevertheless the opposite of each other. This fact is essential to our grasp of the relationship between Grendel and Beowulf" (p. 116).

Siegfried, when announcing himself to the Burgundians and stating to them the purpose of his visit to their land, never so much as refers to Kriemhild or his desire to obtain a wife.[4] Rather, he explains his purpose in the following terms:

> Mir wart gesaget mære   in mînes vater lant
> daz hie bî iu wæren   (daz het ich gerne erkant)
> die küenésten recken   (des hân ich vil vernomen)
> die ie künec gewunne;   dar umbe bin ich her bekomen.
>
> Ouch hœre ich iu selben   der degenheite jehen,
> daz man künec deheinen   küener habe gesehen.
> des redent vil die liute   über élliu disiu lant.
> nune wil ich niht erwinden   unz ez mir wérdé bekant.
>
> Ich bin ouch ein recke   und solde krône tragen.
> ich wil daz gerne füegen   daz si von mir sagen
> daz ich habe von rehte   liute unde lant.
> dar umbe sol mîn êre   und ouch mîn houbet wesen pfant. (107-09)

> I was told repeatedly in my father's country that the bravest warriors that King ever had were to be found with you, and I have come to see for myself. I have also heard such warlike qualities ascribed to you that (according to many people in all the lands about) a more valiant prince was never seen; nor shall I desist till I know the truth of it. I, too, am a warrior and am entitled to wear a crown, but I wish to achieve the reputation of possessing a land and people in my own sole right, for which my head and honour shall be pledge! (29)

According to Siegfried's words, what has attracted him to Burgundy is not Kriemhild's reputation for beauty, as he had declared at home, but her brother's reputation for bravery and other warlike qualities. By defeating a king with such a reputation, Siegfried intends to legitimate his own right to the crown he would otherwise inherit from his father. The basis for wearing a crown, in Siegfried's mind, is established by victory against another crowned warrior, the representative and protector of another kingdom.

---

[4] These two motives are for Siegfried hardly distinguishable, though for the Burgundians (as well as modern readers) wooing a wife and conquering a territory are incompatible, if not mutually exclusive, activities. Thus, Beyschlag finds that Siegfried's "allzu polterndes Auftreten am Wormser Hof"—his all too brash swaggering at Worms—is directed solely towards the wooing and winning of Kriemhild, from which it follows that Siegfried never posed a threat to Gunther and that there was therefore no necessity for getting rid of him (p. 211). All that it would take to make Siegfried go away peacefully is possession of Burgundy's princess. Beyschlag seems uncritically, indeed unconsciously, to accept the premise that a princess must be disposed of by her relatives.

It never even occurs to Siegfried that Gunther would base the legitimacy of his own rule on any principle other than his readiness to defend the kingdom in single combat with his own hands or to authorize another warrior to fulfill that role for him.[5] At the same time, Siegfried's challenge articulates a foreign policy initiative:

> ez enmúge von dînen ellen   dîn lant den fride hân,
> ich wil es alles walten.   und ouch diu erbe mîn,
> erwirbest dus mit sterke,   diu sulen dir undertænec sîn.
>
> Dîn erbe und ouch daz mîne   sulen gelîche ligen.
> sweder unser einer   am andern mac gesigen,
> dem sol ez allez dienen,   die liute und ouch diu lant. (113,2-14,3)

> Unless you can protect your country by your own valour I shall rule the whole of it: but if you can wrest my inheritance from me this shall be subject to you. Now let us stake our patrimonies one against the other, and whichever of us two proves victorious let him be master of both lands and peoples. (29)

The terms of the duel and those of Siegfried's foreign policy are identical. Not only does he intend to establish his own legitimacy as king of the Netherlands, but he expects to establish the basis for future relations between the Netherlands and Burgundy. One of these will subordinate itself to the other, according to which kingdom possesses the more able champion. Siegfried equates his marriage to Burgundy's princess with the subordination of that entire kingdom to his rule. Marriage, kingship, and the state's relative sovereignty are all to be legitimated with a single duel.[6]

---

[5] An alternative criterion for the authority to rule is property ownership, which Frakes rates as "the most obvious and important means of access to political power and authority" (p. 64). This is very likely the principle on which Gunther and his court operate and which it would seem that Siegfried understands rather well, as he indicates through his attention to fine clothing and equipment in preparing himself and his small entourage for the expedition to Burgundy. For Siegfried, however, finery does not suffice as a claim to political power and authority. Rather, the reason he gives the Burgundians for wishing to meet Gunther in combat is legitimation of power through success in battle. The finery, then, appears only to signify that his challenge is to be taken seriously. It signifies his claim, but it does not establish his right.

[6] Haymes's entire approach to the *Nibelungenlied* is keyed to understanding Siegfried's wooing in terms of *minnedienst*—service performed for a reward. Three aspects, in particular, of Siegfried's behavior do, in fact, support Haymes's interpretation: first, Siegfried's courtly upbringing and the narrative's presentation of his attraction to Kriemhild in terms of courtly love; second, Siegfried's assistance to Gunther in repelling an invasion by Kings Liudegast and Liudeger; and third, Siegfried's invisible participation in the contest with Brünhild followed by his public fetching of Nibelung warriors as an honor guard to accompany Gunther and his new-won bride to Worms. But this is only half the picture

From the grounds that Siegfried gives for his challenge to the Burgundians, we can infer that a warrior's fame has a double-edged function, namely, both to establish his individual status at home and to determine relations between neighboring kingdoms. Just as the Danish and Saxon kings Liudegast and Liudeger would never have invaded Burgundy had they known Siegfried to be her protector, the Geats' neighbors hold themselves in check so long as they know Beowulf to be alive. Beowulf rules peacefully through fifty winters largely because his reputation staves off invasion from abroad. The champion's reputation not only secures his status within his own society, but his fame actually achieves foreign policy objectives by securing the kingdom.

The dissemination of reports about the conduct of champions plays an important role in helping warriors, each a champion in his own realm, no matter how small, to form indispensable and unavoidably hierarchical relations. When Siegfried comes to Worms, Gunther must either fight him, designate a champion to fight for him, or acquiesce. Gunther seems never to consider meeting Siegfried in single combat himself, and Ortwin, the only Burgundian to volunteer to substitute for him, is rejected out of hand by Siegfried as being unworthy of him, a judgment with which the Burgundians do not argue. Gunther would, therefore, be wise simply to acquiesce, subordinating himself and his kingdom, including his sister, to Siegfried, just as Liudeger will surrender upon the instant of recognizing his opponent as Siegfried. Siegfried, then, has nothing further to profit from Liudeger's death

---

and half the meaning of *dienst* (service) as it is used in these passages. The other sense of *dienen*, meaning "feudal subservience," is linked to Siegfried's challenge, translated by Haymes in the following words: "Which ever of us shall defeat the other, it will all serve him, both lands and people" (p. 52). In this instance, service is forced by one upon the other through combat. These two meanings of *dienst* represent radically different and, as the Nibelungen calamity shows, mutually exclusive approaches to establishing feudal relationships. That both systems are functioning simultaneously in the Nibelungen context is made most apparent by the wooing styles required by Kriemhild and Brünhild to which Siegfried and Gunther both respond inappropriately. Siegfried is not, as Haymes oversimplifies, "motivated entirely by *minne* to seek Kriemhild" (p. 65). Rather, he is motivated in large part by his desire to establish his reputation (though perhaps also by his wish to make friends, to belong) but modifies his approach in the face of Burgundy's unwillingness to meet him on his own terms. Siegfried's "service" on behalf of Burgundy against the Saxons and Danes can similarly be interpreted from two perspectives: his willing subordination to Gunther in order to gain access to Kriemhild and his demonstration of personal qualities contributing to a reputation that legitimates his claims to kingship as well as to the woman of his choosing. The same can be said for Siegfried's errand to fetch the Nibelungs. On the one hand, he demonstrates anew his right by force to be their lord. On the other, he pretends to a subordination to Gunther that has no basis in fact but is required if he is to be successful in the performance of *minnedienst*. These contradictions are present at every turn, creating ever more complex problems and thus leading inexorably towards disaster. The dual wedding mixes the practices of two cultures—with catastrophic results.

and actually treats his captive with utmost courtesy, in the manner befitting an honored guest. Liudeger will even be allowed to continue ruling his Saxons, though he could presumably be required to serve Siegfried, either with payments of tribute or military assistance. Only if he proved disloyal would Siegfried wish to harm him.

This is precisely the relation between Siegfried and Alberich, captain of the Nibelungs. Siegfried makes himself master of the Nibelungs by slaying their princes, Schilbung and Nibelung. He is then opposed by Alberich, "der wânde sîne herren rechen dâ zehant, / unz er die grôzen sterke sît an Sîvride vant" (96,3-4)—"who hoped to avenge his masters there and then, till Siegfried's huge strength was brought home to him" (28). Thus, Siegfried makes himself lord of the Nibelung treasure, coming into possession of the magic cloak of invisibility. But equally important, he comes into possession of the Nibelung fighting forces, henceforth to be captained in Siegfried's name by Alberich: "Die dâ torsten vehten, die lâgen alle erslagen. / . . . Albrîch der vil starke dô die kameren gewan. / Er muose im sweren eide, er diente im sô sîn kneht. / aller hande dinge was er im gereht" (98,1-99,2)— "All who had dared fight lay slain there . . . and, after swearing oaths to Siegfried that he would be his humble servitor, Alberich was made lord treasurer. Indeed, he was in all ways ready to do [Siegfried's] bidding" (28). Guaranteed by an oath similar to the contract solemnized and sealed by a duel, Alberich's obedience and loyalty to Siegfried must be absolute. Alberich's survival, like Troy's, depends on his honoring that oath. If the oath is kept, then Alberich will be left alone to rule the Nibelungs without interference from Siegfried until such time as Siegfried has need of the Nibelungs' services.

On that day, he returns to call upon his subjects. But instead of assuming that they have upheld their oaths of loyalty even in his absence, he does something that at once tests them and at the same time reconfirms his own legitimacy as their sovereign. The scene describing his return has been largely overlooked, perhaps because of its apparent insignificance to the larger story of murder and revenge.[7] From the perspective of epic culture,

---

[7] Haymes (as noted above) does not overlook this scene. Rather, finding Siegfried's behavior "silly" (p. 102), he dismisses this aspect of the scene from consideration and focuses entirely on its significance in the context of Siegfried's *auxilium* to Gunther (p. 56). From Brünhild's point of view, Siegfried's subordination to Gunther is demonstrated simply by his arrival with the contingent of Nibelung knights. She need never know anything of Siegfried's deception of his own men. For the audience, however, the contests at Brünhild's castle at Isenstein and at Alberich's castle in Nibelungenland are comparable and thus invite an assessment of similarities and differences in the two scenes. Siegfried deceives the Nibelung giant guarding the castle gate and then the dwarf Alberich in order to test their loyalty to their absent lord (himself) as well as to reenact his dominance over them, the basis for his right to claim their obedience to him. At Isenstein, by contrast, he uses deception to lend Gunther the impression of strength and with it the right to his loyalty and submissive obedience. Siegfried's expedition to fetch a Nibelung honor guard is, in fact, part of his deception of Brünhild. The

however, the scene very succinctly articulates the principles upon which political, military, and economic relations are established. Desiring the Nibelungs to serve as a military escort for Gunther and his newly-won bride on their journey to Worms, Siegfried goes in person and alone to the Nibelung castle to summon them to his service. The scene is presented as follows:

> Dô kom er für die porten: verslozzen im diu stuont.
> jâ huoten si ir êren,   sô noch die liute tuont.
> anz tor begunde bôzen   der unkunde man;
> daz was wol behüetet.   dô vant er innerthalben stân

> Einen ungefüegen   der der bürge pflac,
> bî dem ze allen zîten   sîn gewæfen lac.
> der sprach: "wer ist der bôzet   sô vaste an daz tor?"
> dô wandelte sîne stimme   der herre Sîfrit dâ vor.

> Er sprach: "ich bin ein recke,   nu entslíuz úf daz tor.
> ich erzürne ir eteslîchen   noch híuté dâ vor,
> der gerne samfte læge   unt hete sîn gemach."
> daz muote den portenære,   dô daz her Sîfrit gesprach.

> Nu hete der rise küene   sîn gewæfen an getân,
> sînen hélm ûf sîn houbet.   der vil starke man
> den schilt vil balde zuhte,   daz tor er ûf swief.
> wie rehte grimmeclîchen   er an Sîfriden lief!

> Wie er getorste wecken   sô manegen küenen man!
> dâ wurden slege swinde   von sîner hant getân.
> dô begonde im schermen   der hêrlîche gast.
> dô schuof der portenære   daz sîn gespéngé zerbrast.

> Von einer îsenstangen;   des gie dem helde nôt.
> ein teil begunde fürhten   Sîfrit den tôt,
> dô der portenære   sô krefteclîche sluoc.
> dar umbe was im wæge   sîn herre Sîfrit genuoc.

> Si striten alsô sêre   daz al diu burc erschal.
> dô hôrte man daz diezen   in Nibelunges sal.
> er twanc den portenære,   daz er in sît gebant.
> diu mære wurden künde   in al der Nibelunge lant.

---

assumptions necessary to exercise his own authority are the very ones that must be subverted in Brünhild if she is to marry Gunther. This is a contradiction that can become apparent to the audience through the narrative structure of the Nibelung expedition, but only if the assumptions shared by Brünhild and Siegfried are recognized and taken seriously. Haymes's dismissal of Siegfried's combat with his own men as "silly" reflects the difficulty of approaching the work when such key assumptions have become unavailable.

THE CHAMPION AND HIS QUEST

Dô hôrte daz grimme strîten   verre durch den berc
Albrich der vil küene,   ein wíldéz getwerc.
er wâfende sich balde;   dô lief er dâ er vant
disen gast vil edelen,   da ér den risen váste gebant.

Albrich was vil grimme,   starc was er genuoc.
hélm únde ringe   er an dem lîbe truoc,
unt eine geisel swære   von golde an sîner hant.
dô lief er harte swinde   dâ er Sîfriden vant.

Siben knöpfe swære   die hiengen vor dar an,
dâ mit er vor der hende   den schilt dem küenen man
sluoc sô bitterlîchen,   daz im des vil zerbrast.
des lîbes kom in sorge   dô der wætlîche gast.

Den scherm er von der hende   gar zerbrochen swanc.
dô stiez er in die scheiden   ein wâfen, daz was lanc.
den sînen kameræere   wolde er niht slahen tôt;
er schônte sîner zühte   als im diu tugent daz gebôt.

Mit starken sînen handen   lief er Álbríchen an.
dô vienc er bî dem barte   den altgrîsen man.
er zogte in ungefuoge   daz er vil lûte schrê.
zuht des jungen heldes   diu tet Albriche wê.

Lûte rief der küene: "lát mích genesen!
unt möhte ich iemens eigen   âne einen recken wesen
(dem swuor ich des eide,   ich wære im undertân),
ich diente iu ê ich stürbe."   sprach der lístége man.

Er bant ouch Albrichen   alsam den risen ê.
die Sîfrides krefte   tâten im vil wê.
daz getwérc begonde vrâgen: "wie sît ir genant?"
er sprach: "ich heize Sîfrit;   ich wânde ich wære iu wol bekant."

"Sô wol mich dirre mære,"   sprach Albrich daz getwerc.
"nu hân ich wol erfunden   diu degenlîchen werc,
daz ir von wâren schulden   muget lándes herre wesen.
ich tuon swaz ir gebietet,   daz ir mich lázét genesen." (486-500)

Arriving before the gateway he found it barred, for those within were punctilious in discharge of their duty. . . . The stranger fell to pounding on the gate, but the gate was well guarded—he saw standing inside a gigantic watchman, whose arms always lay near to hand.

"Who is that pounding on the gate so mightily?" asked the warden.

"A soldier of fortune! Come, throw open the portal!" answered lord Siegfried from the other side, disguising his voice. "Before the day is out I shall rouse the fighting spirit of some few out here who would prefer to lie snug and at ease!" The gatekeeper was annoyed to hear lord Siegfried say so.

In a trice the giant had donned his armour, put on his helmet, snatched up his shield, and flung open the gate; and how ferociously the burly man rushed at Siegfried! How dare this visitor wake so many warriors! And he began to lay about him with his iron pole, forcing the noble stranger to seek cover under his shield, whose braces this watchman yet managed to shatter. This brought the hero into great peril, so that Siegfried was in no small fear of being killed by the mighty blows of this gatekeeper—a feat that much endeared the man to his liege lord Siegfried!

They fought so fiercely that the whole castle re-echoed and the din was heard in the hall of the Nibelungs. Yet Siegfried overcame the watchman and afterwards bound him, news of which went round all Nibelungland.

Far away through the cavern the fearless kobold Alberich heard this savage fight, and, arming himself at once, rushed to where the noble stranger had laid the giant in bonds. Alberich was very strong and of ferocious temper; he wore a helmet, and chain-mail on his body, and wielded a scourge heavy with gold and on whose thongs seven massive balls were hung. Running at great speed towards Siegfried, he struck such bitter blows at the shield which the hero was gripping that large parts of it were smashed, and Siegfried feared for his life. Flinging his ruined shield aside, the handsome stranger thrust his long sword into its sheath, remembering his good breeding as decency required; for he was loath to slay his own treasurer. Thus, with only his strong hands to help him, he leapt at Alberich, seized the old man by his grey beard, and roughly dragged him to and fro till he shrieked at the top of his voice. This chastisement by the young hero was a painful thing for Alberich.

"Let me live!" cried the dwarf, who was both brave and subtle. "If I could be the bondman of any man except only that one warrior whose subject I swore to be, I would serve you, rather than die!"

He bound Alberich as he had bound the giant before him, and much did Alberich suffer from his might.

"Who are you?" the dwarf managed to ask.

"I am Siegfried. I thought I was well known to you."

"I am very glad to hear it!" replied Alberich. "I have now made the acquaintance of your heroic handiwork and see that you are indeed fit to be a sovereign lord. If you let me live I shall do all that you command." (70-72)

Siegfried is clearly testing Alberich and takes pleasure in the watchman's strength and determination. But in addition to his watchman's abilities, Siegfried is interested in his vassal's loyalty. By threatening Alberich's life, Siegfried discovers the extent to which he can trust him not to join his power to that of some other champion. Alberich's final comment, however, reveals that Siegfried has also put himself on trial in order to demonstrate the legitimacy of his sovereignty.

This scene presents us, then, with the following principles: a sovereign's power is legitimated by his ability to defeat his subordinates in direct combat; the subordinate having once submitted himself to the rule of a superior warrior shall not, even upon pain of death, accept a new master; the sovereign must occasionally offer renewed demonstrations of his superiority; the sovereign must be willing to risk his own life in order to retain the loyalty of his subordinates; and finally, the most convincing demonstration is effected by a lone challenger working with his bare hands.

We have seen, however, that champions do not always work alone. While Siegfried has need of neither assistants nor witnesses either in originally winning his sovereignty over the Nibelungs or in later reasserting it, when he challenges the Burgundians at Worms he is not entirely alone—twelve companions have been chosen to accompany him. Beowulf likewise selects fourteen companions to join him on his overseas mission to cleanse Heorot. Only these companions spend the night with him in Heorot, and only these, reduced in number to thirteen by the death of one, accompany him to the lake in pursuit of Grendel's avenger. Having returned to Hrothgar possession of his own hall, Beowulf takes his leave, promising, however:

> Gif ic þæt gefricge ofer floda begang,
> þæt þec ymbsittend egesan þywað,
> swa þec hetende hwilum dydon,
> ic ðe þusenda þegna bringe,
> hæleþa to helpe. (1826-30a)

> If beyond the sea's expanse I hear that men dwelling near threaten you with terrors, as those who hated you did before, I shall bring you a thousand thanes, warriors to your aid.

The number of one thousand fighting men is, however, also that required by Siegfried to attend him when defending Burgundy against the Saxon-Danish invasion. In light of the principles we suppose to organize epic culture, can we explain why the heroes sometimes shun support altogether, under other circumstances travel with a dozen or so companions, and occasionally even require the backing of as many as a thousand armed warriors?

Siegfried's reputation for invincibility is won when he is alone among the Nibelungs. Since that reputation precedes him to Burgundy, neither Gunther nor his court dare openly accept his challenge, though he is accompanied by only twelve knights. Had he been unaccompanied, would the Burgundians have responded differently? These are, in fact, precisely the conditions that the Burgundians later contrive when they kill Siegfried. They conspire to strip him of his armor, isolate him from his subordinates, and then spear him in the back. Their success in these contrivances depends entirely on trickery, preying upon Siegfried's mistaken belief that he is now among friends.[8]

---

[8] The concept of friendship is taken by Francis Gentry, in *Triuwe and Vriunt in the "Nibelungenlied"* (Amsterdam: Rodopi Press, 1975), to be the key to understanding and resolving tensions among characters in the *Nibelungenlied*. The problem with this approach is that, having presumed that types of friendship are at issue, it misses the point that the term *vriunt* (friend) is often defined only in relation to *vient* (enemy) and particularly to the way in which enemies approach

Upon the occasion of Siegfried's initial challenge to Gunther, however, he had presented himself as an enemy, understanding full well that he must cover his back. His companions, of course, are more vulnerable than he. Their action at his back cannot stave off an attack from the sides or rear indefinitely. What they can do is cover him long enough to allow him to turn around to face off such an attack. Beowulf beds down at Heorot in the midst of his men with the result that Grendel first encounters one of them, Hondscioh, whom he devours. Alerted to what is happening, Beowulf then makes ready to grapple with the monster.

The price of attacking the hero's guard is death, for the attack, no matter how sudden or unexpected, brings the perpetrator within the hero's range. Fear of such reprisal must keep the enemy at bay, preventing it from attacking even the hero's rear guard. The hero's reputation for invincibility thus keeps safe even his companions, who are useful to him as an extension of his own body, with their added senses able to detect attack from all sides, their armor positioned to parry thrusts from the flanks and back, and their flesh to absorb unavoidable wounds, thus decreasing his vulnerability.

Armies massed in numbers large enough to carry out or repel an invasion present a different problem, because the individual warriors will probably not easily be able to recognize one another. Unless a duel is proposed, only through a war of attrition will the heroes on each side be able to distinguish themselves and identify their opposites. Since the Saxons and Danes do not expect to find Siegfried among the Burgundians, his fighting prowess itself must first draw their attention. Meanwhile, some of his own men will inevitably be slain. Consequently, the body of friendly troops allows the hero an opportunity to evaluate the enemy and identify its champions. The size of the opposing army does to some extent dictate the size of the hero's bodyguard.

The function of a hero's fame can thus be expressed by the geometry of concentric circles. Starting alone, he defeats individuals or even small armies, who preserve their own lives by swearing to him their absolute allegiance. Equipped with a small bodyguard, the hero is able to move at will through foreign territory. By making himself useful to beleaguered nobles, he can enlarge his reputation, thus reducing others' willingness to challenge his sovereignty. Accompanied by a bodyguard comprising retainers absolutely loyal to his person and armed with a reputation that discourages potential challengers, he can then return home, where he will serve his own people as a guarantor of their peace. Nevertheless, challenges will arise from beyond

---

one another. An individual's reputation as a potential enemy affects behavior towards him. Siegfried's reputation makes the Burgundians hesitate to treat him as an enemy. He implicitly offers them another possibility—that of accepting him as their master. They take the approach, however, of inviting him in as a guest and allowing him to become a "friend." Since they are never forced publicly to acknowledge his superiority and since he himself lights upon the plan of holding Gunther's stirrup as a sign of his subordination, the Burgundians find themselves in a position to murder Siegfried when his "friendship" becomes problematic.

the sphere of the champion's reputation. Using the system of contractual pledges, he can easily summon knights whose show of strength both in their numbers and in the quality of their equipment or clothing may indicate even to strangers the extent of his personal physical strength. If this display is not sufficient to deter a challenge, the bodyguard's capacity for action would be employed to protect the champion's rear and flank while he demonstrates his invincibility to the satisfaction of the enemy army by dismaying and turning it to rout. The bodyguard's secondary function, then, is to put itself on display as a metonymy for the champion's prowess, while the champion seeks the perpetual enlargement of his fame. Beginning entirely alone, he can win the right to protect other warriors. With them at his back, he can impress others. Siegfried's summoning of the Nibelung escort, then, serves perhaps more to assure Brünhild of Gunther's stature than to provide military protection. The thousand Nibelung warriors at Siegfried's call are presented to Brünhild as a token of Gunther's prowess. Siegfried's wrestling first the guard and then Alberich serves not only to remind *them* of his superiority, but it acts to remind the poem's audience at this critical juncture that the show of power has a genuine basis. The deception of Brünhild thus touches not simply on the determination of an appropriate marriage partner but on all the relations of power significant to maintaining the position of the ruling elites.[9]

Both the champion's bodyguard and his fame are acquired during the quest that he originally undertakes alone and untried. A successful quest accords the individual warrior the status of champion and at the same time secures him against incessant testing. The fame that he goes in quest of thus has an entirely pragmatic aspect. The wider its spread, the less likely he is to meet with challenges and the larger the force of men that he can call upon to increase his bodyguard. This means that the questing warrior should travel as widely as possible and seek to undertake tasks notable for their difficulty. By thus propagating the report of his invincibility and by occasionally assuring himself of his bodyguard's loyalty, he might, like Beowulf, preserve his own and his people's sovereignty for fifty winters—a very long time.

---

[9] Beyschlag understands the factors of power politics in the *Nibelungenlied* to center directly on the claim to Burgundian land and sovereignty ("Anspruch auf Vorrang, Land und Reich"—p. 202), to which Schröder responds that Kriemhild's comment that her husband should be sovereign over "elliu disiu riche" (str. 815,4)—"all these kingdoms"—announces no political aspirations ("keine politische Aspirationen") and by no means expresses the central issue in the dispute between the queens; rather, it is an expression of the joy she takes in having Siegfried for her husband (90). When, however, the problem of power is approached from the perspective of suitors who actively establish and defend their claims, it is possible to understand that Kriemhild must assert her very identity—her status—through her husband's claim to power. "Love" for her husband and suffering caused by his death are neither a purely emotional personal attachment (Schröder), nor a strictly political calculation (Beyschlag), but a complex combination of various factors, not the least of which is Kriemhild's need to find some maneuvering room for herself.

We are not told precisely how the hero's reputation is spread. Presumably there are those among the Nibelung, either the defeated warriors themselves or merchants, artisans, cooks, and others providing logistical support to the army who could tell the tale of Siegfried's deadly industry among the Nibelung warriors. Later, however, during the expedition to Worms, the companions picked to accompany Siegfried may serve not only to cover his flanks and back but also to witness his successes. The army of one thousand Burgundians that accompanies him against the Saxon-Danish invasion does most assuredly bear tales home to Worms, particularly to Kriemhild, of Siegfried's prowess and valor. Beowulf's fourteen companions sit and watch intently, no more than spectators, as he plunges to the bottom of the lake to deal with Grendel's mother. Likewise, during his fatal encounter with the dragon ravaging his country, Beowulf's companions sit immobile until it is too late to save him.[10] They then have the burden of reporting to the rest of the Geats his defeat and the doom that it spells for them all.[11] In addition to Beowulf's companions, Hrothgar's retainers and other nobles travel to take measure of the dimensions of Beowulf's victory: "ferdon folctogan feorran

---

[10] Friedrich Klaeber, in his introduction to *Beowulf*, 3rd ed. (Lexington, Mass.: D. C. Heath, 1950), compares Beowulf to Christ. His eleven companions, who are disloyal and cowardly, except for one, and who abandon him at the dragon fight, are reminiscent of the disciples in the garden at Gethsemane. I would not disagree that the parallel is apt. The question is whether the number of disciples does not rather reflect epic-cultural numerology in a circumstance that further extends the religious conversion of the champion beyond that implicit in David's claim "that all the earth may know that there is a God in Israel" (I Sam. 17:47—see the discussion in Chapter 3 above). Following a pattern that Klaus von See describes in *Germanische Heldensage: Stoffe, Probleme, Methoden.* (Frankfurt: Athenäum Verlag, 1971), especially the chapter "Christliche Elemente der Heldensage"—pp. 148-66, the last *Beowulf* poet (the one responsible for recording the poem in writing) would thus have found the traditional epic-cultural material extremely suitable for the purposes of a Christian interpretation. From our perspective, however, it can be argued that the *Beowulf* poet was doing no more than advancing the argument to its next stage along a path already taken nearly a millennium earlier by the story of a Hebrew-Philistine duel completed by the story of Jesus's self-sacrifice. From the earlier epic-cultural perspective, however, Beowulf's death is catastrophic. As a measure of the discrepancy between these two perspectives on the story stands the element of the dragon's hoard of gold. We shall see in the next chapter that possession of the gold should represent a tremendous benefit to the king and the people for whose protection it will be used. In fact, since Beowulf fails in his protective function, though not for lack of gold, it is clear that he would not have put the gold to its proper use anyway. While from a religious perspective the gold may represent an undesirable temptation towards materiality and its destruction in the fire therefore renders it harmless, from an epic-cultural perspective the gold would have been most useful, had Beowulf thought to offer it to a worthy champion, and its destruction ends all hope for the Geats.

[11] This point is missed by von See, for whom the positive aspects of the king's self-sacrifice are "ohne jeden Zweifel" (p. 162)—"without any doubt."

ond nean / geond widwegas wundor sceawian, / laþes lastas" (839-41a)—
"Folk-chiefs came from far and near over the wide-stretching ways to look on
the wonder, the footprints of the foe." They ride out to see the lake "on blode
brim weallende" (847)—"boiling with blood." Having gone to the lake and
seen the signs for themselves, they immediately set to work composing their
reports:

> þanon eft gewiton ealdgesiðas,
> swylce geong manig of gomenwaþe
> fram mere modge mearum ridan,
> beornas on blancum. Ðær wæs Beowulfes
> mærðo mæned; monig oft gecwæð
> þætte suð ne norð be sæm tweonum
> ofer eormengrund oþer nænig
> under swegles begong selra nære
> rondhæbbendra, rices wyrðra. —
> Ne hie huru winedrihten wiht ne logon,
> glædne Hroðgar, ac þæt wæs god cyning.—
> Hwilum heaþorofe hleapan leton,
> on geflit faran fealwe mearas
> ðær him foldwegas fægere þuhton,
> cystum cuðe. Hwilum cyninges þegn,
> guma gilphlæden, gidda gemyndig,
> se ðe ealfela ealdgesegena
> worn gemunde, word oþer fand
> soðe gebunden; secg eft ongan
> sið Beowulfes snyttrum styrian,
> ond on sped wrecan spel gerade,
> wordum wrixlan. (853-74a)

From there old retainers—and many a young man, too—turned back in their
glad journey to ride from the mere, highspirited on horseback, warriors on
steeds. There was Beowulf's fame spoken of; many a man said—and not
only once—that, south nor north, between the seas, over the wide earth, no
other man under the sky's expanse was better of those who bear shields,
more worthy of ruling. Yet they found no fault with their own dear lord,
gracious Hrothgar, for he was a good king. At times battle-famed men let
their brown horses gallop, let them race where the paths seemed fair, known
for their excellence. At times a thane of the king, a man skilled at telling adventures, songs stored in his memory, who could recall many of the stories
of the old days, wrought a new tale in well-joined words; this man undertook
with his art to recite in turn Beowulf's exploit, and skillfully to tell an apt
tale, to lend words to it.

Beowulf's companions, Hrothgar's retainers, and independent nobles from far
and wide eagerly witness the hero's exploits, even traveling some distance to
do so. Their act of witness includes attesting to the truth of the report,

assessing its magnitude, and ranking the hero among others known to them. Among them, one is a bard, a scop, a singer of tales, who sets to work immediately as the witnesses leave the scene to compose a lay that commemorates the event's most significant aspects. This lay will then serve as a vehicle for transporting the hero's fame as far and wide as travelers can carry it.

Thus it is that Odysseus, as a guest at the Phaiacian court nearly a decade after the close of the Trojan war, following years of wandering far from both Troy and his home in Ithaca, comes to hear the song of his own exploits in the wooden horse. We can infer that his fame has spread, carried by travelers into every corner of the world. Nor is the praise such travelers sing by any means simply idle story-telling. Rather, the information that it conveys will play an important role in the balance of power, for it will determine the readiness of one king to challenge another's sovereignty. Hagen knows who Siegfried is and precisely how dangerous he is because he has made it his business to attend to the reports that have reached him.

The spread of a hero's fame, then, is an integral aspect of the system by which political stability is achieved without resort to war and the heavy cost in lives that such expeditions inevitably entail. Only as established warriors pass their prime should there be the need for renewed testing, competition, quest, and warfare. Once a successor has been identified, the stories of his exploits can spread the report of his daunting size and strength, attesting to his invincibility. Once this process is complete, peace can be restored. Epic culture works to diminish the extent of damage that would result from frequent wars that could very likely annihilate the entire warrior class, leaving the rest of the population vulnerable to dispersal, enslavement, colonization—in short, to every imaginable form of subjugation. Hence the quest—the search for theaters of conflict to serve as the stage upon which a warrior's powers of intimidation can be displayed. The ideal challenge, as we can infer from the *Beowulf* narrative, comes in the form of a magic monster—a dragon or gorgon that holds a population in thrall. In lieu of a dragon, the hero must involve himself in a war. If people are at peace, a war must be manufactured. Epic culture thus only avoids the devastation of war by promoting war. The war that it promotes, however, is of a very different nature than the war that it seeks to avoid. By arriving accompanied by so few men, Siegfried makes it clear that he is seeking a duel with Gunther. Unlike the invasion by Liudegast and Liudeger, which results in significant loss of life, Siegfried's challenge should (in theory) cost at most one life—his own or that of Burgundy's champion.

If Gunther (or Hagen) were to die in combat with Siegfried, Burgundy would suffer a gain, not a loss, for it would gain in Siegfried a champion able to defend his land against the Saxons and Danes, whose invasion is predicated upon the calculation of Burgundy's vulnerability. Were Siegfried known to be Burgundy's protector, the Saxons and Danes would most assuredly demur, as Liudeger's behavior on the battlefield unmistakably demonstrates. Destruction of Burgundy does not follow from Siegfried's challenge but from avoidance of the test he proposes.

Epic culture cannot do away with battle altogether. It can only regulate battle, thus providing a means to control its destructiveness, significantly reducing the number of casualties. It does this by converting the battlefield to a ritual ground. By honoring the ritual procedures governing combat, political hierarchies can be adjusted or reestablished economically. For the purpose of fighting ritual battle, warriors would gather from far and wide—ideally from all corners of the known world. In this way, hierarchies established in the course of championship duels would effectively bind all the participants against the disruption of internecine warfare. This is because the ritual battle provides an opportunity to every individual and, by extension, every local polity to establish a position in a regional political and economic hierarchy.

We might interpret the story of Helen's marriage to Menelaus in light of this practice. In wooing Helen, the Greek kings meet in a test of their strength as warriors, with the understanding that this contest will establish their relationship to one another, such that afterwards all will be allied against any enemy. Helen's selection of one of them as a husband thus betokens his supremacy in the alliance. In an interesting substitution, the movement of her person to Sparta records both the event of a contest and its outcome. To any warrior not invited to the contest but still desiring to establish his position in the pan-Hellenic hierarchy, Helen's body stands (or lies in his bed) as the token of his successful challenge.[12]

The more participants at a ritual battle, the greater the number of witnesses. Reputations may thus at once be established and disseminated. Moreover, the special circumstances of ritual warfare assure the attendance of bards, whose job it was to record and to transmit the results. Medieval tournaments are the most obvious example because the knights were not meant to be killed. In fact, the improper wounding of a knight provided grounds for a transition from relatively harmless ritual warfare to the devastating effects of an unregulated mêlée. In addition to the illegal bowshot during the duel between Paris and Menelaus, we have an example in the *Nibelungenlied* of ritual battle violated. Thousands of knights are gathered at the court of Etzel, king of the Huns. In addition to the Burgundian army, newly arrived to celebrate a midsummer feast, many of Etzel's vassals and allies are present. The knights are fully armed, parading before the observing royalty, showing off their skill by riding the bohort, a ritual clash of mounted knights who charge each other en masse, using blunted lances, which shatter and splinter against enemy shields. The combat is not meant to turn deadly.

> Volkêr der vil snelle   den bûhurt wider reit.
> daz wart sît maneger frouwen   vil grœzlîche leit.

---

[12] As Butterworth observes, "As long as succession descended in the female line, there was bound to be fierce rivalry for the kingship of the more powerful realms" (p. 59); this is a rivalry, we might add, that concentrates itself on possession of the queen.

> er stach dem rîchen Hiunen   daz sper durch sînen lîp.
> daz sach man sît beweinen   beide maget unde wîp.
>
> Vil harte hurteclîche   Hágene und síne man
> mit sehzec sîner degene   rîten er began
> nâch dem videlære,   dâ daz spil geschach.
> Etzel unde Kriemhilt   ez bescheidenlîchen sach.
>
> Done wólden die drî künege   den ir spileman
> bî den fîánden   niht âne huote lân.
> dâ wart von tûsent helden   vil kunsteclîch geriten.
> si tâten, daz si wolden,   in vil hóchvérten siten. (1889-91)

> Volker wheeled round to renew the bohort, and this gave many ladies untold sorrow in days to come, for he thrust his spear clean through the body of that gorgeously turned-out Hun, a blow that was to be lamented by women and maidens alike. Hagen at once spurred to the scene of the joust with sixty of his men at full gallop to cover the Fiddler [Volker] while Etzel and Kriemhild looked on, noting every detail. Nor did the three kings wish to leave their Minstrel amidst their enemies unsupported, and so a thousand knights rode up in intricate formation and haughtily imposed their will. (234)

Volker's blow is held responsible for the grief to come because it initiates earnest warfare: "Nâch swerten und nâch schilden riefen dâ zehant / des marcgrâven mâge von der Hiunen lant. / si wolden Vólkêren ze tôde erslagen hân" (1893,1-3); the dead Hun's relatives "called for swords and shields with the intention of killing Volker" (234). Only Etzel's immediate intervention prevents an outbreak of war between his own knights and his guests. His grounds for stopping the fighting are that he would have failed in his "dienest" (1895,4)—"duty as host" (235)—if one of the Burgundians were killed while being his guest. In other words, guest-host rules establish the conditions for ritual warfare and guard against unrestricted bloodshed. Just as the truce provides for a duel in the midst of battle, special conventions provide for ritual battle between rivals even while remaining at peace with one another. The midsummer festival at Etzel's court is thus an enormously delicate situation that Kriemhild can fairly easily disrupt to accomplish her revenge on the Burgundians. Her desire to hold Gunther and Hagen's fate in her own hands will, in fact, cost the lives of nearly every knight present at the festival, regardless of his allegiances and affiliations. This she accomplishes through her willingness to subvert the guest-host conventions that guarantee protection to potentially hostile warriors while at the same time allowing them to come together fully armed for the purpose of ordering power relations among themselves.

Interestingly, it is the guest-host conventions whose infringement is held responsible for the Achaean invasion of Troy. In the case of Paris's visit to Sparta, the purpose is not ritual warfare. The fact that host-guest relations govern the visit, however, suggests that some mechanism is in place to avert bloodshed between neighbors and rivals. That mechanism must provide for a suspension of hostilities, because international relations, including respect for boundaries, integrity of trade routes, and so forth, could not be maintained otherwise. The theft of Helen and her wealth by Paris directly challenges the existing political order and indicates the need for a series of confrontations. These can be handled in terms of general warfare, or they can be handled within the bounds of ritual battle.

It is interesting to look at the Trojan war in light of this choice. The combatants' single-minded intent to kill one another presents the most obvious objection to regarding the Trojan war as a ritual battle. If ritual battle were meant to be bloodless, as it seems to have been in medieval Europe, the Trojan war would clearly be excluded. Within the context of epic culture, however, ritual battle provides a mechanism not necessarily for avoiding bloodshed altogether but for avoiding the wholesale slaughter of entire fighting forces. On the understanding that a stable political organization can only be established when the heroes have determined a ranking among themselves, a forum must be provided for the display of fighting power and the elimination of rivalries. The Trojans' breach of guest-host protections requires discipline—a renewed demonstration of the basis for hierarchical power arrangements. This demonstration, of course, entails the subjection of Troy to the combined might of the entire political organization that has been challenged. The need to discipline Troy presents the forces assembled against her with an additional opportunity to reestablish relations among themselves. In the event that peaceful relations have persisted for some time, it is probable that champions are aging. Younger men, some of whom have never experienced firsthand the terror of war, may doubt that their elders can live up to their reputations. By bringing together from throughout the region all serious rivals for power, the battle for Troy provides an opportunity for heroes to test themselves and to establish their reputations at the expense of the Trojans and Trojan allies. That they must risk their own lives in this process goes without saying, because the position for which they are vying is the championship—the right to represent against any challenger all the assembled warriors and the peoples they protect.

That the Trojan war could have fulfilled the function of ritual battle is borne out by a number of its features, including the rise of a new generation of heroes, the practice of stripping armor from the corpses of the defeated, the ritual exchange of names, family data, and accomplishments, and the presence of noteworthy volunteers.

An older generation of heroes has passed its prime and is being replaced by a young generation of warriors who have not thoroughly tested themselves and who are not fully convinced by the political organization and the conventions according to which peace is maintained. Only one of the previous generation of heroes remains alive—Nestor, whose sons and grandsons have grown to manhood, apparently without the opportunity to establish their own reputations. Nestor, in fact, constantly holds up the previous generation of heroes as a standard not yet achieved by any of the warriors assembled before Troy's walls.

The fighting itself is conducted so as to emphasize individual accomplishment. The warriors seem to be obsessed with stripping the armor from the corpses of those they have slain, even when this activity opens them to easy attack by exposing their flanks to the enemy. Victory over the common enemy thus seems to hold less importance than the establishment of a reputation for having personally killed a notable warrior.

The pause of opposing pairs to exchange their names and patrimonies before engaging in combat itself constitutes a ritual moment in the battle. Their encounters occur, then, not as Trojan versus Achaean but as one hero against another. The identity of the warrior's victim gives him credentials and establishes his place in the pecking order.

In addition to those of the Achaean allies who, like Odysseus, have come to Troy only at the summons of Agamemnon, their field commander, there are others who are present as volunteers. Most notable among these is Achilles. His participation is motivated only by his desire to "please" Agamemnon by volunteering to help him. He makes it clear that he has no other reason to be at Troy, stating explicitly in the *Iliad* as follows: "οὐ γὰρ ἐγὼ Τρώων ἕνεκ' ἤλυθον αἰχμητάων / δεῦρο μαχησόμενος. ἐπεὶ οὔ τί μοι αἴτιοί εἰσιν· / οὐ γάρ πώ ποτ' ἐμὰς βοῦς ἤλασαν οὐδὲ μὲν ἵππους. / οὐδέ ποτ' ἐν Φθίῃ ἐριβώλακι βωτιανείρῃ / καρπὸν ἐδηλήσαντ'. ἐπεὶ ἦ μάλα πολλὰ μεταξὺ / οὔρεά τε σκιόεντα θάλασσά τε ἠχήεσσα" (1.152-57)—"It was no quarrel with the Trojan spearmen that brought *me* here to fight. They have never done *me* any harm. They have never lifted cow or horse of mine, nor ravaged any crop that the deep soil of Phthia grows to feed her men; for the roaring seas and many a dark range of mountains lie between us." While no personal quarrel with the Trojans motivates Achilles to go to war with them, the war of the Atreides with Troy presents him with the proper context in which to establish his fame as a champion.

It is the quest for fame that takes Achilles to Troy. He, like Beowulf, is young and untried when he leaves home. So inexperienced is he, in fact, that his father sends along Phoenix, an old charioteer, as guardian and tutor to the boy, "νήπιον. οὔ πω εἰδόθ' ὁμοιΐου πολέμοιο" (9.440)—"a mere lad, with no experience of the hazards of war." Nine years later, Achilles has had ample opportunity to distinguish himself. He can boast in the *Iliad*: "δώδεκα δὴ σὺν νηυσὶ πόλεις ἀλάπαξ' ἀνθρώπων. / πεζὸς δ' ἕνδεκά φημι κατὰ Τροίην ἐρίβωλον" (9.328-29)—"I have captured twelve towns from the sea, besides eleven that I took by land in the deep-soiled realm of Troy." But what qualifies Achilles as champion is his conviction—eventually shared by Agamemnon and all the Achaean captains—that only he can stop Hector. This is the point he makes by withdrawing from battle. The great Aias, Diomedes, Menelaus, and Agamemnon himself prove to be unable to stop Hector. After the inconclusive duel between Aias and Hector, the Achaeans see fit to build a defensive rampart to protect the line of ships and huts along the beach. Achilles is scoffing when he says of Agamemnon, "καὶ δὴ τεῖχος ἔδειμε. καὶ ἤλασε τάφρον ἐπ' αὐτῷ / εὐρεῖαν μεγάλην. ἐν δὲ σκόλοπας κατέπηξεν" (9.349-50)—"He has built a wall, I see, and dug a trench along it, a fine broad trench, complete with palisade." Such a wall had been unnecessary so long as Achilles himself stood between Hector and the ships.

Even Hector had conceded to Achilles's reputation: "ὄφρα δ' ἐγὼ μετ' Ἀχαιοῖσιν πολέμιζον / οὐκ ἐθέλεσκε μάχην ἀπὸ τείχεος ὀρνύμεν Ἕκτωρ" (9.352-53)—"Why, in the days when I took the field with the Achaeans," Achilles points out, "nothing would have induced Hector to throw his men into battle at any distance from the city walls." The Trojans' reluctance to face Achilles demonstrates the success of his quest. He has acquired a reputation sufficient to install him as champion and discourage challenges to his status. The Trojan war has served his purpose. The fame of Achilles would hold every enemy at bay, thus securing peace for Phthia into Achilles's old age. And yet Achilles is destined never to reach old age. The repute that he has striven so hard and risked so much to acquire will prove fruitless. Achilles can have the fame he seeks but not the safety it promises him. Why not?

The text explicitly expresses this problem in terms of Achilles's fate. In the *Iliad*, Achilles repeats what he has been told by his mother, herself a goddess, namely:

διχθαδίας κῆρας φερέμεν θανάτοιο τέλοσδε.
εἰ μέν κ' αὖθι μένων Τρώων πόλιν ἀμφιμάχωμαι,
ὤλετο μέν μοι νόστος, ἀτὰρ κλέος ἄφθιτον ἔσται·
εἰ δέ κεν οἴκαδ' ἵκωμι φίλην ἐς πατρίδα γαῖαν,
ὤλετό μοι κλέος ἐσθλόν, ἐπὶ δηρὸν δέ μοι αἰὼν
ἔσσεται, οὐδέ κέ μ' ὦκα τέλος θανάτοιο κιχείη. (9.411-6)

Destiny has left two courses open to me on my journey to the grave. If I stay here and play my part in the siege of Troy, there is no home-coming for me, though I shall win undying fame. But if I go home to my own country, my good name will be lost, though I shall have long life, and shall be spared an early death.

Achilles has come to Troy for one reason and one reason only—to win undying fame. His own life is a price he is willing to pay. Clearly, for Achilles, the fame promised by heroic activity is an end in itself—the highest end that life can offer. When Agamemnon insults Achilles by depriving him of a war prize, a gift from the ranks of warriors betokening the measure of their respect and appreciation for him, Achilles understands his fame to have been diminished. He thereupon withdraws from battle. Since the increase of fame is his only reason for aiding Agamemnon against the Trojans, he may as well go home. If he does not immediately sail away, it is only because he wishes to enjoy witnessing the impact of his withdrawal. He is waiting to see the day "ἤ ποτ' Ἀχιλλῆος ποθὴ ἵξεται υἷας Ἀχαιῶν / σύμπαντας· τότε δ' οὔ τι δυνήσεαι ἀχνύμενός περ / χραισμεῖν, εὖτ' ἂν πολλοὶ ὑφ' Ἕκτορος ἀνδροφόνοιο / θνῄσκοντες πίπτωσι" (1.240-43)—"when the Achaeans one and all will miss me sorely" and Agamemnon "will be powerless to help them as they fall in their hundreds to Hector killer of men." That day does indeed come, and Agamemnon repents of his anger and his ill-conceived act depriving Achilles of the captive girl Briseis. He offers recompense—a long list of gifts by which he hopes to display his respect for Achilles, including not only the return of Briseis and many objects representing great material wealth but also marriage to one of his own daughters and recognition of Achilles as a son. So far as Achilles is concerned, however, the damage done by Agamemnon cannot be repaired. Having learned from Odysseus of Agamemnon's offer, he, at first, says that he will sail away home on the very next day. At this moment, he seems to prefer a safe life in anonymity at home to death at Troy and undying fame. Under the influence of the other emissaries, he gradually modifies his decision, saying to Phoenix that he will decide in the morning whether to go home or stay. Then, implying that he has changed his mind altogether, he insists to Aias that he will not return to battle until Hector attacks his ships. What really keeps Achilles at Troy?

The morning that Achilles would have gone sees the bloodiest battle of the war. The narrative devotes most of Books 11-17 to a description of the carnage. This battle scene rivets Achilles to the spot, "ἑστήκει γὰρ ἐπὶ πρύμνῃ μεγακήτεϊ νηΐ. / εἰσορόων πόνον αἰπὺν ἰῶκά τε δακρυόεσσαν" (11.600-01)—"watching the crisis of the battle and the lamentable rout from the stern of his capacious ship." Achilles seems unable to resist the fascination of the battle, and he is drawn to inquire after one of the wounded. Eventually, he will allow his companion Patroclus to enter the battle. And thus will he himself finally be compelled to fight, to win undying fame, and to meet his own death on the plain of Troy.

It would appear that the choices represented by Achilles's mother concerning his fate are not genuinely available.[13] He withdraws from the battle but waits to see the impact of his action; he sees his prediction fulfilled and plans to sail home, but his ship remains firmly ashore. Standing upon its deck, he is rooted to the field, transfixed by the spectacle of war. His choice is denied him, yet without the intervention of god or man. The paradox of Achilles's fate and the ineluctable pull exerted upon him by battle can, however, be explained from the perspective of epic culture—the understandings that lend meaning to the institution of championship and to the many practices, such as the quest for fame, that support it. From this perspective, Achilles never really has the choice of whether or not to fight.

---

[13] The choices seem to be as genuine to modern readers and critics as they do to the characters themselves. Voegelin, for example, finds that "one may reasonably assume . . . that a healthy specimen like Achilles will have a long and agreeable life if he succeeds to the throne of a prosperous kingdom in a remote region and does not deliberately look for trouble" but notes "that he runs the risk of getting killed sooner or later, if he engages continuously in battle with such intensity that his fame will be imperishable" (p. 66). Thus Voegelin naturalizes the Homeric notion of fate, but according to premises that run counter to the circumstances peculiar to epic culture.

When rejecting Agamemnon's overture of gifts and marriage to a daughter, he imagines the alternate path opened to him by his fate:

> ἢν γὰρ δή με σαῶσι θεοὶ καὶ οἴκαδ' ἴκωμαι.
> Πηλεύς θήν μοι ἔπειτα γυναῖκά γε μάσσεται αὐτός.
> πολλαὶ Ἀχαιΐδες εἰσὶν ἀν' Ἑλλάδα τε Φθίην τε.
> κοῦραι ἀριστήων. οἵ τε πτολίεθρα ῥύονται.
> τάων ἥν κ' ἐθέλωμι φίλην ποιήσομ' ἄκοιτιν.
> ἔνθα δέ μοι μάλα πολλὸν ἐπέσσυτο θυμὸς ἀγήνωρ
> γήμαντα μνηστὴν ἄλοχον. ἐϊκυῖαν ἄκοιτιν.
> κτήμασι τέρπεσθαι τὰ γέρων ἐκτήσατο Πηλεύς·
> οὐ γὰρ ἐμοὶ ψυχῆς ἀντάξιον οὐδ' ὅσα φασὶν
> Ἴλιον ἐκτῆσθαι. εὖ ναιόμενον πτολίεθρον.
> τὸ πρὶν ἐπ' εἰρήνης. πρὶν ἐλθεῖν υἷας Ἀχαιῶν.
> . . . Πυθοῖ ἔνι πετρηέσσῃ.
> ληϊστοὶ μὲν γάρ τε βόες καὶ ἴφια μῆλα.
> κτητοὶ δὲ τρίποδές τε καὶ ἵππων ξανθὰ κάρηνα·
> ἀνδρὸς δὲ ψυχὴ πάλιν ἐλθεῖν οὔτε λεϊστὴ
> οὔθ' ἑλετή. (9.393-403, 405-09)

"If the gods allow me to get safely home, Peleus will need no help in finding me a wife. Up and down Hellas and Phthia there are plenty of Achaean girls, daughters of the noblemen in command of the forts. I have only to choose one and make her my own. There were often times at home when I had no higher ambition than to marry some suitable girl of my own station and enjoy the fortune that my old father Peleus had made. For life, as I see it, is not to be set off, either against the fabled wealth of splendid Ilium in the peaceful days before the Achaeans came, or against all the treasure that is piled up in Rocky Pytho. . . . Cattle and sturdy sheep can be had for the taking; and tripods and chestnut horses can be bought. But you cannot steal or buy back a man's life."

Through nine years of war, Achilles has been willing to trade his life for fame. Now, after Agamemnon's insult and the irreparable damage that it seems to him to have done his fame, he views life as the more precious of the two. He takes for granted that the role he imagines for himself back in Phthia is his for the asking or, rather, for the taking. Clearly, his life in Phthia is built upon the privilege based on his father's status as king. Other men, such as those given command of the forts, have accepted the superiority of Peleus. In making him king, they have accorded him the privileges now claimed by Achilles. But surely, Peleus earned his privileges, most probably through his prowess in battle, through his ability to save and protect his people, and through the reputation that he built at home and abroad. Peleus understands this all too well and so sends his son, now grown almost to manhood, in quest of war. Without establishing a reputation for invincibility, Achilles would not be able to retain any of the privileges he now takes for granted. This is true not just because he might be challenged by other warriors from Hellas, who might well accord him the kingship uncontested, but mainly because of challenges from beyond Hellas. Even if the country's immediate neighbors were reluctant to attack her, some distant land would inevitably produce a challenger. The proof of this is the challenge to Menelaus by Paris. And Paris does not act alone in his challenge—he is backed by Priam and his brothers, including Hector. Inevitably, then, the Trojans or their like will stand at Phthia's door.[14] Inevitably, then, Achilles must meet his challenger, whether it is Hector or another. For Achilles, there is no safety in remaining home, no long life without battle, unless he is willing to live as another's vassal. Then that man could appoint him commander of a fort and choose for his wife Achilles's daughter or take into his bed as a captive slave girl Achilles's own wife. Achilles himself implies as much when he poses the following rhetorical question: "ἦ μοῦνοι φιλέουσ' ἀλόχους μερόπων ἀνθρώπων / Ἀτρεΐδαι· ἐπεὶ ὅς τις ἀνὴρ ἀγαθὸς καὶ ἐχέφρων / τὴν αὐτοῦ φιλέει καὶ κήδεται. ὡς καὶ ἐγὼ τὴν / ἐκ θυμοῦ φίλεον. δουρικτητήν περ ἐοῦσαν" (9.340-43)—"[A]re the Atreidae the only men on earth who love their wives? Does not every decent and right-minded man love and cherish his own woman, as I loved [Briseis], with all my heart?" If Achilles is infuriated by being deprived of Briseis by Agamemnon, would he not be equally incensed by being deprived of his woman by an enemy? If he is ready to wish death upon his friends for this insult, would he not be willing to wish it on his enemies for the same offense? If he is restrained from drawing his sword against Agamemnon, what is to stop him from drawing his sword against the foreigners? He must and he will fight. It is inevitable: if not now, then later, if not the Trojans, then others. The "choice" presented him by his fate represents not two lifestyles but two perceptions. Achilles's belief that he has a choice is a perception that leads to the paradox that is his actual fate—to win undying fame but uselessly, not because he himself cannot live to enjoy his accomplishment but because the war is no longer a ritual war, governed by the terms and protocols of the duel, with its provisions for a peaceful settlement and its prohibition against archery. Achilles—and by extension Phthia—both fall to the arrows of Paris, because when he could and should have been championing the Achaeans in a formal duel, instead he was in his hut nursing the delusion of a return to peaceful life at home. With the breakdown in ritual battle and its possibilities for resolution, Achilles's championship is rendered meaningless. The potential for establishing peaceful relations throughout the region is wasted. Not only must the town and towers of Troy be razed, but the man whose leadership would guarantee stability to the new order is killed in the process. What follows must be a period of disorder, strife, and bloodshed.

There is irony, then, on either side of the fateful choice of Achilles, for his decision to withdraw from battle, and thus from his position as

---

[14] Lynn-George observes that Priam himself equates Troy with Phthia in the *Iliad* (24.486-89), where Achilles's father is suffering with no son at hand "to ward off the harrying, harmful incursions, the gathering forces of destruction in an imagined setting which mirrors the reality of Troy" (p. 207).

champion, initiates the series of events that ends in his return to the fighting at a point when even a victory over Hector in single combat cannot bring the war to a close. Following Hector's loss, the Trojans, knowing full well what is in store for them, will fight with increased determination, claiming many Achaean lives, among them that of Achilles, who falls now not in purposeful duel but to an unseen arrow. Thus, the choice between a long life of obscurity in Phthia and a brief but glorious career at Troy is false, for had Achilles gone home, he would have found no safety there, and had he championed the Achaeans in a duel, he might never have exposed himself to Paris's arrows and thus not had to die at Troy.

The paradoxical fate of Achilles—the false choice that it presents—draws attention to the fact that the quest for "undying fame" poses a serious problem within epic culture. The individual who devotes himself to acquiring that fame as an end in itself cannot function properly as a champion. The purpose behind the institution of championship is to provide for political stability by resolving issues of hierarchy without resorting to all-out war. As soon as a champion's actions begin to put the lives of others in jeopardy, he not only fails in his function but he also subverts the institution that is the culture's primary means for maintaining its own organization.[15]

So great is the wrath of Achilles towards his king, Agamemnon, in the *Iliad* that it leads him to treat his friends—those in whose protection he has enlisted himself—as enemies. In requesting of his mother, Thetis, that she persuade Zeus "ἐπὶ Τρώεσσιν ἀρῆξαι, / τοὺς δὲ κατὰ πρύμνας τε καὶ ἀμφ' ἅλα ἔλσαι Ἀχαιοὺς / κτεινομένους" (1.408-10)—"to help the Trojans, to fling the Achaeans back on their ships, to pen them in against the sea and slaughter them," obviously, he wishes quite literally for their deaths, and, by refusing to fight, he ensures that his wish comes true. From the moment of this wish, every single Achaean death must be credited to his account.

---

[15] Achilles's excesses mark a point of contrast with Odysseus, who, like Achilles, "goes out from home in quest of the achievement of his name," notes Alice Mariani, in her essay "The Renaming of Odysseus," in *Critical Essays on Homer*, p. 219. She adds that Odysseus gets a name that means both a giving and getting of trouble in an act of "mutuality" (p. 218). The name he receives is given by his maternal grandfather at the time of his birth, while the name that he earns is given during a boar hunt on the occasion of his coming-of-age visit to that grandfather. Interestingly, Mariani recognizes in the language of the boar-hunt narrative the features of a duel, "a contest of equals" (p. 218). Indeed, "the effect," she observes, "is quite like that of two warriors rushing upon one another on a battlefield, perhaps in one of the familiar contests of peers in which the others stand apart to witness" (p. 218). Mariani further points out "the various similes in the *Iliad* which compare warriors to wild boars, . . . and in particular XI.414ff. where Odysseus himself, at bay in a circle of Trojans, is likened to one" (p. 218). Odysseus is compared to other warrior heroes, including Achilles, who stand solitary before a hostile world. He is unlike Achilles, however, in the fact that his quest for fame results in pain that he endures, a narrow escape from death, and a lifelong scar to remind him of the mutuality of danger and pain in battle.

Achilles knows and accepts this responsibility, and he believes that his terrible prayer to Zeus is justified by Agamemnon's disrespectful treatment.[16] Agamemnon never was a friend of Achilles, so Achilles's service to him was always motivated by the motive of winning fame. What Achilles has forgotten, however, is that, among the Achaeans, some are, in fact, his friends. If there is anyone among the Achaean forces for whom he cares personally, then he must volunteer to serve Agamemnon. By requesting that Zeus provide for the slaughter of Achaeans, he is himself participating in the slaughter of his own friends. When Achilles glimpses Machaon returning wounded from battle, he is moved by concern for the man to dispatch Patroclus to inquire after him. This slight concern for Machaon betrays Achilles's miscalculation. He will be prevailed upon soon enough to dispatch Patroclus into battle. Only the death of Patroclus can really bring home to him the utter wretchedness of his own position as failed champion.[17]

The audience should perhaps have reason to suspect Achilles's reasoning long before the death of Patroclus. From the beginning, Achilles's death wish for the Achaeans too nearly resembles another such wish—that of Chryses, an Achaean enemy. Chryses is the priest of Apollo whose daughter had been captured by the Achaeans and given as a war prize to their commander, Agamemnon. The priest offers both ransom to Agamemnon and his support of the war effort against Troy in exchange for the return of his daughter. Agamemnon treats the priest with contempt, though the latter carries with him tokens sacred to the god for all to see. As retribution for this contempt, the priest beseeches Apollo, "τείσειαν Δαναοὶ ἐμὰ δάκρυα σοῖσι βέλεσσιν" (1.42)—"Let the Danaans pay with your arrows for my tears." The archer-god's arrows bring on the plague—death in droves, very much like the battlefield slaughter summoned by Achilles. Chryses, unlike Achilles, is a suppliant. He seeks the return of his daughter, not his honor. His prayer for Achaean suffering responds only to the suffering that they inflict on him as an enemy, and, as soon as he has the girl back, he lifts his curse. Chryses is motivated by a father's love, Achilles by a lover's possessiveness. Achilles is preoccupied with his fame, with the gifts that attest to his fame by signifying the honor in which he is held, and with the objects given him for the pleasure that they can provide. He neither protects nor respects anyone. He has forgotten—or perhaps was never made aware—that the quest for fame and glory is a quest for the safety, security, and peace of his own people. In promoting the institution of the duel by offering fame and glory to the

---

[16] Simone Weil remarks, in "The *Iliad* or the Poem of Force," in *Critical Essays on Homer*, p. 155, "Achilles rejoices over the sight of the Greeks fleeing in misery and confusion. What could possibly suggest to him that this rout, which will last exactly as long as he wants it to and end when his mood indicates it, that this very rout will be the cause of his friend's death, and, for that matter, of his own?" Further references will be cited parenthetically in the text.

[17] As Voegelin observes: "Something is badly wrong with the leading Homeric characters; and under one aspect, therefore, the *Iliad* is a study in the pathology of heroes" (p. 65).

successful champion, epic culture unavoidably fosters an attitude that can also be quite destructive and that it must therefore work to curb, perhaps in part through the telling of epic stories that detail the consequences of these attitudes and so act as a form of corrective to such excesses.

CHAPTER FIVE

THE KING AND HIS GIFTS

When the shepherd boy David comes into the Hebrew camp to deliver his father's cheese, he overhears Goliath's challenge to the Hebrews to send out their champion against him, and subsequently he is informed that "גָדוֹל וְאֶת־בִּתּוֹ יִתֶּן־לוֹ וְאֵת בֵּית אָבִיו יַעֲשֶׂה חָפְשִׁי בְּיִשְׂרָאֵל וְהָיָה הָאִישׁ אֲשֶׁר־יַכֶּנּוּ יַעְשְׁרֶנּוּ הַמֶּלֶךְ | עֹשֶׁר" (I Sam. 17:25)—"the man who kills [Goliath], the king will enrich him with great riches, and will give him his daughter, and make his father's house free in Israel". Saul promises to his champion material wealth, permanent status as a member of the king's family, and improved standing for his own family. After David's victory over Goliath, Saul does, in fact, attach him to the royal entourage. Indeed, as David's successes mount, "וַיְשִׂמֵהוּ שָׁאוּל עַל אַנְשֵׁי הַמִּלְחָמָה" (I Sam. 18:5)—"Saul set him over the men of war"—and the people approve Saul's action. But their approval displeases Saul:

וַיְהִי בְּבוֹאָם בְּשׁוּב דָּוִד מֵהַכּוֹת אֶת־הַפְּלִשְׁתִּי וַתֵּצֶאנָה הַנָּשִׁים מִכָּל־עָרֵי יִשְׂרָאֵל לָשׁוּר [לָשִׁיר] וְהַמְּחֹלוֹת לִקְרַאת שָׁאוּל הַמֶּלֶךְ בְּתֻפִּים בְּשִׂמְחָה וּבְשָׁלִשִׁים. וַתַּעֲנֶינָה הַנָּשִׁים הַמְשַׂחֲקוֹת וַתֹּאמַרְןָ הִכָּה שָׁאוּל בַּאֲלָפוֹ [בַּאֲלָפָיו] וְדָוִד בְּרִבְבֹתָיו. וַיִּחַר לְשָׁאוּל מְאֹד וַיֵּרַע בְּעֵינָיו הַדָּבָר הַזֶּה וַיֹּאמֶר נָתְנוּ לְדָוִד רְבָבוֹת וְלִי נָתְנוּ הָאֲלָפִים וְעוֹד לוֹ אַךְ הַמְּלוּכָה. (I Sam. 18:6-8)

> And it came to pass as they came, when David returned from slaying the Philistine, that the women came from all the cities of Israel, singing and dancing, to meet king Saul, with tambourines, with joyful song, and with lutes. And the women answered one another as they danced, and said, Saul has killed his thousands, and David his ten thousands. And Saul was very angry, and the saying displeased him; and he said, They have ascribed to David ten thousands, and to me they have ascribed but thousands; and what can he have more but the kingdom?

Because David is credited with more Philistine deaths, Saul assumes that he will soon usurp him as king. From that moment, Saul regards David as an enemy to himself greater than the Philistines.

On the very next day, he tries to murder David:

וַיְהִי מִמָּחֳרָת וַתִּצְלַח רוּחַ אֱלֹהִים | רָעָה | אֶל־שָׁאוּל וַיִּתְנַבֵּא בְתוֹךְ־הַבַּיִת וְדָוִד מְנַגֵּן בְּיָדוֹ כְּיוֹם | בְּיוֹם וְהַחֲנִית בְּיַד־שָׁאוּל. וַיָּטֶל שָׁאוּל אֶת־הַחֲנִית וַיֹּאמֶר אַכֶּה בְדָוִד וּבַקִּיר וַיִּסֹּב דָּוִד מִפָּנָיו פַּעֲמָיִם. (I Sam. 18:10-11)

> And it came to pass on the next day, that the evil spirit from God came upon Saul, and he prophesied in the midst of the house; and David played with his hand, as at other times; and there was a spear in Saul's hand. And Saul raised the spear; for he said, I will strike David to the wall with it. And David turned outside of his presence twice.

Saul then grows afraid to attack David directly but thinks to contrive his death by sending him against the Philistines, anticipating that eventually David must be slain. This king, who originally had offered prizes in order to be rid of the Philistines, now offers new rewards but this time in the hope that the Philistines will rid him of his own champion. Thinking to use his daughter as a snare, he offers her in marriage as a prize to David for killing more Philistines. (We understand from our analysis in Chapter 3 above that David's initial victory over Goliath did nothing to bring the war to an end. In fact, quite the opposite was true; David's unorthodox use of his sling to slay the giant amounted to a breach of protocol and established once and for all the Hebrews' unfitness for any form of negotiated settlement.) But Saul is disappointed in his expectation, and when David returns well and whole, having fulfilled the king's command that he "אַךְ הֱיֵה־לִּי לְבֶן־חַיִל וְהִלָּחֵם מִלְחֲמוֹת יְהוָה" (I Sam. 18:17)—"only be brave for me, and fight the Lord's battles"—Saul forgets his promise and gives his daughter to another man in marriage. Soon, however, Saul again attempts this stratagem, on the second occasion making his orders more specific, causing David to be instructed that: "כִּי בְּמֵאָה עָרְלוֹת פְּלִשְׁתִּים אֵין־חֵפֶץ לַמֶּלֶךְ בְּמֹהַר" (I Sam. 18:25)—"The king desires no dowry, but a hundred foreskins of the Philistines." In this way "וְשָׁאוּל חָשַׁב לְהַפִּיל אֶת־דָּוִד בְּיַד־פְּלִשְׁתִּים" (I Sam. 18:25)—"Saul thought to make David fall by the hand of the Philistines." David, of course, gladly accepts the challenge and "וַיְמַלְאוּם לַמֶּלֶךְ וַיַּךְ בַּפְּלִשְׁתִּים מָאתַיִם אִישׁ וַיָּבֵא דָוִד אֶת־עָרְלֹתֵיהֶם" (I Sam. 18:27)—"slew of the Philistines two hundred men; and David brought their foreskins, and they gave them in full number to the king"—with the result that "אֶת־דָּוִד כָּל־הַיָּמִים וַיֹּאסֶף שָׁאוּל לֵרֹא מִפְּנֵי דָוִד עוֹד וַיְהִי שָׁאוּל אֹיֵב" (I Sam. 18:29)—"Saul was still the more afraid of David; and Saul became David's enemy continually." David is repeatedly successful against the Philistines, ever increasing Saul's eagerness to see him dead.

Saul's behavior is not at all anomalous. When a champion has won his duel and thus made himself an army's savior, he can expect to be murdered by the very king who previously had promised him gifts for volunteering to risk his life in single combat. The underhanded murder of champions by their kings appears, in fact, to have been endemic to epic culture. After Siegfried has saved Burgundy from the Saxons and Danes and aided Burgundy's king in acquiring Brünhild for his wife, Gunther acquiesces in his murder. The murderous mood between Agamemnon and Achilles is kept partly in check—swords stay in their scabbards—but their enmity finds its way to the surface nevertheless, and their feud takes the lives of many a companion. After David has rid the Hebrews of Goliath and put the Philistines to flight, he is attacked by Saul, who endeavors to slay him with his own hands. The conflict between champion and king is, in fact, not only predictable, but hardly avoidable.[1] When the men of the army and the general population learn that a duel

---

[1] De Boor makes the following comment about Siegfried: "Der fremde Held, der sich den burgundischen Königen unentbehrlich macht und die Hand ihrer Schwester erringt, wächst sich zur Bedrohung des einheimischen Königtums aus. Die Zuneigung wandelt sich in eifersüchtigen Haß und aus ihm gebiert sich die

has been won on their behalf, they regard their champion as a savior—and rightly so. His victory turns aside the privations and dangers of war to which they have been subject; in effect, he removes from them and their families the menace of subjugation, slavery, brutalization, rape, and death. As an expression of their gratitude and in an effort to secure for themselves the permanent services of this savior, the people may be prepared to accept the champion as their new king.[2]

The individual currently enjoying the status of king therefore has every reason to feel threatened under such circumstances. But if his resistance were the only problem to be reckoned with, champions would surely soon find their way to power. The situation is made more complex by two considerations: first, that the attributes necessary to the champion's success in battle—his physical strength, stature, and skill with weapons—are not relevant to the administration of government; and second, that the community's interest is best served by maintaining a separation between the functions of champion and king. The champion must, by the nature of his function, be replaceable. Government, on the other hand, may perhaps benefit at moments of crisis from greater continuity, particularly upon the loss of a champion. So while the champion is a savior, his very success threatens to destabilize the functions of government.

That the hero who steps forward as a volunteer to risk his life in order to put an end to bloodshed represents a grave danger to the society he saves is a central paradox. If the event of the duel is itself problematic, requiring for a successful outcome the strictest adherence to numerous protocols and formalities, its aftermath entails problems of its own, requiring further adjustments and innovations within the culture's institutions and practices. Epic culture must concern itself with these issues and provide for their resolution.

---

schlimme Tat" (p. 46)—"The foreign hero, who makes himself indispensable to the Burgundian kings and wins the hand of their sister develops into a threat to their hold on the kingship. Their appreciation is soon converted to a jealous hatred from which stems the evil deed." In addition to the king's jealousy, however, we need to consider the monstrous dimension of many heroes, including Siegfried, Achilles, and Aias, whose destructiveness threatens even those they serve. The loner-cum-monster is, in fact, thematized in Grendel.

[2] The populace need not necessarily desire a change in leadership, however, especially if the society is constructed with a separation between the roles of king and champion. In the *Nibelungenlied,* there does not appear to be any indication that the Burgundians would like to have Siegfried replace Gunther. Here it may be less the kingship than the championship that is at stake, and the Burgundians are no longer even very clear on proper management of the institution of championship. From Siegfried's perspective, on the other hand, kingship and championship are at first combined, though at the point of his peaceful entry into the Burgundian court, he begins a transition to the Burgundian system. Unfortunately, since he neither seeks nor receives proper instruction into the working of that system, he falls afoul of it, especially its need for secrecy in regard to the deception that is practiced and for which he must be killed.

In other cultures, one of the king's functions may be to staff, equip, and quarter a standing army. In epic culture, the king must assure his community that its military interests are placed in the hands of the most daunting available individual warrior,[3] and it falls on the king to secure the services of that warrior. He may make a selection from among competing local candidates, or he may well find it prudent to attract to defense of the community's interests an exceptionally gifted outsider. To this end, he will offer gifts, prizes, and tokens of status. Thus, when Hagen fails to present himself as champion to meet Siegfried's challenge, Gunther could have offered his unmarried sister as a reward to anyone able to defeat Siegfried. Still failing to obtain a champion by this means, Kriemhild would be offered in marriage to Siegfried for his agreement to champion (rather than challenge) Burgundy. Siegfried's purpose in challenging the Burgundians is thus fulfilled as he acquires clear title both to the status he seeks and to Kriemhild, in return for which he agrees to represent Burgundy against challengers like the Danes and Saxons.[4] Having established his championship of Burgundy, Siegfried may, like Beowulf, return to his own kingdom without greatly endangering the Burgundians, for he offers to return in time of need. The king's gifts thus represent more than simple payment to the champion for services rendered; they define in advance the relationship sought by the king between himself and the successful candidate for champion. Presentation and acceptance of gifts signify agreement about the terms that will govern their mutual behavior.

---

[3] We may suppose that the size of armies would therefore have been greatly reduced, but this is not necessarily the case, and certainly the epic narratives seem generally to indicate that even while a champion need only a dozen cohorts to back him up, as king he may go to war accompanied by thousands. When Siegfried rides to meet the Danes and Saxons numbering forty thousand, he takes one thousand Burgundians with him. On the one hand, we see that he calculates that he can manage with only a fraction of the enemy's force. On the other, the battle itself is not decided by the numbers involved at all. We may, therefore, speculate either that the emphasis on warriors numbering in the thousands is either a later emendation of the story or else it may be that an epic-cultural king had other reasons to assemble an army, for it might be useful to call all his subordinates to witness afresh his power and thus to impress them with the legitimacy of his overlordship. The presence of a large force of men on the field might impress the enemy as well, for if they are organized in accordance with epic-cultural understandings, the size of an entourage would indicate the degree of its champion's formidableness. If, on the other hand, the enemy is not familiar with the special economies of epic-cultural battle, it may be necessary to engage army-to-army until the champion can demonstrate his ability to dominate the field.

[4] Siegfried, of course, never does establish his championship of the Burgundians, because they do not clearly understand the institution of championship. Once he enters their court, he himself loses sight of it, so that where he had begun with a bold challenge to Gunther for control of his land and people, a year later when the Danes and Saxons make war he blushes uncontrollably when he is not taken into Gunther's confidence as a "friend" (155,1-4).

140   CHAPTER FIVE

Achilles withdraws from battle not so much because of his attachment to the girl Briseis herself, but because Agamemnon's confiscation of the gift represents a breach of the relationship between king and champion.[5] Achilles has fulfilled his part of the compact only to see Agamemnon renege on his obligation to pay him the full respect that he is due as Agamemnon's best warrior.[6] Because Agamemnon fails to treat Achilles properly, the latter

---

[5] Gifts and spoils must be meted out by the king to all his supporting warriors but with a careful distinction made for his champion. The tendency to forget the importance of this distinction is reflected in Agamemnon's mistreatment of Achilles and then carried forward by the modern commentator's ignorance of the difference between a champion and a warrior. Leonard Frey, for example, in "Comitatus as a Rhetorical-Structural Norm for Two Germanic Epics," *Recovering Literature: A Journal of Contextual Criticism*, 14 (Summer 1986), p. 68, comments broadly that it is "wisdom on the leader's part to share the spoils of war," where the circumstances in question are Attila's rewarding of Walter and Hagen—men who are not his thanes. Further references to the Frey work will be cited parenthetically in the text. The focus of much of Frey's argument is on Hrothgar and Beowulf, to whom no "spoils" are passed. It is, in fact, Beowulf who brings back a few treasures from the deeps of the Mere which he gives as gifts to Hrothgar and his queen. What Beowulf receives in return are rewards that constitute a part of Hrothgar's wealth, treasure wisely saved for use on an occasion like this one. Hrothgar's followers are thus "ineffectual" only insofar as they cannot defend Heorot against Grendel's predations, which is to say that they are ineffectual as champions. They are, nevertheless, in Frey's opinion, quite willing to die doing their duty and are thus quite honorable as thanes, for they do fulfill their part of *comitatus* ideals requiring reciprocity, loyalty, and generosity (p. 69). Only Unferth, whose "flyting" (verbal attack) betrays his sense of competition with Beowulf, might once have entertained some notion of volunteering alone against Grendel, and Beowulf retorts that, had Unferth been as fierce in fight as in his words, "næfre Grendel swa fela gryre gefremede, atol æglæca ealdre þinum" (591-92—"Grendel, awful monster, would never have performed so many terrible deeds against your chief." In Frey's estimation, Beowulf lives up to the ideal on both sides of the equation, first, by showing up Hrothgar's *comitatus* of "ineffectual thanes" and then in death showing up his own men for standing by when he needed them, though they do "nominally stay within the letter of the *comitatus*-law in 'obeying orders'" (p. 69). Clearly, then, Frey's employment of the *comitatus* relationship to evaluate human character results in this contradiction—that the thanes are both worthy and unworthy. Key terms used but passed over by Frey are "effectual" and "ineffectual." Judgment in these terms requires an understanding of responsibilities more complex, or at least different, from those presented by the *comitatus* model.

[6] "χωόμενος ὅ τ' ἄριστον Ἀχαιῶν οὐδὲν ἔτεισας" (1.244)—"You will be sorry," Achilles predicts to Agamemnon, "that you did not pay respect to the best of the Achaeans." (my translation). The verb "τίω," however, means to pay, to pay recompense for and to value, to treat with honor. Agamemnon's removal of a gift thus displays the reverse of respect towards Achilles, to which the latter responds by reminding the king that he will not be able to protect the men—"οὔ τι δυνήσεαι . . . χραισμεῖν" (1.241-42), for it is Achilles who serves as the Achaeans' protector, their wall of defense—"ἕρκος Ἀχαιοῖσιν" (1.284)—in an

withdraws from the function in which he is needed, and the Achaeans pay with their lives. Agamemnon can be considered a good king and protector of the fighting men entrusted to his command only so long as he accomplishes the fall of Troy with a minimum loss of life. To the extent that Agamemnon is guilty of mishandling Achilles, he must bear responsibility for the Achaean dead.[7] By failing to provide his men with the best available protection, he proves himself to be a poor king.[8]

Agamemnon's error is worth studying because it is not simply a personal failure of judgment. Rather, the source of his error can be traced to a conflict that is inevitable within the domain of epic culture. If the king's decisions and commands are to be effective, they must be authoritative. In order to perform his function, the king requires the loyalty, obedience, and respect of his subjects. The individual performing the function of king requires, in a word, legitimacy—the recognition that he alone is empowered to perform the functions of his office. Such legitimacy can best be communicated to outsiders, newcomers, and doubters through easily recognizable signs that he is, in fact, accorded this authority by his subjects. Outward displays of respect in the language of address required of those who approach the king, special behavior in his presence or even his proximity, and ostentatious display connected to him all serve to convey and perpetuate the king's legitimacy. Considering, however, the army's natural inclination to reward a champion with its respect, loyalty, and obedience, the community finds itself faced with the dilemma either of dividing its loyalties or of making a choice between the two candidates for kingly legitimacy.[9]

---

early Greek world that is, as Lynn-George puts it, "vulnerable and in pressing need of defence and protection" (p. 200).

[7] We saw in chapter 4 that Achilles must bear responsibility for the Achaean dead. Neither he nor Agamemnon bears sole responsibility but each does bear full responsibility.

[8] "With the hurling of the sceptre and the formal withdrawal of Achilles," observes Lynn-George, "the sceptre-bearing king is left to preside over a community that he is pronounced powerless to protect against the blade. This severance from within society puts the necessary conditions for existence and survival not only at risk but in question" (p. 202).

[9] In attempting to interpret the behavior of the Burgundian court in the *Nibelungenlied*, Beyschlag explains that the "oberstes Gesetz des Handelns für die Brüder ebenso wie für den regierenden König die Wahrung der Einheit und Unversehrtheit des Reiches, die Vermeidung oder zumindest Abschwächung gefährlicher Gegensätze ist" (p. 209)—"the highest law of action for the brothers as for the ruling king is the preservation of a unified and inviolate realm—the avoidance or at least weakening of dangerous oppositions." This text raises the question, however, of whether it is possible to weaken dangerous oppositions by eliminating the guest champion with a spear in the back, escorting his relatives to the borders, and depriving his wife of her treasure. The issue of the horde, however, especially as it comes up after the bloodbath in Vienna, seems to suggest that the oppositions, beginning with that between champion and king, may have been more effectively resolved through an open confrontation.

This dilemma permits several solutions. One of the competitors may be killed. If the champion is killed, however, as when Gunther's vassal kills Siegfried, then the community is left without its best defense. Those loyal to the murdered champion may, moreover, plot revenge. If, on the other hand, the king is killed, the community may be subjected to poor government and chronic tumult as a succession of challengers contests the throne. These unsatisfying alternatives can be avoided, however, if king and champion acknowledge each other's status, accepting precisely demarcated roles and displaying tokens or signs that clearly indicate to the community how it is to apportion its loyalties. Such a careful division of loyalties between the two statuses of king and champion is, however, difficult to achieve.[10]

Agamemnon is not king of the Achaeans. Technically, he only commands the Mycenaeans and the inhabitants of villages nearby the fortress town of Mycenae. Nevertheless, he has special authority within both the general assembly of the military forces and the special assembly of kings and captains. While his power is not democratic, it does depend upon the consensus of the other Achaean kings and princes. The war against Troy is not fought at his command but under his direction. He therefore does not offer gifts or status symbols from his own Mycenaean coffers in order to recruit fighting forces. Rather, prizes are generated by the capture of towns and citadels. These prizes are distributed not by Agamemnon but by the fighting men themselves. The distribution of prizes reflects the judgments of the men about the honors due their own kings, captains, and heroes. In this way, the community of fighters directly bestows legitimacy upon individuals who are thus accorded a status of special authority to govern, advise, or represent the army in a duel.

All this is brought to light in the *Iliad* when Agamemnon is advised to give up his prize, the girl Chryseis, to her father, Chryses, who, though a member of a captive community, happens to be the priest of Apollo. His priesthood is a special status recognized even by his daughter's captors, entitling him in their eyes to her release, as follows: "αἰδεῖσθαί θ' ἱερῆα" (1.23)—"they wished to see the priest respected." He achieves this respect by displaying symbols of his own special status, "στέμματ' ἔχων ἐν χερσὶν ἑκηβόλου Ἀπόλλωνος / χρυσέῳ ἀνὰ σκήπτρῳ" (1.14-15)—"[h]e ... carried the chaplet of the Archer-god Apollo on a golden staff in his hand," by acknowledging Agamemnon's status, by bringing him a generous ransom in exchange for the girl's release, and by offering the services of his own priestly function, calling upon the gods to grant the Achaeans' wish to sack Troy and get home safely.

---

[10] Weil attributes to Achilles's and Agamemnon's mishandling of their relationship much of their own and their companions' suffering. "Why should you," she asks rhetorically, "refrain from taking Achilles' girl away from him if you know that neither he nor she can do anything but obey you?" to which she answers, "Thus it happens that those who have force on loan from fate count on it too much and are destroyed" (p. 155).

The troops approve the exchange. Agamemnon, however, is reluctant to part with the girl. Disregarding the priest's status, he takes advantage of his own authority as king and commander of the combined Achaean forces to reject Chryses's request. Chryses then turns to the gods as guarantors of the social order to redress the wrong done him. Apollo obliges by raining arrows of disease upon the Achaean camp.

Achilles calls an assembly of Achaeans to find a remedy to the plague ravaging the camp. Addressing Agamemnon before the men and apparently deferring to his status as commander in chief, Achilles proposes consulting a prophet or priest in order to discover the source of Apollo's anger. Calchas, a prophet of Apollo and credited with bringing the fleet successfully to Ilium, has the answer to Achilles's question but is afraid to voice it, fearing the wrath of Agamemnon, "ὅς μέγα πάντων / Ἀργείων κρατέει καί οἱ πείθονται Ἀχαιοί" (1.78-79)—"one whose authority is absolute among us and whose word is law to all Achaeans." Calchas may as well name Agamemnon. But he fears the monarch's power, observing that "κρείσσων γὰρ βασιλεὺς ὅτε χώσεται ἀνδρὶ χέρηϊ" (1.80)—"a commoner is no match for a king whom he offends." He is clearly aware of the fact that the person enjoying the status of king can abuse the authority granted him. In refusing to give up Chryseis, Agamemnon has already shown himself disposed to consider his own desires rather than his obligations. Against this abuse of his authority, Calchas now demands Achilles's protection "ἔπεσιν καὶ χερσίν" (1.77)—"with words and deeds" (my translation). Achilles has proven to be unequaled in the strength of his deeds; the eloquence of his words, however, is as yet untested. If Calchas puts faith in Achilles's articulateness, it must be based on the respect due him in his status as champion.

Agamemnon grudgingly agrees to return Chryseis, granting that, though he prefers her to his wife, he is willing to give her up: "εἰ τό γ' ἄμεινον" (1.116)—"if that appears the wiser course"—for, as he says, "βούλομ' ἐγὼ λαὸν σῶν ἔμμεναι ἢ ἀπολέθαι" (1.117)—"[i]t is my desire to see my people safe and sound, not perishing." In other words, Agamemnon is now willing to base his actions not on personal desire but in keeping with the responsibilities and obligations of his status. By exposing his selfish motives, however, he has already damaged the king's office. Perhaps in an effort to restore the king's prestige and reassert his authority, he demands that another prize at once be given him. If he alone gives up his prize, he reasons, then his status may be reduced and his authority diminished. In order to reassert his authority, he is prepared to pass on his private loss to one of his subordinates. Indeed, he chooses for this sacrifice the man whose status most threatens his own, Achilles, forgetting that the sacrifice expected of Achilles is already greater than that of any other man in the army. The quarrel between Agamemnon and Achilles, then, has its source in the king's sense of insecurity, his fear of being eclipsed in respect and authority.

On the other hand, the quarrel is deepened by Achilles's apparent ignorance of the king's function: "οὔτε ποτ' ἐς πόλεμον ἅμα λαῷ θωρηχθῆναι / οὔτε λόχονδ' ἰέναι σὺν ἀριστήεσσιν Ἀχαιῶν / τέτληκας θυμῷ· τὸ δέ τοι κὴρ εἴδεται εἶναι. / ἦ πολὺ λώϊόν ἐστι κατὰ στρατὸν εὐρὺν Ἀχαιῶν / δῶρ' ἀποαιρεῖσθαι ὅς τις σέθεν ἀντίον εἴπῃ· / δημοβόρος βασιλεύς, ἐπεὶ οὐτιδανοῖσιν ἀνάσσεις" (1.226-31)—"You never have the pluck to arm yourself and go into battle with the men or to join the other captains in an ambush—you would sooner die," he charges. "It pays you better to stay in camp, filching the prizes of anyone that contradicts you, and flourishing at your people's cost because they are too feeble to resist." In other words, Achilles seems to think that the prizes are earned precisely as they are won— in battle. "ἀλλὰ τὸ μὲν πλεῖον πολυάϊκος πολέμοιο / χεῖρες ἐμαὶ διέπουσ'· ἀτὰρ ἤν ποτε δασμὸς ἵκηται, / σοὶ τὸ γέρας πολὺ μεῖζον" (1.165-67)—"The heat and burden of the fighting fall on me," Achilles complains, "but when it comes to dealing out the loot, it is you that take the lion's share." The king's prizes are greater than those of even the best warrior, and in this way the men acknowledge the king's status. They give him both the greatest credit and the greatest responsibility for bringing the war to a successful conclusion.

It is one thing for the men to acknowledge the king's superior status, another for the king to insist upon it, especially when this comes at the expense of his champion. A rift between these two men means disaster for the whole community. Nestor, the wise counselor, is aware of the danger and attempts to redraw the distinction between the two statuses. Addressing each in turn, he advises both to retreat from their untenable positions:

> μήτε σὺ τόνδ' ἀγαθός περ ἐὼν ἀποαίρεο κούρην.
> ἀλλ' ἔα, ὡς οἱ πρῶτα δόσαν γέρας υἷες Ἀχαιῶν·
> μήτε σύ, Πηλείδη, ἔθελ' ἐριζέμεναι βασιλῆϊ
> ἀντιβίην, ἐπεὶ οὔ ποθ' ὁμοίης ἔμμορε τιμῆς
> σκηπτοῦχος βασιλεύς, ᾧ τε Ζεὺς κῦδος ἔδωκεν.
> εἰ δὲ σὺ καρτερός ἐσσι, θεὰ δέ σε γείνατο μήτηρ,
> ἀλλ' ὅ γε φέρτερός ἐστιν, ἐπεὶ πλεόνεσσιν ἀνάσσει.
> Ἀτρεΐδη, σὺ δὲ παῦε τεὸν μένος· αὐτὰρ ἔγωγε
> λίσσομ' Ἀχιλλῆϊ μεθέμεν χόλον, ὃς μέγα πᾶσιν
> ἕρκος Ἀχαιοῖσιν πέλεται πολέμοιο κακοῖο. (1.275-84)

Agamemnon, forget the privilege of your rank, and do not rob him of the girl. The army gave her to him: let him keep his prize. And you, my lord Achilles, drop your contentious bearing to the King. Through the authority he derives from Zeus, a sceptred king has more than ordinary claims on our respect. You, with a goddess for Mother, may be the stronger of the two; yet Agamemnon is the better man, since he rules more people. My lord Atreides, be appeased. I, Nestor, beg you to relent towards Achilles, our mighty bulwark in the stress of battle.

Achilles is the stronger man, yet Agamemnon rules more people. Achilles owes Agamemnon his respect, and Agamemnon owes Achilles his prize. These are the distinctions.

Instead of relenting, however, Agamemnon is still bent upon exercising his authority: "ἀλλ' ὅδ' ἀνὴρ ἐθέλει περὶ πάντων ἔμμεναι ἄλλων. / πάντων μὲν κρατέειν ἐθέλει. πάντεσσι δ' ἀνάσσειν. / πᾶσι δὲ σημαίνειν" (1.287-89)— in his view, Achilles "wants to lord it over all of us, to play the king, and to give us each our orders"—and this he will not tolerate. Forgetting that Achilles's participation is indispensable to his successful command, he now prefers to do without the help of the champion in the war, rather than to suffer any threat to his own status: "φεῦγε μαλ'"—"Take to your heels, by all means," he encourages Achilles—"οὐδέ σ' ἔγωγε / λίσσομαι εἵνεκ' ἐμεῖο μένειν" (1.173-74)—"I am not begging you to stay on my account." No, the participation of Achilles should not be on his account, he insists, but on account of the men, whose protection and safety should be Agamemnon's chief concern.[11]

Achilles is equally short-sighted. Indeed, he makes an oath before Agamemnon: "ἦ ποτ' Ἀχιλλῆος ποθὴ ἵξεται υἷας Ἀχαιῶν / σύμπαντας· τότε δ' οὔ τι δυνήσεαι ἀχνύμενός περ / χραισμεῖν. εὖτ' ἄν πολλοὶ ὑφ' Ἕκτορος ἀνδροφόνοιο / θνήσκοντες πίπτωσι· σὺ δ' ἔνδοθι θυμὸν ἀμύξεις / χωόμενος ὅ τ' ἄριστον Ἀχαιῶν οὐδὲν ἔτεισας" (1.240-44)—"that the day is coming when the Achaeans one and all will miss me sorely, and you in your despair will be powerless to help them as they fall in their hundreds to Hector killer of men. Then, you will tear your heart out in remorse for having treated the best man in the expedition with contempt." Nestor, however, calls Agamemnon the best man, and Achilles eventually will feel his own heart torn by remorse for having neglected the Achaeans as they fall to Hector in their hundreds. Like Agamemnon, Achilles has lost sight of the fact that his status derives from the men and is designed for their protection. The destruction of the Achaean army occurs in large part because neither king nor champion is sufficiently aware of the dynamics pertaining to his position. Signs of status such as gifts and the public display of respect are meant to enable each to perform his primary function, namely, preserving the lives of his companions. This relationship is reversed, according to Voegelin, when Achilles's anger at Agamemnon's disregard for his tokens of honor renders

---

[11] Donlan has argued that the two men are competing for honor, which is quite true—but that is their error, for they are not mindful of the important differences in status and function that separate them. Donlan, however, drawing upon an interpretive tradition passing through Finley (p. 160; n13), inappropriately applies terms from an altogether different cultural context to identify the society of the *Iliad* as a gift-giving one, characterizing the conflict between Agamemnon and Achilles "as a competition in gift-giving" (p. 160). Gift-giving competitions tax the ability of each contestant to exact huge contributions from their supporters. In order to win, the gift must be so great that it leaves the donors with no remaining gifts in reserve. The winners are temporarily impoverished by the extent of the sacrifice that they make in the cause of winning. None of these conditions can be applied to the world of Homer's narratives. Gifts are of great importance, to be sure, but we come to the best understanding of their function through our analysis of gift-giving within the texts. It is worthwhile to pay attention to gift-giving but not if we prejudge its role in a particular instance.

him "quite willing to let his comrades perish in battle until his intervention is the last and uncontested means for turning defeat into victory" (69).

Agamemnon began the quarrel by reversing the king's function as gift-giver to become a gift-confiscator, which led to Achilles's negating his own function as a preserver of lives. In order to correct the situation, then, Agamemnon offers Achilles great gifts, including marriage to his own daughter. The gifts, however, offered now to placate Achilles, are unacceptable, because if Achilles allows himself to be mollified by the treasures offered him, then he acknowledges his responsibility for the death of so many men.[12] The issue is neither the adequacy of the gifts nor the status relations between the two men but instead recognition and acceptance of the fact that both have failed their function, as a result of which men in their care have died. Agamemnon's belated offer of gifts thus points up the proper function of gift-exchange. In this instance, the king begins by confiscating a gift from his best warrior, who, though he has not been fighting for the sake of gifts, responds by refusing further aid to the king. In this abnegation, he puts aside or rather forgets his feeling for his companions. The offer of gifts, coming after many brutal deaths, now serves not as a reward for saving lives but as a reminder to Achilles that he let them die. In refusing to accept the gifts, Achilles can attempt to ward off acceptance of the consequences of his anger.

Agamemnon is not the best man because he commands more men, but rather he commands more men because he is meant to be the best commander. The very principle upon which the king and champion are sometimes separated into two statuses with two separate functions is that the strongest fighter is not always the one with the best judgment. Agamemnon's role is to exercise his judgment, most especially with regard to the treatment of his hot-headed champion. When kings become preoccupied with their own reputation and champions withdraw from battle, the men begin to die in droves. The *Iliad* is not only the story of the wrath of Achilles, as announced in the poem's opening line, but also of Agamemnon's insecurity. The disaster, measured in the numbers of heroes' souls sent down to Hades, should be attributed both to the king and to his champion.

The role of the king may have particular significance in the case of contests, where the primary object is to establish a hierarchy among friendly or

---

[12] This explanation for the refusal by Achilles of the gifts sharply contrasts with other interpretations, such as that of Donlan, who rightly sees that "Achilles owed the obligations of comradeship to his fellow warriors who were being hard pressed in battle" (p. 165). Donlan considers as reasons for Achilles's rejection the omission of a public apology and, should he accept the gifts, his acceptance of obligation—and thus subordination—to Agamemnon, whose offer to make Achilles his son-in-law "far from honoring him, . . . formally defines him as inferior in status" (p. 166). But Donlan's reasoning is based on a misprision of the champion's status, which immediately vies with that of the king. While it is true that "adoption by marriage into the household of a powerful chief" is "a form of marrying-up, typically reserved for wandering adventurers and impecunious suitors" as, for example, the "poor and landless" Odysseus in Crete (p. 165), the champion need not be poor.

allied chieftains. The king's status as supreme commander gives him both the means and the responsibility for managing the ritual battle and establishing conditions under which the individual warriors can test themselves against the enemy in order to be measured against one another. The men compete for honor, doled out in prizes that signify their ranking. Thus, they establish relations among themselves peacefully, though the competition among them represents a very real danger of deadly military conflict among erstwhile companions and allies. The king's function, then, is to manage the aggression of his warriors. A real quarrel like that between Menelaus and Paris provides the Achaean chiefs with the stage that they need for a test of their champions. Once a champion has been selected, however, he must be treated in the manner appropriate to his status. By focusing too intently upon his own honor, Agamemnon loses sight of the responsibilities that he seems so eager to retain. If he has a great deal of authority, it is so that he can transfer over to the new champion the loyalty and trust vouchsafed to his keeping by the men.

Hrothgar finds himself in a situation that is quite different. His quarrel with Grendel has nothing to do with ritual battle and challenges to authority, for Grendel marauds into his hall and devours his people, putting Hrothgar in desperate need of help to rid his land of its uncanny invader. And Hrothgar is a different kind of king. He has no doubt whatsoever that his primary function under the circumstances is to obtain the services of a warrior capable of standing up to the monster Grendel. As "eodur Scyldinga" (663a)—"protector of the Scyldings," it is Hrothgar's function to welcome help, to allow even strangers to hold his hall against Grendel, and to offer them a reward if they succeed. Beowulf hears the report that Hrothgar has "manna þearf" (201b)— "need of men"—and answers the call. Hrothgar, in turn, wishes him good luck, exhorts him to be mindful of his fame (his motive for volunteering), and promises him a reward: "Ne bið þe wilna gad, gif þu þæt ellenweorc aldre gedigest" (660b-1)—"You will not lack what you wish if you survive that deed of valor."

Beowulf does survive. Instantly, his fame is multiplied and carried into every corner of his world. Just as quickly, Beowulf is compared to Hrothgar himself. Of Beowulf, it is said not only "þætte suð ne norð be sæm tweonum / ofer eormengrund / oþer nænig / under swegles begong selre nære / rondhæbbendra" (858-61a)—"that, south nor north, between the seas, over the wide earth, no other man under sky's expanse was better of those who bear shields"—perhaps a fair statement to make after Beowulf's bare-handed victory over Grendel—but in the same breath, that no other man is "rices wyrðra" (861b)—"more worthy of ruling." The singers of praise make the connection, then, between battle success and government. And by proclaiming his excellence in government, they place Hrothgar's status in jeopardy. And yet, as we are told by the narrative, "Ne hie huru winedrihten wiht ne logon, glædne Hroðgar, ac þæt wæs god cyning" (862-63)—"they found no fault with their own dear lord, gracious Hrothgar, for he was a good king." Clearly, he could no longer serve as defender of the people. His goodness, then, refers either to his past glories as a warrior or to his present management of the crisis. The narrator allows both interpretations to stand, reporting that "swylce self cyning / of brydbure, beahhorda weard, / tryddode tirfæst getrume micle, / cystum gecyþed" (920b-23a)—"[t]he king himself walked forth from the women's apartment, the guardian of the ring-hoards, secure in his fame, known for his excellence." As guardian of the ring-hoards, Hrothgar is regarded for his role in distributing wealth and tokens of their status to his warriors. This is an entirely kingly function, depending not at all on skill or reputation in war. However, his fame is also mentioned and his excellence. Does the narrator mean excellence in battle or excellence in using his wealth to maintain a noteworthy force of armed retainers?[13]

The narrative seems carefully to blend these qualities in Hrothgar. Soon after the poem's outset, Hrothgar's curriculum vitae is sketched:

>   þa wæs Hroðgare   heresped gyfen,
>   wiges weorðmynd,   þæt him his winemagas
>   georne hyrdon,   oðð þæt seo geogoð geweox,
>   magodriht micel.   Him on mod bearn,
>   þæt healreced   hatan wolde,
>   medoærn micel,   men gewyrcean
>   þon[n]e yldo bearn   æfre gefrunon,
>   ond þær on innan   eall gedælan
>   geongum ond ealdum,   swylc him god sealde
>   buton folcscare   ond feorum gumena. (64-73)

Then Hrothgar was given success in warfare, glory in battle, so that his retainers gladly obeyed him and their company grew into a great band of warriors. It came to his mind that he would command men to construct a hall, a mead-building large[r] than the children of men had ever heard of, and therein he would give to young and old all that God had given him, except for common land and men's bodies.

Hrothgar's career path is first that of a champion, proving himself in battle, winning the respect of retainers. Only then does he establish himself as a king by subordinating to himself his neighbors. As a symbol that he sits at the center of a hierarchically organized domain, he builds a hall—an administrative seat. To this seat is transported tribute, which serves both as a form of taxation as well as a token of submission. From his high seat, Hrothgar redistributes all the wealth that he collects. The land itself, aside

---

[13] Frey has analyzed the relationship between Hrothgar and his men in terms of the *comitatus*. Though quoting at length from *Germania* 14 (p. 53), Frey's understanding of *comitatus* actually derives directly from feudalism and vassalage (p. 52). Consequently, the feudal ideal realized in the "Battle of Maldon" is held up as a measure for relationships between king and followers in *Beowulf*, with the conclusion that Hrothgar and his thanes fail to realize "the *comitatus* ideal of mutual advantage for leader and following" (p. 55), because Hrothgar rewards a foreign warrior "for doing what the Danish *comitatus* should do" (p. 56).

from common land, is reassigned to territorial chiefs, who now hold it in fief from Hrothgar. The movable wealth is also to be distributed. If Hrothgar collects wealth, it is only so that he has it to redistribute. In time of need, the wealth he has on hand can be put to use in attracting, retaining, and rewarding a new champion. Thus, as Hrothgar passes to kingship, he provides for his own replacement as champion. He must also prepare a transition of kingship for the time to come when death removes him from his office.

Once his hall is built, Hrothgar remembers his promise: "beagas dælde, / sinc æt symle" (80b-81a)—"at the feast he gave out rings, treasure." These gifts secure the loyalty of an entire hierarchy of retainers. Later on, when the king's health and strength begin to fail him, he will summon all the retainers for a festival, at which time one of his sons will assume the ceremonial function of distributing the rings, the treasure, and the land, thus symbolically transferring to himself the retainers' loyalty. Transfer of their actual fidelity, however, depends, as we have seen, on the prince's successful quest for his own name and reputation.

The transference of power is very clearly represented in the *Nibelungenlied*, where it is related how Siegfried came of age. First, the prince is carefully trained in both warfare and manners. He is dressed in fine clothes and placed in the care of "die wîsen, den êre was bekant. / des mohte er wol gewinnen beide liute unde lant" (25,3-4)—"experienced men well-versed in matters of honour as a result of which he was able to win all hearts" (20). In other words, his demeanor on the field and in court is such as to win him respect and loyalty in his own right: "Nu was er in der sterke daz er wol wâfen truoc. / swes er dar zuo bedorfte, des lag an im genuoc " (26,1-2)—"He had grown to be strong enough to bear arms expertly, and he possessed in abundance all the needful qualities" (20). The transfer of loyalty can now commence:

> Dô hiez sîn vater Sigmunt   künden sînen man,
> er wolde hôchgezîte   mit lieben friunden hân.
> diu mære man dô fuorte   in ander künege lant.
> den vremden und den kunden   gap er róss únd gewant.
>
> Swâ man vant deheinen   der ritter solde sîn
> von art der sînen mâge,   diu edelen kindelîn
> diu ladete man zuo dem lande   durch die hôchgezît.
> mit dem jungen künege   swert genámén si sît. (27-28)

When the time was ripe, his father Sigmund had it made known to his vassals that he wished to hold a festivity in company with his dear friends, and the news was borne to other kingdoms. The King bestowed horses and fine clothes on native and stranger alike. And wherever there were noble squires of his line of an age to be knighted, they were invited to his country to take part in the festivity; and when the time came they received their swords in company with the prince. (20-21)

A new generation of warriors, all untested, is coming of age. This is an occasion for ritual battle, for which purpose witnesses must be gathered from the farthest reaches of Siegmund's influence. At the gathering, loyalty is to be secured by the giving of gifts, to which the warriors respond by displaying their zest for battle:

> Von der hôchgezîte   man möhte wunder sagen.
> Sigmunt unde Siglint   die mohten wol bejagen
> mit guote michel êre;   des teilte vil ir hant.
> des sach man vil der vremden   zuo ze in rîten in daz lant.
>
> . . . .
>
> der wirt der hiez dô sidelen   vil manegen küenen man,
> ze einen sunewenden,   dâ sîn sun Sívrit ritters namen gewan.
>
> Dô gie ze einem münster   vil manec rîcher kneht
> und manec edel ritter. . . .
>
> Si liefen dâ si funden   gesatelt manec marc
> in hove Sigmundes.   der bûhurt wart sô starc,
> daz man erdiezen hôrte   palas unde sal.
> die hôchgemuoten degene   die heten grœzlîchen schal.
>
> Von wîsen und von tumben   man hôrte manegen stôz,
> daz der schefte brechen   gein den lüften dôz.
> trunzûne sach man fliegen   für den palas dan
> von maneges recken hende;   daz wart mit vlîzé getân. (29; 31,3-32,2a; 34-35)

It was a magnificent feast, and well did Siegmund and Sieglind know how to win esteem with the lavish gifts they made, so that many people from other parts came riding to their country. . . .
   Then, at midsummer, when his son was knighted, the King commanded seats to be set for the valiant company, whereupon a host of noble squires and knights of high rank repaired to the minster. . . .
   [After the ceremony, they] ran to where many chargers stood saddled, and the bohort in Siegmund's courtyard grew so tremendous that the palace thundered with the din which those spirited warriors made, while you could hear thrust on thrust by young and old, so that the shivering of shafts rang loud on the air and you could see all these knights send the splinters flying far and wide before the hall—so zestfully did they set to. (21)

The ritual battle, or bohort, is followed by a feast, with entertainment by strolling minstrels, whose job it was to lavish praise on Siegfried's entire kingdom. The day ends as follows: "Der hérré hiez lîhen Sívrit den jungen man/ lánt únde bürge, als er hete ê getân./ sînen swertgenôzen den gap dô vil sîn hant./ dô líebte ín diu reise, daz si kômen in daz lant" (39)—"And now the King commanded young Siegfried to bestow lands and castles in fee, as he himself had done when he was knighted, and Siegfried enfeoffed his companions richly, so that they were well pleased with their journey there" (22).

The chief lesson for Siegfried on this day is to give away land and wealth to secure the loyalty and obedience of his retainers. Thus will he gain the reputation of "good king" such as that enjoyed by Hrothgar: "von den rîchen herren hôrte man wol sît / daz si den jungen wolden ze eime herren hân" (42, 2-3)—"Powerful nobles were afterwards heard to say that they would gladly have the young man for their lord" (22). Thus, Siegfried prepares for kingship, but he is still young enough to be concerned foremost with championship. He regards the office of king as conferring upon him the right to defend his realm with his own person: "doch wolde er wesen herre für allen den gewalt/ des in den landen vorhte der degen küene únde balt" (43, 3-4)—"as a valiant knight he aspired to dominion that he might ward off all the violence which he feared for his country" (22).

Hrothgar is a "good king" because he begins by personally protecting and enlarging his kingdom, then gives away to his retainers the land and wealth that they have brought to him, and finally, when the need arises, secures the services of Beowulf at a time when his own strength is no longer sufficient to defend the hall against Grendel's aggression, when his sons are too young to take up arms, and when none of his retainers, loyal as they might be, is capable (as many of them prove with their lives) of ridding Heorot of Grendel. While Hrothgar is in need of Beowulf's assistance, his wife does not wish to see him replaced by Beowulf as the people's new master. He therefore accepts Beowulf's offer of assistance but promises in return that if Beowulf is successful, he "will not lack" whatever he wishes. Beowulf is meant to accept gifts from Hrothgar's hands but not to usurp the kingship itself, though he might well have it in his power to do so.

When Beowulf's success is made known to Hrothgar, the king, because he is a good king, does not forget his promises. He begins by acknowledging the young warrior's accomplishment:

>   Ðæt wæs ungeara   þæt ic ænigra me
>   weana ne wende   to widan feore
>   bote gebidan,   þonne blode fah
>   husa selest   heorodreorig stod, —
>   wea widscofen   witena gehwylcum
>   ðara þe ne wendon   þæt hie wideferhð
>   leoda landgeweorc   laþum beweredon
>   scuccum ond scinnum.   Nu scealc hafað
>   þurh drihtnes miht   dæd gefremede
>   ðe we ealle   ær ne meahton
>   snyttrum besyrwan. (932-42a)

I did not expect ever to live to see relief from any of my woes—when the best of houses stood shining with blood, stained with slaughter, a far-reaching woe for each of my counselors, for every one, since none thought he could ever defend the people's stronghold from demons and spirits. Now through the Lord's might a warrior has accomplished the deed that all of us with our skill could not perform.

This acknowledgment of Beowulf's singular powers is probably all that he really desires of Hrothgar. Nevertheless, the fact is that he could demand a great deal more. If he wished, he could probably seize the kingdom. Hrothgar is apparently sensitive to this possibility, because he next indirectly suggests that Beowulf regard him as a father—that is, perhaps, as someone from whom, if he wished, he could inherit the kingdom: "Nu ic, Beowulf, þec, / secg betsta, me for sunu wylle / freogan on ferhþe; heald forð tela / niwe sibbe" (946b-49a)—"Now, Beowulf, best of men, in my heart I will love you as a son: keep well this new kinship." More concretely, he offers Beowulf his wealth: "Ne bið þe [n]ænigre gad / worolde wilna, þe ic geweald hæbbe" (949b-50)—"To you there will be no lack of the good things of the world that I have in my possession." Beowulf responds: "We þæt ellenweorc estum miclum, / feohtan fremedon" (958-59a)—"With much good will we have achieved this work of courage, that fight." He makes no demands on his host.

Hrothgar stages an elaborate, lavish, and extensive celebration in Heorot to honor Beowulf. The narrator claims that never was a larger company assembled that was better disposed towards its "sincgyfan" (1012)—"treasure-giver." In this instance, all the treasure will be given to Heorot's new hero and his companions. The gifts are all warriors' heirlooms—pieces of rare workmanship or unusual origin, thus particularly laden with symbolic value; a golden standard decorated with a battle banner, a helmet and mail-shirt, a glorious sword, eight horses with golden bridles, a saddle decorated with jewels that had been Hrothgar's own war-seat when he himself had championed his people's interests on the battlefield:

```
Swa manlice         mære þeoden,
hordweard hæleþa,   heaþoræsas geald
mearum ond madmum,  swa hy næfre man lyhð,
se þe secgan wile   soð æfter rihte. (1046-49)
```

So generously the famous prince, guardian of the hoard, repaid the warrior's battle-deeds with horses and treasure that no man will ever find fault with them—not he that will speak the truth according to what is right.

Those in attendance are then regaled with song. The scop elects to tell a story of a friendly visit that turns to enmity, violence, and carnage. It may be that the song is selected for the occasion because of the great potential for conflict between Beowulf and Hrothgar's retainers, whose loyalties may be confused by their admiration for the new champion's success and their jealousy at his rewards. Certainly, Unferth, Hrothgar's erstwhile champion ("he ne uþe, þæt ænig oðer man / æfre mærða þon ma middangeardes / gehede under heofenum þonne he sylfa"—503-05—"he would not allow that any other man of middle-earth should ever achieve more glory under the heavens than himself"), had openly disclosed his personal animosity towards Beowulf (506ff). After Beowulf's success, of course, Unferth becomes "swigra . . . on gilpspræce guðgeweorca" (980-81)—"more silent in boasting speech of warlike deeds," but this is not to say that he would not harbor resentment towards the man now openly acknowledged as "secg betsta" (946a)—"best of men." The situation is precarious and must be handled with skill and tact if it is not to lead to insult, offense, and bloodshed.

The scop's tale ends as follows:

> Ða wæs heal roden
> feonda feorum, swilce Fin slægen,
> cyning on corþre, ond seo cwen numen.
> Sceotend Scyldinga to scypon feredon
> eal ingesteald eorðcyninges,
> swylce hie æt Finnes ham findan meahton
> sigla, searogimma. (1151b-7a)

Then was the hall reddened from foes' bodies, and thus Finn slain, the king in his company, and the queen taken. The warriors of the Scyldings bore to ship all the hall-furnishings of the land's king, whatever of necklaces, skillfully wrought treasures, they might find at Finn's home.

The destruction of the court is symbolized by the person of the queen herself and necklaces, valuable torques given as tokens of the relationship between the royal family and their warrior guard. The removal of the queen follows the death of her husband, while the necklaces are carried off because the men meant to wear them have lost their lives. The scop could be warning that, should Beowulf and his men not be treated now with utmost civility, they may similarly carry off Wealhtheow, Hrothgar's queen, and the necklaces belonging to Hrothgar's bodyguard. When this narrative within a narrative concludes, Wealhtheow responds to it indirectly by advising her husband to satisfy Beowulf with gifts and respectful words without, however, going so far as to give away to him the status which otherwise would go to one of her sons.[14] Her words subtly suggest to her husband the way for him to manage this very delicate situation:

---

[14] Sam Newton, in *The Origins of "Beowulf"* (1993; Cambridge: D. S. Brewer, 1994), pp. 92ff, makes an attractive argument that it is Hrothulf, Hrothgar's nephew, who poses the most immediate and serious dynastic challenge to Hrethric and Hrothmund, Hrothgar's sons. Even if one does want to see in the *Beowulf* narrative some grounds for a legendary exile of Hrothulf from Denmark and emigration to Britain, Wealhtheow makes it clear in her speech that it is the rumor of Beowulf's adoption by Hrothgar that most troubles her. She addresses her husband on the principles that she assumes to be guiding his actions, namely, adoption of Beowulf as a means to acquire a "hererinc." (This word may safely be

CHAPTER FIVE

> Onfoh þissum fulle, freodrihten min,
> sinces brytta! þu on sælum wes,
> goldwine gumena, ond to Geatum spræc
> mildum wordum, swa sceal man don!
> Beo wið Geatas glæd, geofena gemyndig,
> nean ond feorran þu nu hafast.
> Me man sægde þæt þu ðe for sunu wolde
> hererinc habban. Heorot is gefælsod,
> beahsele beorhta; bruc þenden þu mote
> manigra medo, ond þinum magum læf
> folc ond rice, þonne ðu forð scyle
> metodsceaft seon. (1169-80a)

Take this cup my noble lord, giver of treasure. Be glad, gold-friend of warriors, and speak to the Geats with mild words, as a man ought to do. Be gracious to the Geats, mindful of gifts [which] you now have from near and far. They have told me that you would have the warrior for your son. Heorot is purged, the bright ring-hall. Enjoy while you may many rewards, and leave to your kinsmen folk and kingdom when you must go forth to look on the Ruler's decree.

Turning to Beowulf, whom she finds seated beside her two sons, Wealhtheow makes her own gifts, while publicly she states:

> Bruc ðisses beages, Beowulf leofa,
> hyse, mid hæle, ond þisses hrægles neot,
> þeodgestreona, ond geþeoh tela,
> cen þec mid cræfte ond þyssum cnyhtum wes
> lara liðe; ic þe þæs lean geman.
> Hafast þu gefered, þæt ðe feor ond neah
> ealne wideferhþ weras ehtigað,
> efne swa side swa sæ bebugeð,
> windgeard, weallas. Wes þenden þu lifige,
> æþeling, eadig. Ic þe an tela
> sincgestreona. Beo þu suna minum
> dædum gedefe, dreamhealdende!
> Her is æghwylc eorl oþrum getrywe,
> modes milde, mandrihtne hold,

---

translated as "warrior" but might through the compound "army-warrior" also carry the connotation "champion.") "Heorot has been cleansed," she points out to Hrothgar, suggesting to him that a "hererinc" is no longer urgently needed. Furthermore, Hrothulf, whom she believes to be "glaedne"—"kind," "gracious," and "glorious," can be relied on, she knows, to act for the young warriors in their best interest ("þæt he þa geogoðe wile arum healdan"—1181b-2a).

þegnas syndon geþwære,	þeod ealgearo,
druncne dryhtguman	doð swa ic bidde. (1216-31)

Wear this ring, beloved Beowulf, young man, with good luck, and make use of this mail-shirt from the people's treasure, and prosper well; make yourself known with your might, and be kind of counsel to these boys: I shall remember to reward you for that. You have brought it about that, far and near, for a long time all men shall praise you, as wide as the sea surrounds the shores, home of the winds. While you live, prince, be prosperous. I wish you well of your treasure. Much favored one, be kind of deeds to my son. Here is each earl true to other, mild of heart, loyal to his lord; the thanes are at one, the people obedient, the retainers cheered with drink do as I bid.

Twice in her speech, Wealhtheow mentions her desire that Beowulf respect the Scylding heirs, both in his counsel and in his deeds. She points out that a delicate balance has been achieved among the Danes—the earls are true, well-intentioned, and loyal. Retainers and people alike are obedient. And Beowulf, for his help, is to be praised as far as the shores of the surrounding seas, which means that he has nothing to fear throughout Scylding territory. No Dane would dare attack him. If he is mindful of Wealhtheow's thanks, no Dane will have cause to attack him.

Together, Wealhtheow, Hrothgar, and Beowulf, in effect, set the course for future relations between the Geats and Danes. The scop's lay has warned them that a misstep could end in disaster. Wealhtheow seems to see very clearly how best to proceed. In this instance, Hrothgar and Beowulf also play out their roles well; the king offers a profusion of gifts, including valuable weapons especially betokening Beowulf's successful single combat, while, for his part, Beowulf looks for no reward or power beyond the receipt of such tokens. Having volunteered to fight alone, solely for the sake of the victims that he would save and the fame that this will bring him, Beowulf has displayed behavior ideal in a champion. Relying on his own strength, he has met and grappled with a formidable enemy. Now that this contest is over, he treats his hosts with courtesy, making no further demands upon them. Hrothgar and Wealhtheow, in turn, display behavior ideal in a royal couple. They have at heart the best interest of their kingdom. Retaining wealth only in order to bestow it upon their retainers and, when necessary, upon a guest warrior, they manage to attract a champion to their service and then to send him away again in friendship.

Hrothgar treads a fine line between cowardice and poor judgment, knowing when not to take on Grendel, preferring to vacate his own hall rather than lose his life in an act of bravado. His judgment in this instance can perhaps be compared to Beowulf's late in his own life, when his territories are challenged and his hall burnt to the ground by a fire-breathing dragon. Indeed, the parallels are more than coincidental. Both kings rule fifty years.[15] Both lose their halls due to the predation of an inhuman aggressor. Both are powerless against the monster's magic. Yet Hrothgar's kingdom is saved, while Beowulf's is doomed to annihilation.[16]

A king's desire to keep his twisted gold rings rather than distribute them stems from a two-fold miscalculation. First, he calculates that the gold is of some intrinsic worth to him. Second, he forgets that he will someday weaken and need help. Hrothgar, anticipating Beowulf's eventual ascension to kingship of the Geats and foreseeing a long and successful reign in store for him, in fact, warns Beowulf against the latter error, the one to which he will, despite this warning, eventually fall victim:

>   Nu is þines mægnes blæd
> ane hwile.   Eft sona bið
> þæt þec adl oððe ecg   eafoþes getwæfeð,
> oððe fyres feng,   oððe flodes wylm,
> oððe gripe meces,   oððe gares fliht,
> oððe atol yldo;   oððe eagena bearhtm
> forsiteð ond forsworceð;   semninga bið,
> þæt ðec, dryhtguma,   deað oferswyðeð. (1761b-68)

Now for a time there is glory in your might: yet soon it shall be that sickness or sword will diminish your strength, or fire's fangs, or flood's surge, or sword's swing, or spear's flight, or appalling age; brightness of eyes will fail and grow dark; then it shall be that death will overcome you, warrior.

Foreseeing all this, Hrothgar offers himself as an example to the young Beowulf. Misfortune has taken him by surprise, and he recognizes that Beowulf is a candidate for the same fate:

---

[15] Murdoch points out that the two fifty-year reigns connect Hrothgar and Beowulf (p. 70), but, though he cites Hrothgar's admonition to young Beowulf that "age defeats every warrior," he nevertheless fails to see that Beowulf ignores this advice and must therefore bear some responsibility for the Geats' doom. I, therefore, find it difficult to accept Murdoch's description of Beowulf's journey as "a learning process" (p. 62)—unless by this is meant that the audience is educated from it, for Beowulf does not learn how to pass his responsibilities on to a successor. Beowulf may rule as long as his strength enables him to, and even beyond, until his strength is tested by the dragon, but then the shortcomings in his rule become all too apparent, and the fifty years of success are wiped out.

[16] Gunther may also be judged a "good king" at the moment when, like Hrothgar, he waits for the appropriate champion to step forward to meet Siegfried's challenge (str. 119). Of course, Gunther seems to have a reputation for perfidy rather than battle (at least to judge by Siegmund's trepidation on behalf of his son), so there seems to be little chance that he would unwisely venture out against such an opponent.

THE KING AND HIS GIFTS

>   Swa ic Hringdena   hund missera
>   weold under wolcnum   ond hig wigge beleac
>   manigum mægþa   geond þysne middangeard,
>   æscum ond ecgum,   þæt ic me ænigne
>   under swegles begong   gesacan ne tealde.
>   Hwæt, me þæs on eþle   edwenden cwom,
>   gyrn æfter gomene,   seoþðan Grendel wearð,
>   ealdgewinna,   ingenga min;
>   ic þære socne   singales wæg
>   modceare micle. (1769-78a)

Thus I ruled the Ring-Danes for a hundred half-years under the skies, and protected them in war with spear and sword against many nations over middle-earth, so that I counted no one as my adversary underneath the sky's expanse. Well, disproof of that came to me in my own land, grief after my joys, when Grendel, ancient adversary, came to invade my home. Great sorrow of heart I have always suffered for his persecution.

Grendel has deprived Hrothgar of his hall "fela missera" (153b)—"many half years" and this has amounted to a humiliation for Hrothgar, a heartfelt sorrow and a blemish on his fame. Nevertheless, he has lived to see the remedy, Grendel's bloodstained head, brought up to him by Beowulf from the lake bottom where the monster died.

Beowulf, when he has ruled fifty winters, will likewise be plagued by a monstrous invader. Unlike Hrothgar, however, he will not have the patience to endure many half-years of patient waiting for a champion. Still playing the role of his own champion, he will insist upon taking on the dragon himself. Unlike Hrothgar, Beowulf will not have set the stage for a young volunteer to come clamoring for permission to meet the dragon alone. Beowulf will fall to the weakness of his own advancing age but also to his imprudence for failing to recognize the need for a champion.

Worse than Beowulf's death itself, however, is the vulnerable position in which this leaves his people. The gold hoard that had belonged to the dragon is to be of no use to the Geats because Beowulf dies without arranging for a successor. He fails to take advantage of the treasures already at his disposal to attract a new champion for the people's protection. The fact that he himself fights the dragon is proof positive of this fact. After his death, any wealth known to exist in the Geats' possession will therefore invite invasion rather than repel it. The hoard of ancient arms left by the dragon becomes an added liability, not an asset. That it should be burnt upon Beowulf's pyre is not only fitting but prudent. Beowulf has always been successful in acquiring wealth, but he has been unsuccessful in distributing it. With Beowulf's death, the people are bereft not only of their champion but also of their gold-giver, whose function it should have been to arrange for a new champion. Their king no longer lives to distribute the dragon's treasure.

The ancient hoard is of no more use to Beowulf than it was to the dragon. The dragon had lived entirely alone, beyond all society, jealously guarding a treasure that was of no use to it, but the same can be said of Beowulf. Though he has a people, he neglects his function, distracted in his later years by the drives that had made him a success as a young man—the desire for fame and the gifts that signify success in that pursuit. His attachment to gold and weapons are now improperly placed. Good at winning gifts, he is poor at redistributing them. Whereas a champion must accumulate gifts as a measure of his fame, a king has need of wealth only insofar as he is successful in finding a worthy recipient for it. The good king is one who dies leaving to his people not a storehouse full of treasure but a proven champion whose reputation ensures peaceful relations with neighbors and allies against invaders.

Beowulf's death signifies his failure as a king and, in fact, defines that failure in terms of his inability to turn the trick of separating in himself the two statuses and their functions so as to divest himself, as he ages, of the younger man's role. The latter he would have transferred to a volunteer attracted to the land of the Geats by reports of the fire-breathing dragon's ravages, which lay waste to the countryside and threaten to make the villages and forts uninhabitable. The dragon presents Beowulf with the ideal opportunity to test the availability and quality of a possible champion. The fitness of a volunteer, especially if he should propose that he be allowed to fight alone, would be measured by the dragon. Beowulf, however, though conscious of his age, still refuses to consider any volunteer other than himself. He still seeks fame and gold, not appreciating the fact that his own death means destruction for all Geats, because it will advertise the fact to all possible predators that the land is entirely without an adequate protector.

Wiglaf, the warrior who perhaps should have been allowed to test his mettle against the dragon and who does, in fact, deliver the death blow, indicates with the following pronouncement that he fully appreciates what Beowulf's death must mean for the Geats:

> Nu sceal sincþego   ond swyrdgifu,
> eall eðelwyn   eowrum cynne,
> lufen alicgean;   londrihtes mot
> þære mægburge   monna æghwylc
> idel hweorfan,   syððan æðelingas
> feorran gefricgean   fleam eowerne,
> domleasan dæd.   Deað bið sella
> eorla gehwylcum   þonne edwitlif! (2884-91)

Now there shall cease for your race the receiving of treasure and the giving of swords, all enjoyment of pleasant homes, comfort. Each man of your kindred must go deprived of his land-right when nobles from afar learn of your flight, your inglorious deed. Death is better for any earl than a life of blame.

Wiglaf knows what the Geats have in store for them and why. The "domleasan dæd"—"inglorious deed"—of which he speaks is this: "Wergendra to lyt þrong ymbe þeoden, þa hyne sio þrag becwom" (2882b-3)—"Too few defenders thronged about the prince when the hard time came upon him." The expression is, of course, litotes; no Geats at all thronged about their prince. Wiglaf himself rushes to his aid but only after he is in trouble. Against Grendel, Beowulf had known to dispense with a sword, confident in the strength of his grip. In the fight against the dragon, however, he proves that he is no longer the champion that he once had been.

The obligation of thanes is to protect their lord. For this function, he entertains them in the hall and provides them with treasure and equipment including valuable iron helmets and mail shirts. But thanes are meant only to protect the prince against attacks from flank or rear, for his own strength must be great enough to win a victory over the challenger who steps up to face him. When he is not strong enough to meet the challenger himself, then a champion must be found to take his place.[17]

Wiglaf calls for an announcement of the king's death to the general populace in words that recount the names of the Geats' old enemies and recall the grievances that will propel each of them to renew their wars with the Geats when they learn that the Geats' protector is dead.[18] The grim prophecy is

---

[17] Using the *comitatus* as a model for judging this situation, Frey finds that Wiglaf "technically" need not serve Beowulf in the way that Beowulf has served Hrothgar, for Beowulf orders his "*comitatus* group" to "stand off," thus creating a conflict between the *comitatus* bond of obedience and its sworn oaths of comradeship (p. 57). Nor does Frey miss the fact that Wiglaf is a Swede among Geats, just as Beowulf at Hrothgar's court had been a Geat among Danes. Remaining within the constraints of an interpretation of the situation in terms of the *comitatus*, Frey can only understand the foreigner as "acting the role of follower" with the consequence that "the heroic workings of *comitatus* [are] realized along one-to-one human lines" (p. 58). While commenting directly on those aspects of the narrative that point up the differences between king, champion, and thanes, Frey's prejudgment of the social organization works continually against the specificity of his observations, forcing upon them the simpler dualism of a "classic Germanic junior-senior relationship" under which rubric the discrepancies appear to be the "variations the poet has developed" (p. 58).

[18] Contrasting Beowulf's funeral with that of the legendary Scyld (described in the poem's opening lines), Frey points out that the warrior-king's lavish burial carries "the suggestion that heroism has a cultural and clannish immortality about it" (p. 60). Because Beowulf leaves no heir (p. 60), because Wiglaf is "not a future Beowulf" (p. 58), Beowulf's death is fraught with foreboding, suggesting cultural and clannish morbidity. "Scyld's efforts promise establishment and continuity," in Frey's view, "Beowulf's have been ultimately personal and individual, guaranteeing his name and fame and little more" (p. 60). Frey all but states that the king has responsibility for the survival of his people through the provision of an heir—not so much to the throne, as to the name of champion. The elderly king's insistence on fighting alone is inapppropriate, for his death will bring calamity. Responsibility for this transfer of power rests equally, of course, with the warrior most able to perform the duties of champion, for he must seek the name by volunteering to act alone. As Renoir sees it, the failure of both men—the king and his best warrior—therefore cannot be interpreted as a "victory" (p. 130).

taken up and expressed anew most succinctly by a Geatish woman, who sings a "song sorgcearig" (3152a)—"sorrowful song"—ostensibly about Beowulf, but more particularly expressing "þæt hio hyre hearmdagas hearde ondrede, / wælfylla worn, werudes egesan, / hynðo ond hæftnyd" (3153-55a)— "that she sorely feared for herself invasions of armies, many slaughters, terror of troops, humiliation, and captivity." An annihilation like that visited upon Troy is now to befall the Geats.

What the Geatish woman summarizes is developed at greater length in the thane's report to the city. His report is interesting because it recalls two other instances of warfare. The first tale is short and serves as an introduction to the theme of the longer tale that follows.

>   Nu ys leodum wen
> orleghwile,   syððan underne
> Froncum ond Frysum fyll cyninges
> wide weorðeð.   Wæs sio wroht scepen
> heard wið Hugas,   syððan Higelac cwom
> faran flotherge   on Fresna land,
> þær hyne Hetware   hilde genægdon,
> elne geeodon   mid ofermægene,
> þæt se byrnwiga   bugan sceolde,
> feoll on feðan,   nalles frætwe geaf
> ealdor dugoðe.   Us wæs a syððan
> Merewioingas   milts ungyfeðe. (2910b-21)

"Now may the people expect a time of war, when the king's fall becomes wide-known to the Franks and Frisians. A harsh quarrel was begun with the Hugas when Hygelac came traveling with his sea-army to the land of the Frisians, where the Hetware assailed him in battle, quickly, with stronger forces, made the mailed warrior bow; he fell in the ranks: that chief gave no treasure to his retainers. Ever since then the good will of the Merewioing king has been denied us."

The theme of this prediction, as in the tale that follows and the contextual event to which the old woman responds with her sorrowful song, is a king's death in battle. Hygelac had, of course, been Beowulf's king, and his death thus points up the possible miscalculation of going to battle without his champion. Indeed, Hygelac's death has twice previously been mentioned in the poem, first, as Wealhtheow rewards Beowulf for killing Grendel with a torque that he would later, upon his return home, present to his lord Hygelac. Hygelac is wearing this very neck-ring when he is killed, and it then falls

---

Renoir unfortunately elevates the dead Beowulf to the status of "an ideal Germanic king" by ignoring explicit judgments pertaining to the doom about to befall the kingdom (p. 130). Claiming, contrary to all evidence, that the dragon's death saves the kingdom from impending destruction, Renoir finds further value in the treasure despite the narrative's protestations of its uselessness (p. 130).

into the hands of the Franks who despoil his corpse. The torque thus traces the relationship between several events, including Beowulf's success against Grendel, Wealhtheow's proper reward for his service as champion, Beowulf's presentation of his credentials to Hygelac, Beowulf's subsequent service to the Geats as a member of Hygelac's retinue, Hygelac's death, and finally Beowulf's own death and the anticipated return of war with the Franks. This complex overlaying of stories places together in a single context the repeated circumstances of the neck-ring's function as an icon of service sought and rendered. To Hygelac, the torque represents the potential of a service of which he does not avail himself. Beowulf's death thus evokes a memory that the fallen chief "nalles frætwe geaf"—"gave no treasure." The statement applies to both kings, Hygelac and Beowulf. Indeed, neither offers a reward, and the reward therefore goes unearned and unclaimed. In this connection, Beowulf has been both an ineffectual champion, because he was not called upon to perform in that function by Hygelac, and an ineffectual king, because he did not call upon Wiglaf or another to present himself for service as champion. From this perspective, Beowulf's fitness for the Geatish throne is called into question. Was he a good king?

The poem's second reference to Hygelac's death is presented at the moment when Beowulf is weighing his decision to fight the dragon. Two previous battles now come into his mind: his purging of Hrothgar's hall and his great difficulty in coming away from the Frisians and Hetware after Hygelac is killed, at which point Beowulf is beset by such a storm of sword strokes that he can get away only by entering the sea and swimming, though fully armed and carrying trophies of thirty men he had slain. He returns home "earm anhaga" (2368a)—"forlorn and alone"—to Hygd, Hygelac's queen, who offers him "hord ond rice, beagas ond bregostol" (2369b-70a)—"hoard and kingdom, rings and a prince's throne." The hoard and the rings he never distributes—not out of greed but because whenever he stands in need of a champion, as in the present instance, he remembers his own deeds of valor. Hygd's selection of him as king proves a wise choice only as long as his reputation remains intact. If it is learned that his strength is gone, the Geats can expect to be visited again by their enemies, such as the Franks and Swedes.

An attack by the Swedes is, in fact, anticipated by the messenger reporting Beowulf's death to the Geats. The old enmity of the Swedes toward the Geats, expected now to manifest itself in the Geats' destruction, is illustrated by yet another story involving Hygelac, who, in this episode, will exhibit proper kingly generosity by adequately rewarding the men who furnish him with victory. On campaign against the Swedes, Haethcyn, king of the Geats and Hygelac's older brother, has been killed and his warriors put to rout. The survivors spend an anxious night sheltering in the woods, anticipating a slaughter on the morrow. The light of dawn brings with it, however, the sound of Hygelac's trumpet as he brings his reserves to the rescue. Ongentheow, the elderly Swedish king, "hæfde Higelaces hilde gefrunen, wlonces wigcræft" (2952-53a)—"had heard of the warring of Hygelac, of the war-power of the proud one" and so withdraws into the protection of an earth-wall

CHAPTER FIVE

fort, which is soon overrun by the Geats, forcing the Swedish king to pull back into his citadel where two Geats, the brothers Wulf and Eofor, take him on in turn. Wulf is wounded and falls, but his brother then steps up and finishes off Ongentheow.

>   Ða wæron monige   þe his mæg wriðon,
>   ricone arærdon,   ða him gerymed wearð,
>   þæt hie wælstowe   wealdan moston.
>   þenden reafode   rinc oðerne,
>   nam on Ongenðio   irenbyrnan,
>   heard swyrd hilted   ond his helm somod;
>   hares hyrste   Higelace bær.
>   He ðam frætwum feng   ond him fægre gehet
>   leana mid leodum,   ond gelæste swa;
>   geald þone guðræs   Geata dryhten,
>   Hreðles eafora,   þa he to ham becom,
>   Iofore ond Wulfe   mid ofermaðmum,
>   sealde hiora gehwæðrum   hund þusenda
>   landes ond locenra beaga,— ne ðorfte him ða lean oðwitan
>   mon on middangearde,   syððan hie ða mærða geslogon;
>   ond ða Iofore forgeaf   angan dohtor,
>   hamweorðunge,   hyldo to wedde. (2982-98)

> Then there were many who bound up the brother, quickly raised him up after it was granted them to control the battlefield. Then one warrior stripped the other, took from Ongentheow his iron-mail, hard-hilted sword, and his helmet, too; he bore the arms of the hoary one to Hygelac. He accepted that treasure and fairly promised him rewards among the people, and he stood by it thus: the lord of the Geats, the son of Hrethel, when he came home, repaid Wulf and Eofor for their battle-assault with much treasure, gave each of them a hundred thousand [units] of land and linked rings: there was no need for any man on middle-earth to blame him for the rewards, since they had performed great deeds. And then he gave Eofor his only daughter as a pledge of friendship—a fair thing for his home.

The story told to illustrate impending doom for the Geats thus actually ends by recalling the strength and security that they once had enjoyed. The messenger contrasts his baleful vision of utmost misery and hopelessness to come with an image of happier days from the past.

   At the center of his grim assessment, the messenger proclaims that the entire treasure must be burned with the king's corpse. While the destruction of material goods is not explained, it can be inferred that they would be useless to the Geats and indeed would encumber the survivors with an even greater share of woe, because to possess a treasure would entail a fight to retain control over it, and this in turn would mean the death of all who might attempt to pursue such a policy. Therefore, the treasure is better done without.[19] Even lacking a fight to the death over the treasure, the Geats can anticipate dreadful hardship to come. The messenger's concluding remarks leave no ray of hope:

>   þæt ys sio fæhðo   ond se feondscipe,
>   wælnið wera,   ðæs ðe ic wen hafo,
>   þe us secead to   Sweona leoda,
>   syððan hie gefricgead   frean userne
>   ealdorleasne,   þone ðe ær geheold
>   wið hettendum   hord ond rice,
>   æfter hæleða hryre,   hwate scildwigan,
>   folcred fremede   oððe furður gen
>   eorlscipe efnde.   Nu is ofost betost
>   þæt we þeodcyning   þær sceawian,
>   ond þone gebringan,   þe us beagas geaf,
>   on adfære.   Ne scel anes hwæt
>   meltan mid þam modigan, ac þær is maðma hord,
>   gold unrime   grimme geceapod,
>   ond nu æt siðestan   sylfes feore
>   beagas gebohte;   þa sceall brond fretan,
>   æled þeccean, —   nalles eorl wegan
>   maððum to gemyndum,   ne mægð scyne
>   habban on healse   hringweorðunge,
>   ac sceal geomormod,   golde bereafod,
>   oft nalles æne   elland tredan,
>   nu se herewisa   hleahtor alegde,
>   gamen ond gleodream.   Forðon sceall gar wesan
>   monig morgenceald   mundum bewunden,
>   hæfen on handa,   nalles hearpan sweg
>   wigend weccean,   ac se wonna hrefn
>   fus ofer fægum   fela reordian,
>   earne secgan   hu him æt æte speow,
>   þenden he wið wulf   wæl reafode.   (2999-3027)

That is the feud and the enmity, the death-hatred of men, for which I expect that the people of the Swedes, bold shield-warriors after the fall of princes, will set upon us after they learn that our prince has gone from life, he who

---

[19] Hagen's sinking of Kriemhild's Nibelungen hoard into the river Rhine can possibly once have had a significance related to the treasure's potential for attracting unwanted trouble. Clearly, the hoard could be directly useful to Kriemhild in acquiring the services of a champion, but the accumulation in Hagen's possession is a liability, for it attracts rivals, just as once the Nibelungs fought over it and Siegfried, "chancing" on their fight, killed them both and took the prize for himself. If Hagen is unwilling to fight off challengers, the hoard represents a threat to him. But the Hagen presented in the *Nibelungenlied* is clearly not aware of any of these dangers. If the motif of sinking the treasure has any suggestion of its power to attract challengers, that meaning has been lost sight of in the story's present form.

> before held hoard and kingdom against our enemies, did good to the people, and further still, did what a man should. Now haste is best, that we look on the people's king there and bring him who gave us rings on his way to the funeral pyre. Nor shall only a small share melt with the great-hearted one, but there is a hoard of treasure, gold uncounted, grimly purchased, and rings bought at the last now with his own life. These shall the fire devour, flames enfold—no earl to wear ornament in remembrance, nor any bright maiden add to her beauty with neck-ring; but mournful-hearted, stripped of gold, they shall walk, often, not once, in strange countries—now that the army-leader has laid aside laughter, his game and his mirth. Therefore many a spear, cold in the morning, shall be grasped with fingers, raised by hands; no sound of harp shall waken the warriors, but the dark raven, low over the doomed, shall tell many tales, say to the eagle how he fared at the feast when with the wolf he spoiled the slain bodies.

This is their doom, grimmer even than the "servitude" offered by Goliath, comparable to the destruction of Troy, where the men are killed or escape to a difficult exile wandering among peoples hostile to them and the women and children are dragged off to a slavery of concubinage and forced labor, to be expected when a king dies who leaves not an established champion but a treasure, which is now to be read as the unrealized potential for the people's defense. The king's wealth is of no use if it is not put into the service of security. The king must not desire wealth for himself, such that he retain it or the honor it represents at the expense of a champion. The king must, moreover, be able to separate his function and status from that of the champion. Whereas Saul's jealousy of David brings about, in the end, his own demise, Gunther's murder of Siegfried, unlike Saul's failed spear throw, results in the destruction, not only of himself but of his entire military force. Achilles and Agamemnon restrain themselves from naked violence against each other, but the breakdown in relations between them is enough to cause the death of hosts of their men, including their own cherished companions.

CHAPTER SIX

THE QUEEN AND HER LOVERS

Within epic culture, there are a variety of strategies for resolving issues of succession. One divides the functions of king and champion between two males. Gifts of wealth and tokens of status are the practices principally responsible for maintaining a separation between these individuals. As we have seen, however, the relationship between king and champion is, at best, precarious. Furthermore, even when once status, fame, and wealth have been successfully exchanged for a champion's services, although the champion may stay on for a while as a guest of the court, he will eventually move on, either to search for new "adventures" (in effect, opportunities to increase his reputation) or to return to a settled life in his own country.

When he goes, he perforce leaves his host largely dependent once again on the military strength of his vassals and children. To compensate for this loss, an informal alliance may be forged between the king and his champion. Before leaving Heorot, for example, Beowulf offers to help Hrothgar if ever he should find himself besieged. Siegfried binds himself to Gunther both by the relationship established during the former's lengthy stay at Worms, including an expedition to Iceland for the purpose of wooing and winning Brünhild, and by his marriage to Kriemhild, which makes him Gunther's brother-in-law. Such alliances are always uneasy, however, because they depend upon the champion's continued good will. The king can never be sure of his former champion's intentions. He cannot be certain, for example, that his champion will return when needed, and, worse than that, he cannot know that his champion will not himself some day wish to annex the kingdom. And how could the king withstand such a move?

To secure the champion's good will and to dissuade him from challenging his sovereignty, the king might find it prudent occasionally to present him with renewed tokens of their friendship. To this end, he might invite his former champion to great festive celebrations. Such events make an ideal occasion for the presentation of new gifts, and, in this way, alliances can be maintained, renewed, and even strengthened. And yet the burden of such lavish hospitality might weigh upon the king, his court, and his subjects. He might be inclined or even pressured to curtail the obligations of friendship, either by neglecting to hold festivals or by laying plans to rid himself of his former ally. The uneasy relationship between a king and his champion thus later develops into an uneasy alliance between their courts.

Epic culture can address these issues by allowing the functions of king and champion to be carried out by a single individual. By combining the responsibilities for government and security in one person, conflict between king and champion is avoided. The reduction of risk in this area is purchased, however, at the possible cost of good government, since the champion may barely be more than a youth. His qualifications are those of a warrior, not a judge or an administrator.[1] And besides this unavoidable shortcoming, there is the even more troublesome issue of succession. If the king had a son capable of singlehanded defense, the kingdom could be passed on without undue disturbance to internal and external political relationships. When the prince is too young to have proven himself in battle, he might initially secure his vassals' loyalty by distributing fiefdoms and conferring upon them the rings betokening their status as warriors, but he represents an unacceptable substitute for his father in the place of combat between two armies. And it goes without saying that this will be his most immediate test. Whenever a king dies in battle, his people inevitably find themselves beset by challenges from neighbors and distant enemies alike. The kingdom thus suddenly finds itself faced with the proposition of battle behind a champion of untested caliber. Under these circumstances, it is essential to provide for an alternative method for selecting a successor to the twin posts of champion and ruler.[2]

---

[1] Pointing out that Hector is accused "of being always the same in council and in war, unable to brook contradiction," Bespaloff implies that the qualities of a warrior and a counselor are antithetical, which presents difficulties for the man who would be both, for while the warrior must be ever bent upon increasing his reputation, a leader should not be ever bent upon asserting his authority (p. 130).

[2] It is important to distinguish between the problems of succession in a society organized to address the circumstances of epic culture and those of another type of society that may to us appear in many respects similar. Under some epic-cultural circumstances, hereditary kingship can be the preferred solution to the problem of succession. The problem is, therefore, very complex and should not be prejudged.

Haymes, in his very insightful and interesting interpretation of the *Nibelungenlied* adopts the perspective of European royal succession circa A.D. 1200 as a filter for evaluating behavior at the courts of Burgundy and Xanten as presented in the epic narrative. As a result of this identification, the relationship between narrative detail and historical context (defined with respect to issues of succession) is presumed, with the result that such details as are available are employed only as a confirmation that the narrative indeed conforms to the selected interpretive model. It may be the case, of course, that aspects of the *Nibelungenlied* do pertain to the problems of succession in a courtly system that facilitates the central administration of an extended political, military, and economic hierarchy, but we have seen that other aspects of the same narrative focus upon the set of circumstances pertaining to the battlefield and corresponding to the economy of lives central to the formation of epic culture, its practices and institutions. This latter focus is missed by Haymes, however, simply because it is absent from his sources of knowledge about European courts circa A.D. 1200. Whether the European courtly system circa 1200 is an outgrowth of epic culture or an independent alternative to it (and there are further possibilities) is a question that remains to be addressed. Because evidence for both systems is to be found in the narrative, it could well be argued that the latter, in the form that we have it at least, addresses the conflict that must arise if these two cultural systems were to encounter one another. The "relevance" of the epic narrative material to the courtly context circa 1200 thus deserves careful consideration.

This extremely delicate problem is very neatly solved by investing an interim government with the authority to govern and provide for defense by presiding over the selection process. Epic culture provides for this circumstance by designating in advance the person who is to handle the very particular responsibilities of interim government. That person is the queen.[3] The queen rules the land while searching for a new champion to replace her dead husband. If her country is under attack, she is in urgent need of a champion. Her task is to find a knight who is willing and able to ward off the invader. It is unlikely that one of her own vassals would be capable of defending the kingdom, because otherwise the king should never have been killed. She must, therefore, attract the services of a foreign knight.

Knights in quest of fame, fortune, or status can be counted on to travel to the aid of any castle known to be under siege. Such castles lack a champion and are ruled either by an elderly king or a widowed queen. While an elderly king rewards his champion by adopting him (Hrothgar's impulse) or by marrying him to one of his daughters (as Gawan is offered Bene in *Parzival*), a widowed or unmarried queen signifies her approval of a new champion by making him her husband and regent. The queen rewards a volunteer who proves successful in driving off her enemies not with the usual tokens of success—armor and arm rings—but with a crown and wedding ring.

It may happen, however, that when the king dies, his land is not under attack. He may die of natural causes or an accident, or he may die abroad fighting in aid of an ally. Finally, it is possible that the queen would seek to replace an aging king-champion before he should have the opportunity to suffer a defeat. In this instance, she presides over her husband's ritual killing so as to make room for the replacement she has selected.[4] The queen does not, in any of these scenarios, have the opportunity of testing candidates in an actual battle. She must, therefore, simulate the circumstances of battle by staging a well-designed contest.[5]

---

[3] Butterworth accepts it "as a fact that the Mycenaean kings . . . came to power through marriage with, or relationship to, the women of certain dynastic clans" (p. 14). Referring to Sir James George Frazer's argument in *The Golden Bough: A Study in Magic and Religion* (London: Macmillan Publishers, 1907), Butterworth notes "that there was evidence that the right to the kingship was transmitted in the female line, and that it was actually exercised by foreigners who married the royal princesses" (p. 14) and that "it seemed that these men might be of lowly birth, provided that otherwise, for instance physically, they were suitable mates" (p. 15); thus, it is "the women of a royal house who were consistently devoted to a particular cult and to maintaining dynastic connections" (p. 58). Butterworth finds that the function of the royal women in selecting the king is supported by cultic and mythic evidence for a matrilineal social organization.

[4] For this point, I draw upon Butterworth's reconstruction of a matrilinear substrate in the *Odyssey* (see particularly pp. 102-05).

[5] Butterworth presents for example the story of Pelops's winning of Hippodameia, in which "some sort of contest preceded the betrothal, and the strong man won the royal bride" (p. 15).

If the quality she most prizes in a king is his ability to protect the country against invasion, then her contest will take the form of a tournament or a quest. The prize she offers is herself. The warriors vie with one another for her hand in marriage. To the winner, she awards her royal crown and scepter.[6] Those who fail in their bid, because they are the new king's former rivals, must be dealt with carefully. They may be killed immediately following the contest (Iceland), accept the new king as their superior (Ithaka), or pledge themselves in an alliance with the new royal power (Achaea).

The Greek epic tradition depicts kingdoms that are organized along precisely these lines. Helen is won by Menelaus in a contest. The participants in that contest had, however, previously pledged themselves to each other in a mutual defense pact. The losers retain their local independence while forming a regional alliance. When Menelaus's sovereignty is broached by Paris, then, the Achaean allies join together in the war against Troy. Each of the allied kings involved in the expedition against Troy is both king and champion in his own realm. When he goes abroad, each leaves behind him a queen to rule in his absence. These queens are all well qualified as interim rulers, since they govern alone whenever their husbands go abroad. In the event of a king's death, the queen will continue her rule until she has selected and married a successor.

The prophecy that Oedipus would kill his father and marry his mother is really not as unlikely as it first sounds.[7] Whoever kills Laius makes a widow of queen Jocasta, thus initiating her search for a new husband. The man able to kill a champion-king like Laius (who goes abroad accompanied only by a few retainers) would naturally pass any test of strength or valor devised by the queen. Just so, during the contest established by Penelope to select a new husband, Telemachus very nearly strings his father's bow.[8] Since in Thebes championship is bound to kingship and marriage to the queen, Oedipus will inevitably succeed to the throne and marry Jocasta.

---

[6] As Hugo Bekker observes, in "Kingship in the *Nibelungenlied*," *Germanic Review*, 41 (November 1966), 256, "with Brünhilt strength and crown are inextricably united by virtue of her virginity, and a . . . conqueror will—indeed, *must*—have not only her virginity, but also her crown." Further references will be cited parenthetically in the text.

[7] Interpreting myth, Butterworth infers from Oedipus's answer to the Sphinx's riddle that the king was an old man, while the fact that the Sphinx set the riddle implies that the people's affliction was related to the king's age (p. 46). Oedipus's killing of the king would not, in Butterworth's estimation, have been an accident, and the story only conceals this truth. He concludes, therefore, that "Oedipus of course did not marry his mother: he married Laïos' widow, and only by so doing could he become king" (p. 47).

[8] See the *Odyssey* 21.128, to which my attention was called by Kenneth Atchity and E. J. W. Barber in their "Greek Princes and Aegean Princesses: The Role of Women in the Homeric Poems," *Critical Essays on Homer*, p. 21. Further references will be cited parenthetically in the text.

According to the myth, Thebes comes under attack by a monster. As Grendel does, the Sphinx lays waste to the population. Also like Grendel, the Sphinx's magic properties define the qualities of that person who will put an end to the devastation. The Sphinx, however, poses a test not of brawn but of wit. By killing Laius, Oedipus has already proven himself to be the better fighter, so by answering the Sphinx's riddle, he qualifies himself to succeed Laius as chief executive. Publicly, it is the riddle that entitles Oedipus to the crown. The sign of his accession is Jocasta's taking him as her husband.

As chief law enforcement officer, it falls on the shoulders of Oedipus to discover and punish Laius's killer. Sophocles's tragedy emphasizes the king's executive talents, especially as these interface with the Delphic oracle, which offers itself to the various Greek city-states as an outside source of advice, a neutral site for negotiation, and an impartial arbitrator for disputes. The mythic background for the play, however, makes the point that whenever a king dies violently, the selection process installed to replace him will very likely settle upon his killer. Whoever is capable of killing Laius would also be able to prove himself either in battle or in any artificial test of strength and fighting skill. In the older forms of the story, one would expect the Sphinx to have presented a challenge in wrestling rather than riddling.

Laius dies suddenly and unexpectedly after a very brief absence. Queen Jocasta is therefore seemingly unprepared. In the case of a king's extended absence, however, normally the queen must plan for the possibility of his replacement. If he is killed on campaign, she will need to defend herself and her domain against invasion and takeover. In fact, the news of her husband's death could actually precipitate an attack from her neighbors. A queen is therefore obliged to begin the work of identifying and securing the services of a suitable champion even before she learns that her husband has actually met his end.[9]

The warrior without a kingdom and the queen whose husband is away at war have a natural attraction to one another. He has hopes of succeeding to her throne, while she sees the chance to secure herself and her people against naked aggression. He, therefore, most courteously places himself at her disposal. She, for her part, hospitably invites him to stay as her court's guest. Consequently, during the king's absences, his queen and her guests court one another, and because news of the king's death is always imminent, marriage

---

[9] The dilemma faced by Penelope is given another interpretation by Atchity and Barber, who situate the Homeric poems at the crossroads of two cultural systems: a patrilineal Indo-European immigrant male stock (Greek "nobles" and chieftains from the north) marrying princesses of the indigenous Aegean population "presumably as a bid to get control of their lands" (p. 15). Penelope's temptation, then, in the absence of her patriarchal Greek husband, is to "revert" to matriliny by accepting as a second husband one of the indigenous suitors more than willing "to play the suicidal role of matrilineal king-designate, pressuring Penelope to choose one of them to displace Odysseus and the patriarchy" (p. 21). What makes the suitors' gambit suicidal is the fact that the patriarchal Odysseus cannot be expected to accept his wife's selection of a replacement.

between such lovers is not at all an unlikely proposition. The courtly love ritual is, thus, by no means an idle or frivolous pastime.[10]

The trick is for the queen and her lovers to hold such courtship within the bounds of decorum, for the king may yet return. To him, such a man's championship would be unnecessary and his presence odious, for he inevitably would be a rival.[11] The queen must, therefore, hold the interest of her stand-by champion without entirely committing herself to him. The champion must remain near, ever at her call, yet without trespassing into the king's bedchamber.[12] Discretion and secrecy are incumbent upon the "lovers." From the constraints imposed upon them by these circumstances develops the delicate art of courtly love, including knightly love service (*minnedienst*) and the passing of artfully anonymous love notes (*minnesang*).

In Odysseus's long absence, Penelope spins a very fine web between herself and the band of suitors who would marry her. She both attracts them and yet delays in making a commitment to marry any one of them. She must "μνηστήρεσσι φανῆναι" (18.165)—"show myself to my suitors"—while "ἰσχέμεναί τε μνηστῆρας κατὰ δώματ'" (20.330-31)—"holding back and keeping the suitors waiting." Here is how the interaction is described:

ἡ δ' ὅτε δὴ μνηστῆρας ἀφίκετο δῖα γυναικῶν.
στῆ ῥα παρὰ σταθμὸν τέγεος πύκα ποιητοῖο
ἄντα παρειάων σχομένη λιπαρὰ κρήδεμνα·
ἀμφίπολος δ' ἄρα οἱ κεδνὴ ἑκάτερφε παρέστη.
τῶν δ' αὐτοῦ λύτο γούνατ'. ἔρῳ δ' ἄρα θυμὸν ἔθελχθεν.
πάντες δ' ἠρήσαντο παραὶ λεχέεσσι κλιθῆναι. (18.208-13)

When she came near to her Suitors the great lady drew a fold of her shining veil across her cheeks and took her stand by a pillar of the masssive roof,

---

[10] Modern moralizing, such as is expressed by Voegelin's judgment that Paris "should not start an affair with the wife of his host" (p. 65), lacks the recognition that attraction between guests and their hosts' wives has purposes other than carnal appetite. To label Paris's relationship with Helen as an "affair" is to reduce its importance and, in so doing, to rob the war of a cause appropriate to its cost. To assign only Paris responsibility for "starting" the affair is to deny the queen her powers and responsibilities.

[11] Of the period during the transition between a Mycenean world to what he calls the Apolline cult of archaic Greece, Butterworth observes that "matrilineal dynasties evidently became, on occasion at least, centres of savage competition among the more ambitious men of the time, succession to the kingship . . . being decided by brute force" (p. 50).

[12] Such trespass is either "suicidal" or must accompany a murderous intention. At Ithaca, the indiscretion of openly wooing Penelope brings death to the suitors. At Mycenae, the lovers preempt the king's discovery of their transgression by planning his murder for the moment of his return home. In a courtly culture such as we see in Gunther's Burgundy, the issue is one of discretion. Siegfried must be killed because he has boasted to his wife and she has made a public issue of it.

with a faithful maid on either side.
The Suitors went weak at the knees. Their hearts melted with desire, and every man among them voiced a prayer that he might sleep with her.

Odysseus has been absent a full twenty years, and yet his death has never been confirmed. Penelope's function as "interim" ruler is to preserve the kingdom either until its reigning champion should return or until his death requires the selection of a replacement. Before leaving for Troy, Odysseus charges his wife very carefully in this matter, foreseeing a long absence for himself and even allowing for the day when Telemachus grows to maturity:

> ὦ γύναι, οὐ γὰρ ὀΐω ἐϋκνήμιδας Ἀχαιοὺς
> ἐκ Τροίης εὖ πάντας ἀπήμονας ἀπονέεσθαι·
> καὶ γὰρ Τρῶάς φασι μαχητὰς ἔμμεναι ἄνδρας,
> ἠμὲν ἀκοντιστὰς ἠδὲ ῥυτῆρας ὀϊστῶν
> ἵππων τ' ὠκυπόδων ἐπιβήτορας, οἵ κε τάχιστα
> ἔκριναν μέγα νεῖκος ὁμοιΐου πολέμοιο.
> τῷ οὐκ οἶδ' ἤ κέν μ' ἀνέσει θεός, ἦ κεν ἁλώω
> αὐτοῦ ἐνὶ Τροίῃ· σοὶ δ' ἐνθάδε πάντα μελόντων.
> μεμνῆσθαι πατρὸς καὶ μητέρος ἐν μεγάροισιν
> ὡς νῦν, ἢ ἔτι μᾶλλον ἐμεῦ ἀπονόσφιν ἐόντος·
> αὐτὰρ ἐπὴν δὴ παῖδα γενειήσαντα ἴδηαι,
> γήμασθ' ᾧ κ' ἐθέλῃσθα, τεὸν κατὰ δῶμα λιποῦσα. (18.259-70)

"Wife, I do not think all the Achaean soldiers will return from Troy unhurt. For they say the Trojans are good fighters too, both with javelin and bow, and as charioteers, who can tip the scales in an evenly matched battle more quickly than anything. So I cannot say whether the gods will let me come back or whether I shall fall there on Trojan soil. But I leave everything here in your charge. Look after my father and mother in the house as you do now, or with even greater care when I am gone. And when you see a beard on our boy's chin, marry whom you want to and leave your home."

As long as Odysseus remains away and until their son has grown to maturity, Penelope is faced with the problem of "entertaining" her suitors under ever more difficult circumstances. They naturally grow weary of their fruitless quest and desire not only resolution but recompense for the ardor invested in their wooing.

Moreover, Telemachus, Odysseus's son, now twenty years of age, shows signs of his own physical and psychological maturity. He is beginning to assert himself against the suitors. Soon he may be ready to take Ithaca's throne himself, ending his mother's reign and so relieving her of the necessity to accept a new husband.

The suitors, therefore, band together to murder the young man. In their assumption, however, that many together can destroy a prince, they belie their own unsuitability for championship and kingship. Indeed, the suitors' unsuitability is made manifest by their very presence in Ithaca. Any man seeking to establish a warrior's reputation would have found his way to Troy. The men who shrink back from battle are, by definition, unfit for a kingship such as Ithaca's. Nestor, characterizing Aigisthos, the suitor who succeeds in seducing Agamemnon's queen, says, "ἡμεῖς μὲν γὰρ κεῖθι πολέας τελέοντες ἀέθλους / ἤμεθ'· ὁ δ' εὔκηλος μυχῷ Ἄργεος ἱπποβότοιο / πόλλ' Ἀγαμεμνονέην ἄλοχον θέλγεσκεν ἔπεσσιν" (3.262-64)—"[w]hile we who were besieging Troy toiled at heroic tasks, he spent his leisured days, right in the heart of Argos where the horses graze, busy charming Agamemnon's wife with his seductive talk." Nestor tags Aigisthos with the appropriate epithet "ἀνάλκιδος" (3.310)—"cowardly."

Penelope's suitors devise an ambush to kill Telemachus just as Aigisthos and his men set an ambush for the great Agamemnon in order to kill him. Tellingly, Aigisthos and Clytemnestra choose the bath, where they will catch Agamemnon stripped naked and therefore at his most vulnerable. Aigisthos can never perform the champion-king's function because his deceitfulness reveals an attitude unsuitable in armed combat. Even in the later characterization of him by Aeschylus, Aigisthos does not govern the city. Rather, Clytemnestra continues to rule at Mycenae even after her remarriage.[13]

Clytemnestra and Penelope can be compared to each other because the situations in which they find themselves are so similar. Both act as interim monarchs in their husbands' absence, and both encourage the interest of warriors who might be considered as replacements if their husbands do not return from war. Both queens are expected to withstand their suitors' pressure on them to replace the absent king until after receiving a confirmed report of his death. What the suitors desire, however, is a reversal of the usual sequence of significations. Not because they have saved the domain from destruction are they to be rewarded with the king's throne and bed but because they have succeeded in climbing into the royal bed, they hope to be viewed as legitimate monarchs.[14]

---

[13] Another interpretation, by Richard J. Sommer, in "The *Odyssey* and Primitive Religion," *Critical Essays on Homer*, p. 188, emphasizing the matrilinear aspect of society prior to Homer, has it that "the story of Agamemnon's death originally referred to a ritual event, probably repeated at regular intervals, or to a radical change in the character of that event worthy of being recorded in the mythological annals of the tribe. . . . [T]he old king is disposed of by his queen and an outsider who takes the throne to rule by matrilinear right; the avenger, however, is the son of the old king, claiming patrilinear right to the crown" (p. 188). The transition from matrilineal to patriarchal right is demonstrated through the fact that Orestes, the avenging son, now goes unpunished, for the hounding Erinyes are not mentioned by Menelaus, while, in Aeschylus's version, Orestes's "insurrection, approved . . . by Athena, was to have been ultimately successful" (p. 188).

[14] In this instance, the husband's status is dependent upon that of his wife. She selects him for marriage, thus bestowing upon him her status as well as its appurtenances—wealth and power. As Frakes points out: "the issue of female independence or sovereignty is the inevitable obverse of the displacement of female control of property and the insistence on intra-class status—*as dependent*

Penelope detests her suitors but forces herself to accept them in her house. Her role as queen demands that she put aside her personal desire for Odysseus in order to be properly prepared for his replacement.[15] In the *Odyssey*, Clytemnestra, on the other hand, does not even wait for her husband's death but, "ἐθέλουσαν" (3.272)—a "willing lady"—goes to bed with Aigisthos. Having been unfaithful to her husband, she finds herself in the position of plotting ("τεύξας"—11.409) with her lover against the legitimate monarch. Clytemnestra thus selects to be king a man whose outstanding characteristics are a cowardly deceitfulness and selfish pursuit of pleasure.

Having put off the moment of selection as far as possible, Penelope is finally pressured by the suitors to make a choice among them. She, however, sets a contest to identify Odysseus's successor. The test is one of strength, as is entirely appropriate to the norms and requirements of epic culture. And as it turns out, her test will show that none of her erstwhile suitors is worthy to be Ithaca's king. As one of them puts it, "ἀλλ' εἰ δὴ τοσσόνδε βίης ἐπιδευέες εἰμὲν / ἀντιθέου Ὀδυσῆος. ὅ τ' οὐ δυνάμεσθα τανύσσαι / τόξον" (21.253-55)—"our failure with his bow proves us such weaklings compared with the godlike Odysseus." The contest provides for the selection of Odysseus's legitimate successor according to his suitability for the duties of a king, not according to the queen's personal preference.[16] Indeed, even with regard to the

---

on husband's status—as the defining feature of the female's own status, both feudal and general" (p. 206). The same statement must also apply to those men whose sovereignty is dependent on the wife's status. Had Siegfried defeated the Burgundians, he would stand at the head of their army based on his own merit, or, had he won Kriemhild in a contest, he would stand at the head of their army based on the status conferred upon him through her. Since he has won her in exchange for a service performed for her brother, however, he would take with him nothing but his prize and the Burgundians' good will. A volunteer should normally be content with the increase in reputation resulting from his service, but Siegfried's service to Gunther must remain a secret. He therefore takes with him nothing but Kriemhild. But even that betokens some transaction between the men and is enough to arouse in Brünhild the suspicion that something is amiss. This may also explain why, upon departure from Burgundy following the double wedding, Siegfried wishes to refuse Kriemhild her share of Burgundian wealth and fighting men.

[15] Butterworth makes a similar observation: "Although Atreus was evidently regarded as a great king, others who married women of the priestly nobility of Crete were looked on by the Cretans as *ignobiles*, and perhaps because of their brief and undistinguished reigns (as was that of Pleisthenes, the father of Agamemnon and Menelaus) were recorded by history only under the anonymity of the word 'Pleisthenes.' A princess who married one could be said to have married one of the lower orders, a servant, in modern slang 'a tough' (πλεισθένης).... It is very likely that the princesses of the ancient houses felt a real resentment against the brutal intruders: the story that Agamemnon married Clytaemnestra against her will seems to reflect something of the kind" (pp. 15-16).

[16] This interpretation is not incompatible with an alternate version of the story reconstructed by Butterworth, in whose assessment Odysseus and Penelope would never have met before the contest of the bow, through which he is selected

husband whose absence she has been lamenting for twenty years, the qualities that spring to Penelope's mind are those that qualify him for his station. She describes herself as "πόσιος ποθέουσα φίλοιο / παντοίην ἀρετήν, ἐπεὶ ἔξοχος ἦεν Ἀχαιῶν" (18.204-05)—"longing for my dear husband, who had all the virtues, and was the finest man in all Achaea." By contrast, any other would prove "χείρονος ἀνδρός" (20.82)—"a lesser man." Superiority or inferiority in a husband appear in her mind to be identical with superiority or inferiority in the public sphere.

Penelope's test does not provide any consideration whatsoever for the suitor's desirability to her as a partner in her bed.[17] Indeed, her only motivation for agreeing to the contest at this point must be her understanding of her husband's charge providing for her remarriage once Telemachus comes of age. It is the latter's approaching maturity that provokes the suitors to set an ambush to kill him. If he takes the throne now, the suitors will have little profit from a marriage with Penelope. On the other hand, if she takes one of them as a husband, she removes the motive to murder Telemachus. She, therefore, proceeds with the contest, yet still does not hope to increase the pleasure that she herself will have from her life, for, as she says in private: "ἥδε δὴ ἠὼς εἶσι δυσώνυμος, ἥ μ' Ὀδυσῆος / οἴκου ἀποσχήσει" (19.571-72)—"The hateful day is drawing very near which is to tear me from Odysseus' house." Later, standing before the suitors, she announces the contest to them:

κέκλυτέ μευ, μνηστῆρες ἀγήνορες, οἳ τόδε δῶμα
ἐχράετ' ἐσθιέμεν καὶ πινέμεν ἐμμενὲς αἰεὶ
ἀνδρὸς ἀποιχομένοιο πολὺν χρόνον· οὐδέ τιν' ἄλλην
μύθου ποιήσασθαι ἐπισχεσίην ἐδύνασθε,
ἀλλ' ἐμὲ ἱέμενοι γῆμαι θέσθαι τε γυναῖκα.
ἀλλ' ἄγετε, μνηστῆρες, ἐπεὶ τόδε φαίνετ' ἄεθλον·
θήσω γὰρ μέγα τόξον Ὀδυσσῆος θείοιο·
ὃς δέ κε ῥηΐτατ' ἐντανύσῃ βιὸν ἐν παλάμῃσι
καὶ διοϊστεύσῃ πελέκεων δυοκαίδεκα πάντων,
τῷ κεν ἅμ' ἑσποίμην νοσφισσαμένη τόδε δῶμα
κουρίδιον, μάλα καλόν, ἐνίπλειον βιότοιο,
τοῦ ποτε μεμνήσεσθαι ὀΐομαι ἔν περ ὀνείρῳ. (21.68-79)

---

to become her new husband "by force of arms" (p. 112). When the royal couple enters the bridal chamber, then, they celebrate not a reunion but a wedding. In Butterworth's recasting of the story, Odysseus is not an old man. These two stories are alternatives within the *Odyssey*, and each implies the other. Penelope's contest is meant to result in the selection of a husband, not to reunite her with Odysseus, and Odysseus arrives at Ithaka without the expectation that he will simply assume the kingship without a trial.

[17] As Bekker writes of Brünhild, "[S]he is a queen before she is a woman" (p. 255).

"Listen, proud Suitors. You have exploited this house, in the long absence of its master, as the scene of your endless eating and drinking, and you could offer no better pretext for your conduct than your wish to win my hand in marriage. Come forward now, my gallant lords: the prize stands before you. I shall now place the great bow of godlike Odysseus in front of you. Whoever strings the bow most easily and shoots an arrow through every one of these twelve axes, with that man I will go, bidding goodbye to this house which welcomed me as a bride, this lovely house so full of all good things, this home that even in my dreams I never shall forget."

The contest requires that the suitors perform a feat that she had often seen Odysseus working to perfect. The suitors are thus tested against Odysseus's own rare strength and skill. His bow is an uncommon tool that can be bent to the use only of an uncommon man. It functions as a key to the identification, not only of kingly qualities but of those qualities belonging peculiarly to Odysseus. The bow's use in this contest guarantees not only that the best man attain to Odysseus's throne and bed, but it provides a measure for guaranteeing that Odysseus's successor meet a certain standard.[18]

The bed of Odysseus is, in fact, not a piece of movable freestanding furniture but an integral element of the house: the bed chamber is built around the living olive tree that serves as a bedpost. The royal marriage bed is, thus, like the throne and the space between two armies cleared for a duel—to occupy any one of these spaces is to accept responsibility for the others. The king's marriage bed cannot be entered without consideration for the burdens, responsibilities, and liabilities of championship and governance. Penelope is aware of this, as any good queen must be, and, in fact, it is why she upbraids the suitors for talking only of their own desire. Awarding a champion with the prize of herself makes sense when such an action means that a queen can secure the long-term services of a capable defender for her domain. Penelope clearly expects no such service from any of her suitors. She offers herself as a prize only to forestall the criminal plotting of her son's murder by the ruthless men in her hall and manipulates her lovers for whatever the ruse may be worth.

Brünhild, queen of Iceland with five hundred warriors at her immediate command, rigorously employs precisely the same criteria and standards as Penelope in selecting a husband for herself. We are left to surmise what may have placed her in need of a husband, for the *Nibelungenlied* does not say. She has neither a father nor a brother to help her make a match, and, indeed, she does not want assistance, for she is fully prepared to select her own mate.

---

[18] Referring again to Brünhild, Bekker notes that she is accustomed to thinking of kings in terms of physical strength and prowess: "The conditions she poses serve to lure a *worthy* suitor, presupposed by her to be of the same view as she, to the effect that he will not marry for love, but for strength, that he will not be prone to become the slave of passion, but will be king also in the realm of this nebulous thing called love" (p. 257). A contest of strength is meant to be understood by contestants as agreeing to the principle that superior physical strength is to be the basis for the marriage.

To this end, Brünhild institutes a contest "umbe minne" (326,4)—"[w]ith her love as prize" (53). Contestants for her hand are to meet her in three events: the javelin throw, shot put, and broad jump. The man who would marry her and make himself her king must qualify in her tests of physical strength: "swer ir minne gerte, der muose âne wanc / driu spil an gewinnen der frouwen wol geborn. / gebrast im an dem einen, er hete daz houbet sîn verlorn" (327, 2-4)—"[W]hoever aspired to her love had, without fail, to win these three tests against her, or else, if he lost but one, he forfeited his head" (53). The terms of Brünhild's contest guarantee that her husband will be physically strong, determined, and self-confident.[19]

By putting to death unsuccessful suitors, Brünhild removes them from further competition for her power. She will never be faced by an unruly mob of suitors who remain in her hall consuming her wealth and trying to set the agenda for her selection of a new king. Nor will the husband she selects be speared in the back by a former rival.[20]

---

[19] Bekker observes, "It is part of Brünhilt's philosophy of kingship that she must be taken with a show of force, as it is Sifrit's philosophy to take a wife or a crown by force" (p. 256). What Bekker calls "philosophy," I call "culture." Either term might lead to an exploration of the grounds for such a marriage criterion, a question that Bekker does not, however, pursue.

[20] Although the narrative in its present form does not recognize Hagen as Kriemhild's suitor, a comparison with Siegfried and an assessment in terms of expectations for a champion suggest that an earlier version of the story would have made Hagen Siegfried's rival. The fact that Hagen has not declared himself as a suitor for Kriemhild is paralleled by the otherwise strange circumstance of Siegfried's spending more than a year as a guest at Burgundy without mentioning his interest in Kriemhild as the reason for his visit. If we accept Hagen to be Gunther's leading warrior and, moreover, as indicated by his knowledge of Siegfried's exploits, to be properly schooled in epic-cultural practices, it can be further assumed that, prior to Siegfried's arrival, he may even have performed occasionally as Gunther's champion. Like Unferth at Hrothgar's court, however, there are some challenges that Hagen will decline to take up. It is he who counsels others against meeting Siegfried in combat. He then stands by as the Burgundians react to the announcement of an impending invasion, and he allows Siegfried to assume the leading role in Burgundy's defense, though he does distinguish himself in the fighting. He himself counsels that Gunther consult with Siegfried in the matter of wooing Brünhild. In short, Hagen never presents himself as Burgundy's champion so long as Siegfried is present. Only Hagen's behavior following Siegfried's death can be termed "heroic." Indeed, once in Vienna, Hagen (with Volker at his side) meets Etzel between the armies with an insulting challenge: "'Ez zaeme,' sô sprach Hagene, 'vil wol volkes trôst, / daz die herren væhten ze aller vorderôst, / alsô der mînen herren hie ieslîcher tuot'" (2020)—"'It would well grace the People's Protector were he and his great nobles to fight foremost of all,' said Hagen."

The battle between Burgundians and Huns is a deadly contest on a massive scale orchestrated by Kriemhild in what may be regarded as a posthumous version of the nuptial games in which, however, no bride is to be won. It ends just as Brünhild's contests are meant to have ended, with the death of the unsuccessful suitor—in

The terms set by Brünhild for her contest reveal her to be a queen thoroughly versed in the principles of epic culture. She has but one thought, and that is to provide herself with a champion likely to outlast challenges from any quarter. She may possibly have lost a husband-king-champion once already[21] and is now going to great pains to assure herself that it not happen again.

Siegfried subverts her contest in order to assist Gunther in his quest to marry her. That Siegfried is able to affect her stratagem is a sign of his own thorough understanding of epic culture's practices. That he is willing to deceive her, however, reflects his disastrously mistaken unconcern for the experience out of which those practices had grown. Siegfried is seduced by his desire to win Kriemhild for his wife into accepting an alliance with her brother without first irrefutably demonstrating his own superiority. He strikes a bargain with Gunther: the gift of Kriemhild, Gunther's sister, in exchange for help in surviving Brünhild's tests. Brünhild's contest, however, like the test of Odysseus's bow proposed by Penelope, is designed to identify precisely that male uniquely qualified for marriage to the queen within such a culture. To subvert Brünhild's contest is to reject the wisdom of epic culture and thus to invite universal destruction.

The deception of Brünhild proceeds according to a stratagem based on the correct anticipation by Siegfried of her thought processes and judgments. He knows enough about her and about Gunther to realize that Burgundy's king would be no match for her. Accordingly, he advises Gunther to give up his quest. But Hagen, Gunther's chief advisor, suggests that Siegfried assist Gunther. Such assistance, of course, directly contradicts the principles of championship. The champion must be seen to be capable of standing alone against any adversary, even the most daunting. And it must be assumed that

---

this case, a man who failed to declare himself formally as a candidate for Kriemhild's hand. Had Hagen put himself forward in defense of Burgundy to meet Siegfried in a single combat as he now advises Etzel to do, he could well have expected to be offered the king's sister both as a reward and as an incentive not to challenge the king for his throne. With Siegfried's assumption of duties as the king's champion and subsequent marriage to Kriemhild, Hagen is by no means neutralized. If he does not kill Siegfried in a face-to-face confrontation, he may be quite willing to spear him in the back, as happens in our version of the story. Hagen's familial status and, specifically, his rights, duties, and responsibilities vis-à-vis the ruling family are conspicuously unclear. The ambiguity of his status parallels that of Siegfried, who initially presents himself as a challenger, soon allows himself to be treated as a guest, and eventually takes the role of defender. Kriemhild would resist Hagen, then, not only because he is the murderer of her husband (a situation that occurs in Hartmann von Aue's *Iwein*) but more importantly because he has not legitimated his claims to her through single combat. In other words, Hagen's murder of her husband initiates a process of clarification by which Kriemhild begins to sort out what had been murky, even contradictory, relationships at the Burgundian court.

[21] The text as it stands can perhaps more easily be taken as it is by Bekker to indicate that she is a virgin (p. 256).

every champion will eventually have to face such an adversary as he comes to the assistance of his weaker companions and allies. Brünhild's contest is designed to identify the warrior who can perform such a rescue, not one who will require rescuing.

Siegfried has with him the magic cloak that he won from Alberich and the Nibelungs. The magic garment gives him the strength of twelve men and makes him invisible. In addition to increasing Siegfried's strength, the cloak affords him a quality not usually seen in champions—deceitfulness. As the narrator puts it, "Ouch was diu selbe tarnhût álsô getân / daz dar inne worhte ein ieslîcher man / swaz er selbe wolde, daz in doch niemen sach. / sus gewán er Prünhilde, dâ von im léidé geschach" (338)—"He wooed the splendid woman with great subtlety, since the cloak was of such a kind that without being seen any man could do as he pleased in it. In this way he won Brunhild, though he had cause to rue it later" (54). But subtlety is quite inappropriate in the wooing of a queen like Brünhild, for she is looking for a man who can stand her test of brute force and courage.[22]

---

[22] Frakes interprets the contest as stemming from a desire to avoid marriage (pp. 146, 150, 154-55). Brünhild's contest does not, however, indicate her unwillingness to marry but simply her unwillingness to marry the wrong man. One might argue that Brünhild does not have the freedom to do otherwise. Submission to the socio-political and martial necessity of selecting an appropriate defender for her realm is not the same thing as accepting the humiliation of a patriarchal marriage. In short, a queen acting as does Brünhild is, in many respects, the equal of the men who constitute the set of her potential suitors. As Frakes observes of Kriemhild's handling of her second marriage, she "marries for the same reason that motivates Gunther, Siegfried, and Etzel, who upon deciding to marry, 'knew' and 'loved' their prospective spouses in exactly the same way that she 'knew' and 'loved' Etzel. . . . No role is played by love, affection, sentimentality, or anything of the kind" (p. 156). Where Frakes attributes male and female marriage intentions alike to "status, wealth, and power," as well as to "propagating the dynasty" (p. 156), Bekker comes much closer to the mark with his assessment of Brünhild's reluctance to become Gunther's bedpartner. "Her *kingship*," notes Bekker, "is all-important, and it will not do to speak of Brünhilt's *Virginalitätswahrung* if by that is meant a resolution on her part never to marry. If that were Brünhilt's aim, she simply could refuse ever to marry, could abolish the games, and remain the virgin-queen. Actually, for all we know, Brünhilt may be eager to marry, but her readiness to do so is subservient to something more important, the necessity, namely, that a would-be husband be qualified to do justice to her status by displaying his right to kingship via the display of his strength. Brünhilt's view of marriage is therefore anything but sentimental. Wishing to avoid a misalliance, she is rational and pragmatic, ready to strike a utilitarian, political bargain which will do honor to her kingship" (p. 255). In underscoring and repeating the word "kingship," Bekker emphasizes the queen's responsibilities as ruler when she is, for all practical purposes, a king, not a king's wife. Bekker's interpretation wants only an explanation for the singular importance of superior individual strength in the structure of kingship within Brünhild's culture, which sees the queen's role as

It is precisely the quality of invincibility that must be faked in order to convince Brünhild of Gunther's suitability.[23] The Burgundians suggest assembling a retinue of thirty thousand to accompany them. Siegfried knows better: "'Swie vil wir volkes füeren,' sprach aber Sîvrit, / 'ez pfliget diu küneginne sô vreislîcher sit, / die müesen doch ersterben von ir übermuot'" (340,1-3)—"However great an army we take, the Queen has such dreadful ways that they would all have to die" (54). The conditions of epic battle dictate that its outcome will not be decided by the number of warriors involved on either side. Operating under the same premise as when he had originally approached the court of Burgundy at Worms accompanied by only twelve men, Siegfried now proposes that the wooing party to Iceland number only four warriors. The size of the party is meant as a signal to Brünhild that her suitor, like her, regards himself as invulnerable.[24] He presents himself as

---

relating directly to the acquisition of a champion to provide for the realm's security.

[23] Brünhild, as Bekker points out, believes in her own invincibility "and needs not fear a mere quartet of visiting Burgundians" (p. 252). Such a belief is, of course, a key indicator of epic-cultural understandings and thus maps the cultural common ground between Brünhild and Siegfried. As Bekker writes, "Brünhilt and Sifrit also share the view that the right to kingship depends on physical strength" (p. 254).

[24] Bekker very aptly argues that the number twelve is a device of consequence both for Siegfried's prowess, symbolized by his Tarnkappe (magic cloak), and Brünhild's virgin strength: "Sifrit kills twelve giants (94); Gernot and Giselher use twelve carts—taking four days to make three trips—to get the hoard to the ship that will take the gold to Worms (1122); Kriemhilt, when preparing to depart for Gran, manages to take twelve trunks of gold with her (1280), as if to symbolize her inalienable rights to the hoard at large" (p. 255). Bekker continues with his speculations about these pertinent issues, noting, on the other hand, with respect to Brünhild, "[d]uring the preparations for the Islant-games, twelve men have difficulty hauling the stone that is to be used by Brünhilt and her suitor (449). Not only is Brünhilt capable of picking up the stone unaided, she also throws it over a distance of twelve *Klafte* (463), the length of twelve men" (p. 258). In short, "the number twelve lies close to the essence of Sifrit's power" (p. 255), while the strength of twelve is linked to Brünhild's shield and spear, in possession of which she "awes Hagen" (p. 258). For Siegfried, the strength of twelve is a matter of consideration when negotiating for an appropriate partner to meet his own challenge to duel in a "bridal contest" for Kriemhilt, for he turns down Ortwin on the grounds that "twelve Ortwins could not stand up to one Sifrit" (p. 256). Because Siegfried's strength is measured in terms of twelve men combined, however, it is possible to judge that Brünhild's strength "comes perilously close to equalling his" (p. 258). Thus, the number twelve links the two wooing expeditions, the duel (never fought) at Burgundy, the bridal contest at Iceland, and Siegfried and Brünhild with each other. After Brünhild's deception through the use of the magic cape, the "hundredfold of twelve [the number of men accompanying Sifrit and Kriemhilt on their visit to Worms] necessarily causes Brünhilt to wonder about Sifrit's evident strength . . . and about the discrepancy between his strength and his assumed vassalage" (p. 256).

a warrior possessed of the confidence to venture out virtually alone on a quest even across the seas. A whole host of knights is a matter of no concern to a man like him. Siegfried himself embodies the qualities of Brünhild's ideal mate. He has ridden alone among the Nibelungs and, undaunted by their numbers, has slain their princes and made himself master of their treasures. The point of the deception is to make Brünhild believe that Gunther is such a man—a man like Siegfried.

This is accomplished by projecting onto Gunther Siegfried's physical strength and his reputation as a warrior. Dressing themselves in Burgundy's costliest garments, the four warriors make an impressive display of their empire's wealth and power, for they are described as wearing the following: "[v]on Márroch ûz dem lande und ouch von Lybîân / die aller besten sîden die ie mêr gewan / deheines küneges künne, der heten sie genuoc" (364,1-3)— "[t]he best Moroccan and Libyan silk that a royal family ever acquired" (57). Such rare and exotic materials stand as a direct testimony to Burgundy's reach, whether through tribute or trading. Court tailors require seven weeks to stitch garments sufficient to clothe each of the four men in three suits of clothing per day for four days. Thirty maidens perform the work.

> Die árâbîschen sîden   wîz alsô der snê
> unt von Zázamanc der guoten   grüene alsam der klê,
> dar in si leiten steine;   des wurden guotiu kleit.
>   . . .
>
> Von vremder vische hiuten   bezóc wól getân
> ze sehene vremden liuten,   swaz man der gewan,
> die dahten si mit sîden,   sô si si solden tragen. (362,1-3; 363,1-3)

> They threaded precious stones into snow-white silk from Arabia or into silk from Zazamanc as green as clover, making fine robes. . . . Whatever handsome linings they could lay hands on from the skins of strange water beasts, wondrous to see, they covered with silk. (56)

This finery itself contributes to the deception, because, without Siegfried's good offices as Burgundy's champion, the court's treasures would have fallen into the hands of the Danish and Saxon kings Liudegast and Liudeger. The wealth directly represents the extent and security of Gunther's sovereignty, from which Brünhild will infer that he is a champion.[25]

---

[25] This inference is so compelling that a scholar like Haymes, though having no inkling of epic-cultural economies and practices, attempts to cast the *Nibelungenlied*'s conflicts in terms of a clash between hereditary power and the rising importance of an administrative cadre and concludes, from the emphasis on finery in the wooing expedition to Iceland and from Gunther's pretending to carry out the games, that Gunther is "pretending to a physical power he does not possess" (p. 95). Haymes here all but recognizes the warrior's attributes as a third quality quite independent of both heredity and service. As Haymes acknowledges, "No one actually challenges Gunther's traditional claim, it is his current claim based

The deception cannot be achieved just by the implication of Gunther's sovereignty and power. It requires for its complete success the telling of a direct lie, for not only does Brünhild insist upon marrying a warrior capable of subordinating all others to himself, but she assumes a determination of hierarchical ranking to be the precondition of every male-male relationship. Siegfried accordingly instructs Gunther, Hagen, and Dancwart: "Sô wir die minneclîchen bî ir gesinde sehen, / sô sult ir, helde mære, wan einer rede jehen: / Gunther sî mîn herre, und ích sí sîn man" (386,1-3)—"When we see the adorable woman with her retainers about her, noble warriors, you must abide by this one story—that Gunther is my overlord and I am his vassal" (59). The importance of this detail is later underlined by Brünhild herself. When Siegfried introduces Gunther to Brünhild as his liege lord, Brünhild replies as follows: "ist er dîn herre unt bistú sîn man, / diu spil, diu ich im teile, unt getar er diu bestân, / behabt er des die meisterschaft, sô wirde ich sîn wîp" (423,1-3)—"If he is your lord and you are his liegeman, and provided he dares essay my sports (whose rules I shall lay down for him) and proves himself the winner, I shall wed him" (63). In other words, Brünhild is now adding a new stipulation to the conditions for marrying her. Not only must her challenger defeat her in the three athletic events, but he must also really be Siegfried's liege lord. Otherwise, "ez gêt iu allen an den lîp" (423,4)—"it will cost you all your lives" (63). This final pronouncement, of course, proves prophetic. All four men will later die as a result of their duplicity in this matter.

Obviously, Brünhild has grounds for her new stipulation. Seeing another warrior presented as Siegfried's better, she begins to sense a distortion in the hierarchy's formation. Indeed, this subtle point is so well understood by Siegfried that he is able to anticipate her uneasiness and to deflect the question that could have undone the deception. Before the wooing expedition even reaches Iceland's shores, Siegfried instructs his companions always to act as

---

on the king's fitness for his task that Siegfried calls into question" (p. 93). "Fitness" refers to Siegfried's capacity to defend the interests of the court in battle. It is this fitness that Brünhild's contest is designed to prove. For her, as Bekker recognizes, "the essence of kingship adheres to the person wearing the regalia" and not, as for Kriemhilt, to "the regalia themselves" (p. 253). The reason that the deception works only imperfectly can easily be accounted for in its incompatibility with what Brünhild must already know about Siegfried through his incomparable reputation. The clash then comes between an assumption that wealth derives directly from an individual's demonstrated battle prowess and the belief that tokens of power and wealth can safely be traded in an intercourtly economy that enables kings to maintain their position without risk of life on the battlefield. (This function of property ownership is the principle identified by Frakes as "the most obvious and important means of access to political power and authority"—p. 64). But eventually the deception comes to light as a double deception, for not only has Siegfried conspired with the Burgundians to subvert Brünhild's carefully contrived marriage games, but the conspirators expose the self-deception involved in their plot, for which, to a man, they pay with their lives.

though he were Gunther's vassal. He himself engages in the most convincing performance by holding the stirrup for Gunther to mount his horse in sight of the ladies observing their arrival from the castle of Isenstein. Such an act would not be performed by one king for another unless he had been forced to it through a defeat in combat.

Despite this performance, however, Brünhild is slow to be convinced of Siegfried's subordination, for Siegfried is already known to Brünhild just as he once had been to Hagen—not necessarily through a previous meeting but through his reputation. In a scene that neatly replays Siegfried's arrival at Worms, a member of Brünhild's court reports to her that, even though he personally "ir deheinen nie mêr habe gesehen" (411,2)—has "never set eyes on any of them" (62)— one of the visitors "gelíche Sîfrîde" (411,3)—"bears a likeness to Siegfried" (62). "[N]u brinc mir mîn gewant!" (416,1)—"Bring me my robes," responds the queen—"unt ist der starke Sîfrit komen in diz lant / durch willen mîner minne, ez gât im an den lîp. / ich fürhte in nicht sô sêre daz ich wérdé sîn wîp" (416,2-4)—"[I]f strong Siegfried has come it is at peril of his life, since I do not fear him so much that I should consent to marry him" (62). Brünhild has jumped to the conclusion that her suitor is Siegfried, whom she admits fearing. Nor is she unwilling to marry him. When she says she will not consent to marry him without a test, she reveals that she has been entertaining the idea of dispensing with her customary procedure. Rejecting that temptation, she reasserts her determination to follow through with the practices demanded of her in her position as queen.[26]

While Gunther goes unrecognized, not for a moment does the queen hesitate in identifying Siegfried as the small party's commander. She must be relying for this judgment solely on the strength of Siegfried's reputation. Indeed, she remains assured that if any of Siegfried's companions were worthy of her notice, she or one of her court would certainly be able to recognize him. Quickly attiring herself in special clothes of state and accompanied both by "vil manec schœniu meit, / wol hundert oder mêre, gezieret was ir lîp" (417,2-3)—"bevies of pretty girls, a full hundred or more and all of them elegantly dressed" (62)—and "degene dâ ûz Îslant, / die Prünhide recken. die truogen swert enhant, / fünf hundert oder mêre" (418,1-3)—"knights of Iceland to the number of five hundred or more . . . sword in hand" (63)—Brünhild goes to greet the man that she believes has come to marry her. She addresses her words directly to him, confident that he is

---

[26] Frakes, for all his attention to female characters' status and independence of action, does not recognize that Brünhild presents an important exception to the rule that "men decide when and whom to marry" (p. 53). While pointing out that "women do not initiate 'groom-quests'" (p. 53), Frakes ignores the fact that they do sometimes hold nuptial contests. Brünhild's marriage is not forced, nor does it "disguise the brutality and humiliation . . . of patriarchal marriage" (p. 66). Indeed, Brünhild's contest foregrounds the brutality that awaits her husband once he assumes his duties as champion-king, while, insofar as she exercises her full responsibility for disposing of her own person, her marriage is anything but patriarchal.

worthy of this honor: "sît willekomen, Sîfrit, her in ditze lant" (419, 3)—
"Welcome, Siegfried, to my country."[27]

This is the "error" anticipated by Siegfried, for Brünhild's recognition of Siegfried, in fact, presents the Burgundians with the single greatest obstacle to the success of their deception. To counter the effects of his own reputation, Siegfried has taken pains to give the impression that Gunther is his master, leading out Gunther's horse and holding his stirrup upon disembarking from their vessel. As the narrator points out, such a service has never before been performed by Siegfried. In holding Gunther's stirrup, he acts the part of a squire. Only a vassal would perform this service, which is precisely the interpretation that Siegfried intends will be put on his action. Indeed, it was performed for the benefit of observers in Brünhild's court: "daz sâhen durch diu venster die frouwen schœne unde hêr" (398,4)—"this was seen by those proud and comely women through the loopholes" (61).

Brünhild at first fails to take note of this dramatic display. Siegfried, however, is prepared even for this eventuality because he has not underestimated the difficulty of overcoming the prejudicial effect of his fame. When Brünhild persists in directing her attention toward Siegfried, he is ready with a bald-faced lie.

> "Vil michel iuwer genâde,   mîn frou Prünhilt,
> daz ir mich ruochet grüezen,   fürsten tohter milt,
> vor disem edelen recken,   der hie vor mir stât,
> wande er ist mîn herre: der êren het ich gerne rât.
>
> Er ist geborn von Rîne,   waz sól ich dir ságen mêr?
> durch die dîne liebe   sîn wir gevarn her.
> der wil dich gerne minnen,   swaz im dâ von geshiht.
> nu bedénke dichs bezîte: mîn herre erlâzet dichs niht.
>
> Er ist geheizen Gunther   unt ist ein künec hêr.
> erwurbe er dîne minne,   sone gérte er nihtes mêr.
> ja gebôt mir her ze varne   der recke wol getân:
> möhte ich es im geweigert han,   ich het ez gérné verlân." (420-22)[28]

---

[27] "Brünhilt," as Bekker recognizes, "takes it for granted that it is Sifrit who has come to woo her, and not that other man in white (399), whose biography is given to her by Sifrit (420ff.), because she had never heard of Gunther before" (p. 257). Brünhilt's not having known about Gunther is in itself highly significant, because it must indicate that he has done nothing to earn a formidable reputation. We may recall that Siegmund does know who Gunther is but is more concerned about Hagen and the danger he presents.

[28] McConnell has pointed out to me (in correspondence) that the deception moves through three phases; optical, verbal, and physical/optical, achieving in the end what he refers to as a metaphysical deception that goes far beyond tricking the Icelandic woman, for it actually undoes the cultural constructs by which both courts function and thus brings on their destruction.

"You accord me too much favour, my lady Brünhild, magnanimous Queen, when you deign to salute me before this noble knight, who, as befits my lord, stands nearer to you than I—an honour I would gladly forgo! My liege is a prince of the Rhenish lands—what more need I tell you?—and we have voyaged here to win your love. For whatever the fate in store for him he means to make you his wife. Now consider this while there is time, since my lord means to hold you to your terms. His name is Gunther, and he is a king most high. If he were to win your love, he would have nothing left to wish for. The handsome warrior commanded me to sail here, but, had it been in my power to deny him, I would gladly have refrained." (63)

Siegfried here claims to be in Iceland strictly against his own will, because only if Siegfried were Gunther's vassal could this be true. Siegfried's earlier performance of a squire's duties now comes into play by lending credence to these words. Otherwise, Brünhild might well have asked him whether he had, in fact, suffered a defeat at Gunther's hands. That is a lie that, even under the present circumstances, would have been too much for Siegfried. The deception is meant to encourage Brünhild to ascribe superior power and strength to Gunther without doing damage to Siegfried's reputation. Such a ploy cannot, however, succeed within the system of Brünhild's assumptions about warfare and politics. Siegfried's deception shows that he has knowledge of that system, a knowledge that he uses to subvert it. In his effort to gain access to Kriemhild, Siegfried has begun to adopt the system prevailing among the Burgundians. The expedition to acquire Brünhild for Gunther, however, places Siegfried in the position of exploiting his marginal position between the two cultures to further his own entry into Burgundian society. The immediate cost of this move is a disregard for Brünhild's integrity, not only as an individual but especially in her function as Iceland's queen—a function to which she has already subordinated herself entirely.[29]

---

[29] As Bekker puts it, "Sifrit's true guilt is . . . not quite as much constituted by his violation of the dignity of Brünhilt as a woman as by his violation of the principle of kingship. . . . [Sifrit] should have recognized the validity of the principle represented (and propagated) by her" (p. 262). Bekker argues that violation of this principle affixes to Siegfried responsibility for Brünhild's instigation of his death, because she eventually discovers that as a result of his (in)action, "her life over the past decade has been a lie, and therefore an insult, not to her honor as a woman—or rather, not as Worms would define such an honor—but as queen disdained by the only true king because he is the strongest. This king cheated her into marrying a second-rate king and caused her, the crown-bearer of Islant, to become guilty of violating the code by which kings must live" (p. 260). Siegfried's error thus becomes the occasion, ten years after the fact, of his own undoing. It is not necessary, however, that we understand Siegfried's failure to recognize the principle of kingship to hinge on his omission to "take" Brünhild when he had the chance to do so (p. 259), for as Bekker himself points out, her subduer must take her crown along with her virginity (p. 256). Siegfried's behavior is not to be measured, then, by whether or not he is the first to have intercourse with her but by whether he accepts the duties of kingship,

Siegfried's speech is crafted on the premise that there can be only one type of relationship between the two men—a hierarchical subordination of one to the other. Either Siegfried must be superior to Gunther, or Gunther truly is his master. The actual state of affairs, the alliance between Gunther and Siegfried, is never suspected by Brünhild because such a relationship is not part of her vocabulary. Indeed, such a pact is new for Siegfried himself. He is gambling that Brünhild will naturally assume that one of the two men must be the other's master, for, on this point, there could be no dissembling. A king would never pretend to be his vassal's squire. A king spends—and risks—his life establishing his status, and he relies on the identification of his person with that status in order to secure himself in his position.

Nevertheless, Brünhild remains skeptical. She has never heard of Gunther, whose identity is made known to her only when Siegfried introduces him. She reserves some doubt and expresses it to Siegfried in a new condition: "*ist er dîn herre unt bistú sîn man*" (423,1)—"*[i]f* he is your lord and you are his liegeman" (63; my emphasis)—only then will she marry Gunther. If he is not Siegfried's master, "ez gêt iu allen an den lîp" (423,4)—"it will cost you all your lives" (63). This is a threat that her suitors do not take seriously enough.

The contest between Brünhild and Gunther has all the hallmarks of a formal duel: terms clearly specifying what is at stake for both sides, a space cleared between the hosts of armed men (here rather unevenly represented) whose job it is to witness the contest's fairness, and armor noteworthy for its size and heaviness:

> Der rinc der was bezeiget,   dâ sólde daz spíl geschehen
> vor manegem küenen recken,   die daz solden sehen
> mêr danne siben hundert.   die sach man wâfen tragen:
> swem an dem spil gelunge,   daz ez die helde solden sagen.
>
> Dô was komen Prünhilt.   gewâfent man die vant
> sam ob si solde strîten   umbe elliu küneges lant.
> jâ truoc si ob den sîden   vil manegen goldes zein.
> ir minneclîchiu varwe   dar under hêrlîche schein.
>
> Dô kom ir gesinde.   die truogen dar zehant
> von alrôtem golde   einen schildes rant,
> mit stahelherten spangen,   vil michel unde breit,
> dar under spilen wolde   díu vil mínneclîche meit.
>
> Der frouwen schiltvezzel   ein edel porte was.
> dar ûfe lâgen steine   grüene sam ein gras.
> der lûhte maneger hande   mit schîne wider daz golt.
> er müeste wésen vil küene   dem diu frouwe wurde holt.

---

specifically, responsibility for the defense of Brünhild and her people. His failure, then, is the failure to marry, for he is her conqueror in both her tests.

> Der schilt was under buckeln, als uns daz ist gesaget,
> wol drîer spannen dicke, den tragen solde diu maget.
> von stahel unt ouch von golde rîch er was genuoc,
> den ir kameræere selbe vierde kûme truoc. (433-37)

> The ring was marked out in which the games were to be witnessed by over seven hundred bold fighting-men that were seen there under arms and would declare who had won the contest.
> And now Brünhild had arrived, armed as though about to contend for all the kingdoms in the world and wearing many tiny bars of gold over her silk, against which her lovely face shone radiantly. Next came her retainers, bearing a great, broad shield of reddest gold, with braces of hardest steel, under which the enchanting maiden meant to dispute the issue. For its baldrick her shield had a fine silk cord studded with grass-green gems whose variegated lustre vied with the gold of their settings. The man whom she would favour would have to be a very brave one: for this shield which the girl was to carry was (so we are told) a good three spans thick beneath the boss; it was resplendent with steel and with gold, and even with the help of three others her chamberlain could scarce raise it. (64-65)

The novelties here are Brünhild's gender and the related fact that Gunther seeks to make her not his vassal but his wife (although this difference is politically insignificant). Because of Brünhild's gender, however, details that might usually be viewed as "natural" to the formal duel seem distorted, even grotesque. The parodic and exaggerated aspect of this duel reflects, however, not on Brünhild but on her opponent, Gunther. His weakness is made to seem ridiculous. He soon appears laughable for ever having thought himself her match.

> Alsô der starke Hagene den schilt dar tragen sach,
> mit grímmegem muote, der helt von Tronege sprach:
> "wâ nu, künec Gunther? wie verlíesen wir den lîp!
> der ir dâ gert ze minnen, diu ist des tíuvéles wíp." (438)

> "What now, King Gunther?" stalwart Hagen of Troneck asked fiercely, on seeing the shield brought out. "We are done for—the woman whose love you desire is a rib of the devil himself!" (65)

Just as Hrothgar traces Grendel's descent back to Cain, Hagen traces Brünhild's origin to the devil. Like Eve, whose genesis as a mate for her husband is from his rib, Brünhild would have been created to be the devil's mate, not Gunther's. Brünhild's ferocious and daunting appearance changes Hagen's perception of her from the beautiful to the monstrous. Brünhild, like monsters and superhuman opponents, also has special properties that make her an ideal test of the men who would be her husband, her champion, and her king.

Because Brünhild is extraordinarily strong, the duel with her appropriately tests Gunther and Siegfried's physical strength. But because she is a woman, her contest tests also their (and the audience's) understanding of and appreciation for her culture's practices. The three Burgundian men are, in fact, caught off guard by the degree of danger to which they find themselves unexpectedly exposed. Brünhild at first appears to Gunther "sô wol getân" (392,2)—"so well formed"—that he exclaims, "si müese wérdén mîn wîp" (392,4)—"she must become my wife"; she is both *"schœne"* and "wol gekleit" (417,1)—"beautiful" and "well dressed" (my translations). Gunther, boasts Hagen in his name, "trûwet wol erwerben ein also schœne magedîn" (424,4)—"trusts himself to win a handsome young woman such as you" (63). In other words, he trusts that any warrior such as Gunther, Hagen, or Dancwart (Hagen's brother) would be safe in battle with a woman. The sight of her in her armor, however, gives the Burgundians cause to reevaluate their mission. Brünhild is, in fact, described in terms strongly reminiscent of Goliath's presentation in I Samuel:

> Dô truoc man der frouwen swære unde grôz
> einen gêr vil scharpfen, den si álle zîte schôz,
> starc unt ungefüege, michel unde breit,
> der ze sînen ecken harte vreislîchen sneit.
>
> Von des gêres swære hœret wunder sagen.
> wol vierdehalbiu messe was dar zuo geslagen.
> den truogen kûme drîe Prünhilde man. (440,1-3)
>
> They thereupon carried out for the lady a great spear, both sharp and heavy, which she was accustomed to throw—it was strong, and of huge proportions, and dreadfully keen at its edges. And now listen to this extraordinary thing about the weight of the spear: a good three-and-a-half ingots had gone into its forging, and three of Brünhild's men could scarcely lift it. (65)

At this sight, Gunther and his companion Burgundians are dismayed, just as one would expect of lesser warriors. Gunther wishes to fall back, literally saying to himself, "wære ich ze Burgonden mit dem lebene mîn, / si müeste hie vil lange vrî vor mîner minne sîn" (442,3-4)—"If I were safe and sound again in Burgundy, she would not be bothered by my wooing" (65). The figure that the king cuts here is made ridiculous by the reminder that he is making love, not war. The fact is that, like Penelope's suitors, this king never himself willingly embarks on an expedition of war. Indeed, when eventually he does find himself surprised by the necessity to fight, it is in the context of a visit to his sister and her husband. His hesitation to defend Burgundy against challenges from Siegfried, Liudegast, and Liudeger is simply reaffirmed when he finds that combat with Brünhild requires that he put his life at risk.

Dancwart views the situation in the same terms as his brother and his king. "mich riuwet inneclîchen disiu hovevart" (443,2)—"I heartily regret our visit to this court," he says (my translations): "nu hiezen wir ie recken: wie verlíesen wir den lîp! / suln uns in disen landen nu verdérbén diu wîp? / Mich müet daz harte sêre, daz ich kom in diz lant" (443,3-44,1)—"We have always borne the name of heroes, but what a shameful way of dying if we are to perish at the hands of women! I bitterly rue ever having come to this country" (65). But Brünhild's contest is perfectly honorable, and it is the Burgundians' behavior that gives real cause for shame. Dancwart wishes only for his sword and declares, "unt het ich tûsent eide ze einem vride geswarn, / ê daz ich sterben sæhe den lieben herren mîn, / jâ müese den lîp verliesen daz vil schœne magedîn" (445,2-4)—"had I sworn a thousand oaths to keep the peace, that bewitching young lady would have to lose her life before I would see my dear lord die" (66). Dancwart admits that he would break the oaths that bind opponents and so guarantee the duel's efficacy. This uncanny duel reveals the weakness in Dancwart's understanding. He is much like Pandarus in his misprision of the situation. Brünhild actually overhears Hagen expressing a similar wish for his battle gear and confidently commands her retainers as follows: "nu er dunke sich sô küene, sô traget in ir gewant, / ir vil scharpfen wâfen gebet den recken an die hant" (447,3-4)—"[s]ince he fancies himself to be so brave, bring these knights their armour, and give them their sharp swords too" (66). Brünhild's demeanor, her armor, and her strength, as she proves, are all those of a champion. Only her sex is contrary to the norms. Consequently, the Burgundians do not respect her as an opponent, and Hagen intends to tame "dér fróuwen übermuot" (446,4)—"the woman's arrogance" (my translation).

Neither Hagen nor his companions, including Siegfried, recognize the queen's principal function to identify an adequate defender for her domain. It is the Burgundians' intention from the outset to subvert her selection process. In his willingness to aid the Burgundians, Siegfried betrays the extent to which he himself has lost sight not only of Brünhild's roles and functions as queen but also his own proper behavior as champion, would-be husband, and future king. Siegfried, by taking sides with men who would break their oaths and spoil the ritual duel, undermines the institution by which his own championship is made meaningful.

The narrative's pointed ridicule of Gunther has the effect of displaying the utility of Brünhild's strange customs. Her courtly ways may seem absurd, but they expose to view—unfortunately not her view—Gunther's shortcomings. Consequently, the wooing expedition itself is thrown into an ever more questionable light.

But the duel is not actually fought between Brünhild and Gunther, as appears to be the case, but between Brünhild and Siegfried, who is made invisible by the magic properties of the cape won from the Nibelungs in the same fight in which he also acquired his reputation for invincibility. Siegfried's deception, then, does not so much give him an unfair advantage as it enables him to pass that advantage over to Gunther. In essence, Siegfried is cloaking Gunther in the two-fold protective mantle of his reputation, built on previous exploits, and his strength. Brünhild is fairly defeated but not by the man she sees in front of her. She ought, by the terms of the contest, to yield to marriage; however, it should not be marriage to Gunther. By all the terms of the duel, Siegfried is Brünhild's rightful husband. She is not interested in her husband's person but in his capabilities, which include both his fame, won in the past, and his present fighting ability. The man she selects for marriage, on both counts, is Siegfried. The face and body of Brünhild's husband are, for her, only markers for that individual who fulfills the functions of champion, king, and lover. By holding Gunther's stirrup and then cloaking him in the appearance of his own strength, Siegfried lends credibility to Gunther's otherwise hopeless proposal of marriage.

Grudgingly, unable to pierce the Burgundian deception, Brünhild eventually agrees to duel Gunther. She still mistrusts him, however, and cannot be fully persuaded that he is deserving of her respect. Indeed, after he appears to have defeated her in spear-throwing, the boulder-toss, and the leap, "Prünhilt diu schœne wart in zorne rôt" (465,3)—"[f]air Brünhild flushed red with anger" (68). But she respects her practices more than her personal feelings and so "ein teil si lûte sprach" (466,1)—"in a voice not altogether quiet" (my translation)—she immediately commands, "vil balde kumt her nâher, ir mâge unt mîne man! / ir sult dem künec Gunther alle wesen undertân" (466,3-4)—"[c]ome forward at once, my kinsmen and vassals! You must do homage to King Gunther" (68). She has selected a husband for herself, a champion and king for her people. They, too, understand the significance of the event: "Dô leiten die vil küenen diu wâfen von der hant, / si buten sich ze füezen ûz Burgonden lant / Gunther dem rîchen, vil manec küener man. / si wânden daz er hête diu spil mit sîner kraft getân" (467)—"Then those brave men laid down their weapons and knelt before the great King Gunther of Burgundy in large numbers, in the belief that it was he who with his unaided strength had performed those feats" (68). But, in fact, the duel has been won through trickery. The Burgundians are cowardly cheats who have no right to the homage being paid their king. The transfer of power is completed according to the terms of the duel: "dô nam in bî der hende diu maget lobelîch. / si erloubte im daz er solde haben dâ gewalt" (468,2-3)—"clasping [Gunther] by the hand, Brunhild gave him express authority to rule over her country" (68).

But there is one more station at which the queen will test her husband's mettle. Because the queen legitimates the champion as king by making him her husband, epic culture interchanges the battlefield, the throne, and the royal marriage bed. Brünhild, therefore, still has a last venue for confirming her husband's strength, courage, and determination. She turns their wedding night into a wrestling match that Gunther cannot win.

The event that causes Brünhild to be upset is Kriemhild's marriage to Siegfried. In Iceland, it was Siegfried's ploy to insist that he was Gunther's vassal, yet now he is being given Gunther's only sister in marriage. In the strictly hierarchical world of champion-kings, tokens of status must be unambiguous. The marriage between Siegfried and Kriemhild violates the code of significations through which a king's power and authority are secured. Thus, Brünhild weeps to see Kriemhild "sitzen nâhen dem eigenholde" (620,3)—"sitting beside a liegeman" (86). Gunther promises to explain this apparently uneven match at some later date, but Brünhild will not be placated and determines to use the last means still remaining to her—the power to refuse her husband in bed.[30]

When that night comes, "der degen küene" (633,2)—the "dauntless warrior" (88)—dims the lights and makes ready to take her in his arms to lavish caresses and endearments upon her, but she flies into a rage and declares, "ich wil noch magt belîben (ir sult wol merken daz) / unz ich diu mære ervinde" (635,3-4)—"I intend to stay a maiden till I have learned the truth about Siegfried" (88). And that truth is that Siegfried should be her husband, not Gunther. Were she to learn about the deception, she would have every reason to consider her marriage null and void, but knowing her to be unarmed and, in fact, dressed only for bed, Gunther flatters himself with the calculation that he should now be capable of forcing her.

> dô wart ir Gunther gehaz.
>
> Dô ranc er nâch ir minne unt zerfúorte ír diu kleit.
> dô greif nâch einem gürtel diu hêrliche meit;
> daz was ein starker porte, den si úmb ir sîten truoc.
> dô tet si dem künege grôzer léidé genuoc.
>
> Die füeze unt ouch die hende si im zesamne bant,
> si truoc in ze einem nagele unt hienc in an die want,
> do er si slâfes irte. die minne si im verbôt.
> jâ het er von ir krefte vil nâch gewúnnén den tôt. (635,4-637)

> Gunther grew very angry with her. He tried to win her by force, and tumbled her shift for her, at which the haughty girl reached for the girdle of stout silk cord that she wore about her waist, and subjected him to great suffering and shame: for in return for being baulked of her sleep, she bound him hand and foot, carried him to a nail, and hung him on the wall. She had put a stop to his love-making! As to him, he all but died, such strength had she exerted. (88)

The wrestling match is always the ultimate test of strength for two champions. When their weapons are used up, smashed, or broken, they must resort to bare-handed strength. Brünhild, like Grendel and Grendel's mother, is endowed with strength beyond that of a normal woman or man. She, in fact, would be quite capable of crushing Gunther to death. Unlike Grendel's mother, however, Brünhild's strength is put, like a champion's, in defense of her people and her domains.

Gunther submits to Brünhild in the terms of submission offered by a vassal, such as Alberich's submission to Siegfried. She, however, does not desire a submissive husband. The terms of her wedding contest specified a

---

[30] It is in order to confront this contradiction, not because she resists marriage per se, that Brünhild confounds Gunther's expectation of having sex with her on their wedding night.

man able to defeat her in three tests of strength. To find now that she has taken a husband unable to give her any more security than she could give herself is to recognize her marriage to be a mockery. He is left hanging on his hook through the entire length of the night. By morning, Gunther has lost all his power: "ob er ie kraft gewunne, diu was an sînem lîbe klein" (639,4)—"If Gunther had ever been possessed of any strength, it had dwindled to nothing now" (88).

The parallels between Brünhild's public duel to select a husband and the private duel held in their bed underlines the parallels between a queen's acceptance of a new husband in her bed and her legitimation of his right both to kingship and championship. Her authorization of a lover to enter her bed is a sign of her permission for him to represent her in duels for her domain, her wealth, and the fate of her people.

The fact that Siegfried must enter Gunther's bed in order to subdue the queen for him is a hyperbolic statement of the intimate relationship between marriage, championship, and kingship in epic culture. Gunther cautions his champion not to "make free with" Brünhild in any way. But the issue of penetration, important to the definition of violation from Gunther's perspective, is a moot point for Brünhild. For her, the duel is a form (albeit specialized) of coupling. In defeating her, Siegfried has already made love to her. When, in her bed, the contest turns to wrestling, Siegfried struggles fiercely with her "daz ir diu lit erkrachten unt ouch al der lîp" (677,3)—until "her joints cracked all over her body" (92)—whereupon "wart si Guntheres wîp" (677,4)—"she became Gunther's wife" (my translation).[31] Note the sudden and extreme change in her demeanor:

> Si sprach: "künec edele, du solt mich leben lân!
> ez wirt vil wol versüenet, swaz ich dir hân getân.
> ich gewér mich nimmer mêre der edelen minne dîn.
> ich hân daz wol erfunden, daz du kanst frouwen meister sîn." (678)

> "Let me live, noble King!" said she. "I shall make ample amends for all that I have done to you and shall never again repel your noble advances, since I have found to my cost that you know well how to master a woman." (92)

Her temper has turned sweet because she has been thoroughly convinced, at last, that her husband really can "master" her or can wrestle her and subdue

---

[31] Frakes points out that at the moment when the struggle ceases and Brünhild "becomes Gunther's wife" Gunther is not yet in the bed (p. 122). The end of the struggle changes Brünhild's disposition so that she will now allow Gunther to penetrate her, be it immediately, minutes later, or at a later date. Whether Siegfried took advantage of the doubled cloak of darkness and invisibility to ravish her is perhaps of interest to Gunther but not to her. While Frakes finds it important that penetration occurred but unimportant by whom (p. 120), Brünhild believes that it is unimportant whether or not there has been penetration but important who has defeated her in a test of "naked" physical strength.

her. For her, these are the qualities of an ideal lover.[32] She wishes not for tender caresses but instead a display of his physical power. Siegfried's promise to Gunther "daz ich ir niht enminne" (656,2)—"that I will not make love to her" (my translation) is rendered meaningless from her perspective, because she herself has regard not for his sexual performance but for his wrestling.[33] As a wrestler, Gunther makes an inadequate lover and spends his

---

[32] Brünhild's moment of transformation is paralleled by Kriemhild's insistence, upon concluding the celebration of her wedding to Siegfried, that she retain her share of Burgundian men. Frakes identifies this passage in the *Nibelungenlied* (696,1-2) as an important example of the way in which marriage is used to disenfranchise a woman of her power and property. Despite her husband's intervention to disallow her her rightful share of property and an armed retinue, Kriemhild manages to effect an "intrusion . . . into men's business" and so to retain the rights to at least a small portion of her wealth and power (p. 71). Thus, Kriemhild, who as a Burgundian princess had almost no say in selecting a husband (though apparently she might refuse to marry) and who was used for her exchange value by her royal brothers in their endeavor to obtain Siegfried's services for the wooing expedition to Iceland, now begins for the first time to assert herself in the quest for a power outside of her husband's identity and control, especially as, at this moment, his position is made very weak by the fact that the service he has performed must remain a secret. If, as Frakes very correctly observes, Kriemhild's movement vis-à-vis power and independence runs opposite to that of Brünhild in a chiasmus that runs through the length of the narrative (pp. 148, 156, 164), the double wedding marks the point at which these lines cross. Kriemhild, through her association with Siegfried and the calamity that befalls her when he is murdered, passes from a passive object of male political exchange to a woman who plans, controls events, and amasses military power, eventually transforming herself into the warrior that had once earned Brünhild the reputation of having "monstrous" customs. The process that begins when she refuses to relinquish her right to a Burgundian guard (Frakes calls attention to this passage with a particularly detailed analysis—pp. 70-73) then escalates as, acting as a king, she employs wealth to acquire the services of warriors "den armen unt den rîchen" (1128,1)—"rich and poor alike" (148)—and she eventually is at all times accompanied by a bodyguard of twelve royal companions (1391). In the last scene, she takes the final step, wielding in her own hands her dead husband's sword, using it to kill his murderer. At this moment, lack of strength is the only quality to separate her from being the kind of queen that Brünhild had been or becoming a warrior like Siegfried.

[33] Brünhild's perspective is radically different from that of late-twentieth-century society, which might well consider Brünhild's experience to be a kind of gang rape perpetrated by Siegfried and Gunther (see, for example, Frakes—pp. 17, 120, 154-55). Brünhild's refusal to have sex with her husband is based on the fact that he seems not to be the man she thought he was. The "rape," then, as Frakes points out, is not defined by sex, but neither is it characterized "primarily by power and violence" (p. 123), for the capacity for violence is the very quality that Brünhild most seeks in the man with whom she would willingly have sex. The wrong done Brünhild is defined by her husband's *incapacity* for physical violence and penetration.

night hanging from the wall. Here again, from her perspective, Siegfried is the only man who has a legitimate claim to be her husband, even though she is kept in the dark by the deception played on her. The ring that he takes from her finger and the girdle that he takes from around her waist symbolize a marriage relationship that exists between them regardless of intercourse and superseding any sexual intimacy that Gunther later enjoys with her.

Brünhild is in essence married to two men simultaneously but according to two conflicting marriage codes. The impossibility of such a double marriage's succeeding reflects the conflict between the two cultural codes that are apparently in competition with one another. The one code assigns to marriage the role of selecting and legitimating new champions, while the other code employs marriage as a means for making and cementing alliances. The one code requires of the queen that she bestow herself and the crown on a man whom she must first test for the ability to serve as her champion, while the other code requires that the princess serve as a medium of exchange in a political economy based on nonaggression or mutual assistance between rival courts. The one arranges for the queen to exchange status and position for security, while the other provides that the men will exchange security directly with each other. The one assumes that a challenge for control of the court is imminent, and the other allows for some willingness to leave matters as they are, to exchange wealth or property without resorting directly to violence. The two codes are incompatible,[34] and when they are inadvertently or care-

---

Brünhild's sudden loss of strength and her transformation into a woman who can only act through the intercession of male courtiers may not be believable for twentieth-century readers, or, as Frakes puts it, "within the realm of patriarchal myth as politics in which marriage is the ultimately defining and legitimizing experience for women" (p. 252). But it is believable in an epic-cultural context judged in terms of the queen's successful completion of her search for an appropriate champion and mate. Until that moment, however, she is the active, controlling, and dominant party in the "courtship" ritual. Frakes accounts for Brünhild's strength and the imagery that portrays her as the rapist by interpreting that when she refuses "to consummate marriage with the king, she challenges the entirety of male ideology and thus becomes by definition the aggressor" (p. 123). She does indeed challenge an ideology, but it is not a "male" ideology any more than the epic-cultural ideology in whose defense she fights is a female ideology. Gender has a central role in governing the function of individuals in both ideologies, but those functions are not defined by gendered opposition. It is a fundamental error in cultural (and thus textual) analysis to presume to know in advance the values and functions placed on gendered distinctions. The result of this error is the discovery, Frakes notes, that "the thirteenth-century text already seems to presage the twentieth-century" definition of rape (p. 123).

[34] Recognizing but failing to understand the conflict between the two types of queen, de Boor simply judges the function with which he is unfamiliar to be ahistorical ("außerhalb aller Geschichtlichkeit"—p. 49). Kriemhild's role as a gift meant to bind the champion's services to the king, on the other hand, he finds to be compatible with history. Behavior, function, and historical reality are here indistinguishable terms. Brünhild's function as an independent arbiter to make the selection of a new champion-king is never recognized, because it is

lessly mixed, the mechanisms designed to curb the spread of violence break down with disastrous consequences for everybody.[35]

Kriemhild's marriage with Siegfried, then, is contracted under the terms of a marriage arrangement alien to Brünhild. Whereas under Brünhild's code, as we have seen, the queen is encouraged to attract lovers—men ready to submit at her command to any danger, prove themselves in any test she may set, and enter into any battle in her defense—under Burgundy's code, the queen is the property, first, of her male relatives, then of her husband. Her body serves as a physical token in the agreement between her brothers and her husband, with her chastity functioning as an index of their control over her but also of their self-control, for in delivering Brünhild to Gunther, Siegfried must refrain

---

summarily dismissed as a departure from the construction of reality that de Boor assigns to the poetry but that should actually be ascribed to an entire cultural system familiar to de Boor and, indeed, to contemporary criticism in general. Based on his assumptions about the historically possible, de Boor is able to state with authority: "The domain which the historical frame here described would have allowed a Burgundian queen for her development would have been the stance of a prominent member of the national-Burgundian enemies of the great Frank. . . . From this basis a female role could have been created which would have been related to that of [other] poetry —that of a great intriguer who rendered her weaker husband pliable to her plans and made his physically powerful lieutenant her tool" (pp. 49-50). Like the Siegfried who first arrives at Burgundy, however, de Boor notes that the Brünhild we find in the text extends beyond the "heroic-ideal reality" into the supernatural ("das Überwirkliche"—p. 50).

[35] Haymes is correct in assessing that "Brünhild serves as something of a social arbiter in the Siegfried story and it is her conviction that the social order is awry that leads directly to the confrontation with Kriemhild and thus to Siegfried's death" (p. 101). Though recognizing Brünhild's role as arbiter, Haymes nevertheless fails to associate the conditions of her contest with Siegfried's "puzzling challenge to Gunther upon his arrival in Worms" (p. 101), for he never for a moment takes seriously the assumptions behind either's insistence on a duel. Thus the values of *minnedienst* are incorrectly assigned to Siegfried, while to Gunther and Burgundy are ascribed adherence to "traditional" values favoring hereditary transfer of royal power. *Minnedienst* is a practice taken on by Siegfried, however, only after he enters into the Burgundian context. Regardless of the finery in which he dresses himself and his companions for their grand approach to the Burgundian court, Siegfried's challenge makes it clear that he initially expects to have to prove himself in battle for the honor of marrying Kriemhild. Entering into the court without the clarification of the proposed duel, Siegfried indeed "lays the grounds for his own destruction through his thoughtless adherence to these two foreign ideals," according to Haymes (p. 101). Brünhild serves as an arbiter by insisting on the duel that Siegfried had been willing to forego at Burgundy. In order to maintain his "foreign" practices in the Burgundian context, Siegfried and the Burgundians together must deceive her. Through the deception, Siegfried once again ducks his own values. This time, ironically, he uses his ability to duel and his knowledge of dueling custom to subvert the social order dependent on that practice. It is not the custom of heredity away from which Siegfried turns but instead the practice of the duel as the sole criterion of sovereign legitimacy.

from intercourse with her out of respect for his partnership with the king. When Kriemhild insults Brünhild with the term "mannes kebse" (839,4)— "vassal's whore" (my translation)—she draws on the connection between sexual mores and gender as a key feature in the cultural construct, for coitus with Siegfried is judged differently according to the cultural code being employed. From the perspective of Brünhild's Islandic marriage code, the outrage is not that she has been compromised by sex with a man not her husband but that the man able to force himself on her sexually did not then bind her to himself; instead, he gave her to another in a marriage that she now discovers to have been a sham. Kriemhild's use of the term "kebse" (whore) also impugns the king's potence—and thus his status—as the sole male with sexual access to the queen.[36] Because both queens have been living for some time under codes contrary to their background, it may be possible that they now intend and understand the insult according to both codes. Brünhild is to comprehend that she was deceived in her marriage and that her husband's status is under attack. Kriemhild, on the other hand, claims superiority on both counts, that she is married to the superior warrior and to a king without stain.

According to the terms of their agreement, the two kings are to regard themselves as equals. Siegfried's return to Xanten and his life there independent of Burgundy works well for both parties so long as the definition of their relationship is never put to the test. Siegfried's obvious independence becomes a problem for Brünhild, however, for her marriage is predicated upon Siegfried's acceptance of Gunther as his better, and she therefore contrives a meeting precisely in order to examine this discrepancy. Thus, when they do come together, Siegfried and Gunther's mutual commitment to maintain parity will be tested under the most trying of circumstances. Indeed, the events at Worms make it apparent that the delicate relationship between the kings is compromised by their relationships with their wives.

The betrothal of Hrothgar's unmarried daughter, Freaware, provides Beowulf with an occasion to reflect on the delicacy of marriages. Her name

---

[36] Schröder makes a distinction between two meanings of Kriemhild's accusation as "objektiv eine Übertreibung des wahren Sachverhalts, jedoch subjektiv keine bewußte Verleumdung" (objectively an exaggeration of the true state of affairs but subjectively not a conscious defamation—p. 91). The words of this statement (particularly "Übertreibung" and "Verleumdung") are taken directly from a similar comment by Beyschlag, to which the latter adds that "Brünhild wird im Epos in Wirklichkeit nicht gekebst" (p. 198), by which must be meant that Siegfried kept his agreement with Gunther and did not penetrate Brünhild when he had the chance. But if we take "kebse" as does Brünhild in her next remark, "Wen hâstu hie verkebset?" (840,1), it means not penetration but the (double) insult, and we might with Brünhild well ask: who has been "verkebset"? Kriemhild is the one used as a token in an exchange among males; is she not then a "kebse"? Yet Siegfried trades away to another man the woman that he has won in the contest. Brünhild is also a "kebse." Both women are involved in the trade; both are "gekebset" by the men's plan to avoid conflict. Either one of them can escape this designation, however, by denying the kings their equality.

indicates her role as "guard" of the "lord"—her husband, who will be the son of Froda, king of the Heatho-Bards. Indeed, the purpose of the marriage is to put an end to the violence between these two groups: "þæt he mid ðy wife wælfæhða dæl, / sæcca gesette" (2028-29)—"that with this woman he settle their portion of deadly slaughters, of feuds" (my translation). But Beowulf anticipates that in this instance, as in others when a prince has fallen, no matter how satisfactory the bride, the spear will be given but a short rest: "Oft seldan hwær / æfter leodhryre lytle hwile / bongar bugeð, þeah seo bryd duge!" (2029-31)—"Yet most often after the fall of a prince in any nation the deadly spear rests but a little while, even though the bride is good." This interregnum is brief because, as the rival groups sit in the hall at their beer, they wear the weapons that brought death to each other's fathers, all of which remind them that they are in the company of those who did the killing; inevitably such memories fan into flame the desire for vengeance, and thus the result is a sudden outbreak of violence, upon which the oaths will be broken on both sides and "weallað wælniðas, ond him wiflufan æfter cearwælmum colran weorðað" (2065-66)—"his wife-love after the surging of sorrows will become cooler" (my translation). To guard against such an outbreak, the warriors in both camps must practice a perfect self-discipline extending over a period of weeks and months or, as in the case of the Huns and Burgundians, even of years.

Though a history of warfare between Huns and Burgundians is not part of the narrative, it is clear from the moment that the Burgundians cross the Rhine that they have entered hostile territory. The farther they travel, the more precarious their safety. The uneasy peace that at first prevails between the Huns and their guests should be attributed not to Kriemhild, who quickly sets about inciting an act of violence, but to the kings, whose determination it is to avoid war, even under the most volatile circumstances. Both sides do, however, expect their agreement to be upheld through and by their mutual connection to Kriemhild. Thus, Etzel never suspects her to be deceiving him in inviting her male relatives for a visit, and her brothers are nearly equally slow to appreciate the fact that she will gladly sacrifice them to the project of her revenge. Even Hagen seems to believe that the relationship between the Burgundian and Hunnish courts can be managed so as to exclude Kriemhild's influence.[37] The men demand honor from[38] and grant honor to each other,[39]

---

[37] Thus, the Burgundians put aside their profound misgivings in order to give Etzel's ambassadors a tolerably cordial reception. Pointing out that Hagen asks after Etzel but not Kriemhild, Schröder observes that "Hagen sind die hiunischen Gesandten allein um Etzels willen willkommen" (the Hun ambassadors are welcome to Hagen solely for Etzel's sake—p. 114).

[38] Etzel's ambassadors imply that the Burgundians' apparent avoidance of Etzel and his lands is interpreted as a sign of tension and even enmity, which, if not corrected through a visit to Etzel's court in Vienna, may provoke the Hun to anger (strs. 1448-49).

[39] It is as though the men's assertion of their commitments to one another demanded the exclusion of Kriemhild's wrongs from all consideration. They

keeping their peace as long as they can and exercising restraint even after violence erupts—first with an accidental killing during the bohort, then even as naked aggression begins to express itself.

The marriage code by which a princess serves as a token of good faith in an exchange among males is shown by the *Nibelungenlied* to be vulnerable in two ways.[40] The first is because the bonds between the males and the female who passes among them are not powerful enough to stem the forces of competition and revenge and the second because, in a structure of male-male bonds, the female is allowed no play for independent action, although she is capable of exploiting the slightest scope of action inadvertently granted her by the men to assert herself, especially against those who have abused her function as peace-maker to take advantage of each other. Kriemhild's revenge is aimed principally at Hagen, but the destruction that she unleashes engulfs them all. Through their part in killing Siegfried, Kriemhild's brothers make a mockery of her service as a peace-token and deny her any role for the future. Her revenge, then, is not only or perhaps not primarily for the loss of her husband as a beloved friend but also for her brothers' abuse of the marriage into which they had placed her. Her revenge involves another marriage into which she enters in order to destroy them.

Kriemhild is not simply bent on destruction, for the power to destroy and the power to rule are the same. Thus, working from a point of absolute powerlessness[41] at the court of her brothers after the murder of her husband, Kriemhild parlays her personal power ever more forcefully, beginning with the personal promise made to her by Rüedeger, adding Etzel's desire to please her, and thence manipulating male-male bonds and animosities to control—if imperfectly—the action of thousands of warriors. Through the course of this terrible struggle, it becomes clear that in Kriemhild's circumstances power must be measured in absolutes.[42] The hoard, her legacy from Siegfried, rep-

---

appear to put aside their knowledge that Hagen's betrayal of Kriemhild involved Siegfried's murder. Schröder notes that the black spot on Hagen's honor has faded; the monstrous and despicable deed appears no longer to be held against him in the "male world" (p. 119). Of course, it is not only Hagen's honor that is at stake but also the society's well-being. In either case, time may also mollify Hagen's critics. From this perspective, Hagen's guilt in Siegfried's murder may be mitigated by the fact that the victim had some culpability in his own death, for in giving his wife the ring and girdle secretly wrung from Brünhild, Siegfried broached male-male confidences.

[40] As Murdoch sees it, this work may be taken as "a warning that alliances implied by the marriages do not always work" (p. 151).

[41] Schröder calls it a forced inactivity—"erzwungene Untätigkeit"—that ends with her decision to remarry, through which she wins back her lost freedom of action (p. 112).

[42] Thus, where Schröder judges her existence to have become "vollends sinnlos" ("absolutely meaningless"—p. 18) through the vengeful passion that consumes her friends together with her enemies and herself, it is also possible to see that her existence would have been absolutely meaningless unless she could succeed in reasserting herself. The fact that the cost of that self-assertion is total

resents a royal treasury—funds necessary for her if she is to rule. Though she eventually accomplishes her revenge despite Hagen's having deprived her of the hoard's use, she finally appreciates its value. That is, she completes the transformation from a passive peace-token exchanged among men into a sovereign queen with the means and understanding to maintain and protect herself. If her intent was not initially to have wealth and power,[43] by the end of her life she has learned that there was no other way for her to function.

The promises made to Kriemhild by Rüedeger represent the first opening to her, after Siegfried's death, of some maneuvering room, for while men's promises cannot always be trusted, they can occasionally be trusted, and such an occasion is all that she requires.[44] The affection her new husband feels for

---

annihilation for all places this catastrophe in the category of other epic-cultural breakdowns, such as occur when the duel is not fought, its protocols neglected, or a champion abused by the king he serves.

[43] In Schröder's words, "Kriemhilt hat für die in der Werbung Etzels steckenden macht-politischen Möglichkeiten anfangs überhaupt keinen Blick"—"Kriemhild has at first no eye for the possibilities of power politics that reside in Attila's marriage proposal" (p. 106).

[44] Schröder points to Kriemhild's initial lack of interest in Etzel's proposal of marriage as evidence that the power she can acquire through him is of interest to her not for its own sake but only insofar as it serves as a means to her revenge, because she changes her mind when Rüedeger, wooing in Etzel's name, promises her in private that he personally will avenge her for any wrongs done to her (str. 1255). Yet this exchange makes it clear that Kriemhild is not principally moved by Etzel's promise of marriage but instead by Rüedeger's promise of help. She marries Etzel in order to avail herself of Rüedeger's promise. Rüedeger, wooing in Etzel's name, is accepted by Kriemhild as a partner, though without a sexual component to their relationship. Here Kriemhild has adopted the values originally held by Brünhild, when Siegfried was wooing in Gunther's name.

Kriemhild promises herself no advantage directly from Etzel, because she has discovered to her deep sorrow that a marriage according to the Burgundian code deprives the queen of any and all real power to protect either herself or those she loves. Schröder completely misses this point when he interprets her revenge motives in terms of love rather than power: "Es geht ihr also um den unvergessenen Geliebten und nicht um verlorene Ehren und eingebüßte Macht, für die sie überdies seit ihrer zweiten Heirat reichlich entschädigt worden war"— "What matters to her is her beloved, whom she has never forgotten, and not lost honor or diminished power, for which she had been richly compensated through her second marriage" (p. 104). As Schröder sees it, "Kriemhilt verfügt als Gattin Etzels über die Machtmittel des mächtigsten Herrschers der Welt"—"As Attila's wife Kriemhild disposes of the means to power of the world's most powerful ruler" (p. 97)—but Kriemhild has learned from the theft of Siegfried's hoard that those means are not at her disposal unless she exercises direct control over them. The wealth has to be held in her own name, protected by men whose loyalty is pledged directly to her. The other side of the exchange, her possible value as a potential peace token, has been negotiated between Rüedeger (acting for Etzel) and the males of the Burgundian court, and she will feel no compunction about undermining it. For she has now learned to make the all-important distinction between the two mutually exclusive systems.

her, as implied by their pillow talk (1400-07), opens a second avenue for her to misuse the system in which she is meant to serve as a peace token exchanged among the ruling men but which, in fact, affords them the opportunity to catch one another at a disadvantage.[45] Etzel's inclination, however slight, to please his wife by accommodating her request, gives her the power to bring down the whole court and the army that supports it. In a system that works by depriving the queen an active role in her own function, the *Nibelungenlied* makes it clear that no promises would be given her, no accommodation made. The queen must either be demonized, or else she should not be used as a token in male-male exchange but allowed to choose her own husband, aggregate her own lands and wealth, and entertain as many lovers as she likes. That is the choice that the *Nibelungenlied* places before its audience.

---

[45] The Burgundians' motives in arranging for Kriemhild's second marriage pose an interesting problem. Schröder suggests that, because she is a persistently grieving widow, she continues to trouble Burgundian politics as the embodiment of its bad conscience (p. 112). If we define Burgundian politics (as Schröder does not) in terms of its marriage code, Kriemhild's grief stands as an indictment of Burgundian trustworthiness. Instead of bad conscience, it is more likely a bad reputation that troubles the Burgundian leaders. Their success in finding her an appropriate husband would thus represent an important step towards the Burgundians' rehabilitation of their reputation.

Chapter Seven

HILTIBRANT AND THE PROBLEMS OF FREE-AGENCY

Of the texts we have so far identified with epic culture, only the "Lay of Hiltibrant" makes the duel its structuring topos. The action takes place in the space between the armies, with the entire narrative structured as a word-for-word and blow-for-blow description of the verbal and physical exchange between a father and son upon their meeting. And yet, without the discovery of the duel's economy and then the elaboration of practices and institutions related to it, we would not advance very far with a cultural analysis of this poem. While it is clear that Hiltibrant does not expect to meet his own son in battle and that his first impulse upon learning the truth is to present his son with tokens of his pleasure at this surprise, it is difficult to comprehend why the son is so insistent upon denying the possibility of their relationship and why even the father will eventually acquiesce in a battle to the death.

All of the texts we have looked at so far depend upon their audiences to supply some understanding of the epic-cultural milieu, especially as relates to the fact that in the course of a battle the principal warriors will inevitably meet for a decisive combat "untar heriun tuem" (3)—"between two armies." Because this central understanding must be brought to each narrative by its audience, the connection between battle dynamics and the formal battlefield duel is not apparent. Thanks to the sheer volume of passages descriptive of battle in the *Iliad*, however, it has been possible to reconstruct circumstances quite alien to our experience and thus beyond our comprehension. The sixty-five lines of the "Lay of Hiltibrant," by comparison, offer too few details to support the development of any such inferences. Indeed, as I hope to demonstrate, an understanding of this Germanic lay depends upon the full sequence of understandings accumulated through the incremental process of analysis and discovery completed in the foregoing chapters.[1]

The *Odyssey* exemplifies the process of incremental accumulation by which our study has progressed to this point. Though traditionally paired with the *Iliad*, the connection between epic culture and the *Odyssey* is not at all evident, for Odysseus never fights a duel and his use of a bow to eliminate the suitors runs directly counter to epic-cultural protocol. The queen's distinctive role in epic culture (discovered through analysis of the *Nibelungenlied*) does, however, provide a basis for recognizing Penelope's relationship with

---

[1] Renoir similarly finds that this text can only be interpreted in light of previous elucidations of the themes that it expresses. "[T]he poem," he writes, "hits us with a phenomenal concentration of thematic materials leading in the same direction" (p. 145). Though stating emphatically that "the oral-formulaic approach provides us with the only empirically ascertainable context likely to inform our interpretation of the text," he nevertheless leaves untouched the question of oral-formulaic themes' origins (p. 131).

her suitors to be entirely appropriate within an epic-cultural context. Once this connection has been made, the *Odyssey* presents us with an opportunity to observe and understand further aspects of the culture of which we might otherwise have remained unaware, particularly that of the delicacy of the queen's position during her husband's prolonged absence and the sensitivity of her role at the critical moment if and when he returns home. While the battlefield itself remains beyond the immediate concern of the *Odyssey*, the battlefield topos and especially the epic-cultural understandings appropriate to it do inform the audience's interactions with the narrative, though inversely, in that Odysseus's use of the bow, his disguises and false stories, and his decade-long personal struggle to get back home all can be judged in relation to the codes of behavior that regulate conduct on the field of battle. The battlefield topos is of course given frequent, though brief, mention in the *Odyssey* through reference to the Trojan war, but it is also referred to at greater length, as in the description of Patroclus's funeral on the plain before Troy (Book 23).

Identification of the *Odyssey* with epic-cultural practices prompts us, then, to reconsider the problem of the bow; though its use is prohibited by the protocols of single combat, in the *Odyssey* it serves as a symbol of royal power and legitimacy. Penelope herself chooses the bow as the instrument for measuring her suitors' qualifications. Her selection of it for this purpose and Odysseus's use of it to dispatch the suitors thus poses a question that otherwise would not have been raised, namely: should Odysseus not, in keeping with the behavior demanded by his status as a warrior-chief, face his rivals on an equal footing and man to man? Such a question, if it cannot be answered, will either reveal a serious contradiction within the interpretive model or, if it can be answered, will lead to additional insights, expansion, and elaboration of the model.

We may thus distinguish between questions arising from assumptions current within the culture sponsoring the research and questions arising from assumptions that may have been current within the culture being reconstructed. With respect to the "Lay of Hiltibrant," a question of the former type arises from the fact that Hiltibrant is willing to proceed with the combat even after discovering his opponent to be his own son. Hiltibrant's reluctance only reinforces the impression that his perspective and ours must be the same. From the standpoint of epic-cultural understandings, however, the question is far more complex, for the taboo on shedding a kinsman's blood has to be contextualized within a complex network of prohibitions, constraints, protocols, and expectations.[2] Unlike the other texts with which we have worked thus far, ones that, in addition to posing questions, also provide a wealth of narrative material from which to draw inferences about the circumstantial context, this text's brevity offers a bare minimum of circumstan-

---

[2] Renoir explains Hiltibrant's ability to overcome his hesitation to kill his own son in terms of a "heroic code" (p. 135), but it seems to me necessary to contextualize the code itself, so that Hiltibrant's obedience to it can be understood to be a rational, albeit terribly difficult, decision.

tial detail. We shall, therefore, have to draw heavily upon the inferences of the preceding chapters to contextualize each of the poem's details and so to reconstruct an understanding of the relationships among them.

The close blood tie between Hiltibrant and Hadubrant is thematized for the audience by the narrator very early in the lay, a dozen lines before Hiltibrant himself is made aware of it: "sunufatarungo iro saro rihtun. / garutun se iro guð hamun, gurtun sih iro suert ana, / helidos, ubar ringa, do sie to dero hiltiu ritun" (4-6)—"a son and his father set right their armor, belted their battle shirts, girded on their swords, the heroes, over chain mail, when they rode to this battle." The father-son relationship will, in fact, be mentioned repeatedly throughout the lay, so that there can be no doubting its noteworthiness or its centrality. Hiltibrant, "Heribrantes sunu" (7, 44, and 45)—"Heribrant's son"—is himself, though old, still referred to in connection with his own father's name, both by the narrator and by Hadubrant, Heribrant's grandson. Throughout the poem, then, no matter what the topic of a line or strophe, an ongoing recognition of the father-son relationship continuously informs the audience's assessments.

Hiltibrant's first words go to the identity of his young opponent's father. But before Hadubrant can reply, the narrator quite unobtrusively states that "Hadubraht gimahalta, Hiltibrantes sunu" (14)—"Hadubrant spoke out, Hiltibrant's son"—thus restating for the audience the relationship already named in the second line.[3] Answering "Hiltibrant hætti min fater: ih heittu Hadubrant" (17)—"Hiltibrant was the name of my father, I was named Hadubrant"—the son's first speech simply confirms the narrator's statement. Issuing as they do from two independent sources (narrator and character), these reiterations serve an important purpose, for in addition simply to repeating and thus underscoring the significance of the paternal-filial connection, they establish this connection in the audience's mind as objectively given, so that the audience will judge the son to be in error when he refuses to accept his father's revelation. As opposed to the audience's certainty that Hiltibrant is alive is set Hadubrant's certainty that his father is dead, which leads to his judgment that the older man is attempting a cunning deception aimed at weakening his resolve to fight, against which he therefore steels himself by refusing even to entertain the possibility that this old Hun retainer might indeed be his own father. Hadubrant's determination to survive the imminent combat thus expresses itself in a self-inflicted blindness to every circumstance beyond the immediate constraints imposed by the contingencies of the duel between two armies.

---

[3] Thus, while Renoir is undoubtedly correct in observing the formulaic character of these lines, I think it is clear that the formula is here lent poignancy by the contradiction between its content and that of the speech it introduces. The unsettling effect of such a juxtaposition might eventually, after its use four times in this poem, actually color an audience's future reactions to it in other contexts, for the audience will learn that such phrases as "X spoke, son of Y" may be problematized by a father's and son's ignorance of each other's whereabouts.

Hadubrant commits himself wholly to his function as champion by setting aside the circumstances, the events, and the complex history of personal and social experience preceding the present conflict and the moment of its resolution. The young champion rejects at this moment his identity, including his personal history and experience, in favor of an entirely formal identity determined by the status, the role, and the function of a champion. From the warrior's perspective, this formal identity is without past or future, existing only for the duration of the event. In order to ready himself for the duel, Hadubrant restricts his sense of self to those features prescribed for the army's duly authorized representative, and he expects no less of his counterpart.

The older warrior's request to know the younger's identity is thus accepted by the younger only insofar as such information has some bearing on the ensuing combat, for, on the one hand, the potential for each man to add to his own prestige hinges on his opponent's lineage and reputation, but if either of the combatants already possesses a reputation with the power to inspire awe, he may use his credentials to intimidate his opponent. The exchange of words between warriors is, indeed, a customary prelude to single combat, as can be inferred from the fact that the narrator explains that Hiltibrant spoke first because "her uuas heroro man" (7)—"he was the hoarier man." The issue is not whether to speak but who should speak. Following custom, it was Hiltibrant who "fragen gistuont" (8) —"put the questions."

These questions are a fixed set, of the sort as follows: "hwer sin fater wari / fireo in folche" (9-10)—"who his father might be, a man among his people." The elder presumes, wrongly, that the young warrior's father is at this moment serving as a warrior among his own people. The father then elaborates his question by offering his younger counterpart an alternative: to tell "hwelihhes cnuosles" (11)—"of which clan" he comes, for, as Hiltibrant explains, these two pieces of information are intimately connected, such that if he is told either one, he will immediately know the other: "ibu du mi enan sages, ik mi de odre uuet" (12)—"[t]ell me but one, and I know the other." Knowledge of the young man's clan will enable the elder to identify both his father and the people the father serves. Conversely, the name of the father would identify the younger champion's home clan.

This simple equation depends upon two important assumptions, one about a similarity between fathers and sons and the other about their relative proximity to home. Hiltibrant first assumes the young champion's father to be a warrior of great repute, a conclusion that must mean a young man is unlikely to become a champion unless his father before him has proven his worth in single combat. The supposition that fathers are like their sons is, of course, not merely an inversion of the commonplace that sons should be like their fathers. Common experience in family life shows that sons do not always possess their fathers' qualities. Hiltibrant judges, however, that, in this instance, son and father must indeed be alike, because the young man is, as Hiltibrant thinks, away from home. It is Hiltibrant's business as a champion to be informed about "al irmindeot" (13)—"all the earthly breed." Like Hagen, his competence depends in part on assessing the strength of challengers and defenders, and, having once served those he now faces,

Hiltibrant should know more than a little about its leadership. He thus knows it to be without a recognized and established champion, nor is he mindful of the possibility that any champion's progeny (least of all his own!) may have risen to the responsibility of defending land and people. He concludes, therefore, that the young man facing him comes as a volunteer from elsewhere, seeking to build his fame through service to others.

If this were correct (it is not), then the father he leaves at home, "in folche," must be famous; only then is the young champion forced to go abroad to establish his fame, because at home he has no opportunity for proving himself. In the first place, foreign attack is deterred by the father's reputation. We have already seen how the Geats' neighbors leave them in peace as long as Beowulf is thought capable of defending them. Such appears also to be the case in Siegmund's kingdom. But second, if a hostile power were ill-advised enough to attempt an attack, the father would probably assume personal responsibility for repelling it, thus depriving his son of the opportunity to prove himself. Therefore, when the son of such a champion grows to manhood, he must leave the orbit of his father's protection in order to find the opportunity to fight and to establish his own fame. In this event, he goes off in search of beleaguered strangers to whom he may offer his services.

These are the considerations implied by Hiltibrant's double question. For those audiences living according to knowledge of epic-cultural conventions, such considerations would be self-evident. For us, on the other hand, these considerations are made possible only with reference to our reconstruction (however incomplete) of epic-cultural circumstances, practices, and conventions.

Hiltibrant's claim to knowledge of "al irmindeot" is not meant, of course, to pertain to every living individual, to every male, or even to every male warrior. The unstated limitation to this proposition is represented by the peculiar context in which it is uttered—the formal duel taking place "untar heriun tuem." In accordance with the protocol governing their meeting, Hiltibrant's questions presume his younger opponent to be the duly authorized representative of the army in front of which he now stands. In this very specialized context, the number of likely champions is quite limited, and it is no great feat to know all their names. It is, in fact, in quest of such a name, known to all people far and wide, that younger warriors must go abroad, whether, like young Beowulf, as volunteer defenders or, like young Siegfried, as aggressive challengers. The fact is, however, that Hiltibrant's boast to know "al irmindeot" is mocked by his failure to know his own son. Hadubrant, contrary to all Hiltibrant's expectations, is among his own people. Hiltibrant has miscalculated; his assumptions are faulty. He has overlooked one very real possibility—the one created by his own actions. The audience, knowing his error before he does, is put in the position of revisiting his reasoning and the assumptions on which it is based.

The narrative's rhetoric implicates the father-son relationship on two levels: explicitly as plot (father and son meet on the battlefield representing opposing armies) and implicitly in the premises that must be furnished by the audience (fathers are like their sons; warriors with a great reputation remain at home among their own people while their sons go abroad and place themselves in the service of foreigners). As the lay develops, however, it will be discovered that both of these premises are false: the son is in important respects quite unlike his father, and the father has been thirty years in the service of foreigners, while the young man, though his father is a renowned living warrior, has assumed responsibility for the protection of his people. Since the lay's premises are never made explicit, however, and are left for the audience to supply if it is to make sense of Hiltibrant's questions, then it is not only to the old warrior but also to the audience itself that mistaken assumptions must be attributed. The rhetorical subtlety of the lay consists in the inconspicuousness with which the audience is led first to employ a set of assumptions, later finding itself caught in its own mistake. It is given the opportunity to revise these assumptions so as not to make the same mistake again, not only in the context of its interactions with this and other narratives but within the domain of all its interactions.

The lay repeatedly calls upon its audience's familiarity with the epic-cultural context and thus upon the assumptions with which it determines its own disposition to act within that context. It constantly draws on our reconstruction of epic culture for our ability to interpret its lines. Having identified himself to his father, for example, Hadubrant very briefly tells what he knows of both their stories; the son left at home, the father gone abroad. Hiltibrant is known to have traveled eastward together with Theoderic and "degano filu" (19)—"numerous blades"—because he had aroused Otachre's "nid" (18)—"enmity." The cause of this enmity is not told nor is a reason given for the exile's return now after some thirty years ("sumaro enti wintro sehstic"—50—"sixty summers and winters") wandering in "ur lante" (50)—"alien territory."

These matters might, however, be inferred from a knowledge of the social issues identified with epic culture. Hiltibrant is clearly a champion. This is his role now in the single combat with his own son, but it has been his role continuously, stretching all the way back to the days before his exile, when he lived in Otachre's kingdom where he had a wife and child, whom he left behind when he fled with Theoderic. As Hadubrant tells it, "des sid Detrihhe darba gistuontun / fateres mines: dat uuas so friuntlaos man" (23-24)—"on this voyage Theoderic had much need of my father: that was such a friendless man." Theoderic had many enemies and required the service of warriors but especially of a champion like Hiltibrant, for "her was eo folches at ente; imo was eo fehta ti leop: / chud was her chonnem mannum" (27-29)—"he was always at the forefront of massed men: to him fighting was exceedingly dear. He was known to keen men." Fighting at the head of the troops, seeking out battle, establishing his name among warriors everywhere—these are all characteristics associated with an epic-cultural hero and champion. Hiltibrant left Otachre's territory, then, as Theoderic's champion. Upon Hiltibrant's return to the place of his departure, he is still serving as champion, appearing alone between the two armies and wearing as symbols of his service "wuntane bouga, / cheisuringu gitan, so imo se der chuning gap" (33-34)—"the wound rings, imperial rings in spirals, which the king had given him." That king is identified only as "Huneo truhtin" (35)—"keeper of the Huns."[4] Whether this means Theoderic, Attila, or another is impossible to determine.[5] These details are important because they help to establish the context for Hiltibrant's departure, his thirty-year exile, and his return. The departure is tied to Otachre's enmity and Theoderic's need.

Hiltibrant, eyeing his son, judges from his equipment that he has a "herron goten" (47)—a "good master"—who rewards service properly—first and foremost with the best available armor and weapons.[6] This positive assessment is measured by Hiltibrant inversely against his own life and the fact of his exile, observing of his son that "noh bi desemo riche reccheo ni wurti" (48)—"in this realm never yet have you been an exile." This realm is (or was) Otachre's, and the implication of "noh" is that in Otachre's realm, eventual enmity and subsequent exile are to be expected—witness Hiltibrant's personal experience. Hiltibrant thus implicitly connects the fact of his exile with lack of proper reward and recognition by the king he once served. The source of enmity between Otachre and Hiltibrant, though not stated, may well have been the same as that between Agamemnon and Achilles or between Saul and David—the jealousy and insecurity of a king in the presence of an awe-inspiring warrior, a savior who could easily seize the throne and to whom, in any case, must be given great treasures and tokens of special status. The parallels between Hiltibrant and David, Otachre and Saul are strengthened by the fact that Hiltibrant leaves his wife when he flees and that he flees rather than killing the man in whom such enmity has developed.

Let us note once again that our ability to recreate a plausible context for Otachre's enmity depends upon our comparative reading of narratives such as the *Iliad* and I Samuel, whereas the Germanic audience must be thought capable of reconstructing this context based on understandings that were current and far closer to home, whether known from oral history or direct personal experience. The encounter between father and son on the battlefield is a problem not only from a modern perspective, for it clearly troubles Hiltibrant and would trouble Hadubrant too if he allowed himself to consider it seriously. The source of the error is, therefore, of concern and must be traced to circumstances of which neither characters nor audience seem to have been fully aware. Even the Germanic audience will, therefore, need to furnish its own explanation for Otachre's enmity and Hiltibrant's flight, for it is

---

[4] Here the poem accords closely with the details of Dietrich's status as "guest" at Etzel's court in the latter half of the *Nibelungenlied,* in which Hildebrand, though old, is still a redoubtable warrior, as demonstrated by his survival of the battle with the Burgundian chiefs, Hagen and Gunther.

[5] Theoderic as a historical figure is identified as an Ostrogoth. Whether such a distinction is meaningful in this context is impossible to say. In the *Nibelungenlied,* Dietrich is a friend and ally of Etzel/Attila.

[6] Renoir finds this mention of armor to be "superfluous within the semantic requirements" (p. 135) and thus included primarily as an indication (through its gleaming) of the theme of the hero on the beach.

only in light of this that Hiltibrant's actions can properly be judged. The text's rhetoric thus first creates the conditions under which an audience might engage itself in recreating a context for the story's action and then discretely supplies the details useful to the audience in formulating a judgment.

What, then, was Theoderic's status when Otachre was king and Hiltibrant his champion? It is possible that Theoderic was Otachre's champion, with Hiltibrant one of his companions, like the relationship between Achilles and Patroclus under Agamemnon's command. But if this were the case, why would it always be up to Hiltibrant to take the point position and to represent the army, then as now, in its battles? Is it not more plausible that Theoderic and Otachre, both kings, had been at war, with Hiltibrant in service of one of them? Had he served Theoderic and killed Otachre's champion, why should he have fled Otachre afterwards? And why would he have left his wife behind under such circumstances? Clearly, he must initially have been in service of Otachre, perhaps facing and defeating Theoderic's champion. Then, when Otachre behaves unappreciatively (as Agamemnon did) or even treacherously (as Saul did), Hiltibrant might have no choice, if he is not to kill Otachre or be killed by him, but to offer his services to Theoderic, just as David is driven to seek protection with the king of Gath. There need be no stigma in Hiltibrant's shifting his service from Otachre to Theoderic, especially if the former has rewarded him with murderous treachery rather than gifts and tokens of status.[7]

It might further be inferred that Hiltibrant's wife, like David's, is likely to be one of the king's daughters. The marriage may have arisen either directly or indirectly from the champion's usefulness to the king. When David arrives at the camp where the Hebrews anxiously anticipate battle with the Philistines, he is told that Saul has promised his daughter in marriage to whomever steps forward and slays the giant. When Agamemnon determines to placate Achilles, he likewise offers to make him a son-in-law as an enticement to return to battle. Where Agamemnon's profferment of a daughter follows upon a severe breach between himself and his champion, Saul's precedes it.

In a series of tests or tasks much like those required of the Greek hero Heracles, David is sent out by Saul to what the king hopes will be his destruction. These tests, however, to the king's surprise, only further confirm his champion's invincibility—a quality now more threatening than useful from the private perspective of a man afraid of losing his own status. Saul thus offers David a position within the royal family as a son-in-law but only

---

[7] On the grounds that there is nothing in the tradition to support this view, Haymes objects (in private correspondence) to my characterization of Hiltibrant as a free agent. But we must account for the facts in the poem. A conflict between our analysis and the tradition proves nothing, for it may well be that the traditional names were joined to the narrative after the latter had been in circulation for some time already. The Hiltibrant met with in our lay may differ in some respects from the Hildebrand of tradition, just as the Otachre of our lay may differ from the historical Odoacer.

on the condition that he bring as a wedding present "a hundred foreskins of the Philistines," thinking thereby "to make David fall" (I Sam. 18:25). David, however, comes back with twice the number of trophies stipulated. The hero is eventually married to Saul's daughter Michal but without alleviating any of the king's anxiety, so that while David makes himself ever more indispensable in the war effort against the Philistines, Saul becomes obsessed with ridding himself of his imagined rival. It is to be expected that when the king fails to establish a stable relationship with his champion the latter may withdraw his services, perhaps going abroad to serve others. As was inferred earlier (in Chapter 4), every great warrior has the opportunity to act as a free agent on the international market, an aspect of the hero's status that David makes use of only most reluctantly. He eventually sees no choice but to seek shelter from Saul's murderous plots among the Philistines, repairing eventually to Gath, where he enters the service of its king, A'chish, who, in turn, gives him Ziklag as a place to live and, possibly, as a source of revenue. So it must have been with Hadubrant, who enters Theoderic's service only when Otachre's enmity leaves him no other choice.

With respect to David, Achilles, and Hadubrant, we see a relationship between the king's enmity, marriage (proposed or actual) to the king's daughter, and the champion's alienation from the king's service. Indeed, the father's enmity interferes with the champion's continued association with his daughter, regardless of marriage bonds between them, which in such cases are anyway intended primarily to consolidate and to regulate the extremely unstable relationship between king and champion. The complexity of such relationships is indicated by Saul's use of his daughters on the one hand to bind David's loyalty to him while at the same time inducing his son-in-law to expose himself to mortal dangers, both in open battle with the Philistine army and within the palace, where he goes about unarmed and thus vulnerable to ambush. Just so, the Burgundian court makes use of Siegfried's obligations as an in-law to summon him to their defense against the Saxons and Danes, thus affording themselves an opportunity to stab him in the back when he goes unarmed among "friends" on a hunt. If Hiltibrant's wife were Otachre's daughter, her child would be his grandson, and both of them would be safe despite his terrible enmity towards their husband and father.[8] These are the circumstances under which Hiltibrant flees Otachre and abandons his wife and child.

Hiltibrant's long voluntary exile, the circumstances of his return, and the terrible predicament from which it seems no longer possible that he will extricate himself reveal the erroneousness of his assumptions, those expressed in the questions that he puts to his younger opponent now as well as those that determined his actions thirty years before. In assuming that fathers stay at home while their sons go abroad in order to build their own

---

[8] In the *Nibelungenlied*, Kriemhild chooses to remain with her mother and brothers even after the murder of her husband, apparently because she feels that her youngest brother can best comfort her and in some measure stand in for ("ergetzen") Siegfried (1080,3).

reputations, Hiltibrant has neglected to consider the story of his own life—the case of a father abandoning wife and child to wander abroad in exile. His present reasoning simply repeats an error made thirty years previously, when he apparently neglected to consider his wife in any way other than as an instrument in his relationship with Otachre.

The awful fact of a father and son meeting one another in a ritual combat is not, then, the result of fate or cruel chance. Rather, Hiltibrant has been guilty of a very serious misprision, one no less serious than that now committed by his son. For if Hadubrant momentarily reduces his identity strictly to the outlines prescribed by his status as the army's representative in a formal duel, Hiltibrant has already lived an entire lifetime under these very restrictions. Hiltibrant understands all too well the factors that might compel a champion's sojourn abroad—both the need to acquire a name for himself and the likelihood that this will engender enmity in the king he serves. While either of these alone gives sufficient grounds for leaving home, Hiltibrant never considers factors that might induce a champion to give some thought to those he has left behind. He thus spends the better part of his life fighting others' battles while leaving in someone else's protection his wife and the son who now stands before him as physical proof of his error, even uttering the reproach that his father "furlaet in lante luttila sitten / prut in bure, barn unwahsan, / arbeo laosa" (20-22)—"left behind in the country insignificant a wife in the house and a son not yet grown—nothing to inherit."

The more difficult challenge to which Hiltibrant discovers himself called to respond is not to give battle but to confront his own past. It is thus doubly ironic that Hiltibrant should declare to his son, "du neo dana halt mit sus sippan man / dinc" (31-32)—"you never yet took up combat with a man so closely related"—when it is he himself who has failed for years to give thought to his family. Offering his son the bands from his arms, he reveals his own failure to understand how great a distance his thirty-years' absence has placed between them. Hadubrant finds it impossible to believe his father's words, in part because he has been told since childhood that his father is dead but more importantly because he operates on a different set of assumptions, one that forbids him to believe that a father worth the name would willingly leave a wife and child so long without the benefit of his personal protection. Even if they are members of the chief's family, the fact is that that chief is now without a proper champion. In abandoning Otachre to whatever may befall him, Hiltibrant must also abandon Otachre's entire polity, including its population of women and children. He has instead spent his life offering protection to strangers, even going so far as to serve the Huns, whose tokens of status he proudly wears and which he now uncomprehendingly attempts to present his son as a sign of the honor in which he holds their blood relationship: "want her do ar arme wuntane bouga, / cheisuringu gitan, so imo se der chuning gap, / Huneo truhtin" (33-35)—"From his arms he twisted the wound rings, imperial rings in spirals, which the king had given him, keeper of the Huns," saying: "dat ih dir it nu bi huldi gibu" (35)—"[t]his I give you out of loyalty."⁹ To Hadubrant, however, the rings are a sure sign that this old man could never be his father, for the gesture affronts the son's respectful belief that his father died abroad before he could return home to the service of his family. Thus, though Hiltibrant has discovered his son, he is wrong to think that they could not be more closely related.

Unlike Hiltibrant, Odysseus marooned on Calypso's island weeps daily for home—not particularly for the pleasures of which he is deprived, for he lives with a beautiful goddess eager to grant him eternal life.¹⁰ What he misses is the wife and child whom he knows to be in need of him.¹¹ Indeed, his return home occurs just in the nick of time, as the suitors are plotting death for Telemachus. For Hiltibrant, this return has not been assiduously enough sought, and it comes too late to make a difference either to wife or to son. Hiltibrant and his son are at this point entirely alike and unalike—a contradiction of which neither can be aware but which must be played out in a duel predestined thirty years before by the father's departure.

Once Hiltibrant sees that Hadubrant's will is implacable and that his own attempts to abort the duel will only strengthen his son's resolve, he acquiesces, calling upon God to witness the fact that "wêwurt skihit" (49)—"a calamity is taking place." While "wêwurt" may be translated in terms of

---

[9] Renoir translates this as "token of loyalty" (p. 135).

[10] One line of interpretation sees Odysseus's relationship to a series of dangerous females as a new patriarchal ideology expressing itself against its matrilineal past. According to this analysis, Odysseus defies the role of sacrificial king by surviving his encounters with powerful and threatening females. Sommer thus describes the episode of "Odysseus's sojourn on the island of the cave-goddess Calypso" in the following terms:

> On the one hand she is the "Concealer," that is, as Goddess of Death she harbours the dead god during the time when, as the feeble winter sun or as the sun during its nocturnal disappearance, he is dormant and obscured. On the other hand, traces remain of an escape from death similar to the others, in Odysseus's refusal to accept immortality at Calypso's hands. The immortality which she promises can most coherently be explained as meaning one thing: an immortality *beyond* death, originating perhaps in an apotheosis and devout reverence post-humously accorded a sacrificed king. But Odysseus does not wish the immortality of a semi-divine hero; he wants a life, the life of a mortal man. (pp. 203-04)

If this general thesis is correct, as it very well might be, it leaves unspecified the cultural dynamics of the new patriarchy in which Odysseus must remain alive, apparently so that he can perform functions of defender and householder that now, in presumably changed cultural and material circumstances, supersede the sacrificial function preeminent within the foregoing matrilineal construct. The king's participation in a duel may, of course, be viewed as a form of sacrifice, and this connection may actually be responsible for reviving the memory of dormant matrilineal customs and practices.

[11] "Home," writes Lynn-George, "is not simply a goal finally achieved after a lengthy passage through distant lands: it is a site introduced from the first book of the epic in its emphatic need of defence and protection" (p. 213).

woeful fate, Hiltibrant's acceptance of it, coming only after Hadubrant's refusal to countenance a gesture of good will, suggests that the fatefulness of this particular calamity was something that could and should have been avoided. While Hiltibrant himself does not (or cannot) pause to consider how his own actions may have precipitated the awful predicament that he either kill his own son or be killed by him, the poem's rhetoric has positioned the audience to recognize the fact that some of Hiltibrant's assumptions have been erroneous and, therefore, to look perhaps more critically at his present circumstances. The alternatives before which Hiltibrant stands—"nu scal mih suasat chind suertu hauwan, / breton mit sinu billiu, eddo ih imo ti banin werdan" (53-54)—"so now shall my own child hew me with his sword, fell me with his battle axe—either that or I have to become his slayer"—need not be viewed as inevitable if one has as one's parameters not only the immediate situation but the life span as a whole. The poem's inclusion of the elder warrior's biography is not simply a formula appropriate to instances of single combat, for in retrospect the temporal sequence may be regarded as causal. Honor and duty may indeed constrain the warriors' choices at the moment of their meeting. Nevertheless, if a wounded sense of honor played a role in Hiltibrant's departure, then the poem suggests a reevaluation of such a decision in light of its consequences.

The last extant lines indicate that the two warriors, who have thrown their javelins, drawn their swords, and hewn away each other's shields, are evenly matched. It is impossible to tell from the course of action which man will win. And this affords us the opportunity not only to interpret the text as we have it but to predict the ending that it is lacking.

The text that has come down to us appears to break off before the lay's conclusion. The incomplete manuscript was written down by medieval monks on the blank cover leaves of a book having nothing whatever to do with these characters or their situation. It is thought that the blank material was simply too valuable to leave unwritten, and that two monks, discernible in their two different hands, took turns, perhaps as a writing exercise, filling the book's endpages with a text that seemed to be of the right length neatly to fill the space. The crowding of the last lines suggests the second scribe's realization that the space would be used up before the text could be completely copied.[12] If these inferences are correct, then the number of lines missing is probably very few.

From a modern perspective, the more moving ending would be the son's murder of his father. Modern culture has long preoccupied itself with the Oedipal situation in which son kills father. And leaving aside this Freudian interest, a concern for the greatest possible dramatic effect would also favor the son, for whom the moment of recognition, bringing with it the unexpected discovery that he has become his own father's killer, should be terrible. Indeed, Aristotle's assessment of Oedipus's tragedy focuses not on the

---

[12] See Hartmut Broszinski, "Einführung: Datierung und Schrift" in *Das Hildebrandslied: Faksimile der Kasseler Handschrift mit einer Einführung von Hartmut Broszinski* (Kassel: Johannes Stauda, 1985).

incest taboo but upon the reversal from good fortune to bad. From the perspective of a tragic reversal, Hadubrant's discovery of his father's identity promises a moment of desperate self-knowledge. From both Freudian and Aristotelian perspectives, then, Hadubrant should slay his father.

To these views may be added Hadubrant and Hiltibrant's joint assessment that, because of the elder's advancing years (his age might be somewhere between fifty and sixty), the younger man has the greater likelihood of winning. Hadubrant sees age as the grounds for his opponent's deceitful claim to be his father: "[D]u bist dir," he tells him, "alter Hun, ummet spaher, / spenis mih mit dinem wortun, wili mih dinu speru werpan. / pist also gialtet man, so du ewin inwit fortos" (39-41)—"You, old Hun, are immeasurably cunning. You would snare me with your words, thus deliver me to your spear. Grown so aged, you readily rely on your craftiness." This is an accusation with which, at least regarding the possible diminution of his strength, Hiltibrant can only concur, saying, "doh maht du no aodlihho, ibu dir din ellen taoc, / in sus heremo man hrusti giwinnan" (55-56)—"Indeed, now you can easily—if your fighting prowess serve you well—win the armor of such a hoary man." In suggesting here that the younger man will prove the better fighter, the lay lends resonance to psychological and dramatic attitudes that favor the son's killing his father as the best ending in terms of the greater emotional and artistic effect as well as enjoying the greater plausibility.[13]

Our understanding of epic culture indicates, however, that the outcome of this duel will upset probability, the dictates of classical poetics, and the expectations of modern psychology. We have already observed the extent to which the unstated commonplace (like father, like son) in Hiltibrant's initial question informs the rhetorical design of the narrative. Indeed, Hiltibrant is living proof that the champion's father is like his son, for he is the champion he expects his opponent's father to be. The son, too, has proven to be a champion, perhaps his father's match.

Telemachus, seeing that none of the suitors can string his father's bow, takes the weapon into his own hands and would easily string it, were his father not to catch his eye and signal him not to make the attempt. Unlike Odysseus on the occasion of his return home, however, Hiltibrant does not make himself known to the son under circumstances appropriate to recognition and acceptance, and thus the test between them cannot be stopped with a gesture or even a declaration but will proceed until one is victorious, the other dead. Just as Telemachus proves himself capable of performing feats equaling his father's in strength and skill with weapons, Hadubrant is likely some day to match his father in strength and skill. And like Telemachus, he is probably the only man from the region able to do this. But where Telemachus is perhaps just reaching the point of proving himself capable of defending Ithaca, Hadubrant has already assumed the role of his country's defender. Because Hadubrant is Hiltibrant's son, he, above all others, can replace Hiltibrant as the people's protector. Consequently, if Hadubrant is

---

[13] Medieval sources suggest that the story ends with the death of Hadubrant. See Renoir (p. 135) and von See (p. 143).

killed in this present contest, then the people will be deprived of their champion. If Hiltibrant kills his son, however, his obvious age makes it improbable that he will be able to serve for long before falling victim to a new challenger from abroad, thus leaving his people in a predicament very similar to that of the Geats upon the death of the elderly Beowulf. Hadubrant's death at his father's hands is to be measured, then, not only in terms of either man's personal tragedy but rather in terms of the vision of doom that it spells for the entire society. The father's victory will thus be doubly bitter, for he will know that he has killed his own son and he will eventually understand that he has destroyed the people's promise of future peace and stability. The son, by contrast, if eventually he learns that he has indeed felled his own father with the blade of his sword, will understand that his father had abandoned his family to serve the Huns. To the people, moreover, Hadubrant's victory presents immediate evidence of his viability as their protector. From their perspective the father is, in any case, elderly and has for thirty years been of no use to them. They have found in the son a protector who has already been winning their admiration, their respect, their gratitude, and their trust. His success promises them an extended period of peace and stability. They should greet his triumph with widespread rejoicing. If the son wins, then, his victory is neither psychologically bitter nor dramatically thrilling. In the event, however, that the father wins the battle, he at once bereaves himself of his son and the people of their protection. His victory plunges his people into despair. To an audience steeped in epic-cultural values, the son's death would be far more disturbing than the father's.

The "Lay of Hiltibrant" is quite unlike the *Nibelungenlied* in that the duel, once proposed, proceeds inexorably to fulfillment, despite the fleeting attempt to abort it. In this instance, the circumstances of the battlefield duel, the importance of the protocols and their strict observation, and the underlying understanding that an economy of lives supports or even insists on the faithful preservation of this institution are recognized and accepted without question by the poem's characters as well as its audience. Father and son have not only their own relationship to concern themselves with but also their obligations to the kings whose rings of office they carry, to the ranks of men on either side, silent witness to the contest that will spare their lives and chart their common future, and to the women and children whose future is at stake. Unlike the breach of faith by the Trojan bowman Pandarus, here the protocols are so strictly adhered to that Hiltibrant is prepared to submit to them, even when it means taking his own son's life. Within this context, however, there is room for sober recognition, first of the personal sacrifice to be made by both champions but then also of their vulnerability to the peculiar accident to which they have fallen victim. Indeed, the poem demands an examination of the premise on which this accident is based—the possibility, or rather probability, that such a father and son will eventually meet each other alone between two armies.[14]

---

[14] Making the point that, based on the poem's employment of themes commonly used in oral poetry, "we should expect the father and the son to face each

The people's dependence on a champion for their freedom from constant warfare requires that they acquire the services of the best man available. The man who would preserve his own people from war must, for his part, establish a personal reputation for invincibility. These needs are complementary and promote the warrior's quest. Once the warrior has successfully performed his task, however, he becomes a threat to the king whom he has served. He then has the impetus either to journey on to volunteer his service elsewhere or, when his fame has reached sufficient proportions and been extended far and wide enough, to return home, bringing with him for his people the gift of a secure and peaceful future.

When, like David, the champion emerges not from the royal family but from a less prominent household, then the implicit threat to the royal family drives him out of his own homeland. On the other hand, his size and strength put him in the way of tempting offers in exchange for his services. Gahmuret (Parzival's father) is simultaneously offered the rule of three realms and marriage to three queens. Odysseus, though sorely needed by his wife at home, frequents the bed of the sorceress Circe during the sojourn of one year, is trapped for years by the goddess Calypso, who wants him for an eternal mate, and is eyed as a potential husband by the Phaeacian princess Nausikaa.[15] Like David among the Philistines, Hiltibrant takes service with the Huns—despised enemies, as can be inferred from Hadubrant's insulting taunts, when he describes his opponent as "alter Hun, ummet spaher" (39)—"old Hun . . . immeasurably cunning." The great warrior always has a place in someone's service; the problem is that he may not be able to find a permanent home for himself anywhere. Champions are thus forced into free-agency, frequently changing allegiance, so that they may well confront as enemies their former "ring-givers." If the system continues to develop in this direction, a very small caste of super-warriors will find itself in circulation, offering its services to the highest bidder as lesser members are killed off, with the result that the ranks of these elite individuals will constantly be pruned. The survivors are rewarded with ever-increasing fame but at the sacrifice of all personal relationships, because even their wives and children must be forsaken as they move on in a state of perpetual exile. Worse than their personal loss, the champions are no longer capable of delivering that protection for which the people look to them.

---

other in combat," Renoir goes so far as to call this the poem's "lesson" (p. 146). In other words, though we *should* expect a combat between father and son, we might fail to do so without the poem's intervention. The interplay between the poem's themes must further lead us to combine, on the one hand, rejoicing at the father-son reunion but also, once the combat begins, sorrow in anticipation of the hero's victory, a paradox that Renoir calls "brutal" (p. 146).

[15] Atchity and Barber attribute Nausikaa's interest in Odysseus (like that of Circe and Kalypso) to a "pre-[Indo-European] Aegean matrilineal system" in which her selection of him as her husband would likely make him king of Phaiakia (p. 18).

The volunteer, always a free agent, coming and going as he pleases, may be inclined toward friendship through the bestowal of gifts in recognition of his accomplishments. Marriage into the king's family and the issue of children from that marriage might strengthen the champion's commitment. Nevertheless, the pressures driving him out would appear to be even more powerful than the bonds of loyalty tying him down. If these pressures are not checked, the champion will inevitably leave sons behind in one or more of the halls at which he sojourns, thus giving rise to the distinct possibility either that he will later face one of his own sons in a contest or that one son will eventually slay another, a half-brother.[16] Our analysis of the "Lay of Hiltibrant" suggests, then, that in cases of enmity between ruler and champion, exile of the latter should be avoided and that the differences between them be settled immediately, even at the ruler's expense and even if this means the champion killing his patron and seizing rule for himself. The warning for ruler and populace is a stern one—placate the champion and avoid his enmity at all costs. The warning for champions is equally stern—establish and uphold ties of loyalty to a people, for otherwise the institution of championship will become self-consuming.

---

[16] This nearly occurs when Parzival and Feirefiz, two sons of Gahmuret, meet in combat in *Parzival*.

CHAPTER EIGHT

THE TALE-SINGER'S FUNCTION

In this book, I have taken the position that implausible aspects of ancient narrative should be neither dismissed as "poetic license" nor attributed to the vagaries of transmission via oral and scribal traditions; rather, our incomprehensions (as they arise) should be attributed primarily to the cultural discontinuity between epic-singing societies and our own. And yet, if the distance between ourselves and epic culture is not altogether unbridgeable (as the foregoing chapters are meant to suggest), then the capacity for communication across such a temporal gulf must repose in part within narrative itself, whether oral or written, poetry or prose. We should therefore reconsider these narratives specifically in relation to cultural boundaries, which may be either endogenous, as between generations or among polities within a relatively stable cultural system, or exogenous, as between a migrant group and the settled polities it encounters.[1]

The study of cultural communication is further complicated by the sheer plenitude of available media. With so many avenues of communication in simultaneous use, study and assessment of the impact from any one upon the culture as a whole must be hopelessly speculative. This limitation does not

---

[1] My use of the term polity throughout this chapter reflects the influence of Renfrew's definition in "Peer polity interaction and socio-political change" (pp. 7-8). Here is the core of his definition:

1 Within a given region with a human population, we shall term the highest order social units (in terms of scale and organisational complexity) 'polities.' It is predicted that, when one polity is recognised, other neighbouring polities of comparable scale and organisation will be found in the same region. . . .

2 When a significant organisational change, and in particular an increase in complexity, is recognised within one polity, it is generally the case that some of the other polities within the region will undergo the same transformation at about the same time.

3 . . . [W]e can predict that several further new institutional features will appear at about the same time. These may include architectural features, such as monumental buildings of closely similar form; conceptual systems for communicating information . . . and customs (including burial customs) indicative of ritual practices reflecting and perhaps reinforcing the social organisation.

4 The observed features will not be attributable to a single locus of innovation (at least not in the early phases of development), but . . . will be seen to develop within several different polities in the region at about the same time.

5 It is proposed that the process of transformation is brought about . . . as a result of interaction between the peer polities.

hold, however, for the case of hostile neighbors between whom the opportunity for cultural exchange is extremely limited, for contact occurs but infrequently and then only under the most restrictive conditions. From the perspective of research into the communication of culture, then, polities at war present an opportunity of rare promise.

It is indeed a most interesting and curious circumstance that the practice of substituting a duel for general warfare has to be agreed to by parties on the verge of battle or else already engaged in it. Successful conduct of a duel thus requires the highest degree of cooperation between precisely those least disposed to it, for we may presume that even if the warring parties were inclined to give the duel serious consideration, they would mistrust one another and might very well secretly hold their own commitments to be purely provisional, pending a favorable outcome. The danger of renewed bloodshed, therefore, is always perilously close, and resorting to such a precarious and unpromising arrangement as the duel gives us some sense of the desperate circumstances under which it is tried. These drawbacks may be mitigated somewhat, however, by the spectacle of single combat itself, for the combined sight of the enemy's champion in action and its own laid low may persuade the vanquished army to accept its defeat and keep its oaths. The victors, on the other hand, stand to gain from having tried the duel whether or not the vanquished honor their word, for the removal of a prominent fighter from the enemy ranks tips the balance in their favor while increasing their confidence in obtaining a victory, though they must still fight for it. Thus Tacitus may not have been far off the mark with his comment that the Germanic peoples regarded even duels conducted with captives as auspicious, for any actual trial of men, equipment, and technique would provide some indication of what was to be expected from the coming battle.

Considering that the particular geometry to which the epics refer affronts common-sense assumptions about strength in numbers, only as two military forces spend ever more time in the field reducing each other's numbers do they acquire an understanding for the consequences of prolonged fighting, which, in turn, prepares the warriors on both sides to accept the idea that single combat might serve as a reasonable substitute for general battle. Linking patterns of experience and circumstance on a field rich in images and actions, the battlefield sets parameters of a context that then serves as the basis for discourse. The field of death thus provides a fertile common ground upon which cultural innovation and cross-cultural communication develop.

Those people first exposed to the circumstances of epic-cultural battle may themselves very likely have been slow to appreciate its significance and to make appropriate adjustments. They certainly could not have anticipated nor even comprehended the extent of its destructiveness until they had witnessed the annihilation of their armies, not just once but repeatedly, for the economy of single combat makes itself apparent only as military forces utterly expend themselves in the course of warfare so catastrophic that neither side can count itself victorious. It is then left to the survivors to recognize the futility of further attempts to achieve a military conclusion and consequently to seek alternative means of resolving their conflict. It is also they who, in the course of time, will have had the opportunity to observe that battle consistently boils down to a decisive meeting between the two most daunting men on the field and who thus conceive the idea of deliberately placing the battle's outcome in the hands of a champion whom they appoint for the purpose.

While this innovation first presents itself in the medium of physical combat, its development depends upon verbal interactions, first, among the individuals on either side as they attempt to come to grips with the destruction to which they are witness, and then later, crossing the battle lines in the shape of a challenge, a formal invitation to lay aside weapons, if only provisionally, in order to experiment with what amounts to a new cultural practice.

Many of the legendary accounts examined in chapter 1 make an explicit link between the proposal to try the duel and the expectation of mutual destruction resulting from prolonged battle. Indeed, they carry unmistakable traces of the interdependence between verbal and martial media, for, according to these reports, as shown in Herodotus, the challenger accompanies his proposal to meet in single combat with a brief explanation to the effect that "ὡς χρεὸν εἴη τὸν μὲν στρατὸν τῷ στρατῷ μὴ ἀνακινδυνεύειν συμβάλλοντα" (9.26.4)—"there was no need for the two armies to risk their lives in a general engagement." As articulated on the battlefield, the reason for submitting to the procedure is always the same:

> "Quousque bellum super cunctum populum commovetur? Ne pereant, quaeso, populi utriusque falangae, sed procedant duo de nostris in campum cum armis bellicis, et ipse inter se confligant. Tunc ille, cuius puer vicerit, regione sine certamine obtenebit." (Gregory 2.2)

> "How much longer is war going to devastate an entire people? In my opinion the armed forces of both peoples should not be slaughtered, but two champions chosen one from each side should meet fully armed on the field of combat and should fight it out between them. That side whose champion is victorious should take over the territory in dispute without further contest."

> "Ecce, quantus populus ex utraque parte consistit! Quid opus est, ut tanta multitudo pereat? Coniungamus nos ego et ille singulari certamine, et cui voluerit Dominus de nobis donare victoriam, omnem hunc populum salvum et incolomem ipse possideat." (Paul 5.41)

> "See how many people there are on both sides! What need is there that so great a multitude perish? Let us join, he and I, in single combat and may that one of us to whom God may have willed to give the victory have and possess all this people safe and entire." (248)

> Ut paucorum impendio, inquit, complurium pericula redimantur, publicam stragem privato discrimine praecurrere liceat. (Saxo 132)

"As the majority may be brought out of danger at the cost of one or two lives, we could forestall a general catastrophe by hazarding single persons." (80)

In each case, however, the appeal to reason depends upon implicit acceptance of an unstated premise in support of which the speaker offers no evidence, namely, that a battle allowed to run its course will ultimately result in a mutual catastrophe. The battlefield audience is presumed to understand that, should the armies rely on warfare to settle the issue, a multitude must perish. Yet, even when the opposing sides have been at war with one another for some time and thus have been witness to the same events, their appreciation of the utility of a duel would not necessarily be reached simultaneously, and when the hostile groups were strangers to one another, as we are told was the case in all the instances just cited, those suggesting the duel could not have expected the enemy to share their understanding of the duel's economy and thus to accept their proposal. Nevertheless, only by issuing a challenge could they test the state of the enemy's comprehension of these issues. And if, as often must have been the case, the offer to duel was declined, battle would have commenced. Under these circumstances, verbal exchange would actually precede physical combat, which, as it progressed, would illustrate the assertion that, absent an agreement to duel, battle must eventually consume the whole of both forces. In this instance, the experience of battle itself enables the warriors to perceive the connection left unstated in the verbal challenge, because during the course of battle they may observe that combat breaks into a series of duels and that the enemy's champion is the one ultimately to be dealt with if a victory is to be won. If issued before a battle begins, the verbal challenge reframes the impending contest as the test of a proposition, namely, that the same results could be achieved without loss of more than one life if all involved submitted the issue between them to the judgment of a duel.

Even when the challenge is rejected, the champion who utters it expedites matters by drawing the eyes of the opposing warriors to himself, focusing their attention on his display of battle prowess, and so hastening their realization that if they cannot stop him, they cannot win. As soon as this point has been made, and once it is seen that the champion cannot be downed from a safe distance, the enemy will begin to realize that the duel presents a reasonable means for coming to terms. Recognizing, however, that this "argument" will take some time to make, the champion may have to repeat his challenge. Coming forward "morning and evening" (I Sam. 17:16) in the manner of Goliath addressing the Israelites, he periodically punctuates the battle with a repetition of his proposal, thus both reminding his audience of the proposition to be proved and testing to see whether they have begun yet to make the central observation.

The battlefield speeches either remind their audience of conditions already completely understood, or else they predict what is to come. In either case, the brief explanation works in conjunction with experience—whether past or future—to present an argument in support of the duel. Removed from the context of that experience, the suggestion to try a duel makes no sense at all. And this introduces a new problem, for once instituted, the duel brings peace, thus separating people from the foundational experience on which is constructed their new way of managing violence. Introducing stability into a world that has fallen into nearly complete chaos, the practice of single combat paradoxically removes the conditions of warfare from which it springs. Conceived in the recurrent trauma of witnessing armies going down to death, challenges shouted across the battle lines are designed for use in war, not peace. And so, just as prolonged exposure to the geometry of battle gradually persuades warriors to make a trial of the duel, prolonged peace deprives them of experience with that same geometry, with the result that counterintuitive understandings begin to fade, until the hostile polities inevitably relapse into war.

Such breakdowns do not necessarily undermine the new system; they reinforce it, because every transgression unleashes a new wave of killing that cannot be brought under control either until the supply of fighting men is all but exhausted or until the commitment to single combat has been renewed. Rather than rejecting the duel, then, the survivors would, with fresh conviction, determine to abide by its protocols and, indeed, to maintain awareness of their importance and to ensure their observance. The process of reinforcement thus results in a steady elaboration of the new cultural system through the continuous adaptation of existing practices and the adoption of new ones.[2] Subsequent adoption of noncombative rites may then provide for the public expression of mutual respect for commonly held symbols, thus extending the basis for trust even among hostile polities. In a further step, sacred precincts mark off neutral territory to serve as a fixed neutral location in which to hold periodic meetings for the affirmation of generally accepted premises upon which the continuation of peaceful relations depends.[3] The practice of the duel, in this way, gradually becomes enmeshed in an increasingly complex structure of peacetime institutions ever better able to engender cooperative understandings without recourse to war.

Despite the recurrent reconfiguration of such social institutions, however, the duel's function would never be entirely assured, especially given the fact that the relationship between these polities is defined by their antagonism. Peace is, at bottom, inimical to the structure of epic culture. Given a long

---

[2] Renfrew recognizes three distinct categories of interaction: "(a) competition (including warfare), and competitive emulation (b) symbolic entrainment, and the transmission of innovation (c) increased flow in the exchange of goods" (p. 8).

[3] These are all examples of the symbolic entrainment referred to by Renfrew. Though he does not state that competition, symbolic entrainment, and increased flow in the exchange of goods should occur in any particular sequence, the case that we have before us would seem to proceed in precisely the order in which Renfrew lists them. Naturally, war must have been intermittent, but I would argue that each outbreak of war necessitates beginning again from scratch to reestablish in its turn each appropriate practice and institution, starting with the agreement to duel, moving on to the elaboration of protocols, and so on.

enough period without the salutary effects of war, ritual combat might devolve into a form of theater and contests of arms into sport. When, then, war does break out anew, the use of the duel as a final bulwark against the annihilation of fighting forces has to be rediscovered and reinstituted. Yet at what cost, for each relapse means a new episode of relentless killing, a relearning of the fundamental geometry lesson paid for in lives.

I recapitulate as follows: because the duel serves to establish political boundaries and to regulate the movement of people across them, it provides for the formation, definition, and stabilization of polities in relation to each other as well as in relation to the geography with which they become associated.[4] As soon as relations between geopolitical units are stabilized, however, the primary venue for communication can no longer be situated between the battle lines, for battle itself should now occur far less frequently. As hostile interactions decrease, moreover, so increases the need for mutual reassurance with respect to understandings and agreements, for without regular reaffirmation of mutual respect for sovereignty, integrity of borders, access to trade, and so on, the parties will be inclined to test one another, if not in open war, then indirectly through their common institutions. Therefore, as epic culture becomes ever more fully articulated, its interactions move to new venues and require the development of new practices and the exploitation of new media. Under such circumstances, the performance of epic poetry provides a medium for the exchange, not of explicit assurances but of the understandings upon which the cultural system is founded. Epic narrative supplements other media constitutive of dueling culture by carrying the memory of those circumstances most easily forgotten in times of peace—the dynamics of battle itself.[5]

Like other cultural media, oral poetry has a double function. On the one hand, each practice and institution serves as a medium for the symbolic exchange through which the culture lives; each medium carries vital information. On the other, each medium constitutes a practice in its own right, thus providing yet another venue for interaction; to this extent, the medium is itself the cultural message. Though there has been understandable confusion between our epic poems and the tale-singing functions occasionally mentioned within them, we can now distinguish between the kind of song composed to commemorate Beowulf's victory over Grendel and an epic song like *Beowulf*, for while the former carries the message of a young warrior's demonstrated ability in single combat, the latter draws attention to the prac-

---

[4] Where Renfrew and his colleagues in archaeology are interested in peer polity interaction as an explanation for the process by which similar symbolic products develop simultaneously among relatively independent polities, observations made here suggest that peer polity interaction may explain the process by which the polities define and then maintain relationships among themselves.

[5] Murdoch observes that the *Nibelungenlied* and at least one other poem (*Kudrun*) carry the same message, to wit: "the need once again to cope with political chaos and the need for constant control, with the warning rider that damage cannot always be contained" (p. 150).

tices and institutions in which such information has a use. Each medium thus operates on at least two levels at once; it carries the information that provides individuals with a context in which to act, but it also carries the code by which individuals define the parameters for their action.

The first perspective is the more readily observable. We have already noted the way in which familiarity with warriors' relative strengths and knowledge of their whereabouts plays a decisive role in determining whether or not a war will be initiated. Similarly, information that a chief requires assistance is interpreted by a would-be champion as an occasion to prove himself. If he is successful, he will require witnesses who can compose a song to celebrate his exploits—the sort of report that could have kept Burgundy free of attack and did enable Beowulf to rule the Geats in peace for fifty years. The *Odyssey* portrays singers permanently installed in the princely houses of Ithaka and Phaiakia as being informed (though not equally well) of events at Troy. The Phaiakians are sufficiently knowledgeable about Odysseus to treat him with extraordinary care. The suitors, on the other hand, are ill-enough informed about Odysseus to disregard the possibility of his return. Information of this sort is, then, a valuable commodity.

Just as the duel substitutes for a general battle, so may a song obviate the need even for a test of arms. The potential for such substitutions is delicately suggested by the propensity for epic-cultural poetry to represent the exchange of narratives within the frame of the narrated action. Even within the scope of the most compact of epic poems, the "Hildebrandslied," we find Hadubrant relating a fifteen-line oral verse account of his father's deeds, which constitutes (in Alain Renoir's words) a "mini-epic within the poem" (137). This mini-epic is told literally at the site of the duel, between the two armies at the moment of hostile confrontation, and it nearly has the effect of forestalling the conflict, for it leads to Hiltibrant's recognition that his opponent is his own son, to whom he responds by offering gifts and implying that such closely-related men should not fight. Thus the narrative nearly substitutes for the duel, though this substitution is rejected. The consequences of the younger man's refusal are, however, implied by the frame poem, with the effect that the frame poem's audience, unlike Hadubrant, may be slightly more inclined to give thought to the circumstances in which such a meeting might occur and thus to seek a way out of the dilemma. While the framing poem would not likely have been told at the point of combat itself, the parallelism in its reference to that setting does position it as a possible substitute for the duel, on the condition that it receives an appropriately attentive hearing.

The continuous exchange of symbolic data required for the ongoing operation of the epic-cultural system might be accomplished by merchants, by warriors traveling in quest of opportunity, or even perhaps by professional news agents traveling about for the rewards of carrying such information to those in need of it. The bearers of such tales have the specialized function of helping to maintain maximal order between and within polities, thus directly reducing the loss of life and so indirectly working against social breakdown. Exchanges of this kind are, therefore, quite necessary to epic culture and must be institutionalized within it. The dissemination of such information clearly does not, however, require the services of highly skilled poets or singers capable of producing the complex narratives with which we are concerned. As opposed to the legendary materials at which we have looked, all of the epic narratives warn of dire consequences to be met with due to neglect of protocols, practices, and institutions directly or indirectly connected with the duel. The telling and retelling of tales such as these serve, then, as a check on the individual members of each *oikos* or mead hall by reinforcing understandings won—perhaps long ago—from the painful experience of unregulated warfare.

Both the information-bearing report and the code-defining epic song require transmission by individuals moving among the hostile polities. Because of the sensitive nature of the messages being carried, however, messengers affiliated with one of the affected polities would not have much credence. Consequently, a need arises for the exchange of songs. To this end, singers may gather at a neutral site, a kind of festival already serving as a venue for other epic-cultural practices such as martial contests and religious rituals. Another solution may have been presented by a regional guild of independent singers moving freely among hostile polities. Furthermore, exchanges of this sort require either a facility with translation or the development of a *koine* especially for the purpose.

Gregory Nagy (summarizing A. M. Snodgrass) points out that many of these conditions are met in Greece during the eighth century B.C., the era in which the Homeric poems became fixed in the form in which we now find them, a period that Nagy calls a "watershed in the evolution of Hellenic civilization" because it observed the emergence of a "strong trend of intercommunication among the elite of the city-states—the trend of Panhellenism," which we see reflected in the Olympic Games as well as the sanctuary and oracle of Pythian Apollo at Delphi.[6] These Nagy calls "monumental feats of intersocial organization and also of intercultural synthesis" (7), but the same may be said of Homeric epos, because it "synthesizes the diverse local traditions of each major city-state into a unified Panhellenic model that suits most city-states but corresponds exactly to none; the best example is the Homeric concept of the Olympian gods, which incorporates, yet goes beyond, the localized religious traditions of each city-state" (7). Concluding from this correlation that "the Panhellenic nature of Homeric Epos is due not only to its composition but also to its proliferation" (7), Nagy recognizes Homeric poetry to be a "masterpiece of organization not only in an artistic but also in a social dimension" (9). However, where Nagy assumes the establishment of the city-state to be a prerequisite for proliferation of the poems, I wish to suggest that in the composition and performance of the poems rival peer groups discover a venue in which they can begin to define themselves as

---

[6] See Gregory Nagy, *The Best of the Achaeans* (Baltimore: Johns Hopkins Univ. Press, 1979), p. 7, and A. M. Snodgrass, *Arms and Armour of the Greeks* (Ithaca: Cornell Univ. Press, 1967). Further references to the Nagy work will be cited parenthetically in the text.

polities.[7] The fact that Homeric diction and themes, the Olympian gods, the Olympic games, the sanctuary at Delphi, and the constitution of the city-state all exhibit a Panhellenic quality simply indicates their usefulness as media in a process of peer polity interaction. That the same international quality applies to the tale-singers may be inferred from the existence of poetic organizations or guilds such as the Homeridae of Chios and the Kreophuleioi of Samos, both of which, Nagy reminds us "had a heritage of strong Panhellenic affiliations" (9).

Because our sources are not confined to one linguistically, historically, and geographically bounded group, however, we are confronted with a further question about the formation and distribution of epic culture. The line of inferences that we have followed here leads to a definition of the tale-singer's function not only within Panhellenic culture of, say, the eighth century B.C. but indeed wherever epic culture may have manifested itself, as can be determined in relation to the composition (and to a lesser extent the transmission) of narratives such as those we can group together under the rubric of epic culture. And this returns us to an earlier comment about the rather curious circumstances under which epic-cultural geometry pertains, for either every surviving remnant of epic-cultural narrative results from a more or less continuous web of peer-polity interactions linking together Hebrews, sub-Mycenean Greeks, and a variety of Germanic peoples or else the range of epic-cultural narrative reflects parallel but independent cultural genesis. Even if we assume independent development, however, we must still presume a recurrence of the conditions of warfare that give rise to the distinctive and anomalous combat geometry upon which epic culture is based. It becomes necessary to decide, then, whether independent development must extend also to the conditions of warfare, including not only weapons technology but also other more general technological and social developments that enable weapons manufacture. For example, the Late Bronze Age development of a slashing sword follows from achievements in metallurgy and mining, but the ores themselves can only be obtained via trade. The answer to the question of independent development can only be reached via an interdisciplinary analysis of evidence drawn from archaeology, anthropology, sociology, and history. What I hope I have shown here, however, is that no such study should proceed without reference to the poetics of warfare and especially to the tale-singer's function.

---

[7] Nagy's assumption of sequence is indicated only by his use of the past perfect in this sentence: "We also know that the *Iliad* and the *Odyssey had* proliferated throughout the city-states at the time that they reached their present form" (p. 7; my emphasis).

APPENDIX

THE LAY OF HILTIBRANT—A TRANSLATION

I heard it told
that champions met each other alone,
Hiltibrant and Hadubrant, between two armies.
A son and his father set right their armor,
belted their battle shirts, girded on their swords,
the heroes, over chain mail, when they rode to this battle.

Hiltibrant spoke out, Heribrant's son, for he was the hoarier man,
wiser through experience, he put the questions,
few words, who his father would be,
a man among his people:
"—or of which clan do you come?
Tell me but one, and I know the other,
child in kingdom. Known to me is all the earthly breed."

Hadubrant spoke out, Hiltibrant's son:
"This much told me our people,
old and wise ones, who were living way back,
that Hiltibrant was the name of my father, I was named Hadubrant.
He went eastward—fled Otachre's enmity—
hence with Theoderic and his blades so numerous.
He left behind in the country insignificant
a wife in the house and a son not yet grown—
nothing to inherit. He rode eastward.

"On this voyage Theoderic had much need
of my father: that was such a friendless man!
He was immeasurably angry with Otachre.
The truest blade who went with Theoderic,
he was always at the forefront of massed men:
to him fighting was exceedingly dear.
He was known to keen men—
for I'm not deluded he still has life."

"Almighty God be my witness," quoth Hiltibrant, "from heaven above,
that you never yet took up combat with a man so closely related!"
From his arms he twisted the wound rings,
imperial rings in spirals, which the king had given him,
keeper of the Huns, saying: "This I give you out of loyalty."

Hadubrant spoke out, Hiltibrant's son:

"With a spear should one acquire gifts,
point against point.
You, old Hun, are immeasurably cunning.
You would snare me with your words, thus deliver me to your spear.
Grown so aged, you readily resort to your craftiness.
It was sea voyagers who told me,
coming west over the Vandals' sea, that a battle had carried him off:
dead is Hiltibrant, Heribrant's son."

Hiltibrant spoke out, Heribrant's son:
"Well do I see in your armament,
that you have at home a good master,
that in this realm never yet have you been an exile.
Now alas, ruling God," quoth Hiltibrant, "a calamity is taking place!
I wandered sixty summers and winters through alien territory.
There I was assigned to a place among the missile slingers.
As nobody at any castle could fasten murder to me,
so now shall my own child hew me with his sword,
fell me with his battle axe—either that or I have to become his slayer.

Indeed, now you can easily—if your fighting prowess serve you well—
win the armor of such a hoary man.
He would indeed be most despicable," quoth Hiltibrant, "among the Easterners,
if he were now to deny you battle, now that it suits you so well,
a deadly encounter. Let each test his courage, see whether
he will boast of the spoils this day, and which will have in his power
both these chest plates!"

Then first they both let their ashes stride
in sharp showers, so that they stood in the shields.
Then they stepped together. Battle trappings dinned.
They hewed most harmfully at the bright shields,
until their linden wood grew small in their fists,
gouged by the weapons . . .

WORKS CITED

Primary Sources and Translations

The Battle of Maldon. Edited by E. V. Gordon. New York: Apple-Century-Crofts, 1966.
Beowulf. Edited by Friedrich Klaeber. Lexington, Massachusetts: D. C. Heath, 1950.
Beowulf. Translated by E. Talbot Donaldson. New York: W. W. Norton, 1975.
The CD-ROM Bible. Chicago: Judaica Press, 1995.
Diodorus Siculus. *Diodorus of Sicily with an English Translation by C. H. Oldfather.* The Loeb Classical Library. Cambridge, Mass.: Harvard University Press, 1953.
Gregory of Tours. *Gregorii Episcopi Turonensis Historiarum Libri Decem.* Edited by Rudolf Buchner. Darmstadt: Wissenschaftliche Buchgesellschaft, 1970.
_____. *The History of the Franks.* Translated by Lewis Thorpe. Middlesex: Penguin Books, 1974.
Herodotus. *Herodoti Historiae.* Edited by Karl Hude. Oxford: Oxford University Press, 1975.
Herodotus. *The Histories.* Translated by Aubrey de Sélincourt. Suffolk, England: Penguin Books, 1978.
Das Hildebrandslied. Edited by Hartmut Broszinski. Kassel: Johannes Stauda, 1985.
"The Lay of Hiltibrant." Translated by Victor Udwin. Appendix.
Homer. *Iliad.* Edited by David B. Monro and Thomas W. Allen. London: Oxford University Press, 1969.
_____. *The Iliad.* Translated by E. V. Rieu. London: Penguin Books, 1950.
_____. *Odyssey.* Edited by Thomas W. Allen. London: Oxford University Press, 1974.
_____. *The Odyssey.* Translated by E. V. Rieu. London: Penguin Books, 1946; London: Penguing Books, 1991.
Livy. *Livy.* Translated by B. O. Foster. The Loeb Classical Library. Cambridge: Harvard University Press, 1960.
Das Nibelungenlied. Edited by Helmut Brackert. Frankfurt: Fischer, 1977.
The Nibelungenlied. Translated by A. T. Hatto. London: Penguin Books, 1988.
Paul, the Deacon. *History of the Langobards.* Translated by William Dudley Foulke. Philadelphia: University of Pennsylvania, 1907.
Paul, the Deacon. *Pauli Historia Langobardorum.* Edited by L. Bethmann and G. Waitz. Hanover: Hahnsche Buchhandlung, 1878.
Polybius. *The Histories.* Translated by W. R. Paton. The Loeb Classical Library. Cambridge: Harvard University Press, 1979.
Saxo Grammaticus. *The History of the Danes.* Translated by Peter Fisher. Totowa, New Jersey: Rowman and Littlefield, 1979.
Saxo Grammaticus. *Saxonis Grammatici Historia Danica..* Edited by Johannes Mattias Velschow and Petrus Erasmus Müller. Copenhagen: Libraria Gyldendaliana, 1839.
Tacitus. *Germania.* Translated by M. Hutton. In *Agricola, Germania, Dialogus.* The Loeb Classical Library. Cambridge: Harvard University Press, 1980.

Widsith: A Study in Old English Heroic Legend. Edited and translated by R. W. Chambers. New York: Russell & Russell, 1965.

Wolfram von Eschenbach. *Parzival.Wolfram von Eschenbach.* Edited by Karl Lachmann. Berlin: Walter de Gruyter, 1926.

Secondary Sources

Anderson, J. G. C. *The Germania of Tacitus.* Oxford: Clarendon Press, 1938.

Andersson, Theodore. *A Preface to the "Nibelungenlied."* Stanford: Stanford University Press, 1987.

Atchity, Kenneth. "Andromache's Headdress." In *Critical Essays on Homer,* edited by Kenneth Atchity, 159-65. Boston: G. K. Hall & Company, 1987.

Atchity, Kenneth, and E. J. W. Barber. "Greek Princes and Aegean Princesses: The Role of Women in the Homeric Poems." In *Critical Essays on Homer,* edited by Kenneth Atchity, 13-36. Boston: G. K. Hall & Company, 1987.

Bekker, Hugo. "Kingship in the *Nibelungenlied.*" *Germanic Review* 41 (November 1966): 251-63.

Bespaloff, Rachel. "Hector." In *Critical Essays on Homer,* edited by Kenneth Atchity, 127-31. Boston: G. K. Hall & Company, 1987.

Beyschlag, Siegfried. "Das Motiv der Macht bei Siegfrieds Tod." *Germanisch-Romanische Montasschrift* (1952): 95-108. Reprinted in *Zur Germanisch-Deutschen Heldensage,* edited by Karl Hauck, 195-213. Darmstadt: Wissenschaftliche Buchgesellschaft, 1965.

Broszinski, Hartmut. "Einführung: Datierung und Schrift." *"Das Hildebrandlied": Faksimile der Kasseler Handschrift mit einer Einführung von Hartmut Broszinski.* Kassel: Johannes Stauda, 1985.

Butterworth, E. A. S. *Some Traces of the Pre-Olympian World in Greek Literature and Myth.* Berlin: Walter de Gruyter & Company, 1966.

Chambers, R. W. *"Widsith": A Study in Old English Heroic Legend.* New York: Russell & Russell, 1965.

Davidson, Hilda Ellis. *The Sword in Anglo-Saxon England: Its Archaeology and Literature.* Woodbridge, England: Boydell Press, 1994.

de Boor, Helmut. "Hat Siegfried gelebt?" *Beiträge zur Geschichte der deutschen Sprache und Literatur* 63 (1930): 250-71. Reprinted in *Zur Germanisch-Deutschen Heldensage,* edited by Karl Hauck, 31-51. Darmstadt: Wissenschaftliche Buchgesellschaft, 1965.

de Vries, Jan. "Das Motiv des Vater-Sohn-Kampfes im Hildebrandslied." *Germanisch-Romanische Monatsschrift* 34 (1953): 257-274. Reprinted in *Zur Germanisch-Deutschen Heldensage,* edited by Karl Hauck, 248-84. Darmstadt: Wissenschaftliche Buchgesellschaft, 1965.

Dillery, John. "Reconfiguring the Past: Thyrea, Thermopylae, and Narrative Patterns in Herodotus." *American Journal of Philology* 117 (1996): 217-54.

Donlan, Walter. "Duelling with Gifts in the *Iliad*: As the Audience Saw It." *Colby Quarterly* 29 (1993): 155-72.

Drews, Robert. *The Coming of the Greeks.* Princeton: Princeton University Press, 1988.

———. *The End of the Bronze Age.* Princeton: Princeton University Press, 1993.

Ducrey, Pierre. *Warfare in Ancient Greece.* Translated by Janet Lloyd. New York: Schocken Books, 1986.

Eagleton, Terry. *Literary Theory*. Minneapolis: University of Minnesota Press, 1983.
Fenik, Bernard. *Typical Battle Scenes in the Iliad: Studies in the Narrative Techniques of Homeric Battle Description*. Wiesbaden: Franz Steiner Verlag, 1968.
Finley, Moses I. *The World of Odysseus*. New York: Viking Books, 1954.
Frakes, Jerold C. *Brides and Doom: Gender, Property, and Power in Medieval German Women's Epic*. Philadelphia: University of Pennsylvania Press, 1994.
Fraser, Sir James George. *The Golden Bough*. London: Macmillan Publishers, 1907.
Frey, Leonard. "*Comitatus* as a Rhetorical-Structural Norm for Two Germanic Epics." *Recovering Literature: A Journal of Contextual Criticism* 14 (Summer 1986): 51-70.
Geary, Patrick J. *Before France and Germany*. New York: Oxford University Press, 1988.
Gentry, Francis. *Triuwe and Vriunt in the "Nibelungenlied."* Amsterdam: Rodopi Press, 1975.
Greenblatt, Stephen Jay. *Shakespearean Negotiations*. Berkeley: University of California Press, 1988.
Hanne, Michael. "Peasant Storytelling Meets Literary Theory: The Case of *La Finta Nonna*." *The Italianist* 12 (1992): 42-58.
Haymes, Edward R. *The "Nibelungenlied": History and Interpretation*. Urbana: University of Illinois Press, 1986.
Herder, Johann Gottfried. *Herder und der Sturm und Drang*. Volumes 1 and 2. München: Carl Hanser Verlag, 1984.
Jackson, W. T. H. *The Hero and the King*. New York: Columbia University Press, 1982.
Kant, Immanuel. *Werkausgabe*. Edited by Wilhelm Weischedel. 12 Volumes. Frankfurt: Suhrkamp, 1977.
Kirk, G. S. *The Iliad: A Commentary*. Volume 1: Books 1-4. Cambridge: Cambridge University Press, 1985.
Klaeber, Friedrich. Introduction to *Beowulf*. 3rd edition. Lexington, Massachusetts: D. C. Heath, 1950.
Knox, Bernard. Introduction to *The Iliad*. Translated by Robert Fagles. New York: Viking Books, 1990.
Lea, Henry Charles. First Published as Parts I and II of*Superstition and Force: Essays on the Wager of Law, the Wager of Battle, the Ordeal, Torture*. Philadelphia: H. C. Lea, 1866;*The Duel and the Oath*. Philadelphia: University of Pennsylvania Press, 1974.
Lord, Albert B. *The Singer of Tales*. New York: Atheneum Press, 1973.
Lynn-George, Michael. "Apects of the Epic Vocabulary of Vulnerability." *Colby Quarterly* 29 (1993): 197-221.
McConnell, Winder. *The "Nibelungenlied."* Boston: Twayne Publishers, 1984.
Mariani, Alice. "The Renaming of Odysseus." In *Critical Essays on Homer*, edited by Kenneth Atchity, 211-23. Boston: G. K. Hall & Company, 1987.
Murdoch, Brian. *The Germanic Hero: Politics and Pragmatism in Early Medieval Poetry*. London: Hambledon Press, 1996.
Nagler, Michael N. "Penelope's Male Hand: Gender and Violence in the *Odyssey*." *Colby Quarterly* 29 (1993): 241-57.

Nagy, Gregory. *The Best of the Achaeans*. Baltimore: Johns Hopkins University Press, 1979.
Newton, Sam. *The Origins of "Beowulf."* Cambridge: D. S. Brewer, 1993.
Oakley, S. P. "Single Combat in the Roman Republic." *Classical Quarterly* 35 (1985): 392-410.
Pleiner, Radomír. *The Celtic Sword*. Oxford: Clarendon Press, 1993.
Rankin, H. D. *Celts and the Classical World*. London: Aereopagita Press, 1987.
Redfield, James M. "Imitation." In *Critical Essays on Homer*, edited by Kenneth Atchity, 113-26. Boston: G. K. Hall & Company, 1987.
Renfrew, Colin. "Peer polity interaction and socio-political change." In *Peer Polity Interaction and Socio-Political Change*, edited by Colin Renfrew and John F. Cherry, 1-18. Cambridge: Cambridge University Press, 1986.
Renoir, Alain. *A Key to Old Poems*. University Park: Pennsylvania State University Press, 1988.
Schröder, Werner. *"Nibelungenlied"-Studien*. Stuttgart: J. B Metzler, 1968.
Snodgrass, A. M. *Arms and Armour of the Greeks*. Ithaca: Cornell University Press, 1967.
_____. *An Archaeology of Greece*. Berkeley: University of California Press, 1987.
Sommer, Richard J. "The *Odyssey* and Primitive Religion." In *Critical Essays on Homer*, edited by Kenneth Atchity, 187-211. Boston: G. K. Hall & Company, 1987.
Thorpe, Lewis. Introduction to *The History of the Franks*, by Gregory of Tours. Baltimore: Penguin Books, 1974.
Udwin, Victor. "Autopoiesis and Poetics." In *Textuality and Subjectivity*, edited by Eitel Timm, 1-13. Columbia, South Carolina: Camden House, 1991.
_____. "Experience Interrupted: The Dynamics of Literary Interpretation." Ph.D. diss., University of California, 1985.
_____. "Der materiale Signifikant." In *Materialität der Kommunikation*, edited by H. U. Gumbrecht and Ludwig Pfeiffer, 858-77. Frankfurt: Suhrkamp, 1988.
_____. "Reading the Red Ball—A Phenomenology of Narrative Processes." *Papers in Comparative Literature* 5 (1988): 115-26.
Van Wees, Hans. *Status Warriors: War, Violence, and Society in Homer and History*. Amsterdam: J. C. Gieben, 1992.
Verbruggen, J. F. *The Art of Warfare in Western Europe During the Middle Ages: From the Eighth Century to 1340*. Woodbridge, England: Boydell Press, 1997.
Vivante, Paolo. "Rose-Fingered Dawn and the Idea of Time." In *Critical Essays on Homer*, edited by Kenneth Atchity, 51-61. Boston: G. K. Hall & Company, 1987.
Voegelin, Eric. "Order and Disorder." In *Critical Essays on Homer*, edited by Kenneth Atchity, 62-83. Boston: G. K. Hall & Company, 1987.
Von See, Klaus. *Germanische Heldensage: Stoffe, Probleme, Methoden*. Frankfurt: Athenäum Verlag, 1971.
Weil, Simone. "The *Iliad* or the Poem of Force." In *Critical Essays on Homer*, edited by Kenneth Atchity, 152-59. Boston: G. K. Hall & Company, 1987.
Whitman, Cedric H. "Image, Symbol, and Formula." In *Critical Essays on Homer*, edited by Kenneth Atchity, 83-105. Boston: G. K. Hall & Company, 1987.
Yadin, Yigael. *The Art of Warfare in Biblical Lands in the Light of Archaeological Study*. New York: McGraw-Hill, 1963.

INDEX

Achilles 39, 40, 45, 78, 86, 90, 140-141, 142, 143-144, 207
   and the balance of power on the battlefield 62-64, 65, 71, 85
   and the contest 109
   and Hector 87-89
   as "hero" 13-14
   as failed champion 134, 145-146
   death of 91
   enmity with Agamemnon 133-134, 137, 164, 206, 208
   "fate" of 130-133
   his quest for fame 128-129, 134-135
   invincibility of 53, 59-60, 96
   monstrous dimension of 138
   the "swift-footed" 59-60, 70
Agamemnon 44, 56, 63, 82, 84, 86, 128, 132, 133, 173, 207
   attempts to conciliate Achilles 130-131
   as king 140-147
   disrespects Chryses 134, 142-143
   enmity with Achilles 129, 137, 164, 206
   murder of 92, 172
   proclaims the destruction of Troy 77, 80-81
   see also Clytemnestra
Aias 62, 66, 71, 83, 85-88, 90, 91, 101-102, 128, 130, 138
Anderson, J. G. C. 18
Andersson, Theodore 3
archery, prohibition against 91-96, 108
Atchity, Kenneth 71, 168, 169, 214

Barber, E. J. W. 168, 169, 214
battle
   disproportionate numbers in 1, 2, 12, 47, 49, 62
   outcome determined by strongest individual 45, 63, 64, 70, 85

Bekker, Hugo 168, 174, 175, 176, 177, 178, 179, 183, 184
Beowulf 11, 16, 58, 65, 66, 67, 98, 122, 124, 148, 153, 221
Beowulf 66, 120, 128, 139, 140, 195-196, 204, 221
   aids Hrothgar 96-97, 110-111, 151-152, 165
   and Christ 122
   and his companions 122-123
   as champion 96, 106-107, 110-111, 147
   as king 114, 121, 157-161, 222
   death of 44, 76, 157-161, 213
   fights Grendel's mother 103-104
   his quest for fame 110-111
   honored and advised by Hrothgar and Wealhtheow 152-157
   invincibility of 53, 90
   wrestles Grendel 91, 97-101\
Bespaloff, Rachel 60, 78, 166
Beyschlag, Siegfried 6, 64, 112, 121, 141
Bible, the 38, 46
   see also Samuel, I
Broszinski, Hartmut 211
Brünhild 90, 113, 114, 137, 165, 173-174, 192, 194-195, 197, 198
   deception of 64, 113, 115-116, 121, 177-193
   her contest 175-179, 185-189
   her knowledge of Siegfried 182-183
   monstrous dimension of 186
Butterworth, E. A. S. 110, 125, 167, 168, 170, 173-174

challenge 5, 9, 73, 81, 83, 98, 99, 101, 119, 121, 124, 125, 127, 129, 131-132, 139, 142, 147, 153, 155, 159, 163, 166, 169, 176, 177, 180, 187, 193, 203, 204, 213, 218, 219, 220
Cunincpert's 38-39

duel without one 72
a Gaul's 32
Grendel's 105
Goliath's 3-4, 6, 71, 77, 104, 136-137
Hector's 84
Hector's on behalf of Paris 7-8, 79, 84, 132
Hyllus's 29, 31
Keti and Vigi's 41
a Langobard's 36-37
man of Retenu's 27-28
a Saxon king's 42-43
Siegfried's 1-3, 8, 49, 64, 78, 113-114, 119-120, 124, 139, 156, 194
a Slav's 44
Chambers, R. W. 42, 43
Clytemnestra 172-173
comitatus, the 140, 148, 159
companions 1, 2, 48, 64, 67, 68, 73, 75, 76, 87, 88, 90, 91, 93, 96, 98, 99, 105, 109, 119, 120, 122, 123, 130, 137, 142, 145, 146, 147, 151, 152, 164, 178, 181, 182, 187, 188, 192, 194, 207

David 4-5, 7, 106, 164
  as anti-champion 38, 78, 104-105, 136-137, 206-208, 214
Davidson, Hilda Ellis 17-18, 65, 66-67, 71, 91
de Boor, Helmut 64, 81, 137, 193
Dillery, John 13
Diodorus Siculus 29, 31
Diomedes 53-55, 58-59, 71, 73-74, 85, 87-88, 90, 93, 94, 95, 101, 105, 128
dismay 4, 40, 42, 46, 55-56, 58-59, 62, 64, 65, 73, 74, 85, 86, 104, 108, 121, 187
Donlan, Walter 10, 21, 145, 146
Drews, Robert 30
Ducrey, Pierre 12
duel
  defined 10
  economy of 46, 74-75, 124-125

general battle, contrasted with 6, 28, 49-51, 125
judicial 15-16
modern assumptions contrasted with 12-21
numerical superiority contrasted with 11-12, 46, 51-52, 62, 217
sovereignty, and 9, 10
terms of 5-8, 9, 82, 90, 113
theater, as 9, 32
duels involving
  anonymous champions of the Alamanni and Suebi 35-36, 218
  anonymous champions of the Aspitti and Langobards 37-38
  anonymous champions of the Slavs and Danes 44-45, 218-219
  Athisl and Frovin 39-40
  Athisl and Keti 41
  Beowulf and Grendel 96-101, 107, 110
  Beowulf and Grendel's mother 103-104
  Brünhild and Gunther 185-189, 190-191
  David and Goliath 4-5, 104-105
  Hector and Achilles 88-89
  Hector and Aias 62-64, 83-88, 101-103
  Hiltibrant and Hadubrant 6-7, 65-66, 201-215
  Hyllus and Echemus 28-31
  Marcus Valerius and a Gaul 32
  Menelaus and Paris 7-8, 79-82
  Siegfried and Alberich 116-119
  Siegfried and Gunther or Hagen 1-6, 64
  Siegfried and Liudeger 47-50
  Sinuhe and the man of Retenu 27-28
  Titus Manlius and a Gaul 32
  Uffi and two Saxons 42

Eagleton, Terry 22
epic culture 10, 11, 12, 28, 32, 33, 38, 46, 81, 89, 96, 105, 110, 115, 119,

122, 124-125, 127, 130, 133, 134, 137, 138-139, 141, 165, 166, 167, 173, 176, 177, 179, 180, 189, 191, 193, 198, 200, 201, 204, 205, 212, 213, 216, 217, 220-221, 222, 223, 224

Fenik, Bernard 53, 59, 68, 73, 74
Finley, Moses I. 19
Frakes, Jerold C. 14, 113, 172, 178, 181, 182, 191, 192-193
Frazer, Sir James George 167
Frey, Leonard 140, 148, 159

Geary, Patrick J. 35
Gentry, Francis 119
Goliath 5-6, 7, 8, 36, 38, 77, 78, 107, 136, 137, 164, 187, 219
   challenges the Israelites 3-4
   defeat of 104-106
   monstrous size of 3-4
Greenblatt, Stephen Jay 20
Gregory of Tours 34-37, 38
Grendel 90, 97-101, 107, 111, 120, 140, 147, 151, 155, 157, 159, 160-161, 169, 186, 221
   as non-champion 97, 106, 110, 138
   magic properties of 98-99, 190
Gunther 4, 64, 110, 112, 116, 121, 124, 138, 165, 170, 173, 176, 178, 194, 195, 198, 206
   and the deception of Brünhild 115, 177, 179-193
   as king 6, 47, 137, 139, 142, 156, 164
   at Etzel's court 75-76, 126
   challenged by Siegfried 1-2, 5, 9, 113-114, 119-120

Hadubrant 6-7, 8, 65-66, 81, 202-206, 208-214
   as champion 203, 212-213
   death of 212-213
   recites verse at site of duel 222
Hagen 2, 48, 110, 124, 181, 183, 188, 197, 203, 206

as advisor 177
as failed champion 64, 77-78, 139
at Etzel's court 75-76, 126, 140, 196-198
Hanne, Michael 21
Haymes, Edward R. 1, 77-78, 113-116, 166, 180-181, 194, 207
Hector 62, 66, 70, 73-74, 78, 94, 130, 132, 145
   and Achilles 87-89
   articulates terms of the duel between Paris and Menelaus 7-8, 79
   as champion 81
   as counselor 166
   challenges Achaean heroes to duel 34, 84
   death of 71, 80, 133
   duels Aias 83-88, 101-103
   his fear of Achilles 63, 89, 129
Helen 8-9, 79, 82, 87, 89, 125, 127, 168, 170
Herder, Johann Gottfried 15
Herodotus 28, 31, 45, 218
Hiltibrant 6-7, 8, 65-66, 200-214, 222
   as champion 203, 205
   enmity with Otachre 205-209
"Hiltibrant, Lay of" 6, 9, 65, 200-201, 213, 215, 222
Hrothgar 97, 99, 107, 110-111, 140, 165, 186
   advises Beowulf 96, 156-157
   as king 123, 147-149, 151-157, 167

Iliad, the 8, 9, 10, 11, 13, 16, 17, 19, 20, 34, 45, 46, 53-56, 60, 62, 63, 65, 70, 71, 73, 74, 78, 79, 81, 83, 95, 101, 105, 107, 128, 129, 132, 133, 134, 142, 145, 146, 200, 206, 224
invincibility 46, 53, 59, 60, 87, 91-92, 96, 120, 121, 124, 214
   Achilles's 59, 96, 131
   Beowulf's 101, 107
   Brünhild's 179, 187
   David's 207
   Diomedes's 58

Goliath's 6
Grendel's 97-99
Gunther's (faked) 179
Siegfried's 2, 49, 52, 53, 119, 188

Jackson, W. T. H. 16

Kant, Immanuel 22
Kirk, G. S. 11
Klaeber, Friedrich 122
Knox, Bernard 13-14
Kriemhild 1, 2, 8, 9, 13, 81, 121, 122, 139, 163, 165, 173, 177, 178, 184, 189, 193, 194-195
 exercising power 192, 197-199
 wooed by Siegfried 111-112, 113-114
 revenge of 77, 126, 176, 196

Lea, Henry Charles 15-16
Livy 32
Lynn-George, Michael 60, 62, 63, 65, 93, 132, 141, 210

McConnell, Winder 2, 183
magic 53, 98-99, 190
"Maldon, Battle of" 67, 71, 98, 148
Mariani, Alice 133
Murdoch, Brian 13, 98, 156, 197, 221

Nagler, Michael N. 92
Nagy, Gregory 223-224
Newton, Sam 153
Nibelungenlied, the 1, 3, 8, 9, 13, 16, 46, 51, 53, 55, 75-76, 77, 81, 113, 119, 121, 125, 138, 141, 163, 166, 175, 192, 197, 199, 200, 206, 208, 213, 221

Oakley, S. P. 32, 45
Odysseus 94, 124, 169, 170, 173, 175, 200-201, 214, 222
 and the quest for fame 133
 and the suitors 91-93
 at Troy 73, 128, 130
 in Crete 146
 his absence from Ithaka 170-172, 174
 his return home 212
 on Calypso's island 210, 214
Odyssey, the 11, 19, 92, 167, 172, 173, 174, 200, 201, 222, 224
Oedipus myth, the 168-169
 and "The Lay of Hiltibrant" 211-212

Parzival 215
Paul the Deacon 37-39
Penelope
 and the contest 168, 173-175, 177
 and the suitors 169, 170-172
 as interim ruler 171
Pleiner, Radomir 33
Polybius 33-34

Renfrew, Colin 11, 216, 220-221
Renoir, Alain 23-24, 58, 98, 111, 160, 201-203, 206, 210, 212, 213-214, 222

Samuel, I 3-5, 8, 9, 36, 104-105, 122, 136-137, 187, 206, 207-208, 219
Saul 4-5, 104, 106
 his jealousy of David 136-137, 164, 206-208
Saxo Grammaticus 40-42, 43, 44-45
Schröder, Werner 2
Siegfried 4, 6, 8, 46, 54, 55, 66, 71, 90, 110, 122, 124, 165, 170, 173, 176, 194, 195, 198, 204, 208
 and the deception of Brünhild 113, 177-193
 and the Nibelungs 51-52, 115-118, 163
 as champion 139
 at war with the Saxons and Danes 47-51, 72-73, 75
 his challenge of Gunther 1-2, 3, 5, 9, 64, 113-114, 120, 121, 156
 his coming of age 149-151

INDEX

his son 81
his wooing of Kriemhild 111-112, 113-114
invincibility of 2, 52-53, 96, 119
monstrous dimension of 98, 138
murder of 64, 77-78, 81, 137, 142, 164, 197
Snodgrass, A. M. 17, 21, 223
Sommer, Richard J. 172
suitors 91-93, 169, 170-174, 187, 222

Tacitus 34, 35, 217
tale-singer, the 216, 222-224
  at Heorot 124, 152-153
  at the Phaiacian court 124, 222
  see also Hadubrant
Telemachus 81, 93
  and the contest 168, 212
  and the suitors' murder plot 171-174

Thorpe, Lewis 36

Van Wees, Hans 19-21, 64
Verbruggen, J. F. 59, 75
Vivante, Paolo 60
Voegelin, Eric 8-9, 70, 81-82, 130, 134, 145, 170
Von See, Klaus 76

Wealhtheow
  advises Hrothgar 153-154
  rewards Beowulf 154-155, 160-161
Weil, Simone 134, 142
Whitman, Cedric H. 13, 53, 59-60
Widsith 42-43

Yadin, Yigael 17, 27

DAVIS MEDIEVAL
TEXTS & STUDIES

Scholarly editions and studies devoted to those aspects of the European Middle Ages that include English, Germanic, Latin, and Romance languages and literatures; music; philosophy; and rhetoric.

1 Hugo Bekker. *The Poetry of Albrecht von Johansdorf.*
2 John J. Hagen OSA. Translator. *Gerald of Wales, Jewel of the Church: A Translation of* Gemma Ecclesiastica *by Gilardus Cambrensis.*
3 Norris J. Lacy. *The Craft of Chrétien de Troyes: An Essay on Narrative Art.*
4 Margaret Winters. Editor. *The Romance of Hunbaut: An Arthurian Poem of the Thirteenth Century.*
5 Henry Ansgar Kelly. *Chaucer and the Cult of Saint Valentine.*
6 Margaret Jennings CSJ. Editor. *The* Ars Componendi Sermones *of Ranulph Higden OSB.*
7 Katharina M. Wilson. *Hrotsvit of Gandersheim: The Ethics of Authorial Stance.*
8-9 Emil J. Polak. *Medieval and Renaissance Letter Treatises and Form Letters.*
   1. A Census of Manuscripts Found in Eastern Europe and the Former USSR.
   2. A Census of Manuscripts Found in Part of Western Europe, Japan, and the United States of America.
10 Victor Morris Udwin. *Between Two Armies.* The Place of the Duel in Epic Culture.